LONDON RECORD SOCIETY
PUBLICATIONS

VOLUME XLVIII

SUMMARY JUSTICE IN THE CITY

A SELECTION OF CASES HEARD AT THE GUILDHALL JUSTICE ROOM 1752–1781

EDITED BY

GREG T. SMITH

LONDON RECORD SOCIETY
THE BOYDELL PRESS
2013

First published 2013

A London Record Society publication
Published by The Boydell Press
an imprint of Boydell & Brewer Ltd
PO Box 9, Woodbridge, Suffolk IP12 3DF, UK
and of Boydell & Brewer Inc.
668 Mt Hope Avenue, Rochester, NY 14620–2731, USA
website: www.boydellandbrewer.com

ISBN 978–0–900952–53–1

A CIP catalogue record for this book is available
from the British Library

The publisher has no responsibility for the continued existence or
accuracy of URLs for external or third-party internet websites referred to
in this book, and does not guarantee that any content
on such websites is, or will remain, accurate or appropriate

Papers used by Boydell & Brewer Ltd are natural, recyclable products
made from wood grown in sustainable forests

Printed and bound by
CPI Group (UK) Ltd, Croydon, CR0 4YY

CONTENTS

ACKNOWLEDGEMENTS

Funding for this project was provided by the Social Sciences and Humanities Research Council of Canada and the University of Manitoba. I am grateful to both bodies for the financial support necessary for completing the project. The archival staff of the former Corporation of London Record Office, especially former City Archivist Jim Sewell, Juliet Banks, Vivian Aldous, Jessica Newton and Elizabeth Scudder, and later the staff of the London Metropolitan Archive, now home to these records, have shown me every courtesy in working with City archives and sharing their knowledge of London's administrative history. A small team of research assistants, including Mary Clayton, Kevin Palendat, Catherine Quirk, Trevor Sampson, Tim Wales and especially Rob Stansel, provided more advice and insight as they assisted with the transcriptions, and I am very thankful to each of them for their diligence and editorial assistance. Madeleine Chartrand provided excellent assistance with the index. Tim Hitchcock suggested the idea of creating a London Record Society volume to me and has answered many queries since. I am also grateful to John Beattie, Stephen Heathorn and Jim Oldham for comments on the introduction, and Simon Devereaux, Christopher Frank, Drew Gray, Peter King, Norma Landau, Andrea McKenzie, Ruth Paley and Bruce Smith for advice on various transcriptions or on the introductory material. For the London Record Society, Vanessa Harding helped facilitate the early proposal and Robin Eagles and Caroline Barron have patiently overseen its slow maturation. I am most grateful to my wife Denise for her constant support and encouragement.

ABBREVIATIONS

Abram	Abraham
ads/ats	(ads, possibly short form of *adversus*) on the prosecution of
agt	against
Ass^t	assault
B	Bridewell
C, Cx, C+	appearing in left margin where fees are usually noted, indicates cases where the magistrate convicted the accused and assessed a fine
C.	appearing after a proper name in the main entry is short for constable. All notations of constable (C., Const., Cble., etc.) have been standardized to 'C.' in the interests of space.
Chd	charged
Co:	County
Comm^{rs}	Commissioners
D^d, d^d, d'd	Discharged
D^o., do.	Ditto
D^{o}C	Ditto Compter
d^{o}C.	ditto Constable
Exaiacon, Examicon, Examon	Examination
Exeson	Execution
fr	from
friv^s	frivolous
fur, fu^r	further
GL	Guildhall Library
Ga, Gas, Gu^s	Guinea, Guineas
Ho:	House
L	London
LMA	London Metropolitan Archives
LW, LWH	London Work House
Ma^r	Master
Midx, Middx	Middlesex
Mre	Matter
N	Newgate
Nunc	now

OBP	*Old Bailey Proceedings*
P	poor or pauper (no fee taken by clerk, presumably)
par, pish, psh	parish
PC	Poultry Compter
pl	plaintiff
ppty	property
pr, pr^d	produced
pson	person
pties	parties
Pros^x	Prosecutrix
R	Recognizance issued; though sometimes used to indicate a person was bailed. The R can appear crossed out (R̶), with a cross beside it (Rx or R+) or simply as the letter (R) and has been fairly transcribed in each case.
RX	Notation of a recognizance, clearly crossed through with an 'X'.
sum^d	summoned
ux, uxor	wife of
WC	Wood Street Compter
W^{h}man	Watchman
W^o	Widow
Wp, Wpp	Worship
W^t, Warr^t	Warrant
Xtian	Christian

Editorial insertions

[blank]	a blank gap in the original
[illegible], [i̶l̶l̶e̶g̶i̶b̶l̶e̶]	illegible entry or an illegible entry also struck out

INTRODUCTION

The common point of entry into the criminal justice system in England was the local justice of the peace. When disputes between neighbours or strangers arose, or once it was determined that a criminal offence had possibly occurred, usually by the alleged victim, one of the first steps to take would be to approach the local justice of the peace for a warrant to arrest someone on suspicion of the charge. Over time, by way of royal charters, statutes and customary law, justices of the peace – or magistrates – had gained the authority to discharge a range of administrative, criminal, and civil matters. Their work was done without the aid of a jury and without a formal trial procedure. In some cases the magistrates were restricted in their powers while in other cases the expectation had emerged that these custodians of the peace would exercise their good judgement to arbitrate and mediate when necessary, and adjudicate or punish when required and permitted. Magistrates had the assistance of local sheriffs and their constables, whose roles as the muscle before the law underwent a significant transformation over the eighteenth century. The evolution of criminal justice administration at the grassroots level, and the related problem of policing the city, was experienced most acutely in London and Middlesex.

The nature and forms of this essential work of social regulation and the administration of law by magistrates in summary proceedings has recently started to emerge from the shadow of historical work on the social and legal history of England. The summary work of JPs has received only limited attention, in part because few records of such summary procedures survive, especially for such a unique setting as London, prior to the nineteenth century, before summary justice proce- dure was formalized. This volume provides a valuable complement to the recently published work of county JPs while also providing a unique insight into the preliminary trial process in the period before London's magistrates' courts were officially constituted. With the discovery and publication of more justices' notebooks and other records of pre-trial procedures, a clearer picture is beginning to emerge of how in prac- tice offenders and victims of crime were initiated into the formal legal procedures of trial and punishment, or how bylaws and other local regulations were imposed in daily practice.

We are learning more about the nature of summary justice and routine pre-trial preliminary investigations before the nineteenth century as historians turn their attention to summary justice work more generally.[1] One contemporary work by James Burrow, Master of the Crown Office, offered an abridgement of settlement cases heard by pairs of JPs and which eventually proceeded to the King's Bench, but such formal recounting of the JP's work is exceptional.[2] A small number of surviving notebooks produced by other eighteenth-century justices have been published in recent years.[3] Some of the more conscientious (or pecuniary-minded) magistrates kept rough minute books to record their decisions on each matter, and to account for the fees they collected for performing their duties. The notes kept by these magistrates generally confirm what we have assumed about pre-trial practice or summary justice from formal rules of practice laid out in statute and also from the many extant justices' manuals, of which Richard Burn's *Justice of the Peace and Parish Officer* is perhaps the best known. But since most of the JP's work was carried out in the parlours, sitting rooms, or the makeshift courtrooms of the various justices at a point in a dispute before formal proceedings began, and before formal records were generated in the form of indictments or depositions, there was not always a careful record taken of the proceedings.

THE POWERS OF LONDON'S ALDERMAN JPs

In the City of London, the task of administering the law to keep the peace fell on the shoulders of the City's civic elite. The power of the

1. D. Oberwitiler, 'Crime and Authority in Eighteenth Century England: Law Enforcement on the Local Level', *Historical Social Research*, 15:2 (1990), 3–34; S. Flynn and M. Stevens, 'Petty Criminals, Publicans and Sinners: Petty Sessions Records in the Berkshire Record Office', *Journal of the Society of Archivists*, 16:1 (1995), 41–53; G. Morgan and P. Rushton, 'The Magistrate, the Community and the Maintenance of an Orderly Society in Eighteenth-Century England', *Historical Research*, 76:191 (Feb. 2003), 54–77; P. King, 'The Summary Courts and Social Relations in Eighteenth-Century England', *Past & Present*, 183 (May 2004), 125–72; D. Cox and B. S. Godfrey, eds., *Cinderellas and Packhorses: A History of the Shropshire Magistracy* (Woonton Almeley, 2005); F. Dabhoiwala, 'Summary Justice in Early Modern London', *English Historical Review*, 121:492 (June 2006), 796–822; P. King, *Crime and Law in England, 1750–1840: Remaking Justice from the Margins* (Cambridge, 2006). The most thorough analysis to date of the records reproduced here is D. Gray, *Crime, Prosecution and Social Relations: The Summary Courts of the City of London in the Late Eighteenth Century* (Basingstoke, 2009).
2. Sir James Burrow, *A Series of the decisions of the Court of King's Bench upon settlement-cases; from The Death of Lord Raymond in March 1732: To which is Added A Complete Abridgment of the Substance of each Case, and two Tables of the Names of them*, 2 vols. (London, 1768); idem, *Continuation of the Decisions of the Court of King's Bench, upon Settlement-cases, By Four additional Years, ending in July 1772* (London, 1772); idem, *A Second Continuation (Down to Michaelmas sessions 1776) of the decisions of the Court of King's Bench upon settlement-cases* (London, 1777).
3. E. Silverthorne, ed., *The Deposition Book of Richard Wyatt, J.P., 1767–76* (Surrey Record Society, 30, 1978); E. Crittall, ed., *The Justicing Notebook of William Hunt, 1744–1749* (Wiltshire Record Society, 1982); R. Paley, ed., *Justice in Eighteenth-Century Hackney: The Justicing Notebook of Henry Norris and the Hackney Petty Sessions Book* (London Record Society, 1991); G. Morgan and P. Rushton, eds., *The Justicing Notebook (1750–64) of Edmund Tew, Rector of Boldon* (Surtees Society, 2000).

Lord Mayor, as chief magistrate of the Corporation, and past mayors to act as Justices of the Peace was established very early in London's history. Uniquely, the City Justices could conduct their summary business sitting alone. This power was formally recognized in a series of charters beginning with that secured from Henry VI on 26 October 1444, which confirmed upon the mayor, Recorder and any aldermen who had served the office of mayor the power to act as Justices of the Peace so long as they remained aldermen. It was therefore no longer necessary in the City for commissions of the peace to appoint particular persons as Justices. The charter's privileges would operate in perpetuity as new aldermen were elected and later charters (1462, 1550, 1608) confirmed these powers.[4] The list of eligible aldermen to serve as JPs was expanded to include the next three senior aldermen below the mayor by a charter of Charles I in 1638, and a further six who had served as sheriff were added by virtue of a 1692 charter.[5] Each such expansion of the commission was made to address the growing business of the city government, including its administration of criminal justice.[6]

GUILDHALL AS THE VENUE FOR CITY JUSTICE

London's Guildhall had long served as a place for the administration of justice, possibly since the construction of the Great Hall around 1411. Various civil and criminal courts held regular sessions in Guildhall's rooms and London's citizens probably came to know Guildhall as a location for the discharge of all manner of legal business, including the place to find the sitting alderman JP. The Outer Chamber of Guildhall was the venue for the Lord Mayor and aldermen to transact their judicial business and this chamber seems to be the so-called 'Justice Room'.[7]

By the eighteenth century, the population of the City had swelled considerably and the daily business of the magistrates was growing more voluminous and complex. In the early eighteenth century many aldermen shied away from their obligations as JPs and thus by the 1730s the bulk of the magistrate's work in Guildhall had devolved to only a few men. When the former mayor Sir Richard Brocas, an especially active alderman magistrate, died in 1737, it became clear that to avoid a log jam in the summary business, other eligible aldermen would need to step up. On considering the problem, the Court of Aldermen

---

4. [P. E. Jones], 'The City Justices and Justice Rooms' (Historical Notes, unpublished paper, Oct. 1956), LMA: COL/AC/13/005/19.
5. Charter of Charles I (1638) and William & Mary (1692).
6. J. M. Beattie, *Policing and Punishment in London 1660–1750: Urban Crime and the Limits of Terror* (Oxford, 2001), p. 11.
7. [P. E. Jones], 'The City Courts of Law', *The Law Journal*, 93 (18 Sept. 1943), 301.

resolved on 22 November 1737 that all aldermen capable of sitting as JPs should attend at Guildhall every weekday from 11 a.m. to 2 p.m. by rotation, and that attorneys who attended to the Lord Mayor in the Mayor's Court were also to attend in rotation.[8] This would spread the burden of administering the law more equitably across all of the eligible aldermen, and would go some way to preventing future problems from the concentration of such work into only a few hands. The attorneys of the Mayor's Court were asked to select a clerk to assist the Justices at Guildhall and nominated Mr Christopher Robinson.[9] From December 1737, then, the aldermen and their attending attorney were organized in a rota to sit in a part of the Matted Gallery of Guildhall with the proceedings recorded by a clerk.[10]

Even with the aid of the additional magistrates, in less than three years the solution was proving inadequate. In a petition to the Crown in June 1740, the Court of Aldermen argued that the duties of JPs 'are by many Acts of Parliament very much increased' and requested the Crown to extend the commission to all aldermen.[11] George II agreed and a charter of 1741 finally extended the commission to include all twenty-five sitting aldermen. With all of the aldermen and the Lord Mayor now included on the rota the public administration of justice at Guildhall could settle into a regular, daily routine. The annual rota was drafted around the time of the Lord Mayor's election and individual aldermen knew well in advance when their justicing time was set.[12] This reorganization of magisterial duties among the aldermen regularized the practice of magistrates sitting daily at Guildhall, and summary justice in the City began to take on a new level of permanence and reliability.[13] They were also public hearings, and many London newspapers reported on the business conducted there.

The Guildhall Justice Room was open every weekday, except for holidays and other special occasions. For example, an unusual entry after the proceedings on 28 October 1761 notes that Guildhall was closed until 16 November to accommodate the preparations for the Lord Mayor's Day. In December 1782, the aldermen agreed to add a Saturday sitting to their rotation, no doubt a response to the press of

---

8. Repertory of the Court of Aldermen, LMA: COL/CA/01/01/146, f. 29 (22 Nov. 1737), f. 51 (29 Nov. 1737).
9. LMA: COL/CA/01/01/146, f. 72 (3 Dec. 1737).
10.. Beattie, *Policing*, pp. 108–13, 417–20.
11. LMA: COL/CA/01/01/148, f. 290 (17 June 1740).
12. A copy of the printed rota for the mayoral year 1751–52 may be found glued in the first minute book in the series reproduced here (LMA: CLA/005/01/001).
13. In 1748, before the completion of Mansion House, the room on the main floor originally intended as the Swordbearer's Room was reassigned as a justice room ([P. E. Jones], 'The City Justices and Justice Rooms', *Transactions of the Guildhall Historical Association*, 3 [1963], 35). A more recent history of the Mansion House Justice Room may be found in S. Jeffery, *The Mansion House* (Chichester, 1993), pp. 196–7, 214–17.

business, but in the minutes reproduced here the Guildhall magistrates only sat from Monday to Friday.[14]

The Lord Mayor continued to sit as one justice in the rotation until the Mansion House was completed in 1752. Thereafter, the mayor conducted his own judicial business in one of the rooms on the principal floor of the Mansion House, possibly as soon as the Mansion House was opened, but certainly from 1756, as Mayor Marshe Dickinson reported in his diary that his Worship sat for part of each day in his Justice Room 'despatching publick business'. The Guildhall and Mansion House justice rooms operated in parallel.[15] A separate set of minute books from the Mansion House Justice Room survives for extended portions of the period: 1784–1790, 1800–1803 and 1819–1821.[16]

Though in law both justice rooms had jurisdiction over the entire City, in practice, once the Mansion House Justice Room was operational, an informal jurisdictional division of business between the two courts emerged. This division was one of geography rather than procedure or the nature of the cases. Those incidents arising east of the north–south line created by King Street and Queen Street would fall to the Lord Mayor at the Mansion House, and those from the west side went to the sitting aldermen at Guildhall.[17] According to Pulling, this division seems to have continued into the early to mid- nineteenth century.[18]

ATTORNEYS IN WAITING AND CLERKS

The minutes of the proceedings before the magistrates were kept by a clerk who was also one of the attorneys assigned to the Mayor's Court, known as the attorneys of the Outer Court. These attorneys, four

14. LMA: COL/CA/01/191, f. 16 (3 Dec. 1782).
15. GL, MS 100, cited in Jeffery, *Mansion House*, 196.
16. The seventy-three surviving Mansion House minute books document a more concentrated time period, covering November 1784 to November 1790 and November 1800 to September 1803 completely, followed by one final volume from August 1819 to August 1821. LMA: CLA/004/02/001–073.
17. J. Fletcher, 'Statistical Account of the Constitution and Operation of the Criminal Courts of the Metropolis', *Journal of the Statistical Society of London*, 9:4 (Dec. 1846), 290. P. E. Jones has suggested that the division of business varied from time to time but then, over time, became more fixed. See 'City Justices', but also see [P.E. Jones], 'Historic Courts XVII-Guildhall', *Law Times*, 233 (15 June 1962), 327–28, where he suggests an alternate division. Around the turn of the nineteenth century, the Mansion House Justice Room also became the court for hearing cases brought forward by the water bailiff. Such cases were clearly indicated in the court's rough records or minute books, and the cases themselves usually concerned disputes over forms of illegal fishing, either with illegal nets or bait or for fishing on a Sunday, as well as other disputes among persons within the water bailiff's jurisdiction.
18. A. Pulling, *A Practical Treatise on the Laws, Customs, Usages and Regulations of the City and Port of London* (London, 1842), p. 29.

in number, also 'waited' on the mayor in his other judicial roles, and thus gained the name of attorneys in waiting. The earliest surviving set of records of the mayor's judicial business recorded by the attorney comes from April 1624; these records were called the Lord Mayor's waiting books by a later archivist. Another set of records, called the charge books, covers intermittently the Lord Mayor's activities over the period 1686–1733.[19] The Lord Mayor and aldermen were likely to be men of business and finance rather than men trained in the law, and so relied on the legal counsel of their in-house attorneys. One of these four attorneys was always present to attend to the sitting Guildhall magistrate, be he the mayor or an alderman, to advise him in all matters of law relating to the cases which came before him. These attorneys were expected to be well acquainted with summary procedures and to make themselves masters of the office and duty of a justice of the peace and the law relating thereto. They were thus paid professionals, and indeed we know that in 1783 they were each paid £43 6s. 8d. for their 'attendance on the sitting Justices at Guildhall from Lady day 1782 to Lady day 1783', and in 1786 they were paid 13s. 4d. per day.[20] Before ordering payment, however, Mr Chamberlain was ordered to compare the bill they presented 'with the Minute Books of the Business done' and we can see in the records that nearly every day's minutes end with a note written in a different hand, presumably that of the alderman, indicating which attorney attended followed by the alderman's initials.[21] In the records transcribed here, the names of the attorneys appearing most often are the four men listed in *Browne's General Law List* as the attorneys of the Lord Mayor's court: Thomas Beach, George Hawles Houstoun, William Nash and George Rhodes. Beach also served as the coroner for the City and Southwark, though it is not clear when this combined role began.[22]

The proceedings were all recorded by a clerk who appears from the minutes to have taken an active part in the daily proceedings. It would appear that the clerk, or clerks who also attended, one of whom was a Mr Robert Holder (his initials appear in the entries for 5 and 8 January 1776), was more actively involved than the attorneys. One can imagine the clerks interacting with the crowd awaiting their moment before the magistrate: taking down names, details of their place of commitment and the constable's name in advance of the hearing. This seems especially clear on some days when there are two hands in the text and one

19. Beattie offers an analysis of the Lord Mayor's charge books and their contents in *Policing*, pp. 103–108.
20. LMA: COL/CA/01/01/191, ff. 203–204; LMA: COL/CA/01/01/194, f. 173.
21. LMA: COL/CA/01/01/191, ff. 203–204.
22. *Browne's general law-list; for the year 1779. Being an Alphabetical Register of the Names and Residence of all the Judges Serjeants Counsellors Doctors Proctors Public Notaries Commissioners of Bankrupts Attorneys Officers, &c.* (London, [1778]), p. 77; Fletcher, 'Statistical Account', 289.

is simply filling in the blanks, and on days when a substantial amount of detailed text has been entered but then struck through with the notation 'No Attendance', such as the entry for 6 June 1781.

By 1786 there may have been problems with regular attendance by the attorneys as the Court of Aldermen struck an agreement with three of the four attorneys to terminate the practice of the attorneys in waiting attending the sitting justices at Guildhall. They would be replaced by clerks who were also qualified in the law.[23] George Rhodes objected to this change, pleading 'that his necessities would not permit him to accept of a decrease in his income' and that he was 'ready and willing to give strict and due attendance'. But the court was unmoved and having agreed earlier in January of that year to appoint an assistant to Daniel Gunston, the clerk, they were now of the opinion that the regular services of the attorneys were no longer needed and that 'no further Attendance on the said Justices should be required of the Attorneys of the Outer Court in future'.[24] From then on, the two roles of attorney and clerk were combined in one person.

THE POWERS OF THE JUSTICE OF THE PEACE

Magistrates were frequently the first authorities to become involved in a dispute between two parties and the disputes ranged from potentially civil or criminal actions, to regulatory matters, to matters of Poor Law administration. Because of London's sizeable population, the Guildhall Justice Room (and its Mansion House twin) was busier than its rural counterparts. The volume of business guaranteed a regular crop of routine cases, but also increased the chances that more intriguing or complicated issues would come before the justices too. Like their rural counterparts, the alderman magistrates provided the venue for preliminary complaints arising within the City and acted as gatekeepers to the many formal courts and tribunals to which disputes could proceed. But in contrast to the country justice, the types of cases that came before the Guildhall Justice Room reflected very much the pressures of a growing, urban metropolis. There are no disputes arising from the game laws, for example, and in theft cases even the goods that were stolen were more likely to be manufactured, commercial or imported goods (linen, sugar, rum, nutmegs, pepper) than livestock or grain. A careful examination of these records, with so many disputes arising in

---

23. The four attorneys were offered Freedom of the City by way of compensation.
24. For the appointment of Gunston's assistant, William Henry Whittell, see LMA: COL/CA/01/01/194, f. 71. The report leading to the elimination of the payment of the attorneys is at LMA: COL/CA/01/01/194, ff. 173–5.

the streets, shops, public houses and warehouses, affords the reader a unique feel for eighteenth-century London's bustling, urban character.

Under the 1555 Marian committal procedures, in a felony case the JP was officially limited to taking written statements from the alleged victim and perhaps witnesses, and from any suspects accused of the offence. If necessary he could bind over witnesses to appear at trial. The most trivial of claims might be dismissed, but any allegation of a felony was supposed to be left for the determination of a judge and jury (at the Old Bailey for cases arising in London), while claims of a misdemeanour offence were to be forwarded to the county quarter sessions or the City's sessions of the peace. Over time, magistrates had assumed a considerable degree of discretionary power in investigating the substance of the charge and, as we shall see, in gathering both condemnatory and exculpatory evidence. What the magistrate was forbidden from doing was what was called 'compounding' an offence, or settling a matter of criminal import, which should rightly go to a trial before a jury. Serious offences, or felonies, like murder, rape, treason, forgery, could not be settled by a magistrate or magistrates alone and had to be sent on to the grand jury for trial at a court of assize.

In many minor actions, however, JPs, sitting two or three together or in London the lone alderman magistrate, had the power simply to settle the case and prevent it from proceeding any further or else convict and impose a punishment. Indeed it was expected that responsible JPs would use their power and position both to weed out the most frivolous cases and prevent them from consuming valuable court time later on. They were expected to use their influence and standing as men of power and station within the community and, using their discretion, try to finesse a settlement or agreement between the two parties through a range of negotiation and arbitration tactics to prevent further litigation. This was possible before a formal charge was laid and when the JP could get the parties to speak to one another preferably face to face. This was precisely the setting in most of the cases recorded in the records produced here. The Justice Room minute books make it plain that the aldermen and Lord Mayor in their judicial roles were concerned with arbitration and mediation in the first instance. There were no formal guidelines on how this arbitration and mediation should work in practice, and each magistrate was left to make his own decisions. What is clear, however, is that these interactions in pre-trial and summary proceedings played an extremely important role in the administration of justice and placed the JPs in the role of gatekeepers to England's criminal justice system.[25] Their actions served as an initial filter to the continuous stream of human disputes that ran past the courts. Prominent legal voices like Sir William Blackstone were decidedly uneasy

25. N. Landau, *The Justices of the Peace, 1679–1760* (Berkeley, 1984).

with the discretionary powers of JPs in summary proceedings; Blackstone commented sharply on what he saw as their excessive extension and their 'mischievous effects'.[26] But even he had to concede that the advantage of summary justice was that it was 'extremely speedy' and for the busy aldermen magistrates, time was money.

BUSINESS OF THE GUILDHALL JUSTICE ROOM

The magistrates were well connected with the other legal venues in the City and could expedite the administration of justice when circumstances warranted. The remarkably rapid process from arrest to conviction in some cases is revealed by these records. Take the case of a servant named William Goodchild, arrested on 29 June 1780 and charged with theft. On 30 June he appeared before Alderman Hart who heard the complaint of the victim, his master, a grocer named Joseph Travers, and his witness, one William Hewitt, a warehouseman also under his employ. Goodchild's case moved within days to the Old Bailey, which happened to be in session, and he was tried, convicted and sentenced to six months' imprisonment by the end of the Old Bailey sessions on 11 July. Although this may have been an example of efficient justice from the prosecutor's point of view, the case also demonstrates how eighteenth-century criminal procedure might deny the accused sufficient opportunity to prepare a defence, to gather witnesses and possibly to secure legal counsel.

The number of cases that went on from the Guildhall Justice Room to trial at the Old Bailey was small. Only 67 cases from the sixteen-month selection reproduced here went to the Old Bailey. That said, when the number of cases proceeding to the Old Bailey is compared to the total number of Old Bailey trials for a particular month, the proportion of trials originating at Guildhall is often closer to 10 per cent (7 of 67 in June 1752, 8 of 84 in February 1778, 7 of 61 in February 1781, and 5 of 68 in July 1781). A handful went to the quarter sessions. The remainder of the disputes were settled on the spot in some way, resulting occasionally in a minor sanction, or the parties were simply dismissed as the alderman determined there was no felony, or no felonious intent. In prosecutions for theft, the magistrates were concerned with establishing the basic facts behind the dispute. This was important because it set the stage for the future of the case. They also sought to gain some sense of the character and intentions of the accused. In trifling matters, this could be ascertained by a few pointed questions directed to the accused and to the constables who normally presented them upon a charge.

---

26. W. Blackstone, *Commentaries on the Laws of England* (Oxford, 1765–9; facsimile of first edn, Chicago, 1979), iv. 278.

But when allegations of serious crime were brought to Guildhall, the magistrates made an attempt to pull together as much evidence as possible. The accused could be subjected to a prolonged, pre-trial examination and re-examination on the lines outlined by Beattie in his study of Sir John Fielding's magistrate's court.[27] The minute books reveal the City magistrates engaged in similar practices, taking an active role in these pre-trial procedures and using their powers to detain in order to buy time to collect further evidence, especially in cases that might result in a felony charge. Indeed, it is possible to trace a number of cases that stretch over several days. Suspects were remanded to either the Wood Street or Poultry Compter to await further examination. In the meantime, constables were sent out to search premises, gather evidence and assist with building a credible case for the prosecution. In one case, the constable William Payne was asked by Alderman Hayley to investigate a suspected arson, directing him, as he later testified at the Old Bailey, 'to go and take a survey of the building, and give my opinion of it'.[28] Payne not only produced a plan of the house but cut off a piece of wood allegedly burned in the fire and produced it at the trial along with a number of other pieces of physical evidence. In other instances, witnesses were solicited and suspected stolen goods were advertised in the newspapers along with requests for persons with information to appear before the Justices.[29] William Robson, charged by a watchman in May 1752 on suspicion of stealing a parcel of cobblers' tools and some old shoes, was remanded to Wood Street Compter 'for further Examinacion till the Goods are Advertized'.[30] Clearly the City alderman justices, like their Bow Street counterparts, were using all available policing resources in order to build solid, evidence-based cases that could support a formal charge.

The absence of plea bargaining that John Langbein argues was a characteristic of Old Bailey and other early modern English trials might partially be explained by a better understanding of the range of negotiation and arbitration that occurred in the very earliest stages of a claim.[31] The minute books provide ample evidence of how the magistrates imposed their will in the preliminary proceedings, frequently finding a suitable but lesser sanction for actions that in a criminal trial

---

27. John Beattie has demonstrated how John Fielding was expanding the JP's role outside of the City in his Bow Street court. See J. M. Beattie, 'Sir John Fielding and Public Justice: The Bow Street Magistrate's Court, 1754–1780', *Law and History Review*, 25:1 (Spring 2007), 61–100; idem, *The First English Detectives: The Bow Street Runners and the Policing of London, 1750–1840* (Oxford, 2012).

28. *Old Bailey Proceedings Online* (www.oldbailey.org, version 7.0, 12 Nov. 2012), April 1779, trial of Thomas Hilliard (t17790404–36). This directive is not mentioned in minute book entries for 23 Mar. 1779, reproduced here.

29. For examples see the proceedings on 5 and 9 June 1752, 18 Dec. 1775, 23 Jan. 1778, 4 Feb. 1778.

30. 29 May 1752.

31. J. H. Langbein, *The Origins of Adversary Criminal Trial* (Oxford, 2003), pp. 18–20.

could well result in a capital sentence. Prior to any 'pious perjury' that a trial jury may have committed in finding felons guilty but on lesser charges, leading to a 'partial verdict', we see in these minute books how magistrates were also routinely finding lesser charges in which to frame the alleged wrong in the first place, and holding out alternative sanctions as an inducement to the prosecutor to forego a trial, and to the accused to mitigate the risk of a trip to Tyburn.[32]

Langbein surmised that the pre-trial process 'generated a large quantity of pre-trial confessions' which, when entered into evidence at trial, made for expeditious proceedings.[33] There is evidence of confessions leading to commitments for jury trial in the Guildhall minute books. But it is perhaps possible that confessions made by the accused also became the basis not for a swift trial, but for a negotiated settlement leading to a discharge before a formal charge was ever laid. Elizabeth Norris, for example, charged with felony (the theft of a silver watch), 'confess'd under a Promise of favour' and, there being 'no other Evidence', was discharged.[34]

Evidence and witnesses supporting the accused were supposed to be ignored in the pre-trial examination.[35] But again, the minute books document the appearance of character witnesses, masters, employers, parents and others whose participation sometimes helped to steer the accused away from trial, with the magistrate's blessing. James King, charged with stealing a load of iron from St Paul's church was remanded by Alderman Smith 'to Produce some Person to his Character' (4 September 1777). When five men were picked up by the constable for being idle and disorderly, one of the men produced his master and landlord and another his father and both were discharged (19 March 1779). Henry Ducker escaped a trial for 'feloniously stealing three Tires & a Piece of Iron' when his master appealed for, and was granted, his discharge (22 February 1781). In an earlier case from 1752 it is interesting to note, from what is originally entered in the minute book then struck through, how the alderman magistrate was at first considering leniency to one of two men charged with pickpocketing, ordering him to Wood Street Compter until his master appeared. However, something changed his mind and instead the man was committed to Bridewell – effectively a sentence – while his accomplice was committed to Newgate and stood trial alone at the Old Bailey. In other cases, one could argue with Blackstone that the magistrates were pushing the envelope of acceptable practice and determining on matters of proof

---

32. J. M. Beattie, *Crime and the Courts in England, 1660–1800* (Princeton, 1986), pp. 268–70. Examples of pre-plea bargaining are at 10 May 1762 (James Haines and Bridget Taafe), 12 Dec. 1775 (Alice Miller), 2 Jan. 1775 (Henry Hickey), 10 Sept. 1777 (Mary Hoff).

33 J. H. Langbein, 'The Criminal Trial before the Lawyers', *University of Chicago Law Review*, 45:2 (Winter 1978), 21.

34. 14 July 1780.

35. Langbein, *Origins of Adversary Criminal Trial*, p. 43.

and thus guilt or innocence without the aid of a trial by jury. Thus Mary Taunton, charged by a mercer with 'feloniously stealing 31 Yards of black silk Lace Value 30s & upwards', was summarily discharged by the alderman, there being 'no proof'. Richard Morgan was charged with feloniously stealing some tobacco from Fresh Wharf. The minute book records 'He was acquitted of the Felony for want of Proof' but was then re-charged on the lesser crime of being a suspected pilferer and committed to Bridewell. No jury heard the case, no prosecutor appeared to address the 'want of Proof' but he was acquitted of one charge and convicted of another.[36]

A simple count of business before the magistrates suggests that the bulk of the magistrate's work concerned routine legal administrative work: issuing warrants or backing those issued by other magistrates, and taking affidavits. However, the vast majority of the time-consuming business recorded in these surviving minute books deals with the administration of the criminal law. Gray's sample of business coming to the Guildhall magistrates shows an almost even division of legal business between alleged property offences, regulatory offences and cases of interpersonal violence.[37]

Offences against the peace

Offences that would fall under the broad category of interpersonal violence form a significant proportion of magisterial business at Guildhall. The wide range of offences against the peace that included assaults, batteries, physical threats and heated insults constituted a regular portion of the weekly courtroom fare. Both men and women appear in the roles of complainants and alleged perpetrators though, in the main, violent offences that were brought to the attention of the authorities were committed by men on other men. This pattern is reflected in these minutes too. Only a small proportion of these disputes brought before the sitting aldermen went any further in the courts. As the minutes show, most such cases were settled on the spot and the parties discharged.

Guildhall Justice Room and the regulation of the City and the poor

The Guildhall Justices were also concerned with enforcing a range of regulatory issues including those relating to both commerce and public space, and those relating to morality and the poor. One finds examples of individuals being charged with exercising their trade on a Sunday (Richard Jutsum, a butcher, 8 March 1781) and brought forward by a parish overseer of the poor. Cart drivers, porters and hackney coachmen

36. 5 Dec. 1775 (Richard Morgan).
37. Gray, *Crime, Prosecution and Social Relations*, p. 20, Table 2.1.

appear regularly, charged with obstructing traffic, loading or unloading goods at inopportune times, or 'plying' in streets where they were not licensed to do so. Drivers also appeared as complainants, charging their passengers with failing to pay all or part of their fare or when, as a result of a dispute over the fare, things turned physical. City bylaws against traffic or bullock-hunting are other examples from the range of regulatory matters facing the Justices but the minute books suggest that their roles as local administrators and regulators of other bylaws had been largely pushed aside by the growing business of criminal justice administration.[38]

The regulation of the labouring population, the poor and those who were supposed to help them also fell under the purview of the alderman magistrates. City constables were particularly active in bringing forward people who were in breach of vagrancy laws, public order regulations and moral concerns including prostitution. In October 1781, nine men and one woman were summoned by the Overseer of the Poor in the parish of St Botolph without Aldersgate to explain why they had refused to pay their share of the poor rate.[39] Warrants were issued on the request of overseers of London parishes to arrest runaway husbands and fathers whose actions had now left their families dependent upon parish relief. Another interesting intervention in the personal lives of complainants to the Guildhall Justice Room came in the form of settlements for poor women who wanted a separation from their husbands. The magistrates intervened in a few of these instances, imposing what amounted to separation agreements and scheduled maintenance payments. A small number of cases appear which relate to master and servant law. Idle workers or those who had deserted their employment without leave from their master were subject to the sanction of the JP. The magistrates were empowered to punish such infractions with imprisonment in the house of correction.

The Gordon Riots, London's most explosive urban event in the period, are captured briefly in these records as well. Only one minute book survives from June 1780, covering the business from 28 June to 26 July. Four hearings from that minute book concern the Gordon Riots and one led to a trial at the Old Bailey. It is highly likely that other rioters came before the alderman magistrates, but their appearances were recorded in the preceding minute book, now culled from the archive.

Constables and policing

Constables appear frequently in the minutes of proceedings at Guildhall. In their official capacity, constables assisted the magistrates in

---

38. Gray devotes a chapter to bullock-hunting in his *Crime, Prosecution and Social Relations*, ch. 7.
39. See Thomas Wheeley et al. (26 Oct. 1781).

conducting the business of administering the law. Constables had the power to detain suspects until they could be brought before a JP for the preliminary investigation into the matter. Constables were required to take those they had arrested before a magistrate as soon as reasonably possible, and also had the power to remove a suspected felon from his home at night and gaol him until he might be taken before a magistrate.[40] The records also show the numerous warrants issued for the arrest of individuals to answer the charge of assault or theft, as well as warrants to search premises for stolen property. The active role of constables in the City revealed in these minute books, and the dozens of names represented, adds weight to the suggestion that London was reasonably well policed in the last third of the eighteenth century.

Some constables appeared frequently before the magistrates, in some cases for many years running. Tracing the individual 'beats' of some of the more active constables reveals how some developed certain specializations in terms of the types of cases they became involved in. William Prosser (first appears 12 June 1781) can be found in many garment/weaving/fabric cases. Others, like James Emmerson and Barnabas Linton, were regularly employed by the West India Merchants and knew the docklands and the networks for fencing stolen imported goods very well.[41] William Payne was a remarkably active constable, who took a particular interest in using his position as constable to bring about the moral reform of the City. He appears in numerous cases of brothel clearing, literally loading up a cartload of suspected prostitutes and bringing them before the sitting aldermen.[42] On 19 August 1777, the clerk is careful to note that Payne, who had rounded up a dozen suspected prostitutes, was 'paid 3s. for a Cart for these women'.

Officials involved in policing the City were regulated by magistrates too. When Thomas Ross, a zealous watchman, arrested a couple and brought them before Alderman Sainsbury for 'going to a bad House' he ruled that as there was 'no Indeceny, nor disturbance' the couple were to be discharged. Moreover, the constable William Cooke, who had brought the parties to Guildhall on behalf of Ross, was reprimanded by the alderman for arresting them in the first place.[43]

40. See R. Burn, *The Justice of the Peace and Parish Officer*, 2 vols. (London, 1755), under 'Arrest'. Also see Beattie, *First English Detectives*.
41. See R. Stansel, 'Merchant Prosecutors and Public Justice in the Port of London, 1750–1800' (unpublished MA paper, York University, 2009).
42. The satirical sketch by C. Williams, 'City scavengers cleansing the London Streets of impurities' (1816), which graces the cover of Gray's book is nevertheless a remarkably accurate depiction of William Payne's tactics. See entries at 18 Dec. 1775, 19 Aug. 1777, 27 Aug. 1777 and 5 Feb. 1778 for examples of Payne's campaign against 'loose idle and disorderly women and Common Prostitutes'. For an excellent account of Payne's life and work see J. Innes, 'The Protestant Carpenter – William Payne of Bell Yard (c.1718–82), the Life and Times of a London Informing Constable' in her *Inferior Politics: Social Problems and Social Policies in Eighteenth-Century Britain* (Oxford, 2009), pp. 279–341.
43. 3 July 1780.

JUSTICE ROOMS AS 'COURTS'

Although the alderman justices attempted to mediate disputes and to avert felony prosecutions in some cases, the minutes suggest that in general the aldermen were not inclined to impose penalties. There are no cases reproduced here where offenders were sentenced directly to a whipping. However, by sending people to Bridewell or the house of correction, as happens in a number of cases, there was a likelihood that physical punishments would be imposed. Those cases where individuals were sent to Bridewell as a punishment (more than 80 such cases here) show how summary proceedings might resemble a court. But the magistrates did not determine felony cases where there was credible evidence to support a formal charge. In some cases the magistrate might separate certain individuals from a group, committing the accessories or those unlikely to face trial by jury to Bridewell while the principals in the case were sent on to the Old Bailey.[44]

The Guildhall Justices might be said to have been operating more formally as a court in those instances where they heard and determined on a case and administered a punishment. As mentioned above, such instances were, strictly speaking, few in number and occurred in matters within the purview of the alderman's jurisdiction as a JP. A more liberal interpretation of the business of summary justice as the work of a summary 'court' sees the whole range of adjudications determined by the sitting magistrates as essentially mini trials. King and Gray have promoted this view, arguing that since most people actually experienced the law at the summary level and did not pursue their disputes in the courts of assize or quarter session, their summary hearing and any determination that came out of it was in effect a trial.[45] The elision of the permitted exercise of summary powers by magistrates into the concept of 'trial' may introduce a troubling confusion of procedure and blurs the fine distinctions that were made and understood at the time between what could and could not be determined at law without the benefit of a judge and jury.

OUTCOMES AND PUNISHMENTS

It may be helpful to examine briefly those types of cases in which the magistrates used their power to punish individuals for their actions. The discretionary power accorded to Justices of the Peace in punishing minor offences or offences related to vagrancy allowed them to select from a range of sanctions. Fines were one option, imprisonment for

44. See the case of Philip Doyle and John Webster charged with stealing tobacco, 11 June 1752.
45. King, 'Summary Courts'; idem, *Crime and Law in England*; Gray, *Crime, Prosecution and Social Relations*.

a period of time in Bridewell or either the Wood Street or Poultry Compter was another.

Settled and discharged

The vast majority of cases were settled and the parties discharged, particularly among the numerous assault prosecutions that were brought. One can imagine that many affrays looked rather silly in the sober light of the morning-after, especially after a night spent in the City Compters; the notation in the minutes that the parties 'settled' their differences probably involved a harsh word or two from the sitting alderman and perhaps required the courtesy of a handshake or verbal apology. I suggest this indicates a mild sanction, deliberately noted by the clerks in contrast to other cases where the notation is only that the accused was discharged. Settlements in assault cases could also involve payment or 'satisfaction' made to the victim. This is in keeping with the predominant interpretation of assault in the eighteenth century as a civil rather than criminal matter.[46] Ann Major, charged with assaulting Catherine Eady, 'proposed to make Satisfaction but having no money consented that the Warrant should be in force against her till after Saturday' when she would have the money to pay to Eady.[47] Gray's analysis of the outcomes shows that women were more likely than men to see their complaint settled at the summary level, rather than proceeding to trial.

Fines and imprisonment

Regulatory offences could be settled by paying a fine, as could some assaults. Edward Cuffley assaulted an inspector of pavements in the City and was fined 5s. Offences judged to fall under the broad vagrancy acts could also be settled by way of fines or imprisonment. However, the only option for imprisonment open to the aldermen was to direct offenders to Bridewell and numerous pilferers were sent there for their punishment.

Impressments and philanthropic organizations

Other options for dealing with the unfortunate or troublesome included the possible enlistment of men into service, especially in high moments of military conflict. In November 1761, in the midst of the Seven

46. See G. T. Smith, 'The State and the Culture of Violence in London, 1760–1840' (Ph.D. thesis, University of Toronto, 1999), pp. 275–335; N. Landau, 'Indictment for Fun and Profit: A Prosecutor's Reward at Eighteenth-Century Quarter Sessions', *Law & History Review* (1999), 507–36; P. King, 'Punishing Assault: The Transformation of Attitudes in the English Courts', *Journal of Interdisciplinary History*, 27:1 (1996), 43–74.
47. 27 Oct. 1761.

Years' War, Thomas Shute was brought to Guildhall for being 'an idle and disorderly Apprentice & deserting his Masters Service' allegedly for the eighth time. Alderman Alexander ordered that he be confined to Wood Street Compter until 'they could get him into the Sea Service' (19 November 1761). At times it appears the magistrates coerced some suspects into joining the military or navy as a way of avoiding a criminal trial. George Venables was charged in March 1779 with 'feloniously stealing a Box of Lace'. As a felony was suspected, this case should have proceeded to the Old Bailey for trial. However, Venables 'agreed to go to Sea' and so no recognizances were issued and no trial occurs at the Old Bailey in the ensuing months. Alderman Peckham convinced or cajoled five suspects to go to sea on 17 October 1781. One might speculate whether a press officer tipped off the alderman that he was in need of men, and hoped his summary business might prove obliging. Nicholas Rogers has portrayed the City magistrates such as Thomas Sainsbury as strenuous advocates of improved impressments, particularly in times of crisis.[48] The officer of a press gang was conveniently on hand to take Thomas Hill off the City's hands in November 1761 and he was 'ordered on board the Tender & the Constable directed to Assist him', suggesting Hill might have had other plans.

Other magistrates used the opportunity of arrest to funnel petty thieves into some of the new philanthropic institutions established in the eighteenth century to address the very problem of the poor, potentially criminal youth. In February 1778, when George Parsons, 'a Boy about 13 years old', was charged with stealing a cheese cake, he indicated to the Justice that he would be 'willing to go to Sea' and was directed to the Marine Society.[49]

The same treatment was used for selected members of the city's urban poor who were living in hard circumstances. Jacob Sibley, picked up by the constable William Payne and charged 'for lodging in the open Air' in February 1778, was recommended to the Marine Society. Mary Smith, charged by the constable Boyse May (9 July 1790) with 'lodging in the open Air', was recommended to St Bartholomew's hospital, as was Mary Watson a few days later.

---

48. N. Rogers, 'Impressment and the Law in Eighteenth-Century Britain', in N. Landau, ed., *Law, Crime and English Society* (Cambridge, 2002), pp. 77–8; P. King, *Crime, Justice and Discretion in England 1740–1820* (Cambridge, 2000), p. 91; Gray, *Crime, Prosecution and Social Relations*, p. 80.
49. The Marine Society, established in 1756 by a group of London merchants including the philanthropist Jonas Hanway, was responsible for taking in young boys and training them for naval service.

EDITORIAL METHOD

The original minute books are held by the London Metropolitan Archive which is now the repository for most of the former Corporation of London Record Office holdings.[1] An earlier set of related records known as the Lord Mayor's waiting books are the precursors to the set partially reproduced here. The Guildhall Justice Room booklets are soft cover, thread-bound notebooks of relatively uniform size and page numbers (approximately 60 pages). It was ordered that they be kept 'in the closet in the Justice Room' for the clerk to 'enter the sums received' for the day's business, to be initialled by the alderman.[2] This certainly seems to be established practice at the time of the first surviving volume from the record series transcribed here. The first volume of the Guildhall Justice Room minute books series begins in May 1752 and the fifty-fifth (and last) ends with the business of 25 March 1796. Each individual book covers approximately one month of business. The books that survive appear to be the remainder after a culling of the records at some point as there are significant gaps between the dates of the books. The first book in the series covers the period 25 May to 19 June 1752 and the second book begins over nine years later on 14 October 1761.

The selection that constitutes this volume includes the first fifteen of the surviving fifty-five minute books, which cover the period 1752–1781. They have been transcribed in full. As these were rough minute books kept largely for the recording clerk's own purposes the entries were not always taken in a careful, secretary hand. The hand changes with the clerk of the day and unique or inconsistent abbreviations or notations are rarely explained; the meaning of yet others remains opaque. The minute books were reviewed and corrected by the clerks perhaps to improve clarity, to correct errors in names or other pertinent details in a case, or to substitute a better word. Occasionally parts of or even entire entries are struck out. One gets the impression that occasionally the clerk began noting down names and details from those awaiting the alderman magistrate's appearance. Then, when the magis-

---

1. The former Corporation of London Record Office gave the Guildhall and Mansion House Justice Room books the reference numbers of GJR/M 1–55 and MJR/M 1–73 respectively. The new record references for the records reproduced here are LMA: CLA/005/01/001–056 and LMA: CLA/004/02/001–073.
2. LMA: COL/CA/01/01/156, f. 116 (2 Feb. 1747).

trate failed to arrive, the sessions were cancelled for the day for 'no attendance'.[3] In order to render a more accurate sense of the minute books these deletions and alterations have been retained and indicated in the text. Illegible deletions have been indicated.

The text has been reproduced in chronological order, largely in the order in which it appeared in the original documents, and in a layout similar to that of the original books, with notations of fees collected, recognizances issued and miscellaneous other comments appearing down the left margin and the rough notes of the proceedings on the right. However, in the interests of space and clarity, the entries have been condensed into paragraphs while text that the clerk inserted either within the original entry or by way of later addenda, sometimes appearing on later pages of the notebook, has been consolidated with the initial entry. In the left column, when a simple numeral appears I have assumed this to note shillings, and have amended the transcription so. The minute books were clearly compiled to record the financial side of summary justice as well as the pertinent legal issues. Additional information regarding the progress of a case, particularly to the Old Bailey, has been noted in a footnote.

A list of commonly used abbreviations that have been retained in the transcription appears at the front of this volume. Nearly all of the contractions in the original text have been maintained to preserve the original feel of the text. Some abbreviations or contractions have been silently expanded for clarity of meaning and ease of reading. The various forms of ye have been modernized to the, their, etc. and the clerk's shorthand for 'per' or 'pro' has been silently expanded when used for person, property, and so on. The designation of a proper name as a constable by a capital C has been applied in cases where the clerk used other abbreviations or the full word. Superscripts in noting monetary amounts have been standardized in lower case form, and the variants of the pound symbol used by different clerks have been standardized. In cases where I have expanded for clarity, the addition is enclosed in square brackets [ ]. Date entries have been standardized, but punctuation, capitalization and abbreviations have been preserved except when minor, silent alterations improved the clarity of the sentence. In the interests of space, some very minor or illegible marks and minor word repetitions have been silently removed as they do not affect the understanding of the court business. Entries have been revised into the least number of paragraphs. A more invasive editorial decision was to remove the recurrence of a standard note found at the top of most new pages in the original notebooks, indicating that the minutes continued from the previous session and under the watch of the same alderman *ad huc*, 'even now'. However, if a new justice's

---

3.   See the entries for 6 July and 31 Aug. 1780 and 29 Jan. 1781 as examples.

name appears in the original (occasionally one alderman stepped in mid-session to replace another called away on other business) this has been noted. The title of Alderman has been inserted in lieu of various contractions, S^r has been uniformly expanded to Sir, and names have been spelled out in full.

I have standardized the sign off by the magistrate and the attorney in waiting at the conclusion of the day's business, where the alderman's initials appear in the margin, before or after those of the attorney. Sometimes these initials appear before the day's business is complete or at unusual points on the page. In most cases I have placed the initialling off at the end of the day's business.

MINUTE BOOKS OF
THE GUILDHALL JUSTICE ROOM
1752–1781

Sir John Barnard, Knt.

Sir Henry Marshall, Knt.

Sir Richard Hoare, Knt.

William Benn, Esq;

Sir Robert Ladbroke, Knt.

Sir William Calvert, Knt.

John Blachford, Esq;

Francis Cokayne, Esq;

Sir George Champion, Knt.

Sir Joseph Hankey, Knt.

William Baker, Esq;

Thomas Winterbottom Esq;

Robert Allop, Esq;

Crisp Galcoyne, Esq;

Edward Ironside, Esq;

Thomas Rawlinson, Esq;

William Whitaker, Esq;

Stephen Theod. Janssen, Esq;

Slingsby Bethell, Esq;

Marshe Dickinson, Esq;

Charles Asgill, Esq;

Richard Glyn, Esq;

Matthew Blakiston, Esq;

Samuel Fludyer, Esq;

(Column headings, left to right: October 1751, November, December, January 1752, February, March, April, May, June, July, August, August.)

Printed rota of Alderman Justices at Guildhall for 1751–52 (LMA: CLA/005/01/001)
City of London, London Metropolitan Archive

Mr Alderman Baker. Monday 25 May 1752.

1s.   John Knight fr WC by John Stone C. ch^d by Wm Sparry a prison^r in the Fleet for an Ass^t It App^d they had ch^d each other but Sparry not appearing he was D^d

1s.   George Lane, Hannah Patch} fr WC by D^o ch^d by John Moore
P^1 & ~~Watchman~~ John Buxton Watchmen & ~~on promising not to Offend again D^d~~ with ~~being~~ loitering abo^t as disorderly persons but being the first Time & promising not to Offend again D^d

P   Owen Berry fr PC by Saml Wyat C. ch^d by Chas Wood for as Ass^t on Agreem^t D^d

P   John Anderson, by Robt Eglington C. ch^d by Eliz^a his wife on Ald^n Janssen's W^t 6th Inst. for an Ass^t Upon Consent of his Wife & promising not to offend again discharged.

1s.   Sum^s for Thos Marshall a Waterman to answ^r on Wednesday next the Informacon of John Bayley & shew Cause why he should not forfiet £5 as being the Owner of a Boat navigated 8th Inst^t bet[ween] Gravesend & London by Mich^{ll} Earle under 18 y^{rs} old Contrary to the Statute 10 Geo: 2^d c. 31.

1s.   ~~John Anderson~~ Affid^t Edwd Thomson

1s.   Indors'd a Winchester W^t of Esqr Green the Mayor & Wm Waldron Esqr 19th Inst^t ag^t John Osman for having his Son a Charge to the psh of St Thomas in s^d City

1s.   Warrant against Richd Badger, James Connoway & Patrick King ads John Gormain for an Ass^t.

1s.   Sum^s for Ja^s Saxx, Wm Hazelton, Wm Simpson, Wm Slayny & John Griffin Watermen to answer the Rulers of the Watermen's Comp^y for Non payment of their Quarteridge

P   W^t ag^t Thos Sanderson ads Sarah Bagwell for an Ass^t

~~Sum^s for Mary Humphrys ads Isable Simpson for Differences between them~~

WB ^{2} TL r^d 7s.^{3}

---

1.   The 'P' in the left margin appears to correspond to Hannah Patch.
2.   William Baker. The sitting alderman's initials normally appear at the end of the day's business.
3.   TL, the clerk, acknowledging receipt of 7s. for the day.

Mr Alderman Alsop by Sir Henry Marshall.[4] Tuesday 26 May [1752].
Wm Corrison fr WC by Henry Dobbins C. ch^d by ~~Wm Matt^{us}~~
~~Watts~~ Hillyard on Suspicion of Felony in Stealing Nails &
Lead ~~his~~ Abo^t 50^{lb} W[eight] of Lead his property the pros^r
provd ~~the~~ such Goods were Stolen from him and John Steel a
Smith prov'd the prison^r sold him sevl small parsells of Lead
rolled up together ~~but~~ tho' the pros^r co^d not prove the Identity
of the Lead but the prison^r voluntarily offered to pay the pros
for his Lead which amounting to a Confession to the Satisfaction of his wpp on their Oaths com^d to N[ewgate].

R+[5]   Matt^{us} Hillyard of St And^{ws} Holborn Carpenter   £ 20
        John Steel of Cow Cross Smithf^d at the Key   £ 10

C nil   James Collins fr WC by James Rudge C. ch^d by him for
James   Swearing 2 prophane Oaths abo^t 1 °Cl this morning in the psh
Rudge   of St Mary Aldermanbury Who being convicted & paying the
rec^d penalty 2s. D^d

1s.   Affid^t Mary Burgess

1s.   Lagh Dickenson, Solomon Cooper, Wm Hutchins} fr PC by
nil[6]   Fran^s Philpot ch^d by Eliz^a White & Thos Lilly for an Ass^t upon
        them with a Stick by Dickenson & ag^t the Other 2 for Attempting
        to rescue him after taken. The Ass^t was prov'd ag^t Dickenson
        but no Evidence ag^t the Other 2 they were D^d. As ~~well~~ Also
        was Dickenson on an Agreem^t with the Pros^x.

1s.   W^t ag^t Josiah Ferry & Eliz: his wife ats Jane Brown for an Ass^t

P   Warr^t ags^t Mary Newman ats Eliz Edlington for Ass^t

1s.   Warr^t ags^t Wm Hogdon ats Mabel Devall for an Ass^t

1s.   Warr^t ags^t Wm Lee ats John Bradshaw for an Ass^t

1s.   Warr^t ags^t Wm Hart ats Peter Butler for an Ass^t

1s.   Warr^t ags^t Mary Hughes ats Sarah Young for Ass^t

---

4. Presumably, Alderman Marshall is substituting for Alderman Alsop, who was scheduled in
    the rota for this date.
5. 'R+' or 'Rx' seems to indicate that a recognizance was issued in the amounts indicated. At
    other points, the R is struck through with a large cross, which I have transcribed here by
    'RX'. Most, but not all, cases in which the recognizance is so marked proceed to trial.
6. 'Nil' as positioned in the margin seems to refer to either or both Cooper and Hutchins.

P   Warr^t ags^t ~~Eli~~ Margaret & Mary Cotterell ats Frances Mercer for an Ass^t

P   Warr^t ags^t Ann Henshaw ats Mary Gould for an ass^t

1s.   Warr^t ags^t James Smith ats ~~Ann~~ Joseph Major & Ann his Wife for an Ass^t

1s.   Sum^s for Thos Stevens ads Andrew Roberts for profane Swearing this Morning

      HM 9s.   TL r^d 9s.

Mr Alderman Gascoyne by Mr Alderman Ironside. Wednesday 27 May [1752].
      Richd Meekens, Thomas Davis} by Richd Jones C. ch^d by Alice Brocas on Lord Mayor's W^t 23^d Inst^t for an Ass^t Which was proved on her Oath ag^t them both they were D^d on the following Bail

3. 4   Stet ~~Richd Meekens an Apprentice to Saml Jarvis of Snowhill L. Turner~~   } £40

Rx   Thos Davis App^r to his Father John Davis of Nag's head Cor^t Snowhill Watchmaker } 40

L[ondon]^7 The Said John Davis   20
           Wm Bannister of the Old Bailey Vict.   20

1s.   Thos Marshall app^d upon ~~S^r H Marshall's W^t~~ Mr Ald^n Baker's Summons ~~yesterday~~ on Monday last ~~for~~ to answer the Informacon of John Bayley Who prov'd by Informacon upon Oath that on the 8th of May Inst^t a Boat of which Marshall admitted himself to be the Owner was plyed for passengers & navigated by John Marshall Michael Earle ~~from~~ between London ~~for~~ & Gravesend the s^d Earle being under the Age of 18 Years which was also prov'd by s^d Bayley, and s^d T. Marshall not paying £5 the penalty a W^t of Distress was granted ag^t him

3s.   James Saxx, Sam^ll Slayny, Wm Simpson} app^d upon Mr Ald^n Baker's Summons Monday last for non paym^t of their Quarteridge due to the Watermen's Company And Ja^s Blabyhalf-

---

7.   3. 4 is likely the charge of 3s. 4d. for fees. 'Rx' indicates the recognizance issued. The 'L' indicates the case was to proceed to the London sessions of the peace, which it did, but the two accused were discharged from their recognizances and there was no trial (LMA: CLA/047/LJ/04/119).

penny[8] a Beadle of s^d Compa[ny] prov'd upon Oath they had all neglected to attend the Sumons's of s^d Compa[ny] [illegible] Whereby they incurred the Penalties following vizt Saxx 18.6 for Non Attendances & 3.6. for Quarteridge, and Slayny 1s. for Non Attendance & 3.6 Quarteridge and Simpson was excused having a reasonable Excuse he was forgiven the penalties of Non Attendance & 2s. 6d. app^d to be due for Quar[terage] W^{ts} of Distress were granted ag^t them all But they agreed to give their Notes for the penalties wch Mr Church accepted of So were D^d.

1s.   W^t ag^t Mary Crispin & Eliz^a Cooke ads Mary Norris for an Ass^t

1s.   W^t ag^t Hannah Trustee ads Sarah Waterfield for an Ass^t

1s.   W^t ag^t George Heath ads Eliz^a Edwards for an Asst.

1s.   W^t ag^t Eliz: Emmett ads Mary Berrysford for an Ass^t

1s.   W^t ag^t Robert Webber ads Eliz^a Dukes for an Ass^t

1s.   Indors'd a Middx W^t of 16th Inst^t from Justice Quarrill ag^t Jos^h Quimes & John Bilsom ads James Gray for an Ass^t etc.

       Twelve shillings & Eight pence. E. Ironside   TL r^d 12s. 8d.

Mr Alderman Ironside by Mr Alderman Gascoyne. Thursday 28 May [1752].
       George Eaton fr PC by the keeper John Lyng C. ch^d by Richd Firth a Watchm^n with being a Vagrant taken up last night in Smithfield half naked who appearing to be disorder'd in his Mind he was com^d to LWH.

1s.   W^t ag^t Jos^h Poole ads Ann his wife for an Ass^t

       Evan Evans by George Wardley C. ch^d by Jemima Hart Widow on a Middx W^t of Justice Norris & Dekewer dated 27th Aug. 1751 & indors'd by Ald^n Rawlinson 20 April last ag^t him by the name of John Evans with begetting a female Bastard Child (called Susanna) on her Body wch is likely to become chargable to the psh of St John Hackney Middx on the Complaint

---

8.   A will for James Blaby Halfpenny, waterman of St Nicholas, Deptford, Kent, can be found at The National Archives (TNA), PROB 11/818/168.

of Nehemiah King Churchw^dn & Richd Dann overseer on their Oaths Com^d to PC for want of Sureties.

C.G.   T.L. r. 1s.

Mr Alderman Rawlinson. Friday 29 May [1752].
Wm Robinson fr WC by John Fry C. ch^d by Miles Beck a Watchman on Suspicion of stealing a parcell of Coblers working Tools & old Shoes he stopp'd him with near Smithfield abo^t 2°Cl this Morn Ord^d back to WC for fur^r Exaiacon till the Goods are Advertized.

P   W^t ag^t James Cox ads Margaret his wife for an Ass^t

1s.   Indors'd a Middx W^t of Justice Gower dated 20th Inst^t ag^t John Rush ads Wm Connor for unlawfully breaking out of the Tower Gaol & making his Escape

T.R.   T.L. r^d 1s.

Mr Alderman Whitaker by Mr Alderman Chitty. Monday 1 June [1752].
P   Eliz^a Williams by Richd Nash C. ch^d by Eliz^a Parsons on Mr Ald^n Chitty's W^t 30th Inst^t for an Ass^t. It being frivolous Compl^t & doubtfull who was the Aggressor D^d

1s.   Affid^t Lieu^t T. Davy

P   Miles Bone, Westue Maddox, James Edwards, Chas Lutman } fr PC by Wm Martindale C. ch^d by John Wilson Master of a Hackney Coach & George Sweatman the Driver ag^t Maddox & Lutman for refusing to pay him his fare on an Agreem^t D^d

P   John Wilder by Robt Close C. ch^d by Eliz^a Cooper on his Wpp's W^t 30th May for an Ass^t on an Agreem^t D.^d

P   Samuel Vernon, Eliz.^a Wright} fr WC by John Cook C. ch^d by him with being in an indecent Posture together abot 1°Cl this morning in Friday Street The Woman was on his Oath Com^d to B. for being a common Streetwalker but the Man producing one to his Character was D^d

1s.   Penelope Thomas by John Fry C. ch^d by Mary Beare on Mr Ald^n Scott's W^t 7th April last for an Ass^t . It app^d the parties had taken out Cross W^ts & doubtful who was the aggressor D^d

1s.   Rich[d] Badger brought upon M[r] Ald[n] Bakers Warr 25th May for an Assault upon Agreem[t] discharged.

1s.   W[t] ag[t] Sarah Ripshaw ads John Edwards on Suspicion of stealing sev[l] Goods his ppty.

P   Thomas Bare, Mary his wife} by John Fry C. ch[d] by Rachael Thomas on M[r] Ald[n] Chitty's W[t] 30 May last for an Ass[t]. It app[d] to be a frivolous Compl[t] relative to ~~an[r] matter~~ an affair the prisoner had got ano[r] W[t] for so D[d]

P   Tho[s] Hammond fr PC by Tho[s] Young C. ch[d] by Jonath[n] Granger for being a Carman and misbehaving at his house giving Scurrilous Language etc. on asking pardon & promising not to offend ag[n] D[d]

1s.   W[t] ag[t] W[m] Kirkup ads Isaac Cookson on Suspicion of Stealing a Sum of money the property of Messrs. Cookson Williams & Co.

1s.   Griffith Griffiths fr PC by Jos[h] Brown C. ch[d] by Mary his wife on L[d] Mayor's W[t] 26th May last for an Ass[t] ~~Which was prov'd on her Oath & that she goes in Danger of her Life & John Brown Also deposed that he heard the prison[r] threaten to stab her~~ on an Agreem[t] D[d]

Wm Robinson[9] fr WC by John Fry C. on an Ord[r] Friday last for fur Exaiacon 'till sev[l] Things were advertiz'd that he was suspected to have Stolen. Henry Speller proved that a Cutting Board, 5 Shoemaker's Lasts one Iron Rasp & other things his property were stole out of his Bulk in Turnagain Lane Snowhill in Thursday night last Which was Also Confirm'd by John Speller and Miles Beck a Watchman prov'd he stopped the prison[r] abot 3°Cl on Friday Morning last near Smithfield with a Sack & sev[l] Old Shoes & Implm[ts] of a Cobler's Trade therein and s[d] Speller & his Son prov'd that the Above ment[d] Lasts etc. were part of the things so found in the Sack on their Oaths Com[d] to N.

R+   Henry Speller of Turnagain Lane Snowhill Cobler   £ 20
John Speller ~~the Yr~~ of D[o] his Son   £ 10
Miles Beck of Chick Lane L[ondon] Watchman   £ 10

---

9.   The case proceeds to the Old Bailey under the name Robertson. See *Old Bailey Proceedings Online* (www.oldbaileyonline.org, version 7.0, 12 November 2012), June 1752, trial of William Robertson (t17520625–59).

Paul Wood a Boy fr PC by Geo: Frost C. ch^d by Thos Letts with stealing a p^r of Stockings out of Mr Rushback's Shop in Bishopsgate Street. The prison^r voluntarily impeach'd his Accomplices & W^ts were granted ag^t them So the prison^r was remand^d back fur Exaiacon.

nil W^t ag^t Jos^h Stevens & John Quin on Oath of s^d Paul Wood with being ~~an~~ his accomplices in s^d Felony

nil W^t ag^t M^r [blank] Harvey on same Oath with fel[oniously] receiving Stolen Goods knowingly

P John Pumeroy, Martha Marshall} fr WC by Cornelius Dean C. ch^d by him for being ~~in an indecent posture last~~ in the Streets at an unseasonable Hour last night on promising not to Offend Again D^d.

Wm Wilkinson fr B. by John Smith C. ch^d by Anthony Seal His Master with pilfering 2 drinking Glasses his ppty, But the Prison^r having Impeach'd Thos Dolly of receiving them knowing to be Stolen he was ret^d to WC for further Exaiacon.

W^t ag^t Thos Dolly on Oath of s^d Wm Wilkinson for feloniously receiving Stolen Goods knowing them to be Stolen.

TC TL r^d 5s.

Mr Alderman Janssen by Mr Alderman Chitty. Tuesday 2 June [1752].
1s. Thos Nuttall a Deserter from Lord Lindow's[10] Comp^y 3^d Regim^t of Foot Guards appr^d by Benjn Senior a Corp^l in s^d company on his Oath in parish of St And^w Holborn London. Committed to the Savoy[11] granted a W^t to the Coll^r of the Land tax in that psh to pay him 20s. Reward & gave notice thereof in Writing to the Secretary of Warr [sic].

1s. James Yatman a Journeyman Artificer Blacksmith fr PC by Geo: Frost C. ch^d by his Master John Dodson a Manufacturer of Iron for neglecting ~~his work before finished &~~ the performance of the work on Mr Ald^n Chitty's W^t 12th Inst^t for unlawfully misbehaving himself in his Employm^t. Mr John Dodson the Master Swore that the prison^r. was employed by him in working up Iron and that he neglected the performance

---

10. Probably Alexander Leslie, 6th Lord Lindores [S].
11. A military prison, built in 1695 by Wren. See B. Weinreb and C. Hibbert, eds., *The London Encyclopaedia*, revised ed. (London, 1993), p. 796.

of the work he was employed in by permitting himself to be subsequently retained or employed by ano[r] person before he completed the work w[ch] he was originally employed by s[d] Dodson to perform on his Oath Com[d] to B. for 7 Days.

Paul Wood, Jos[h] Stevens, John Quin[12]}fr PC [and] John Harvey fr WC} by Geo: Frost C on an Ord[r] yesterday for fur Exaiacon ch[d] by Tho[s] Letts with felony, the prison[r] Paul Wood impeach'd Stevens & Quin & swore they were concerned with him in Stealing a p[r] of Stockings out of the Shop of Mr Rushbank in Bishopsgate Street and Letts swore that he see the prison[rs] Wood & Quin in Company Steal them. On Oaths of s[d] Letts & Wood Stevens & Quin were Com[d] to WC and Wood swore that the prisoner Harvey had encouraged him & the other Prison[rs] to steal & many times received Goods they Stole knowing them to be stolen so he was Com[d] to N as an Accessary[sic] on Oath of s[d] Wood, and Wood was on his own Confession Com.[d] as an Evidence to PC.

R+   John Dodson of Threadneedle Street L. £ 20.

nil   Philip Frier fr PC by the Keeper ch[d] by W[m] Pattison & Mary his wife with a fraud in selling ~~him~~ her a parcell of Seals as Sett in Gold whereas they charg'd them to be base Mettall but for want of Evidence D[d].

P   W[t] ag[t] Henry ~~Saunders~~ Hathan ads Judith Austen for an Ass[t]

P   W[t] ag[t] Moses Bellfortee ads Martha Mustifore for an Ass[t]

1s.   Indors'd a Middx W[t] of Justice White 26th May ag[t] John Ganey for forging the name of Harman Verelst & others in order to Cheat the Gov[s] & Guardians of the Hospitall for deserted young Child[n] indors'd by Ald[n] Fludyer

Jos[h] Smith[13] by Rich[d] Nash C. ch[d] by ~~Jos~~ Tobias Pilgrim with picking his Pocket of a Linnen Handkf in Guildhall Which was prov'd on the Oath of James Miles and M[r] Pilgrim Swore it to be his property Val. 1s. on their Oaths Com[d] to PC

---

12. The case against Stevens and Quin proceeds to the Old Bailey. See *OBP*, June 1752, trial of Joseph Stevens, John Quinn (t17520625–27).
13. The case proceeds to the Old Bailey. See *OBP*, June 1752, trial of Joseph Smith (t17520625–9).

R+   Tobias Pilgrim at the Woolpack on Fish str^t hills Hosier } £20

L.^{14} James Miles of Whitecross Street Cooper   10

       John Williams by Jeremiah Maskall C. from PC & charged by John Palmer his Master for being a loose disorderly person and greatly misbehaving himself wch being proved on the Oaths of his Ma^r and Const. Com^d to B for 14 Days.

1s.   John Dawson ads Mr Jesser Sumon'd for keeping sev^l mischievous Dogs to the Annoyance of the Neighbourhood.

1s.   W^t ag^t ~~John Cornish~~ Barbara Baynes ads ~~Thos~~ Mary Parker for an Ass^t

       TC   TL r 4s.

Mr Alderman Asgill. Wednesday 3 June 1752.

P   Hannah Tomlin by Richd Nash C. ch^d by Wm Meynall Ch:w^{dn} of St Bartholomew the Great with being a Lewd woman & common prostitute having a Bastard now chargable to s^d parish, on promising not to Offend again & rid ~~hers~~ the parish of the Charge D^d

1s.   Sarah Howell, Sarah Herring} fr PC by Barlow Sayer C. charging Each other viz Herring ch^d Howell with stealing her Cloak but for want of Evidence of the Felony D^d but the Const. & Henry Brown Watchman prov'd Howell to be a Common Streetwalker   on their Oaths she was Com^d to LWH. But Herring having a good Character D^d .

1s.   W^t ag^t Sarah Wilkin ads Mary Francis for an Ass^t

1s.   Ann Perry fr WC by Richd Harvest C. ch^d by Nicholas Stanley with Picking up a Person in the Street & Insulting & abusing the Constable she appearing not to be a Comon Offender Discharged.

P   W^t ag^t Alex^r Holding ads Mary Clark for an Ass^t

nil   John Dawson app^d upon Mr Ald^n Chitty's Sum^s yesterday ads Mr Jesser for keeping sev^{ll} mischievous Dogs to the Annoyance of the Neighbourhood, on promising ~~to~~ not to Offend ag^n D^d

       3s. CA   TL r^d 3s.

---

14.   Presumably noting London Sessions of Gaol Delivery.

M[r] Alderman Glyn by M[r] Alderman Chitty. Thursday 4 June 1752.

    Elias Levi a Boy fr PC by Elias Mordecai C. ch[d] by Nathan Alexander with being a Vagrant taken up lying in a Dust Tub at night & giving no good Acco[t] of himself on his Oath Com[d] to LWH

P   Jane Bowen fr PC by Matt[w] Baxter C. ch[d] by John Aynge for abusing him & making Disturbance in his house on promising not to offend again D[d]

nil   Sum[s] for George Britain ads James Rudge C. for swearing one prophane Oath last night in the psh of S[t] Alphage

nil   D[o] for George Morgan ads D[o] for Swearing one prophane Curse in the psh of S.[t] Mary Staining on Tuesday last.

P   Edw[d] Bailey fr PC by Elias Mordecai C. ch[d] by Rich[d] Reddish Servant to Mess[rs] Fry & Curst of Aldgate high Street with strolling ab[t] his Masters Door abo[t] 2°Cl this morning & giving no good Accot of himself on his Oath Com[d] to B. for 6 Days.

1s.   Affid[t] Henry Taylor

P   Alexander Holden fr WC by John Ivory C. ch[d] by Mary Clark on Ald[n] Asgill's W[t] yesterday for an Ass[t] on an agreem[t] D[d]

1s.   W[t] ag[t] Peter Mixum ads W[m] Manby & John Cockerell for Attempting to Commit Buggery with them

1s.   Indors'd a Middx W[t] of Justice Fielding's ag[t] Tho[s] Evans, George Meredith and Tho[s] Smokey to plead to an Indictm[t] for assaulting Chris[r] Bows –found in Middx.

1s.   Affid[t] John Johnson

1s.   W[t] ag[t] John Pollard[15] ads Mary his Wife for an Ass[t]

1s.   W[t] ag[t] Barnard Brady ads Eleanor his wife for threatening her hurt

1s.   W[t] ag[t] John Darby ads Ann Ashmore for an Ass[t]

P   W[t] ag[t] Sam[ll] Cooper ads Ambrose Senee for an Ass[t]

---

15. Or possibly 'Rollard'.

1s.   W[t] ag[t] Ann Kitchen ads Mary Coulson for an Ass[t]

1s.   W[t] ag[t] Abigail Piner ads Joseph Keys & Marg[t] his wife for Ass[t]

P   Sum[s] for the Officers of S[t] And[w] Holborn for refusing to relieve Sarah Lewis a poor person

TC   TL r 9s.

M[r] Alderman Chitty by M[r] Alderman Janssen. ~~Adhuc~~ Friday 5 June [1752].

Eliz[a] Bartlett ~~fr~~ by Rich[d] Bromley C. ch[d] by him William Waltho his Serv[t] & James Trinder on Suspicion of stealing a Silver Watch she bro[t] with her into M[r] Bromley's house a publican in Darkhouse Lane this morning abo[t] 6 °Cl, on her own Confession that one John Wilson and another person not taken in Company with her robb'd a person of it that was lying asleep on the Road ~~be~~ nigh Deptford in Kent abo[t] 11 °Cl last night, Ord[d] her to the PC for fur Exaiacon 'till the Watch is advertiz'd etc.

Benjamin Daniel[16] fr WC by John Topham C. ch[d] by Edw[d] Welch with felony, W[m] Gapford Serv[t] to the pros[r] swore the prison[r] came into his Master's Shop in Newgate Street this morning to buy Some Vierges & he show'd him a parcell in a Box when the prison[r] took up the Box & shuffled them in his hands & went away witho[t] buying any, but upon Examining the Box immediately M[r] Gapford miss'd a Quantity & Swore he knew the number in the Box having told them the night before & the Constable Topham & Dan[l] Fenn prov'd upon Searching him ~~17~~ 15 Vierges were found upon him & 2 dropp'd from him ~~on~~ & M[r] Welch prov'd them his propty & that he Suspected the prison[r] often & [illegible] coming to his Shop for such Goods kept the number of Vierges in the Box on their oaths Com[d] to WC

R+   Edw[d] Welch of Newgate street L. Watchmaker   £ 20
L[17]   John Topham of D[o] Worsted man   10
    Daniel Fenn of D[o] Watchmaker   10

2s.   Mary Ayres fr WC by Peter Shepherd C. ch[d] by Jane Jones on Suspicion of Felony, in robbing her ready furnish'd Lodgings

---

16. The case proceeds to the Old Bailey. See *OBP*, June 1752, trial of Benjamin Daniels (t17520625–8). Vierges: a vierge seems to be a metal piece or part, possibly a screw used in watchmaking.

17. Presumably noting London Sessions of Gaol Delivery.

but it app^d the Lodgings were Let to Robt Ayres. Ord^d her to WC for fur Exaiacon & granted a Search W^t to Search the house of one Ferguson a Pawnbroker in Barbican.

C+^{18} George Morgan app^d upon Mr Ald^n Chitty's Sum^s yesterday For
Geo   Swearing, James Rudge C. prov'd the s^d Morgan on Tuesday
Bretton last Swore one prophane Curse in the parish of St Mary Staining Who paying 1s. penalty he was D^d

C+   P   Mary Currell by James Rudge C. ch^d by him for Swearing this Day in the parish of St Mich^{ll} Bassishaw one prophane Oath & John Beazley undertaking to see the penalty Dd.

1s.   Affid^t Jos: Jackson

P   John Hall, Sarah Mungo} fr WC by John Reed C. ch^d by Wm Stanton & Thos Weybridge with the Woman being a Common Streetwalker on their Oaths She was Com^d to LWH but for want of Evidence ag^t the man D^d.

P   W^t ag^t Moses Marshall ads Nathl Catlin for an Ass^t

2s.   Search Warr^t for James Richard Goldsborough in Order to find a Silver Tea Spoon, Two Blanketts and other things stolen from him by Sarah Broughton & suspected to be concealed in the House of [blank] Brown a Pawn-broker upon Snow Hill & one [blank] Keys ano^r Pawnbroker ~~upon~~ in Chick Lane.

1s.   Warr^t ag^t Eliz^a Bayley ads Rebecca Canter for an Ass^t

   Sarah Wilkins by George Wardley C. ch^d by Mary Francis on Mr Ald^n Asgill's W^t 3^d June inst^t for an Ass^t Which being proved on her Oath & Eliz^a Sharp com^d to WC for want of Sureties.

1s.   Affid. Robt Bradley

1s.   D^o John Holdsworth

   John Wilkins by Geo: Wardly C. ch^d by Sarah Prosser on Ald^n Cokayne's W^t 4 February last for stealing a pair of Blanketts etc. out of ~~her~~ his Lodgings but for want of Evidence D^d.

---

18.   Convicted by the magistrate and fined. See Introduction, pp. xxv–xxvi.

P   W^t ag^t Mary Ford ads Sarah Ford for an Ass^t

Warr^t ag^t Mich^l Burrows ats of [sic] Rebecca Bravo for an Ass^t

2s.   Search Warr^t for John Moor ag^t Mary Cuthbert in Order to find a Silk Handkerchief two Shirts & other things lately stolen from him & suspected to be taken by the s^d Mary Cuthbert.

P   Warr^t [blank] Hopkins ats of Wm Hood for an Ass^t.

P   Warr^t ag^t John Barker ats of Jane Pharoh for an Ass^t.

P   Warr^t ag^t [blank] Crocherdale ats of Mary Broadbridge for an assault.

P   Warr^t ag^t Daniel Hamilton ats of Catherine Bolt for an Assault.

Permit pass from [?][19]

S. T. J.   TL r^d 10s.

Mr Alderman Fludyer. Monday 8 June 1752.
P   Dimmock Longstaff by Jere: Maschall C. ch^d by Thos Holmes on Ald^n Cokayne's W^t 6 Inst^t for an Assault upon Agreem^t discharged.

P   Jos^h Littleton fr PC by Thos Henshaw C. ch^d by Bela Broughton with being in Liquor & running about with a Knife in his hand. It app^d there was no Damage done so was D^d.

1s.   Edmund Wentworth fr WC by James Edmunds C. ch^d by Daniel Rice on Ald^n Cokayne's W^t 6th Inst^t for an Ass^t on an Agreem^t D^d

1s.   Mary Ford by Thos Howlet C. ch^d by Sarah Ford on Ald^n Janssen's W^t 5th Inst^t for an Ass^t It app^d to be a Family dispute & frivolous & doubtfull who was the Aggressor D^d.

Eliz^a Taylor fr PC by Jacob Marks C. ch^d by him and Fra^s Macfarson a Watchman with being a disorderly & drunken pson insulting them on their Duty abot 1 ^{o}Cl Sunday morning last wch being provd on their Oaths Com^d to LWH.

---

19.   This phrase has an ink smudge over it.

nil   John Trow fr PC by Tho[s] Ward C. ch[d] by John Tricket on Suspicion of Felony in Stealing a Silver Tankard but for want of Evidence D[d].

3s.   Affid[ts] Friederick Warnken, Johan Henke, & Arend Vogelsang.

         Eliz[a] Goodwin fr PC by Sam[ll] Wiseham C. for begging in the psh of S[t] Swithin L—on his Oath Com[d] to LWH.

nil   Tho[s] Brown, W[m] Key} pawnbrokers by Geo: Levingston C. app[d] upon Ald[n] Janssen's W[t] 5th Inst[t] to Search their houses for sev[ll] Goods stolen from Ja[s] Rich[d] Gouldsbrough, Sev[l] of his Goods were found in Each of their houses but no Evidence appearing ag[st] them to charge them as receivers accessories they were D[d]. The Goods were deposited in the hands of the Const 'till the Principal was found.

         W[m] Curryer, Mich[ll] Notere[20]} fr WC by George Downing C. ch[d] by Benj[n] Crook with ag[t] Curryer Notere with picking his pocket of a silk Handkf on Saturday night last near Ludgate Which was prov'd on M[r] Crooks Oath & the Oath of Cha[s] Pierce to be found upon the prison[r] Curryer Notere he was Com[d] to N. but nothing appearing ag[t] Curryer besides being in the others Company & alledging to be serv[t] to M[r] Burto[ut?] of Fashion Street Spittlef[ds] he was Ord[d] to WC 'till his Master appear and Curryer not giving a good Acco[t] of himself he was Com[d] to B.

R+   Benjamin Crook of Ave Mary Lane L. Clerk of the
         Market   } £ 20
         Cha[s] Pierce of Leadenhall Street Blackwell hall factor }   20

         John Williams fr PC by Peter Winstanley C. ch[d] by Tho[s] Leech a Goldsmith on Suspicion of Stealing a Gold Necklace he stopp'd him with upon offering it to Sale, Ord[d] back to PC for fur Exaiacon 'till it is advertizd etc.

P   W[t] ag[t] Eliz: Burton ads Eliz[a] Pignell for an Ass[t] & biteing her Finger Whereby it mortified & is Cutt off.

P   Warr[t] ag[t] Catherine Boult ads Jane Hamilton for an Ass[t]

         S F   TL r 5s. & p[d] 2s.

---

20.   The case against Notere proceeds to the Old Bailey. See *OBP*, June 1752, trial of Michael Notre (t17520625–28).

Sir John Barnard. Tuesday 9 June [1752].

Eliz^a Williams fr PC by Wm Stevens C. ch^d by John Parsons on Suspicion of stealing his Watch but for want of Evidence D^d but the pros^r proved She attempted to pick him up & Wm Holmes a Watchman proved her to be a Common Nightwalker on their Oaths com^d to LWH.

1s.

Catherine Boult fr PC by George Wardley C. ch^d by Jane Hamilton on Mr Ald^n Fludyer's W^t yesterday for an Ass^t on an Agreem^t D^d

1s.[21]

John Clark, Jane Morris} fr WC by John Stone C. ch^d by Thos Vincent with being disorderly persons but for want of Evidence of that D.^{d} It app^d that the prison^r ch^d Vincent with robbing the Woman of her Handkf last night on Ludgate hill but he app^d to be a Man of Character & only a Drunken Frolick & no Evidence D^d

P

Abigail Piner by Henry Brown C. ch^d by Jos^h Keys & Marg^t his wife on Mr Ald^n Chitty's W^t 4th Inst^t for an Ass^t on an agreem^t D^d

Eliz^a Bartlet fr PC by Richd Bromley C. ch^d by her own Confession for fur Exam^n on Friday last on Suspicon of Steal^g a Watch She deposited with Mr Bromley's Servt on Friday last. The Watch being advertiz'd Thos Carter of Greenwich Carpenter app^d & claimed the Watch but acknowleg'd himself to be so much in Liquor at the Time his watch was lost he ~~co^d. wo^d not Swear it was Stoln~~ laid down to sleep on the Road nigh Deptford in Kent, he wo^d not swear it was Stolen but Mr Carter Swore it was his property & Wm Waltho Servt to the Const proved the prisoner's Confession of [illegible] having been present at the Robbery and Also prov'd the prison^r produced it to him on their oaths com^d PC.

Rx | Thos Carter of Greenwich Kent Carpenter | £ 20
L | Wm Waltho Servt to Richd Bromley a publican in Darkhouse Lane L. | £ 10

P

Geo: Corderoy, Wm White} fr WC by Edwd Muns C. ch^d by Thomas Chamberlain a Watchman for being secreted together in a private Corner near St Pauls Churchyard last night strongly Suspected with an Intent to Commit Buggery ~~together~~ but for want of Evidence D^d

21.   The 1s. notation appears beside Morris's name.

P Wm Cook by Jeremiah Mascall C. ch^d by him with a Suspicion of steal^g a Plank but for want of Evidence D^d

1s. Sarah Needham com^d by his wpp 20th March last to LWH for being a disorderly person, At the Instance of Matthew Arnold Beadle of St Brides D^d

P Warr^t ags^t Samuel Bayley ats Mary his Wife for an Ass^t

1s. Warr^t ags^t Mary Duckett ats Elias Jonas for an Ass^t

1s. Warr^t ags^t Edward Gother ats Susannah his Wife for an Ass^t

  J. B. TL r 5s.

Sir Henry Marshall. Wednesday 10 June [1752].
nil W^t ag^t Theophilus Harboard ads John Dickins & Thos Perryman on suspicion of steal^g at Wadding Chase in Buckinghamshire a Black Gelding the property of s^d Dickins.

nil Affid^t John Dickins.

R ~~John Dickins of Shenley Brookend in Buckinghamshire~~
 ~~Farmer   } £ 20~~
 ~~Thomas Perryman of the parish of Aldenham in~~
 ~~Hertfordshire Farmer } £ 10~~

~~1s.~~ nil Affid^t John Peake

P John Williams fr PC by Peter Winstanley C. on an Ord^r Monday last for fur^r Exaiacon on Suspicion of stealing a Gold Necklace which Mr Thos Leech Goldsmith stopp'd him with in Offering to Sale. The Necklace was advertiz'd & Mary Howell app^d & declared She had lost it out of her Bosom near the place where ~~which~~ the pris^r ~~pretended~~ alledged he found it & having a good Character was D^d.

1s. Affid^t Morgan Jones

1s. D^o Henry Cowell

 Wm Gardner by John Cooper C. ch^d by Chas Pearson on Lord Mayor's W^t this Day for an Ass^t over the Eye Which being prov'd on his Oath & the prisoner confessing etc. & behaving insolently before his wpp Com^d to PC for want of Sureties nil Wᵐ Bothway a Soldier fr PC by Henry Motlo C. chᵈ by Israel Levi a Jew upon the Intrepretation of Michael Abraham who was Sworn, with assaulting him ~~and als~~ in Leadenhall street and was Also chᵈ by the Const for assaulting him & knocking him down. The pties agreed to forgive him so was Dᵈ

P Wᵗ agᵗ Thosˢ Strong ads Isaac Clark for an Assᵗ

1s. Affid. Hannah Goff viva voce

nil Sumˢ for Josʰ Cross ads James Waldrin his late Servᵗ for nonpaymᵗ of his Wages

P Wᵗ agᵗ Sarah Wooley ads Susanna Dallison for an Assᵗ

nil Sumˢ for Thoˢ Blowen ads Josʰ Lee for profane Swearing on Friday last

nil Dᵒ for James Rice ads Dᵒ for profane swearing on Friday last

3s. Affidᵗˢ Fancis [sic] Ardesoif, Charles Fouace, Tho. Barbaud

P Wᵗ agᵗ Jockey Wilson ads Peter Sefton for an Assᵗ

5s. HM TL r 5s.

Sir Richard Hoare by Mʳ Alderman Scott. Thursday 11 June 1752.

P John Woodcock, Wᵐ Smalley} ~~fr~~ by Wᵐ Hughes C. chᵈ by a person who did not appear. The Const said they were chᵈ for an Abuse but for want of Evidence Dᵈ

1s. Wᵗ agᵗ Wᵐ Smalley ads Wᵐ Jones for an Assᵗ

P Margᵗ Jones by Mattʷ Baxter C. chᵈ by him for quarrelling in Leadenhall market & insulting him but promising not to Offend again Dᵈ.

1s. Oath of Wᵐ Evans

  John Hetherington fr WC by John Fry C. chᵈ by Samˡˡ Jarvis with being a disorderly drunken Fellow not appearing to have any visible Means of Livelihood on his Oath Comᵈ to B.

  Thoˢ Chitwood, Susanna his Wife, Susanna Milburn, Penelope

Patterson, Ann Clements, Mary Harboard, Mary Walker[22]} fr WC by John Fry C. ch[d] by Nathan[ll] Winn a Watchman with being loose idle & disorderly persons & common Street-walkers, Which being provd on Oath they were All Com[d] to LWH except Mary Harboard who was D[d] for want of Evidence.

P   Peter Bockumb fr WC by Jos[h] Reed C. ch[d] by Daniel Flude his Master for receiving his Master & not Accounting for it Which being only a Breach of Trust he was D[d]

1s.   Joseph Cross app[d] upon S[r] H. Marshall's Sum[s] yesterday ads James Waldron for nonpaym[t] of his wages But it app[d] that the Serv[t] had greatly misbehaved in his Master's Service w[ch] was proved on Oath of Robert Green that he seduced a Boy the Son of M[r] Cross to lye with his ~~Mas~~ Father's Maid & threaten him M[r] Green proved him to be a disorderly Fellow he was Com[d] to B. for 1 Month his Wpp ord[d] M[r] Cross to pay the wages due which were p[d] before his wpp.

1s.   Affid[t] Rich[d] Taylor

1s.   Mary Steward fr PC by John Butler C. ch[d] by Tho[s] ~~St~~ Towse her Master for a Misbehaviour in ~~her~~ his house ~~on an agreem[t]~~ ~~D[d]~~ there being no foundation for the Charge D[d]

P   ~~Ann Wiser~~ Francis Munks, John Lingley, Elizabeth Jones, Ann Omett, Mary Carmichael, Catharine Patterson, Ann Howard[23]} fr WC by Cha[s] Hill C. ch[d] by him & W[m] Stanton Beadle with being loose idle & disorderly persons associating together picking up persons in the Streets at unseason[ble] hours of Night & resorting to houses of ill Fame on their Oaths Com[d] to LWH Except Jones who bro[t] a pson to her Character so was D[d]

Philip Doyle, John Webster[24]} fr PC by James Emmerson C. ch[d] by Barnabas Linton[25] agt Webster for stealing a parcell of Tobacco Which M[r] Linton swore he see the Prison[r] Webster take out of a ~~ho~~ H[ogshead] on a Brewers Key the property

---

22. A check mark (✓) appears beside each name, except for Harboard's: the notation 'D'd' appears by hers.
23. Check marks appear beside each of the names.
24. The case against Webster proceeds to the Old Bailey. See *OBP*, June 1752, trial of John Webster (t17520625–26).
25. James Emmerson and Barnabas Linton were both constables employed by London merchants. Emmerson was employed by the Hanburys (tobacco traders) and prosecuted other cases at the Old Bailey. Linton later worked for the West India Committee and prosecuted cases on their behalf at the Old Bailey.

of John Hanbury val. 8d. and Mr Emmerson prov'd he stopp'd him with it & also prov'd he detected the Other prison^{rs} Doyle with a Small parcell upon him on their Oaths Webster com^d to PC and the Other Com^d to B.

R+   James Emmerson a Const of the Keys   } £ 10
       Barnabas Linton of Gloucester Court near Bear
       Lane L. Gent   }   10
       To give Evidence ag^t s^d Webster

P

       Ann Thomas fr PC by Barlow Sayer C. ch^d by Jeffery Dun a Watchman with making a Disturbance but promising not to Offend ag^n D^d

P   ~~Henry Hathan~~ Mary Ayres fr WC by Peter Shepherd C. on an Order Friday last for fur^r Exaiacon ~~Ja John Jones prov'd that one Sheet one Brass, one Brass Fender one brass candlesetick & other Goods were Stole from out of Lodgings let to the prison^r and John Berry Servt to a pawnbrok^r in Barbican prov'd the prisoner pawned the Goods on their Oaths com^d to WC~~ John Jones who ch^d the prison^r being sworn said his wife frequently sent the prison^r to pawn his Goods So for want of Evidence D^d

R   ~~John Berry Servt~~

Sir H Marshall by Mr Alderman Scott. Adhuc Thursday 11 June [1752].
C+ 1s.   James Rice app^d upon S^r H Marshall's Sum^s yesterday
Ralph Twyford   ads Jos^h Lee for profane Swearing who prov'd on
Church Warden   Friday last he swore 20 prophane Oaths in the psh of
                 St Faith under St Paul who paying 20s. the penalty D^d

P   Thomas Strong by Sam^{ll} Wright C. ch^d by Isaac Clark on Sr H. Marshall's Warrant yesterday for an Ass^t It app^d the pl was the Aggressor so D^d

P   Henry Hathan by Barlow Sayer C. ch^d by Judith Austen on Mr Ald^n Chitty's W^t 2^d Inst^t for an ass^t It being a frivolous Quarrell D^d

       RS   T L r 5s.

Mr Alderman Benn. Friday 12 June [1752].
       No Attendance.

Thomas Rance, Richd Saunders, Mary Copland} ~~fr WC by Griffith~~

~~Lewis C. charging each other viz the 1st charg'd the Other 2
with making Disturbance at unseasonable hour last night~~

Sir William Calvert by Sir George Champion. Monday 15 June [1752].

1s.   W^t ag^t Eliz^a Jones ads Eliz^a Mullins on suspicion of steal^g 3.
Silver Spoons the property of John Mackay

P   Richd Philips Affid^t viva voce

Mary Hull fr WC by John Parker C. ch^d by the Rev^d W^m
Pinkney with committing ~~great~~ Acts of Vagrancy by Singing
Ballads & greatly misbehaving on his Oath Com^d to LWH.

P   Affid^t Abram Sims touching his Settlem^t

1s.   W^t ag^t Dorothy Drew ads James Drew for an Ass^t

P   W^t ag^t John Cherrydine ads Ann Wood for an Ass^t

G. C.   T.L. r. 2s.

Mr Alderman Blachford. Tuesday 16 June [1752].

1s.   Mary Moore, Bridget Burk} by John Fry C. ch^d by Eliz^a Young
on Ld May^rs W^t 12th Inst^t for an Ass^t. At the pros^r's Request D^d
Burk & the Compl^t ag^t Moore being frivolous D^d her also

1s.   John Ponston, Sarah Newcomb} fr WC by Wm Mills C. ch^d
by him for being together abo^t 1oCl this morning near Chick
Lane & being disorderly persons and Also charges the man for
assaulting him in the Exeson of his Office for want of Evidence
D^d

P   Ann White fr PC by Sam^ll Wiseham C. ch^d by Wm Godfrey
Servt at the City Arms in Lombard Street for coming into
the house yesterday Afternoon in Liquor making Disturbance
therein & annoying the Customers on making Submission &
promising not to Offend again D^d

Myrtilla Hetherington fr WC by Robt Shoesmith C. ch^d by
Henry Barker with being a Common Streetwalker attempting
to pick him up last Night on his Oath Com^d to LWH.

P   Ann Smith by Chas Hills C. ch^d by him for being a disorderly
person committing sev^l Acts of Vagrancy last night. It app^d she
was one of the parish poor of St Andrew Holborn so agreeing
to go to the psh D^d

P   W^t ag^t Rebecca Butler Sarah Rickards & Mary Bun ads Sarah Cox for an Ass^t

1s.   W^t ag^t Ann Meekins ads Mary Langton for an Ass^t

1s.   Affid^t Benjn Reynolds

    JB   TL r 4s.

Mr Alderman Cockayne. Wednesday 17 June [1752].
    ~~Wm Jones fr PC by Jere: Maskall Constable ch^d by Solomon Boost on suspicion of felony~~

    No Attendance

Sir George Champion. Thursday 18 June [1752].
1s.   Affid^t Admiral Bing[26]

P   W^t ag^t Francis Withers ads Walter Clark for an Ass^t

1s.   W^t ag^t Ann Field ads George Perry for an Ass^t

    Thos Wright[27] fr WC by Gilb^t Morewood C. ch^d by ~~John Jenkins a Watchman~~ Thos Shermen on Suspicion of felony. John Jenkins & Ralph Box Watchmen prov'd they found the prison^r in the Cellar of an Empty house in Cow Lane L. belonging to the Earl of Thanet Abo^t 2 o Cl this Morn & a parsell of loose lead lying there which app^d to be fresh Cutt from off the Roof & Mr Shermen Confirmed it on their Oaths Com^d to N.

R+   Thos Shermen of Cow Lane L. perukemaker   £ 20
    John Jenkins of St John's Court Cow Lane Brass Button maker   £ 10
    Ralph Box of D^o Plaisterer   £ 10

P   Wm Oliver by John Fry C. ch^d by Jane Austin on Ld Mayor's W^t 15th Inst^t for an Ass^t on an Agreem^t D^d
        Turn over

    Wm Jones fr PC by Jere: Mascall C. ch^d by ~~Solomon Boost on Suspicon of Felony~~, him for pilfering a Small Quantity of Sugar off Hammond's Key the property of persons unknown. On his Oath Com^d to B.

---

26. Presumably Admiral John Byng.
27. The case proceeds to the Old Bailey. See *OBP*, June 1752, trial of Thomas Wright (t17520625-1).

P   James Caruthers fr PC by James French C. ch^d by George
Mellor on Suspicion of Felony but for want of Evidence D^d

G. C.   TL r 2s.

Sir Joseph Hankey by Mr Alderman Cokayne. Friday 19 June [1752].
P   W^t ag^t Sarah Henley & Mary Speed ads Ann Pugellos for an
Ass^t

1s.   W^t ag^t John Munkus ads Mary Lambert for an Ass^t

1s.   Warr^t ag^t Joseph Wilks ats Eliz^a Taylor for an Ass^t

1s.   Sum^s for Mr Stainsley ads Robt Sturt ~~Driver of a~~ Hackney
Coachman for refusing to pay him his Fare

P   John Stamford, Deborah Knockley} fr PC by Nevil Thompson
C. ch^d by Chas Woolnough a Watchman with being last night
together in an indecent posture on his Oath Com^d the Woman
as a Streetwalker to LWH but the Man d^d on promising not to
Offend again D^d

C+   Justinian Brasegirdle ~~fr~~ by W^m ~~Hill~~ Mills C. ch^d by him with
P   being a Common Swearer, he prov'd he swore 10 prophane
Oaths this morning in St Sepulchre's psh & for want of paym^t
of the penalty or Cha[nce]s of Conviction etc. Com^d to LWH
for 16 Days.

P   W^t ag^t John Masters ads Ann Eades for an Ass^t

P   Sum^s for John Smith a Const. ads Sarah Young for refusing to
Execute a Warr^t ag^t Mary Hughes

4s.   FC   TL r. 4s.

Sir William Baker. Wednesday 14 October 1761.
p^d 6s.   Sarah Scott, Eliz: Baylis, Ann Trevor} fr WC by Philip Price
R.H.   C. ch^d by him for being apprehended ab^t asleep at 11 O'Clock
last Night par. St Faith, being all Vagrants were com^d to B:

1s.   Mary Smith fr WC by John Casbold C. ch^d by James Maxwell
for abusing him by tearing his Cloaths off his back it appearing
they were both in fault. Discharged

Matthew Galpin upon a Summons of the 12th inst. granted by
Ald^n Alexander at the complaint of Saml Munt Carman for

refusing to pay him his Fare for the Carriage of ½ Load of Plumbs from Doublehood Warehouses to his House in the Minories– he was ordered to pay 2s. fare 1s. Sum^s & 1s. Charges wch he did & was d^d.

Chas Stacey fr B: by Daniel Brougham C. ch^d by Ann White, for ass^ting her, he app^d an idle disorderly Person & a fit Person to serve the King & was therefore sent to the C[ompter] till to Morrow; in Order that he might be inspected whether he was a Proper Person.

Wm Newman fr PC by Jacob Aaron C. ch^d by John Howarth ~~on~~ for being a Deserter from out of the Portsmouth Division of Marines – he was ordered to be taken to the Regulating Captains in Mark Lane.

W^t ag^t David Scott ads John Rush for pawning of a Silver Watch his Property.

1s.   D^o against Fra^s Dieous al[ia]s Deous ads John Short Ass^t etc.

W.B.

The Right Honourable the Lord Mayor Elect[28] by Alderman Alexander.
     Thursday 15 October 1761.
     Henry Hayward com^d to WC by Sr Thos Chitty 13 Inst. on Oath of Mary his Wife for assaulting beating & abusing her and threatening to kill her – was bailed as below (by his s^d Wifes Consent)

RX   Henry Hayward of Puddle Dock L: Farrier   } 40
       Saml Saunders of the same Glover   } 20

          RH

~~Mr Ald^n Beckford by~~ Mr Alderman Challenor. Friday 16 October 1761.

C[29] 1s.   Saml Beaumont fr WC by Wm Moreton C. ch^d by him
                   & ~~Jno~~ Edwd Draper for ~~asst~~ greatly abusing the Const.
reced 9s. for   and swearing profanely 9 Oaths this Morning about 3
the use of the   o'Cl: in Smithfield – Par: St Sepulchre he was com^d
Parish.   on Oath of s^d Edwd Draper of swearing 9 Oaths this
Edwd Draper   Day in s^d Pish; & was ord^d to pay 9s wch he did & was
Warden   d^d.

---

28.   Sir Samuel Fludyer.
29.   Convicted and fined. See Introduction, pp. xxv–xxvi.

Wm Fullford, Letitia Martin} fr WC by Jno Tomson C. ch^d by Danl Mardell W^hman in Farringdon W^d w^thin for being apprehended in an indecent Posture tog^r in Bagnio Crt Newgate Street; Mr Dobbs the Ma[ste]r of the Pris^r gave the Man a good Character, & the Woman app[earin]g to be disorderly was com^d to B:

James Peck fr PC by Robt Bradley C. ch^d by Sr Geo: Norman for being found concealed in a Stable in the Bull Inn in Bpsgate St Tuesday Night 12 O'Clock & being seen lurking ab^t there sooner in the Evening; he did not appear to have ~~had~~ a visible way of living nor any person to appear to his Character; he desired to go back to Prison in order to have an Opportunity of Producing some Person to his Char^r.

P Judith Huggins from WC ~~charged by Tho~~ by John Thompson C. charged by Thomas Noble for being a disorderly Person and making a Disturbance at his Ho: she was a very Poor Woman & was reprim^ded & d^d.

1s. W^t ag^t John Palmer ads Sarah Pateman Ass^t etc.

1s. D^o ag^t Thos Graves ads Ann Ux: ejus[30] Ass^t etc.

TC 14/

Mr Alderman Beckford. Monday 19 October 1761.
 Edwd Callan, John McKenley} fr WC by Thos Atkinson C. ch^d by Ja^s Cardin, for raising a great Disturbance & wth many others rescuing a Pris^r in his Custody & violently ass^ting and beating him – he positively said that these two people were present aiding and assisting in the Mob: Mr Callan was bail'd as below & the Man at his own Request sent back till to Morrow, in Order to find Bail.

RX Edwd Callan, Writer at Mr James Parkinson, in Cursitor
Street Writer } 40
The s^d Ja^s Parkinson } 20
Wm Wilks of Whites Alley Liberty of the Rolls
Cabinet Ma^r } 20

1s. W^t ag^t John Williams ads Abram Bizo Ass^t etc.

P Ben: Evans from B: by Saml Inman C. ch^d by Robt Chadwick for ~~making a Disturbance on~~ taking a Pastry Cook's Bun out

---

30. Latin: 'his'.

of his Shop Saturday Night last; it being a trifling Offence & he a very Poor Man, was reprim^ded & d^d.

P   Robt Caffley fr PC per Jacob Aaron C. ch^d by John Chancey for making a Disturbance at his Ho: ~~it being~~ he having been guilty of no Offence was reprim^ded & d^d.

1s.   Aff^t Abram Edlin

P   Ann Griffiths fr PC by Jacob Aaron C. ch^d by a Pson who did not appear ag^t her she was for want of an Accuser d^d.

P   Alexander Holder fr WC by Wm Morton C. ch^d by Henry Biggs for making a Disturbance at his Ho: he was a very poor Man & was for this time reprim^ded & d^d.

1s.   Alex^r Maxwell, Thos Bown} fr PC by Wm Freeman C. chging each o^r as foll: Viz: Bown ch^d by Maxwell for ass^ting him and impressing him without any Authority & for beating him with a Stick – he made Satisfaction & was d^d.

P   John Adley by Thos Hayes C. chd by Eliz. Adley (who was not now Present) for an Ass^t the Pros^x not appearing d^d.

P   Ann Thomas fr PC by Geo: Rea C. chd by John Midhurst for being a disorderly Pson but being guilty of no Offence was d^d.

1s.   W^t ag^t Sarah Sturdy ads Nathl Gillett Ass^t etc.

       Thos Green fr PC by Jer: Maskall[31] C. chd by Henry Burch & Thos Gibbs for stealing this Day in ~~Justice~~ Chester key ware-ho^ses about 8lb. weight of Sugar Value 2s. the pperty of Persons unknown – was (on their Oaths) committed to N.

RX   Henry Burch of Tower St. L: Gangsman   } £ 20
       Thos Gibbs in Crutched Friars Gangsman   }   20

       Will: Beckford   RH

Mr Alderman Alexander. Tuesday 20 October 1761.
       Samuel Thomas, Wm Wasbrough } by R^d Nash C. chd by W^m

---

31. This case proceeds to the Old Bailey. See *OBP*, October 1761, trial of Thomas Green (t17611021–18). The constable Jeremiah Mascle is named in the *Old Bailey Proceedings* on several occasions, beginning in 1746; last name spelled 'Mascle', 'Maschil', 'Maschall' & 'Mascall'. At the trial of William Martin (*OBP*, October 1747, trial of William Martin (t17471014–7)), Mascle identified himself as 'the Constable belonging to the Custom House'.

Axford commander of the Ship called the Marlborough (on M[r] Hammond's Surry W[t] yesterday, back'd by the Lord Mayor same day) now lying at or near Cherry Garden Stairs in s[d] Co: for forcibly and with Violence entering into and taking possession of the s[d] Ship Marlborough cont: Pac.[32] the Cap[n] W[m] Axford swore to the Offense, & they were bail'd as below.

RX   Samuel Thomas of the City of Bristol Leather Dresser £ 400
Sess[s] Will[m] Wasbrough of the same Founder   400
in   W[m] Reeve of the same Merch[t]   200
Surry Monkhouse Davidson of Fenchurch Str. L: Grocer   200

Edw[d] Bartlom fr WC by Tho[s] Craven C. chd by Job Heath (on M[r] Ald[n] Beckford's W[t] yesterday) on suspicion of feloniously stealing 3 Muslin Neck Cloths 2 pair of Shoes & one Pair of Pumps his Property – Tho[s] Craven the Const. produc'd the 3 P[airs] of Shoes – was bail'd as below.

RX   Job Heath of White Cross Street Midx, Cordwainer 20
        Tho[s] Craven of Barbican L: Const.   10

John McKenley from WC by ~~Thomas A~~ Pitt Audley C. charged by James Carden and Edward Bellamy for an assaulting and violently beating them, they made Oath of this offence & he was committed to [blank].

~~W[t] ag[t] Rachel Fileman ads Mary Mason Ass[t] etc.~~

WA

M[r] Alderman Bridgen. Wednesday 21 October [1761]
1s.   W[t] ag[t] Rachel Fileman ats Mary Mason for an Ass[t]

1s.   D[o] ag[t] Mary Shovell ats Winifred Handley & Rob[t] Mackcormick for D[o].

2s.   Affid[t] David Jos[h] Kean & Hercules Gregory

1s.   D[o] ag[t] Jeremiah Clark ats Marg[t] Harrison for ass[t]

P   D[o] Tho[s] Walker ats Sarah Oneal D[o]

1s.   D[o] Eliz: Edward ats Ann Anson for D[o]

P   D[o] ag[t] Mary Smith ats Sarah Wiles for Ass[t]

---

32. Against the peace.

1s.   Dᵒ Hugh Demoreny ats Mary Tarroshire Dᵒ

1s.   Dᵒ Eliz: Mathews ats Mary Evans Dᵒ

~~Dᵒ Eliz Bowles ats~~

1s.   Dᵒ Sarah Duff ats Eliz: Anderson Dᵒ

1s.   Dᵒ George Crowder ats Susᵃ Chapman for Assᵗ

W.B.

Sir William Stephenson. Thursday 22 October 1761.
(No Attendance) his Wp being engaged in the Common Council this Day.

Mr Alderman Nelson by Sir Robert Ladbroke. Friday 23 October 1761.
1s.   Thoˢ Walker by Jno Knapp C. chd by Sarah Oneal on Aldⁿ Bridgens Wᵗ the 21ˢᵗ for an Assᵗ on an Agreemᵗ Dᵈ.

1s.   Mary Smith by Dᵒ C. chd by Sarah Wiles on Dᵒ Warrant for an Assᵗ on an Agreemᵗ Dᵈ.

1s.   Wᵗ agᵗ Zacheus Woolly ats Thoˢ Howson his Master for being a Disorderly Servt & imbezelling his money.

Rachel Fileman fr PC by John Wyre C. chd by Mary Mason (on Mʳ Aldⁿ Bridgens Wᵗ 21ˢᵗ Inst) for assᵗing and throwing Dirt into her House and raising a Mob about her Door; she made Oath of this Offence & she was comᵈ to PC:

Whinifred Scoulthorp fr WC: by Samˡ Saunders C. chd by Eliz: Johnson on Suspicion of stealing a Bolster a Pair of Sheets & some other Things of ~~trifling~~ the Value of about 10s. – there appeared a Suspicion of her being guilty of this Offense, she was ~~yest~~ thereupon remanded for further Examination 'till next Monday.[33]

Jane Rules, Sarah Apper} by Samˡ Inman C. chd by ~~him~~ Matthew Swift & William Paine[34] for being apprehended in a House of ill Fame on ~~Sunday~~ Wednesday Night last in Apollo Court and being a Common Night Walkers they were on the 2 Accusers Oaths comᵈ to B:

33. See below, 26 October 1761 session.
34. Probably the constable, William Payne.

P   Duranse Knoswell fr B: by Jos^h Fletcher C. chd by Thos Siborn on Suspicion of stealing a Palm & Needle two Tools in the Sail Cloth Making ways, it was a very trifling Mre & she was d^d.

P   Frances Wheats fr WC by Hen: Hayward C. chd by [blank] Blower, who keeps the Bear in Thames Street (who was not now present) no Person therefore appearing against her she was d^d.

1s.   W^t ag^t Mary Robins & Mary Shelton ads Thos Pitman Ass^t etc.

1s.   D° ag^t ~~Cath. Ead~~ Ann Major ads Cath: Eady D°

five Shillings
RL

1s.   Jeremiah Clark by Jacob Marks C. chd by Marg^t Harrison (on Mr Alder^n Bridgens W^t 21 Oct. ~~Ult~~ Inst.) for an Ass^t on an Agreement d^d.

19/

Sir Francis Gosling by Mr Alderman Alsop. Monday 26 October 1761.
P   Chas Stacey fr WC by Danl Brougham C. chd by a Pson who was not now pres^t for making a Disturbance ab^t a Week ago; was reprimanded & d^d.

Thos Pocklington Butcher ads Benja: Forfitt for exercising his Trade par: St Faith under St Pauls was exc^d this time being the first

Jno Austin Garratt, Butcher, app^d by his wife, ads D° for the same par St Giles without Cripplegate, was for want of Evidence d^d.

James Bedford Vict. ads D° & Henry Decker for the same par St Gregory; they swore that there were sev^l people drinking in his Ho: and there was a great Noise in his Ho: he was ~~conv^d on their Oaths and ord^d to pay~~ ord^d on the appear: of Bedford's [illegible] wife & 2 Lodger's to [blank]

C. Octob.   Thos Cole Vict: ads D° for the same Par St Gregory by 27th Rece^d by St Pauls – they swore that there were several Compa^s[35]

35. Possibly 'Companions'.

Jn° Jordaine in the Room, and that there was Beer in the Potts; he
£ 0.4.10 was conv^d on their Oaths & ord^d to pay 5s. which he did
& was d^d.

C. R^d Freckleton 3 Cups in Bread Street Inn holder; there were 3
people drinking; the 3 people he s^d that ~~there~~ were drinking;
were ~~not~~ Travailers— but being upon Oath declared it was the
Week before—he was conv^d on their Oaths & p^d 5s. wch he
did & was d^d.

John Davidson, Martha Dale} fr B: by Ben: Boulton C. chd
by Willm Oakman as foll[ows] Viz. Davidson for assaulting &
striking him & the woman for throwing a Pot of Beer over his
Wife; being sworn he said the Man struck him over the Face;
& that the Woman ~~stru~~ threw the Beer over the Cloaths of
Mary his Wife – John Hilliard see the Woman throw the Beer
at Mr Oakman's Wife – see Davidson strike Oakman, he was
bail'd as at the Mark *.

2s. John Davidson & Martha Dale} were chd a 2^d time by Eliza:
the wife of the s^d John Davidson for violently assaulting and
beating her – was bail'd also as below.**

RX * John Davidson of Chancery Lane L. Orace[?] Weaver £ 40
R^d Hudson of Leadenhall Str L. W^h Maker   20
John Hilliard of Chancery Lane L. Porter of Serj^ts Inn   20

RX ** The same Persons became Bail for him a 2^d time for
Davidson on his Wife's Compl^t.

Thos Armstrong ~~Vic~~ Innholder ads Ben: Forfitt & Hen: Decker
for exercising ~~their~~ his Trade as afsd – was excus'd this time.

Sum^s ag^t John Carter & Co: ads Ben: Forfitt for exercising his
Trade of a Butcher Sunday last was sevenight – on Oath of
Forfitt – for Wednesday

1s. John McClarin by Thos Gwin C. chd by Edwd Chapman his
Ma^r for ass^ting and beating him he ask'd his Ma^r pardon, &
they agreed to part, he was d^d.

P John Morgan fr WC by Ja^s Leage[?] C. chd by John Holbard
W^hman belonging to St Sepulchre for being apprehended a
Vagr^t in Fleet Markett. He was a poor Child ab^t 12 years old
& was d^d.

P Mary Sweetman fr WC by same C. chd by W^hman for giving

some Encouragem^t to the Boy— above –it did not appear that there was any Compl^t ag^t her she was d^d.

Whinifred Scoulthorp fr WC by Saml Saunders C. chd by Eliz: Johnson on Suspicion of stealing a Bolster a pair of Sheets & some o^r things her Property.

~~Eliz. Archer~~ Edm^d Hill fr WC by Wm Lee C. chd by Eliz: Archer, for ass^{t}ing and beating her ~~on Sa~~ last night at her own Ho: it app^d on the Testimony of Eliz: Chaddock her Servt she was assaulted by the Man who threw ~~her~~ a Candlestick at her and cut her Eye, at his Request, & ~~on~~ by Pros^x Consent ~~she~~ was rem^{d}ed for fur Examicon.

2s. Jos^h Bond, Mark Taylor} fr PC by Wm Tinn C. chd by Theoph^s Quincey at the Dolphin Darkhouse Lane for making a Disturbance at his House Saturday night last; the[y] ask'd Mr Quincey's Pardon & were d^d.

1s. Mary Robbin[s] by Thos Hayes C. chd by Thos ~~Mary She~~ Pitman for assaulting and beating him in Co: with one Mary Shelton (who was not Pres^t) – on making an Agreement she was d^d.

1s. W^t ag^t John Ellis ads Robt Baptist Ass^t etc.

R. A.

Sir Robert Kite. Tuesday 27 October 1761.
1s. W^t ag^t Saml Nash ads Jane Watts Wid^o his Mistress for disobeying her lawful Commands – on Oath of Wm Watts.

1s. Thos Hilldrup fr WC by Geo: Moore C. chd by Anth[on]y Hardaker a W^{h}man in Cripplegate Ward within for being a Disorderly person much in Liquor and makeing a disturbance on an Agreement D^d

1s. John Langhorn by D^o C. chd by Wm Miles for ass^{t}ing him at the Cross Keys Inn this Morning at 5 o'Clock this Morning – on an Agreement d^d.

1s. Martha Dale fr B: by Ben: Bolton C. chd by Mary Oakman for ass^{t}ing her and throwing Beer over her

1s. She was chd a 2^d time by Eliz: Davidson for an Ass^t but making both Satisfaction was d^d.

Marg^t Wiltshire fr WC by Jno Burdett chd by Jno Lewis for ~~making~~ begging in the parish of St. Gregory & greatly abusing him ~~for~~ on his Oath com^d to B: as a disorderly Pson.

Edwd Burn by D^o C. chd by Richd Parr for stealing a Silver Buckle Val. 2/6 who appear^g to be a poor boy ~~under~~ 12 years Old – he was remanded to WC for fur Examicon till to Morrow, & the Const directed to get his father here at that time.

Ann Major by Saml Saunders C. chd by Cath: Eady (on Sr Robt Ladbrokes W^t 23 Inst.) for an Ass^t – she propos^d to make Satis-facon but having no money ~~she~~ consented that the W^t should be in force ag^t her till after Saturday, when she propos'd to make Sat^n.

1s.   Thos Thorougood, ~~Marg^t Hopkins~~, Susa^a Hopkins} fr B: by Jos^h Fletcher C. chd by Marg^t Hopkins Mo[the]r of said Sus^a Hopkins for ass^{t}ing & violently beating her, it app^d the man had ass^{t}ed her violently – ~~and~~ but the Woman did nothing – he was on her Oath com^d to WC

1s.   Edm^d Hill fr WC by Wm Lee C. chd by Elizabeth Archer for an Ass^t being agreed was d^d.

1s.   W^t against Ben: Dillemore ads John Leverton ~~Ass^t~~ his Ma^r for leaving his Service.

W^t ag^t Terence Connelley ads Mary Gallaway Ass^t etc.

RK

Mr Alderman Master. Wednesday 28 October 1761.
    Henry Follett, f[rom] [blank], Thos Davis, f[rom] [blank]} by [blank] Walklate C. chd by [blank] on Suspision of Robbing their Masters Chas. Barrow & Co.

Jno Carter Summoned by Alde^n Alsop to Answer the Complt of Benja Forfeit for exercise the Trade of a Butcher by selling a neck of ~~n[~~illegible~~]ey~~Mutton on Sunday the 18th Inst. D^d on promise not to Offend again it being in his absence by his Servt it appearing the first Offence D^d

Henry Follet fr PC, Thos Davis fr WC} by Jno Walklate C. chd by Chas Barrow for being concerned in robbing him of a parcel of Capers. Jno Morris saith that Follet & Davis were in the Vault near a Cask where a parcell of Capers had been taken &

were put into a Runlet. That the prisoners were Journey Man Coopers at work in the Vault that the place where the Capers were dis was distant from the work they were remanded to the different Compters for further Examicon.

~~Chas Barrow of Thames Street London Oyelman 40~~
~~Jn° Morris his Servt~~

John Paris[36] by R^d Nash C. chd by John Rogers for picking his Pockett of a Linnen Handkerchief Va^l 1s. his property – the fact was done at Guildhall & he was (on Pros^rs Oath) committed to PC.

RX   John Rogers clk to M^r ~~Roge~~ Crisp in Watling Street Merchant   £ 20

Edwd Burn fr WC by John Burdett C. chd by Richd Parr for stealing a Silver Buckle Va^l 2s/6d his Property – was remanded to WC yesterday by Sr. Robt Kite he being a Boy of tender years (Viz. under 12 years old) was reprim^ded & d^d to his father to be corrected

Douglas Mckenzie by Thomas Lindey C. chd by John Gansford (on Mr Ald^n Cokaynes W^t 8. Inst) for standing indicted tog^r wth o^r Persons at the General Sessions of the Peace holden for the City of London at the Guildhall 14 September for riotously breaking & entering the Back Chamber up two pair of Stairs of the Dwelling House of said John Gansford & Ass^ting him— to wch Indictm^t s^d Douglas Mckenzie had not app^d & pleaded, tho' he before entered into a Recog^ce wth Sureties for that purpose per[sua]nt[?] Pat. per Cert. Cl[erk] P[eace].

1s.   W^t ag^t Mary Barne ads Eliz: Gray Ass^t etc.

1s.   Douglus[?] Discharged Thomas Thorougood fr WC com^d yesterday by Sr Robt Kite for ass^ting Marg^t Hopkins on her Application.

AM

Guildhall being shut up on Account of the preparations for Lord Mayors day, from the 28 Octo^r ~~to 16 November to~~, & kept shut 'till now, in Order to remove the Materials us'd on that Day, therefore No Attendance from the s^d 28 Octo^r to 16 Nov^r.

---

36. The case proceeds to the Old Bailey. See *OBP*, December 1761, trial of John Paris (t17611209–10).

Sir Jospeh Hankey. Monday 16 November 1761.

1s.   W^t ag^t Thos Lawrence ads Jno Ross of the Poultry Compter for escaping out of the Poultry Compter being chd in Execution for a Debt of £ 20.

1s.   D^o agt Malachi Bendon ads Margaret Davidson ass^t etc.

Thos Lawrence Servt to Messers[?] Life of - - - Hungerford Market for driving a Cart with out horse in the parish of St Botolph Billingsgate with[ou]t Name or Number which being Stopt & Sent to the Bull Inn at the request of the Driver to acquaint his Master was Adjourned for a further hearing to Morrow.

1s.   W^t ag^t Mary Harding ats Jane Curtis ass^t etc.

Thos Hill fr PC by John Jebb C.[37] charged by him for escaping out of his Custody; it appeared he had escaped out of his Custody (being deliv^d into the Const. Hands by the late Lord Mayor) the Officer of a press Gang app^d & agreed to take him; he was ord^d on board the Tender & the Const. directed to Assist him.

P   Wm Gilbert fr PC: by Caleb Lee C. chd by Marg^t Gordon & Marg^t Briggs (on Mr Leach's Surry W^t 13 Inst. back'd by Ald^n Cokayne 14th) along with Sarah Rix (not yet taken) on Suspicion of stealing divers Quantities of wearing Apparel the Property of said Marg^t Briggs – on examination of the s^d Wm Mre it did not appear that he was any way concerned in this ~~Affair~~ Felony, he was for want of Evidence d^d.

Jos: Hankey

Sir ~~Jos: Hankey~~ William Baker by Alderman Alexander. Tuesday 17 November 1761.
~~Thomas Morgan by John Walklate C. chd by Cath: Dawson~~
~~(on Sir William Stephensons Warrant yesterday) for assaulting~~
~~beating & abusing her~~

1s.   W^t ag^t ~~Benja Faulker ads Stephen Yates~~ Stephen Yates, ads

---

37. Jebb appears frequently in the *Old Baily Proceedings* as a constable 'for the King on the keys', or 'for the keys'. See *OBP*, January 1760, trial of David Morgan (t17600116–3); September 1761, trial of Patrick Quin (t17610916–51); October 1764, trial of Thomas Jones (t17641017–1); February 1767, trial of John Bottom (t17670218–19).

Benj: Faulkner his Master for assaulting & violently beating him.[38]

1s. Mary Anderson by Jacob Marks C. chd by Mary Cor (on Ald[n] Alsop W[t] 11th Inst) for assaulting beating and wounding her with a Pint Pot – Cornelius Sommers see Pris[r] come into a Ho: to sell Oyster – Prox made a pull at her Oysters & being in Liquor struck Prisr first it app[d] that Prosx was the Aggressor the Compl[t] was dismissed

1s. W[m] Taylor fr PC by Geo: Angell C. chd by Eliz: Clayson for ass[t]ing her and beating her Hat off her Head, & his Companion ran away w[th] it Mary Towers see him strike her, he made Satisfaction & was d[d].

1s Tho[s] Rottam by Jos[h] Ward C. chd by Sarah his Wife (on M[r] Quarrills Midx W[t] 13. Inst. back'd by Ald[n] Cokayne 14[th] ib[id]) for assaulting her in a Violent Manner, & also for running away & leaving her whereby she is likely to become chargeable – the Husband agreed to allow her 3/6d. Per Week with which she was contented, he was on an agreem[t] d[d].

1s. W[t] ag[t] to Search the House of Jacob Abrahams in Gravol Lane Hounsditch for a Quantity of Ribbons stolen out of the Shop of John Kent.

1s. Hannah Beal Abraham, Mary Dutton} by John Bumpus[t?] C. chd by Cath: Steele (on S[r] W[m] Stephenson's W[t] yesterday[ )]for assaulting beating and Abusing her along wth Hannah Brabam not taken, on Pros[x] own shewing there was no Ass[t] but bred a very great Riot & Disturbance – Mary Cassie & her Husband both see heard her greatly abuse Steele; she promis'd to behave well in Future, she & was then d[d].

P Mary Harding by Edw[d] Thorp C. chd by Jane Curtis (on S[r] Jos: Hankey's W[t] yesterday) for assaulting & beating her – Sarah Con heard the beginning, heard Pros[x] call her very bad Names –then being provoked threw Beer at her & a Pint Pot, she made Satisfaction & was d[d].

Tho[s] Preistly sumond by S[r] Jos[h] Hankey yesterday to Answ[r] William Lowen for setting Empty Casks on Sunday last in Alhallows Lane Par: Alhallows the Great – was conv[d] & the money given to Lowen for the parish – Viz: 5s.

38. Both versions of the charge are struck out in the original.

N A

Mr Alderman Beckford by the late Lord Mayor. Wednesday 18 November 1761.

Saunders Joseph[39] by Joseph Ward C. chd by John Kent (on Ld Mayors Wt yesterday) on Suspicion of feloniously stealing a Quantity of Ribbons Va: abt £10:--: it appeared that Lyon Alexander who was prest delivd these Ribbons to the Prisr to sell, & he alledged that he recd 'em from a Man at a public House in Holborn; the Prisr appd only a Person employed to sell these Ribbons as an Acquaintance, & the Prisr swore that he acknowd these Ribbons to be his & that he had them in Exchange for Snuff, his Wife also acknowld the same; Mary Jones sd that Saunders Joseph brot her 6 or 7 pieces of Ribbon, & ask'd her 4d ½ Per yard for it – it was worth near 7d. Per yard – there appeared on hearing a great Suspicion of his stealing these Ribbons he Viz: Lyon Alexander was comd to WC & Saunders Joseph gave Bail for his Appear at next Sesss to give Evidence agt him

RX

Saunders Joseph of Gravel Lane L: Snuff Maker	40	
Isaac Mendez Belisaries of Do petticote Lane Midx	40	
RX To prosecute		
John Kent of Hounsditch L: Cabinet & Chair Maker	£ 20	

Robt Bradley C. sumd ads Mary Satchwell for refusing to take Charge of Ann Lilly; who had stolen from her a Quantity of Silk, he undertook to Produce the woman; & after being absent about an hour & half he returned wth the woman &was for this time reprimded & dd.

Paul Tourquan ads Thomas Dymoke Carman for refusing to pay him for the Carriage of two Hogsheads of Sugar from Coal Harbour to ~~your~~ his House in Great Garden Street – it was agreed to be measured & to appear again on Friday next.

P   Thos Morgan by John Walklate C. chd by Cath: Dawson (on Sr Wm Stephenson's Wt 16 Inst.) for assting beating & abusing her; it apprd that the Woman was ~~abusing~~ desired by the Man to go out of Mrs. Balmer's Shop where he was Servt & she not doing it he turn'd her out, the Asst being justifiable he was dd.

---

39. The case proceeds to the Old Bailey in the trial of Lyon Alexander. See *OBP*, December 1761, trial of Lion Alexander (t17611209–23).

Sir Matthew Blakiston. ad huc Wednesday 18 November 1761.[40]

    Grace Mitchell Carwoman was sum^d ads Sr Wm Stevephenson[sic] to produce the Driver of her Cart N° 2080 for refusing to load. she agreed her Servt sho^d wait on S^r W^m to Morrow Morning to ask his Pardon on wch Cond[iti]on she was to be excused.

    ~~Stephen Yates~~ Ben: Faulkner ~~a~~ by Wm Martindale C. chd by ~~Benja. Faulkner~~ Stephen Yates his Ma^r (on Mr Ald^n Alexanders W^t yesterday) for ass^{t}ing and beating him

    John Edmonds was chd by s^d Stephen Yates his Ma^r for ass^{t}ing and seizing him by the Collar they were both com^d to WC.

    Mary Cowen[41] fr WC by Wm Silvester chd by John Chambers for privately stealing from his Person a Pockett Book & a Tobacco Pouch; he made Oath of the Offence & she was com^d to WC.

RX   John Chambers of Mountague Close, Southwark, Blockmaker} £ 20

    Ann Lilly by Robt Bradley C. chd by Mary ~~Sathwell~~ Satchwell a parcell of Silk Value 5s. from out of her house wch being confirmed on her Oath & the goods found in London [illegible] ged to WC

R   ~~Mary Satchwell of Wheler Street Lond & Wife of Abraham Satchwell~~

    Mary Anderson committed by Order of last Sessions ~~for~~ at the Old Baily for Wilful and corrupt Perjury on the Trial of Thomas Quin for Felony was bailed as below

R   Mary Anderson of Bedford Court Bedford Row Midx Sp^r: £ 80

    Wm Cass of Swan Alley St Jno Str: Midx Farrier   40

    Jno Nicholls of Clem^{ts} Lane Par: St Clements Dane, Midx Broker   40

M: B

Mr Alderman Alexander. Thursday 19 November 1761.

    Thos Shute by Wm Hutchings C. chd by Henry Adamson his Ma^r for being an idle and disorderly Apprentice & deserting

---

40.   The sitting alderman has apparently changed mid-session as the session continues 'ad huc' (as previous).

41.   The case proceeds to the Old Bailey. See *OBP*, December 1761, trial of Mary, wife of — Cowen (t17611209–35).

his Ma^rs Service, it app^d that he had run away 8 times; he was ord^d to WC 'till they co^d get him into the Sea Service

Mary Collett by Jacob Marks C. chd by Stephen Ship Pawn-broker, on Suspicion of stealing a Lawn Apron Val. 6s. his property, Ann Ux R^d Geary rec^d this Apron in pawn from the Pris^r she was com^d to PC

R   Stephen Ship of Long Alley Moorfields Com^42 Midx
Broker } £ 20

1s.   W^t ag^t Jane Launcelot ads Andrew Serle for coming frequently in a riotous & tumultuous manner to his Ho: & there making a great Noise & Disturbance & abusing the s^d Serle.

1s.   D^o ag^t Henry Fossett ads John Wyatt Ass^t etc.

P   Danl Dirkinson fr PC: by Thos Lake C. chd by Solomon Hart for ass^ting and beating him he Promis'd to behave well for the future he was d^d.

1s.   Ann Beury fr B: by Saml Inman C. chd by Edwd Read on Suspicion of picking his pocket of 5 Gu^s & a Moidore on Friday 23^d Octo^r –it app^d that he had taken her into Custody soon after the Fact was com^d – he s^d she was rescued by some Person & not retaken 'till last Night; it app^d the woman was searched immediately after she was chd & nothing found upon her but 2 Gu^s was found upon the bed where they had lain (he acknowledged lying with her) he s^d that he fell asleep on the Bed after he had lain wth her & when he awoke miss'd his money; & found 5 Counters in his Pockett the next Morning instead of his money; he (on being examin'd fu^r) s^d that he co^d not tell what time of the Day he see his money, but that he was certain he had 4 Gu^s & a Moidore when he went into the Room with her in Fleet Lane at Haynes's a Bawdy Ho: On a full Examicon of the whole Mre his Wp was of Opinion that the Man ought not to be sworn, having given such contradictory Accounts ab^t the Mre, she was d^d.

1s.   Alex^r Dibble by James Compton C. chd by Wm Harris for an Ass^t on an Agreem^t d^d.

Tho Groom app^d before his Wp & acknowledged to have been inlisted as a Private Soldier in the 72^d Regim^t on the Eve before last ~~& app^d~~ & the Officer who had inlisted him app^d & took ~~the~~ 20s. & agreed to his being d^d.

42. Comitas = county.

39

WA

M[r] Alderman Bridgen ~~by M[r] Ald[n] Alexander~~. Friday 20 November 1761.
George Deichman ads Tho[s] Hudson Carman for refusing to pay him his Fare for the Car[tage] of 2 Loads of Sugar from Doublehood Warehouses to his Ho: in Bristol Street; his Wp was of an Opinion & ord[d] him to pay 2s./6d. Per Load – 1s Summons & 1s Charges

1s.   Aff[t] Ann Walter

Cha[s] Biggers fr WC by John Stockall C. chd by ~~M~~ Sarah Armstrong ~~for~~ – on hearing it app[d] that she charged Pris[r] on being Serv[t] to a Lodger of hers who had run away w[th] his Goods in Order to cheat her of Rent – there was no Charge ag[t] him he was d[d] –he was a poor Boy 10 years old

James Pentecross sum[d] ~~by~~ ads Hannah Brabham for ass[t]ing and beating her it appearing the Comp[lainan]t was the Aggressor the Pris[r] was discharged.

Tho[s] Wilson by W[m] Beaumont C. chd by him for driving a Cart within the Bill, this day (Viz: Par[h] S[t] Martin Ironmonger Lane) not having a N[o] he residing within the weekly Bills –he was ord[d] to make Satisfaction to the ~~Carman~~ Street Keeper.

W.B.   14/

Sir William Stephenson. Monday 23 November 1761.
1s.   Jacob Levi fr PC: by Tho[s] Knight C. chd by Jacob Taverner for being found concealed in his Ho: ab[t] 5 O'Clock; (in Plough Court Lombard Street) he having done nothing at this time, & having a good Character, was reprimanded & d[d].

1s.   W[t] agt M[rs] [blank] Powell (whose Christian name is unknown[)] ads Eliz: [blank] She now for raising a great Mob ab[t] her Door & greatly abusing her & Profanely swearing Saturday Night last.

1s.   W[t] to search the Chambers of Philip Millard in Lambs Buildings Temple for one wood Stand 3 Wooden blocks one pair of Pinching Irons & 2 pair of Toupie[?] Irons stolen from Robert Marks on his Oath.

1s.   Rose Solomon by John Wyre C. chd by Jane Ruben (on M[r]

Ald^n Cokaynes W^t 17 Inst) for ass^{t}ing her on the 15 Inst. & breaking her Windows; it was a very frivolous complaint & being no material Injury done to Solomon she was d^d.

John Fry fr WC by ~~Nath'l Cr~~ Thos Hayes C. chd by John Biggs for ass^{t}ing and beating him in his Ho: on Saturday night; ~~it was a very frivolous Compl^t~~ he made an Agreement wth Biggs & was d^d fr[om] that Compl^t – but having broke a Quantity of Windows in (Hu[?] Co [blank]

1s. Aff^t Peter Borell

1s. Philip Levi ads Frances Chessman his Servt for unlawfully & without Cause turning her out of his House & Service at an unseasonable time of Night & refusing to pay her her Wages – he was ord^d to pay 4s. Wages 1s. &[?] which he did & was d^d.

Eliz: Wyatt fr B: by John Stockall C. chd by Eliz: Lloyd for stealing a pint pewter pint Va^l about 10d. – she was an idle & disorderly ~~Pson~~ – Jno Simmons Mrs Lloyds Servt see a pot on the Bar, & no body was in the Ho: but the Pris^r – she was greatly suspected of being guilty & was com^d to B.

1s. W^t ag^t Moses West ads Moses West his Ma^r for deserting his Service.

1s. D^o ag^t Eliz: Balmer ads Sarah Hart Ass^t etc.

1s W^t ag^t John Levi ads Dorothy Barrett Ass^t etc.

W S

Mr Alderman Nelson. Tuesday 24 November 1761.
P Ann Griffith fr PC by Robt Bradley C. chd by Saml Robinson & Thos Stokes Watchmen near Bpsgate Ch: yard, for making a great Riot and Disturbance there ab^t 11 O'Cl last Night – it app^d that she was not a Common Night Walker, but a poor Woman a little overcome wth Liquor; she was now penitent & was reprim^d & d^d.

Wm Baldwin fr PC by Thos Gwin C. chd by Wm Hawkins Ch: Wden of St Stephen Coleman Street for making a great Disturbance and greatly abusing him, it app^d that he was an idle & disorderly Person & was com^d to B:

1s. Moses West by Wm Simpson C. chd by his Father Moses West for running away from him and desert[in]g his Service being his Apprentice it appeared he was inticed away by [blank] a Serjeant [blank] [~~illegible~~] and hapend~~ed by~~ ordered to be Disch^d & he ret^d to his Ma^r.

1s.   W^t ag^t James Ilsly ats Robt Maile his Mar for running away from him & deserting his service

1s.   Afft Jno Doxon[?]

1s.[?]   Thos Loyd Carman ats William Hall for Damagain and breaking the Windows of his sister Eliz Hall willfully which being proved on her oath he was adjudged Guilty & fined 10s. ~~but~~ the Reason of wch was to influence him to pay 6: 3d. Charges, wch he promis'd to do--& a W^t of Distress was ord^d to be omitted.

Geo: Crowder by Chas Gough C. chd by Sus^a Chapman for ass^ting and beating her (on Mr Ald^n Bridgen's W^t 21st Octo^r) on an Agreem^t d^d.

John French agt Thos Sharp his Ma^r for ill treating & beating him – the Mre was adj^d 'till to Morrow.

P   Wt agt Wm Waight ads Mary his Wife Ass^t etc.

GN

Sir Francis Gosling. Wednesday 25 November 1761.
1s.   Aff^t Wm Hutchins

1s.   W^t ag^t Barnard Hammond ads Hannah Archer Ass^t etc.

P   D^o ag^t Zechariah Solomon ads Abigail Ux[or]eius D^o

nil   John Comfort by Thos Wrothwell C. chd by Mr Osmond Cook for ass^ting him & striking his Hat off – he was a Messenger to the Lottery – & the Princ[ipal] Dispute was ab^t his taking money of certain persons for their Seats in the Hall & thereby depriving Cook & his Pa[rtne?]^r of the Benefit of their Galleries. 2 Com[missioners] P[ro]mis'd that they sho^d take no money ~~for the time to come~~ he was d^d.

F.G.

Sir Robert Kite. Thursday 26 November 1761.
1s.   W^t ag^t Eliz: Stoughton ads Sus^a Wilkins Ass^t etc.

1s.   Back'd a Midx W^t Per S^r J Fielding dated yesterday.

Ja^s Vale ads Eliz: James for unlawfully taking Possession of a Room rented of him by her Husband –it app^d he had put a padlock on the Room Door & kept her & her child out whereby her Child was greatly hurt –she owed him 5s. 5d. rent; he agreed to forgive this on her going out by to Morrow ~~Morning~~ Eveng wch she Promised to do & the Compl^t was dismiss'd.

2s.   Aff^{ts} John Landall, Ja^s:[?] Hainworth.

Thos Buck ads Thos Armstrong for fraudulently assisting his Ten[an]t in removing certain Goods in Order to hinder him from distraining thereof for Rent; there was no proof ag^t him he was d^d.

1s.   Thos Shaw Drayman ads Joseph Atkins for negligently doing Damage to him by breaking his Windows & also for negligently or by willful misbehaviour obstructing the free passage of his Majys Subjects 24 Inst. in the Poultry; he alledged that his Windows cost mending 2s/4d – & he p^d 1s. Sum^s & the o^r money & was d^d.

P   John Kendale fr PC by Edwd Harris C. chd by Thos Ambler his Ma^r for running away & leaving his Service (he being his Appr^e bound to him for 4 years) & the Ind[entu]re being produc'd app^d to be irregular & the Magistrate having on this Acco^t, no Jurisdiction, was d^d.

1s.   Peace W. ag^t Eliz: Wheatley & Sarah Price ads Mary Bull the first for threatening to stab her & the 2^d for threatening to knock her Brains out.

RK

Mr Alderman Cokayne.[43]
P   Eliz Stoughton by Wm Moreton C. chd by Sus^a Wilkins (on Sr Robt Kites W^t this day) for asst^{t}ing & beating her – the Compl^t was comp[r]omise[d] (the Injury if any being very trifling) & the Pris^r d^d.

Mr Alderman ~~Challenor~~ Master. Friday 27 November 1761.
    Nathl Thring fr PC by Jacob Aaron C. chd by Frances Clarke

43.   Presumably he has stepped in for Kite for this last case.

for ass^{t}ing her ab^t 10 O'Cl last Night in Hand Alley Gravel Lane & attempting to put his Hands up her Petticoats.

Beersheba Wise from D^{o}C by Same C. chd by him for making a Disturbance in Leadenhall Street; she app^d a poor labouring Woman & a little over taken in Liquor & was reprim^d & d^d.

1s.   Back'd a Berks W^t da^t 18 April last, per Mr Aldworth.

1s.   W^t ag^t Chas Roberts ads Mich^l James Ass^t etc.

AM   22 /

Mr Alderman Cokayne for Sir ~~Wm~~ Jos: Hankey. Monday 19 April 1762.

1s.   Thurston Ford by R^d Nash C. chd by Ann Fernley Ford (on his Wp's Peace W^t 16th Inst. being adjourn'd to this Day on Friday last) – for that he had on various Occasions threatened to kill her & in par[ticu]lar on Tuesday last in great heat of Passion threatening to murder her & in Order to compleat his Purpose did wrench open the Door of his Dining Room where she was lock'd up in Order to preserve herself from the Effects of his Rage – Mary Kingston ~~her~~ late Servt to Ford had ab^t 2 Mo[nth]s ago seen her strike her –Cath: Johnson s^d something ab^t touching her Forehead wth a pewter Pott ab^t 2 Mon^s ago – there was a small Mark – it did not hurt her Much –none gave Evidence ~~lately~~ of a late Ass^t etc.—it app^d he was hasty but had not struck her lately

Mr Ford Uncle to The Pris^r, Mr Tyler of Woodstreet Compter} app^d and gave the Def^t a good Cha^r – there app^d no reason to bind him over –the W^t was d^d.

2s.   Ja^s Cooke, Mary Dullige fr PC}by Thos Barratt C. ~~chd by~~ chging each wth some trifling Misdemeanours of no Consequence they were d^d.

Ann Potter by John Ellett a Surry C. (for his Wp^s W^t 16th Inst.), for sending Letters to him & threatening the Life of s^d Markes.

1s.   W^t to search the Ho: of Thos Wilmot Pawnbroker in Bride Alley for a Pot Brass Arms stolen out of St Pauls (on Oath of Isaac Fawcett)

1s.   W^t ag^t Geo: Strench ads John Brown Ass^t etc.

P Wm Ambrose fr WC by Cornelius Hopper C. chd by Joseph Heath for ass^ting one of the serv^ts of Mr Wingott's a Pewterer in Jewin Street – he was penitent & was reprim^ded & (by Consent of Pros^r) d^d.

P W^t ag^t Reb^a Campin & Mary her Dau[ghte]r ads Jane Williams Ass^t etc.

Ann Griffiths fr PC: by Thos Ward C. she by him for being apprehended in Co[mpany] wth a Man (who was not here) & chd for a Felony – she was sent back till to Morrow.

1s. W^t ag^t Jno Bull ads Mary Dao[e?]s Ass^t etc.

6/ F.C.

Sir William Baker by Mr Alderman Alsop. Tuesday 20 April 1762.
1s. W^t to search the Ho: of Thos Wilkins in Cock Lane Smithfield for two Telescopes two cutting Diamonds a Brass Tool & other Goods the Property of Edwd Nairne stolen from him—on his Oath

P Ann Griffiths fr PC: by Thos Ward C. chd by John Owen, for stealing from him 6 or 7s. (this was the Charge he gave to the Const. when she was apprehended) but now co^d not say any thing ag^t her, alledging he was in Liquor; she was therefore d^d.

Eliza: Dennis one of the poor of Coleman Street Parish by Thos Gwyn C. chd by John Townsend Ch: Wden of the said Psh—she was for this time reprimanded & d^d.

1s. Aff^t Matt^w Poole

1s. Warr^t ag^t John Weaver ads of Edmond Stuffs for an ass^t

1s. Attested Geo: Hulbert inlisted into an Independ^t Compa: com^ded by Cap^n John Day.

1s. W^t ag^t Ben: Sanders ads Robt Turvey Ass^t etc.

Mr Alderman ~~Alsop~~ Blunt.[44]
1s. W^t ag^t Alexander [blank] a Carman ads Abram Tappin

---

44. Blunt may have replaced Alsop.

1s.　　Do agt Jane King, John Williams & Sarah Williams ads Reba Kempton & Mary her Dau[ghte]r Asst etc.

P　　Dischd Adelgunda Bull fr B: she was comd by Sr Chas Asgill 13 Inst.

R: B

Recd April 22d 1762 of Mr Jno Franklin three shillings & nine pence being one half of the Conviction money of Richd Harvey on Mims: Convicted at Guild Hall
per W. Wright Ch Warden.[45]

Sir William Stephenson. Tuesday 20 April 1762.

C　　William Page sumd ads Thos Snow for selling him 36 Trusses of Hay on Saturday last in Smithfield Markett all wanting and being short of their due Weight; it appd that this Hay was weighed in Presence of & by John Franklin Clk of Smithfield Markett who deposed to 5 Trusses & more being short of 56lbs—the proper weight—he was convd of this Offence (wch was comd in St Sepulchres Parish) & ordered to pay 7s. 6d. fine & 2s. charges to wch he did & was dd.

Mr Alderman Beckford, by Sir Charles Asgill. Wednesday 21 April 1762.

1s.　　Joseph Thompson by Thos Bracey C. chd by Hannah Cale for Asst ing & beating her (on Mr Aldn Masters Wt 1st Mar:) it having been (on Prosx's shewing) once made up he was dd.

1s.　　Isabel Ward on same C. chd by sd Cale (on Ld Mrs Wt 16 Inst) for assaulting beating & abusing her—it was also a very trifling Complaint, she was likewise dischd.

John Pike sumd ads Thomas Spencer an Hackney Coachman for refusing to pay him for carrying him in his Hackney Coach on No 270 Sunday last from Mincing Lane to the Green Man at Dulwich & round by Dulwich Colledge & back – he swore that he carried him (being called from the White Hart in Grace-church Street) upwards of 12 Miles for which he was ordd to pay 8s/ 6d. – 1s. Sums and 1s. time which he paid and was dischd –the Coachman at Mrs. Moores the Sun in Gray's Inn Lane.

---

45. A loose note appended to the minute book at this point.

1s.   W[t] to Search the Ho: or Appartm[ts] of Marks Davis ats Davids in Shoemaker Row Hounsditch for a Gold Man's Jack Chain and two leafs set in Gold stolen from Gershom Williams – on his Oath.

C   John Frewer Drayman Serv[t] to Mess[rs] Hope & Stubbs chd by Robert Wilks Esq[r] (being the Driver of a Dray N[o] 645) for willfully obstructing the free Passage of his Majys Subjects with his Dray on Wednesday last in Bpsgate Street –he was (on M[r] Wilks' Oath) conv[d] & ord[d] to pay 5s. wch he did & was d[d].

Rec[d] 24 April 1762 of M[r] Nash Five shillings for a fine of Mr Wilks Convicted a Drayman
£ 0: 5: 0   per Tho: Higgs ChurchWarden[46]

C   Tho[s] Wilford Drayman (Driver of ano[r] Dray N[o] 646) chd by s[d] M[r] Wilks for obstructing the free Passage of his Majtys Subjects with his Dray (Par: S[t] Bot. Bpsgate) he was convicted on Oath of M[r] Wilks & ord[d] to pay 5s. wch he did & was d[d]. Sent per Nash to the Par:

4s.   Aff[ts] Martin Shultz, Andreas Tetzloff, Gerhard Lewke} sworn by Tho[s] Recip[?] of London Ship's Master Interpreter.

1s.   Tho[s] Phillips by Jos[h] Weedon C. chd by Hen: Short (on S[r] Tho[s] Chitty's W[t] 15 Inst) for assaulting him and striking him wth a Whip—Minshull Scutt[?] [illegible] Serv[t] to M[r] Short; heard Phillips swear Much & threaten that he w[d] cut him & accordingly saw Phillips strike Short with a Whip before Short ever touch'd him – he was ~~on their Oaths bailed as at the Mark on the o[r] side~~[47] on Agreement Discharged.

Gen[l]   ~~Tho[s] Phillips Jun[r] Apprentice to Tho[s] Phillips his Father~~ }40
Sess[s]   ~~a Carman Stoney Lane Par: S[t] Olave Southwark, Carman~~ }
       ~~Peter Jues[?] of Bot. Lane L: Vict.~~   ~~40~~
R   ~~for the Appear: of s[d] Phillips Jn[r].~~

1s.   Hen[r]ly Short, John Smallman}by R[d] Nash C. chd by Jacob
nil[48]   Mash (on Ld Mayor's W[t] yesterday) for Ass[t] ing beating and otherwise abusing him by knocking a Tooth out and cutting his Lip, with[t] any provocation— there app[d] no Evidence ag[t] Smallman – he was d[d] – the Evidence was ag[t] Short who he

---

46.   This entry appears as a loose note appended to the minute book at this point.
47.   A footnote star here in the original to the recognizance that follows, which appears on the next page of the minute book in the original.
48.   'Nil' seems to pertain to John Smallman who was discharged for lack of evidence.

s^d struck first his Horse, & then himself wth a Broomstick & knocked his Tooth out –on an agreem^t d^d.

P   Mary Atkins by Saml Levi C. chd by Easter Cohen for pawning two pair of Sheets entrusted wth her to wash; she was a poor woman, & the Pros^x being willing to forgive her she was d^d.

7s.   CA

Mr Alderman Alexander. Thursday 22 April 1762.
1s.   Aff^t Wm Warren

1s.   D^o Hen: Smith

P   Sarah Jones fr WC: by Thos Craven C. chd by John Flower (the Ma^r of a parish work house in Beach Lane) for misbehaving in the ~~Employers~~ House–she was reprimanded & d^d.

Joseph Flight sum^d ads John Freelove an Hackney Coachman for refusing to pay him his Fare for carrying him in his Hackney coach N° 70 – on Saturday last was sevenight – Jos^h Harrison Servt to Mr Flight alledged that the Coachman fearing Mr Flight ord^d him to pay 2s. – this the Coachman deny'd on Oath & not chusing to contest this Matter wth him he was d^d.

Isaac Ashur fr PC by Coleman Solomon C. chd by Gershom Williams Esqr (who was not pres^t) on suspicion of stealing a Silver Watch; he had been 2 D[ay]s in Custody, but no regular Charge ag^t him – but it appearing that my Lord Mayor had in past heard this Mre – he was referred to the Ld Mayor.[49]

1s.   W^t ag^t John Fry ads John Morris Ass^t etc.

1s.   D^o ag^t Hyam Jacobs ads Ben: Jacob D^o

WA

Mr Alderman Cokayne for Mr Alderman Bridgen. Friday 23 April 1762.
2s.   Aff^t John Moxam –& Exhibit

P   Mary Watwood by John Edgeley C. chd by Alice White (on his Wps W^t 17 Inst) for ass^{t}ing and beating her – being a poor woman was on asking Pardon dischd.

---

49. This case suggests the division of business between the two justice rooms once the Mansion House Justice Room was operating.

Charity Burgelo fr WC by John Burdett C. chd by Hen: Pen for being a loose idle & disorderly Person and a Common Night Walker, apprehended last Night in Company with a Man in Cheapside, she was [blank].

1s.   Back'd a Midx Bench W^t

Wm Dent fr B: by Wm Boddington C. chd by John Cooke on Suspicion of stealing from him a Pidgeon Pye out of his Shop (a Pastry Cook) on Ludgate Hill – he c^d not give ~~Informacon~~ any Evidence ag^t him but the Pris^r confess'd that he knew sev^l and par[ticular]ly two whose names are John Porter and another who goes by the Name of Jack Country who were concern'd in stealing in many things such as potted Beef Tongues Pulloneys etc. a Wa^t was granted ag^t 'em – he was deliv^d to his fa^r in the Hollow behind St Lukes Church

2s.   Aff^{ts} John Hopley

1s.   W^t ag^t Hannah Windsor ads Jane Lodge Ass^t etc.

1s.   D^o ag^t a Man who goes by the Name of Matt^w Cucumber ads John Wells Ass^t etc.

1s.   D^o ag^t Ann Brady and Chris Clarke ads Eliz Ryan Ass^t etc.

8/   F.C.
        Mr Robinson here this day and p^d the money rec^d by him.[50]

Sir William Stephenson. Monday 26 April 1762.
1s.   Aff^t Thos Frankland Esqr

Joseph Randal by Robt Dean C. chd by Wm Moreton for obstructing the Passage in Mark Lane this Day, and also for swearing 5 Oaths at same time; he was Conv^d of the Offense of swearing and ord^d to pay 5[s.] wch ~~he~~ not doing, he was com^d to B. for 10 D[ay]s.

P   James Byrne, Mary Welsh} fr PC by Merrick Poulter C. chd by Wm Jewell a W^hman in Bpsgate Ward, for making a Disturbance in Bpsgate Street –it app^d the Woman gave Charge of the Man for Ass^t wch was the Occasion of her crying out; the

---

50. Note in a very small hand at the bottom of the page.

Man was a married Man & in Liquor –they were poor people and were now reprim^ded & d^d.

W.S.   R.H.⁵¹

Mr Alderman Nelson by Mr Alderman Alsop. Tuesday 27 April 1762.

1s.   Mary Brown fr WC, Reb^a Dean, PC } by Saml Webb C. chd as fol: viz: Mary Brown chd by Wm Pain for being apprehended loitering at the door of a House of ill Fame in Fleet Lane, & attempting to pick up Men, she app^d an idle & disorderly Person & was on his & Webbs Oath com^d to B. and Rebecca Dean for strolling in Cheapside & attempting to pick up Men was reprimanded & d^d.

1s.   Aff^t Roderick Wilson

1s.   D^o Thos Littler

John Stone ads Edm^d Waller his Ma^r for misbehaving in his s^d Service & Employm^t – Mr Waller was now willing to pay him his wages & making Oath that no Agreem^t for a Mo^s Wages or D^o warning was agreed on – he was ord^d to pay him £4 Wages.

Mary Moore fr PC: by Robt Stevens C. chd by Thos Stoakes Watchman in new broad Street for making a great Disturbance & Noise in the s^d Ward—she app^d a disorderly Person & was com^d to B:

1s.   Attested John Strahan a Private Soldier in the Queens Volunteers

P   W^t ag^t Mary Williams ads Eliz: Flindess Ass^t etc.

1s.   D^o ag^t Edwd Middleton ads Geo: Bransbury on Suspⁿ of stealing a Sheep

R.A.   R.H.

Sir Francis Gosling. Wednesday 28 April 1762.

1s.   Backed a Surry W^t by Mr Hammond per Aldⁿ Cokayne

1s.   Mary Torrent sum^d ads ~~Sarah~~ Eliz: Bowen for assaulting ~~and~~ beating ~~her~~ & abusing her – it appeared a very trifling

---

51. Probably the initials of the clerk.

Complaint, and the woman producing no Evidence of the Offense, she was d^d

Edward Billington app^d upon Mr Alderman Cokaynes Sumons of the 26th Inst at the Complaint of Geo: Bransby for unlawfully taking a Sheep out of a pen belonging to him in Smithfield Markett last Monday –he sho^d have app^d on Monday last but ~~last~~ had not the Sum^s in time, the Pros^r was sent to and directed to appear on Friday.

1s.   W^t to search the Upper Room of a Ho: in Dunning's Alley at the sign of The weavers Hand Roll for a black Silk Cardinal a brown Surtout Coat 3 Linnen Sheets The Property of Hen: Doubtfire on Oath of Hannah his Wife.

Chr^r Clark by Edwd Cheney C. chd by Eliz: Ryan (on Mr Ald^n Cokaynes W^t 23^d Inst.) for an Ass^t (along wth one Anne Brady) the Mre was adj^d till tomorrow

P   Ann Brady & Chris^r Clark upon Ald^n Cokaynes Warr^t of the 23 Inst. ats Elizabeth Ryan for an Ass^t Discharged

Aff^t John Meecham

F.G.   ~~R.H.~~

Sir Robert Kite. Thursday 29 April 1762.
       John Griffiths Ch: Wden of St Bot Aldgate sum^d ads Sus^a Phillips one of their Parish poor for Reb: [blank] –it appeared she required Cloaths (par[ticular]ly a Gown) which she did not appear to want –the Complaint was dismiss'd.

James Wells the Driver of a Cart by Wm Beaumont C. for not having a real N^oame on his Cart –he was ord^d to make Sat^n to the ~~Carm~~ Street Keeper

1s.   Back'd a Midx W^t by Mr James.

1s.   W^t ag^t Wm Glover a Journeyman Carman ads John Andrews his Ma^r for ~~refusing~~ misbehaving in his Employment & neglecting to do his Business & leaving his Service w^thout his License

nil   D^o against Laudadio D'Vital Franchetti ads John Motlow for fraudulently obtaining from him 3 Notes of Hand of the Va: of 36:15:[blank]—wth Intent to cheat & defraud him thereof

Henry Geare, ~~Ann Walker~~[52]} fr WC by Wm Boddington C. chd by James Allen on Suspicion of stealing from him a Brown Silk Gown, a purple Stuff Gown, a Brown Stuff Gown, a Bed Gown a White Dinisty[?] Petticoat & a large Q^y of o^r Goods of the va: of 7s[?] [blank] s^d Property– a Green Petticoat –3 lac'd Caps 2 plain Caps a laced Hand^rchief a Silk D^o a White Apron a Comon Prayer Book a remnant of long Lawn a black Silk lac'd Handkerchief a Shift Body, 2 Remnants of black Lace & one of White, a Pair of Silk Stockings a 2^d Shift Body unmade, a White Apron a pair of double Ruffles an^r Old Silk Handf. 5 Remnants of Ribbons, a Cotton Handk^rf a Neck Cloth a piece of Point a White Handf. a remnant of Linnen 2 Forks (one Mark'd EW.) a Tourele[?] & some Shop Thread, a Tortoise Shell Snuff Box set in Silver a Spanish Dollar, a black Bonnett a blue & White Handkerchief a pair of double Ruffles, wth a lace for 'em unmade, black Stuff for a petticoat & a black Cardinal – the property of Ann Wybourn & Peter Bushby

John Ryal Printseller confirm'd Mr Allen's Testimony— ~~Danl Brown Appr^d to Mr Allen~~ Wm Boddington also confess'd this –they were all 3 sworn – and the two Pris^r s were committed to WC

RX   James Allen of Fleet Street London Gent.   £ 20
        John Ryal of D^o Printseller   10
        Wm Boddington of Salisbury Court L: Baker   10

Jane Elvin fr PC by Wm Martin C. chd by Mary Ferrall her Mistress for assaulting and violently beating her; it app^d a great Abuse from a Comon Menial Servt she was com^d to PC.

RK   ~~RH.~~

Mr Alderman Master. Friday 30 April 1762.
    (No Attendance)

Mr Alderman Challenor. Monday 3 May 1762.
1s.   Back'd a Midx W^t Per Mr Cox

1s.   D^o by Sir Jno Fielding

1s.   W^t ag^t Joseph Alestar ads Mordicai Barew Ass^t etc.

---

52   'Stet' appears over Ann Walker's name, initially crossed out, and it is also underlined. The case against both proceeds to the Old Bailey. See *OBP*, May 1762, trial of Henry Geare, Ann Walker (t17620526–17).

Antho. Richards sum^d ads Jos^h Broadbent Carman for refusing to pay him for carrying a Load of Sugar from Mincing Lane to Ayliff[e] Street Goodmans Field he was ord^d to pay 3s. fare & 1s. Sum^s wch he did

1s.   Mathias Aaron by Saml Levi C. chd by John Wells for an Ass^t (on Ald^n Cokayne's W^t 23^d Ult) on an Agreem^t d^d.

Edwd Jues, Drayman, by Wm Beaumont C. (one of the Street Keepers) for driving a Dray in Cheapside with^t a Name upon it—they went away with^t reporting w[ha]t ~~was~~ done

B.   Reb^a Deane fr WC: by B: Forfitt C. chd by Wm Paine for strolling on Sat. Night last in Cheapside attempting to pick up Men; she was exa[mine]^d here last week & being a known Offender was com^d to B.

P   Ann Chamberlain fr B: by same C. chd by s^d Paine for pick^g up 2 Men a^t 12 O'Cl on Sat. Night last, she, (not being known) was for the time reprim^{d}ed & d^d

P   Charlotte Price fr D^o by same Constable charged by s^d Pain for stroll^g in Fleet Str: & pick^g up sev^l Men – this was the first time she had been here; she was therefore reprim^{d}ed & d^d

2: 4   Mary Parker fr D^o by same Constable charged by s^d Pain for pick^g up a Man in Fleet Street Sat. Night 12 o'Cl – a person app^d to her Character & became bound for her Appear: at next Qua^r Sess^s
RX   Mich^l Hudson of Wyld Street Lincoln's Inn Fields
next Qua^r Sess^s Carpenter £ 40

1s.   Eliz Coombes fr B: by same C. chd by the s^d Const. for pick^g him up on Saturday Night last – a person app^d to her Cha^r & ~~she was~~ P[ro]mising to take Care of her she was reprim^{d}ed & d^d

B   Mary Carter, Eliz Ellis} fr WC by Ben: Forfitt C. chd by W^m
P^{53} Crouch for picking him up on Saturday night last—Eliz: Ellis ~~had~~ was now not well, she was d^d and Mary Carter being a disorderly Person was com^d to B:

nil   Matt^w Woodhouse a Baker ads Thos Finleyson his Servt for ass^t

53. The 'B' notation appears beside Carter's name and the 'P' notation beside Ellis's name in the original layout.

ing & violently beating & abusing him,—the Ma^r acknowl: striking him; & it app^d the man was neglecting the Business & the Ass^t being very trifling he was d^d.

The s^d Thos Finleyson was chd by s^d Matt^w Woodhouse his Master for embezelling a Quantity of Bread deliv^d to him to carry to his Customers & also for neglecting his s^d Ma^{rs} Business & the Comp^t being verified on the Ma^{rs} Oath he was com^d to B:

1s.   Wm Glover a Journeyman Carman by Jno Flemming C. chd by John Andrews his Ma^r (on Sr Robt Kites W^t 29 Ult) for misbehaving in his Employm^t neglecting his s^d Ma^{rs} Business; he made Satisfaction to his Ma^r & was d^d.

Wm Thorn fr PC: by Jos^h Richardson C. chd by Nathl Parker for stealing an Iron Tennant[?] ~~Hand~~ Saw Va: 2s. his Property— he was com^d to D^{o}C.

RX   Nathaniel Parker of Seething Lane L: Carpenter £ 20

P   W^t ag^t a Woman who goes by the Name of French Judith & Sarah Sukee ads Judith Davis Ass^t etc.

P   D^o ag^t John Trenell ads Eleanor Wallone[?]Ass^t etc.

TC   RH

The Honourable Mr Alderman Harley by Mr Alderman Cokayne Tuesday 4 May 1762.

1s.   Wm Beaumont fr PC: by Jno Child C. chd by Thos Plummer for unlawfully Pawning or o^{r}wise disposing of one Suit of Blue Cloth Cloaths entrusted to him to alter, the P[ro]perty of s^d Plummer (on Mr Cox's Midx W^t 1st Inst. & back'd by Mr Ald^n Challenor yesterday) it app^d these Cloaths were del^d to Pris^r (who was a Taylor) & the Pros^r never got 'em again, but not being able to prove that the Cloaths were pawned he was d^d

John Fox sum^d ads Saml Bridgman Carman for refus^g to pay him for carrying a puncheon of Rum from Cross Street St Dunstan's Hill to porters Key —was ord^d to pay 3/6 fare 1s. Sum^s wch he did & was d^d.

4s.   Richd Robinson, ~~John Howard~~, Lawrence Vendry, Ja^s Walters, James Subden} by Wm Martin C. chd by John Steward (on Sr Jno Fielding's Peace W^t 28 April back'd yesterday by Mr Ald^n Challenor) ~~for~~ he having made Oath that he wo^d do or cause some bodily Harm to be done to him—it appᵈ the Prisʳs & Prosʳ were all Shop Mates & it did not appear that there was any Foundation for the Complaint; it appᵈ the Affair happen'd when the Prosʳ was much in Liquor & they were attempting to take Care of him; they were disched.

1s.   Ludadio D'Vital Franchetti, by Thoˢ Rothwell C. chd by John Motlow (broᵗ on Sʳ Robᵗ Kites Wᵗ 29 April) for fraudulently obtaining from him three Notes of Hand of the Value of £36:15: — with Intent to ~~do~~ cheat & defraud him there of –on an agreemᵗ dᵈ .

Mʳ Alderman Blunt nunc. Adhuc Tuesday 4 May 1762.
P   Mary Larkin by Robᵗ Coverley C. chd by Rosalinda Lock (on Lᵈ Mayors Wᵗ 1ˢᵗ Inst) for frequently assaulting beating & abusing her – being a trifling Complaint dᵈ.

1s.   Affᵗ Peter Kekwick

1s.   Dischᵈ Isabella Johnson fr Bridewell Per Mʳ Aldⁿ Cokayne & comᵈ heretofore by him.

1s.   Affᵗ Hannah Noah

1s.   Attested Nichˢ English

P   Richᵈ Morgan by Wᵐ Norman C. chd by the Overseers of the poor of the parish of Sᵗ Nichˢ Cole Abbey (on Sʳ Mattʷ Blakiston's Wᵗ when Ld Mayor) for unlawfully running away and leaving his five Children whereby they are become Chargeable to sᵈ Pish – he was a poor man under Misfortune and was willing as far as lay in his Power to assist in keeping his Family & P[ro]mis'd to do it for the future – he was therefore dᵈ.

R.B.

Sir Robert Ladbroke. Wednesday 5 May 1762.
1s.   Wᵗ agᵗ Sarah Walker ads Mary Cuel Assᵗ etc.

Mary Welsh, Jane Pollard} fr PC: by Robᵗ Stephens C. chd by John Williamson Watchman in Bpsgate Ward, for making a Great Disturbance in Gracechurch Str: John Cavel anoʳ Wʰman confirm'd the Complᵗ (the Offence betwⁿ 1 & 2 O'Clock) they were both disorderly Persons & common night Walkers were comᵈ B.

Mr Fred^k Commorell Ch: Wden of St Thos the Apostle sum^d ads Mary Stratton & Sarah Carpenter two of their parish poor; destitute of the necessaries of Life & to shew Cause he refuses to give them a necessary and proper Allowance of Meat & Cloaths – they both had come from the par^h W^khouse at Kingston in Surry – this Mre was adj^d 'till Friday & the Ma^r of the Workhouse, is then to appear.

1s.   W^t ag^t Mary Sprigs ads Mary Long Ass^t etc.

1s.   D^o Robt Colston ads Alex^r Mill—threat^g to beat him

P   D^o agt Elizabeth Wife of Wm Beach ats Sarah Davis for Ass^t

P   D^o agt Izabella Scarvile ats Catherine Inglesley for D^o

1s.   Aff^t And^w Grinley

        Four Shillings   RL

Mr Alderman Cokayne. Thursday 6 May 1762.
P   Dor^y Shoemaker by Merrick Poulter C. chd by Ja^s: Ripley (on ~~Ald~~ Ld Mayor's W^t 3 Inst.) for ass^ting & beating him; John Slade confirmed the ill usages–he was willing to forgive her— but the Discharge was suspended until she p[ai]d pros^r for the W^t (she hav^g now no money)—afterw^ds she was d^d – his Wp gave the Shill^g to the Pros^r

        Abraham Abrahams by Moses Barnett C. chd by Judith his Wife (on Ald^n Blunts W^t yesterday) for frequently Ass^t ing beating abusing & threatening her. Reb^a Levi confirm'd the Compl^t –& it app^g the woman was in Danger, he was, on the Oath, com^d to WC.

1s.   Isabella Scarvill by Clement Wakefield C. chd by Cath: Inglesley (on Sr R^t Ladbrokes W^t yesterday) for Ass^ting & beating her – being a frivolous Compl^t d^d

1s.   Dorothy Dickinson by John Collinson C. chd by Eliz: Ravenet (on Ald^n Blunt's W^t yesterday) for ass^t ing beating & throwing Water upon her; it app^d the Pros^x had taken her own Revenge – the Pris^r was d^d.

1s.   Aff^t Thos Beare.

1s.   D^o Margaritta Solee[?].

B.   Eliz: Phelps fr WC: by Ben[n] Wright C. chd by John Allen for strolling ab[t] Ludgate Str. & S[t] Pauls Ch: Yard, & pick[g] up a Man & carrying him to her Lodgings – Pain[54] knew her.

1s.   Josph Pinkney, Ann Brown } fr PC: by ~~Sol~~ Moses Barrnett C. chd by him for being apprehended strolling tog[r] at Aldgate
B.   he was a Man of Character (keeping John's Coffee Ho: Corn hill) he was reprim[d]ed & d[d] –& the Woman being a disorderly Person was com[d] to B.

1s.   Back'd a Midx W[t] Per M[r] Berry

B   Rose Solomon fr PC: by Moses Barnett C. chd by W[m] Pain for picking up a Man near Aldgate & being a known Str: Walker was (on his Oath) com[d] to B:

1s.   Eliz: Smith fr PC: by same C. charged by him for being apprehended in a Ho: of ill Fame in Petticoat Lane w[th] a Man upon her Lap who escaped; she was for the time reprim[d]ed & d[d].

P   Ann Deyll fr PC: by Same C. charged by W[m] Pain for being an idle & disorderly Person a Comon Night Walker she was reprim[d]ed & d[d]

B   Frances Terry, Eliz Crane} fr PC: by same C. chd by him &
P[55]   Sam[l] Levi for picking up a Gen[t] ab[t] ½ after 1 this Morning by the Change; the first woman behav'd ill in swearing, & being a disorderly Person was com[d] to B. on their Oaths –the other was d[d].

1s.   Mary Forrest fr D[o]C by same C. chd by him for picking up a Man in Cornhill 1 this Morning –she was for the time reprimanded & d[d].

1s.   Back'd a Midx W[t] by Sir John Fielding

1s.   W[t] ag[t] Cokey Levi ads Sam[l] Jacobs Ass[t] etc.

1s.   Aff[t] John White

nil.   Aff[t] Viva Voce Ann Sewell.

1s.   W[t] to search the House of Mrs. … Blanker[?] in Ducks foot

54. Presumably William Payne, the constable.
55. The 'B' refers to Terry, the 'P' to Crane.

Lane Lawrence Pountney Hill for a Lawn Apron the Property
of John Scott (on his Oath)

12/   R.H. –finis
F.C.

Mr Alderman Alsop. Friday 7 May 1762.
P   Collin McCartie fr WC: by John Wilder C. chd per Marma-
        duke Daniel, for coming into the Ho: of Gibson the Sign of the
        Bell in St Martins Le Grand, it did not appear there was any
        Charge ag^t him, he was d^d.

        John Brockhurst fr PC: by John Johnson C. chd by Israel
        Eltington, for attempting to pick his Pocket last Night; he was
        remanded for fu^r Examicon & to be ~~gone~~ carried to the regu-
        lating Captain, or to the Marine Society.

P   W^t ag^t Mark Abel White ads Eliz: Thompson Ass^t etc.

        Mr Fred^k Commorell Ch: Wden of St Thos the Apostle sum^d
        ads Mary Stratton & Sarah Carpenter two of their Pish poor,
        destitute of the necessaries of Life & to shew Cause why he
        refuses to give them a necessary & proper Allowance of Meat
        & Cloaths – this Mre was adj^d by Sir Robt Ladbroke; and the
        Ma^r of the workhouse directed to appear; and he app^d accord-
        ingly – his Name ~~was~~ is Edward Townsend;—it app^d the poor
        of that parish was farm'd out at Kingston upon Thames, at a
        Sum in Gross [blank]. Stratton complained that there was not
        suff^t Meat & Cloaths; that the Meat provided was not whole-
        some; Carpenter made the same Complaint—R^d Jones ano^r of
        the Parish poor made Complaint that he was put to such work
        as he was unable to do;—the Compl^t wth respect to Cloaths, of
        Stratton was in some degree true; she was ord^d a few Cloaths,
        & being able, was ord^d to go & get into some Employm^t wch
        she agreed to – Carpenter was a little ill, & in some Want – the
        Ma^r of the W^{k}ho: alledged she behaved ill in the Ho: she was
        directed to go & work & reprim^{d}ed – Jones app^d unfit to work;
        ~~they~~ he was directed to give him some Rel[ief]:

R.A.

Mr Alderman Blunt by Mr Alderman Challenor. Monday 10 May 1762.
1s.   Mark Abel White by Clement Wakefield C. chd by Eliz:
        Thompson (on Mr Ald^n Alsop's W^t 7 Inst) for assaulting her
        and throwing Dirt at her, and threatening her Life; it app^d an

idle Complaint and one as much in Blame as the other, he was therefore d^d

P   Mary Silvan fr WC: by Wm Spragg C. chd by ~~him~~ Edwd Goodwin on Suspicion of taking away two Children; ~~Viz~~ the Children were found in Soho Square this Morning; & now having no Suspicion of her she was d^d.

1s.   Arthur Percival fr PC: by Thos Ward C. chd by Ja^s Edwards fr D^oC for abusing him last Night & for taking ½ a Gua of him last Night; to serve the King –(he being a Qua^r Ma^r in the 113 Reg^t of Foot) John Patton—heard him say he gave half a Gua to inlist him; —Jno Clarke W^chman heard the Officer aggravate the Pris^r & on Pretence of laying a wager put half a Gua into his Hand – it being an idle & troublesome affair— the Pris^r was d^d.

      Richd Barratt fr WC: by Ben: Breewood C. chd by Wm Brookbank & Wm Stool, on Suspicion of picking s^d Brookbank's Pocket of a Handkerchief; he was remanded back for fu^r Examinacon 'till tomorrow

1s.   Aff^t Mary Crignoni

1s.   D^o R^d Gibbs.

1s.   Back'd a Midx W^t Per Mr Esdaile.

2s.   James Haines fr PC, Bridget Taafe fr WC} by Thos Bray C. chd by Stephen Dole on suspicion ~~stea~~ of being concerned tog^r in feloniously stealing 5 Guas & a 36s piece of Gold there seem'd to be no direct Proof ag^t them wth respect to the Robbery from that Compl^t they were dischd –but it app^d they were concern'd tog^r in ~~felon~~ keep^g a disorderly Ho: they were defective in Point of proof – they were d^d (being reprim^ded)

P 1s.   Eliz Griffis fr WC: by Wm Crouch C. chd by him for being apprehended in Co: wth a Man in an indecent posture in Stone Cutters Alley; the Man was not bro^t wth her she was therefore d^d.

1s.   Esther Rennall fr D^o by same C. chd by him for being apprehended in the same ho: she was not known & therefore only reprim^ded & d^d.

B   Ann Harper fr WC: by Wm Crouch C. chd by Wm Welsh for picking up a Man & carrying him into her Lodgings – she was an idle and disorderly Person & was com^d to B:

P   Saml Lee, Eliz Dawes} fr WC: by Wm Crouch C. chd by him Wm Welsh, for picking up a Man in a Dark Entry on Ludgate Hill – it app^d they were people of some Character & were dischd.

1s.   Joseph Cole fr PC: by John Scott C. chd by him for Ass^t ing & abusing him ~~last Night~~ yesterday morning –2 o'Clock,– he was now willing to forgive him –he was d^d.

2s.   Evan Harris, John Potter} fr PC: by Wm Martin C. chging each other wth Assaults, wch they had now agreed, they were therefore d^d.

Jacob Cordoza, Mary Sherlock, Hannah Walker, Mary Gardner} fr PC: by Eusebius Windsor & Saml Levi C. chd by Robt Scholey on Suspicion of ~~stealin~~ being concern'd together in stealing upwards of 20 Guas his P[ro]perty –it did not appear that Sherlock & Walker were concern'd they were d^d – the other 2 were com^d for fu^r Examicon & a W^t was granted on the Oath of Scholey & Gardner ag^t [blank]

Eliz Henley & Hannah Degoe on Suspicion of being concern'd tog^r in stealing 10 G^us.

1s.   W^t ag^t ~~Mary Cooke~~ Mary Edwards & Ja^s Saunders ads Eliz: Beaver Ass^t etc.

1s.   D^o agt Isabella Watson agt Mary Grey D^o

1s.   D^o agt Chris: Daughton ads Jos^h Man D^o

P   D^o agt James Hall & Henry Moore ats Mary Whitaker D^o

T.C.

Sir Thomas Rawlinson by Mr Alderman Alsop. Tuesday 11 May 1762.
P   Ann Archer fr WC: by Thos Benbow C. chd by Edwd Abrahams (at the black Bull in Cow Lane) for breaking his Windows, and making a Great Disturbance in his House; it app^d she & her Husband lodg'd in his Ho: & it was them both that were concern'd in mak^g this Disturbance – she was reprim^ded & d^d.

1s.   Richd Barrett fr: WC: by Ben: Breewood C. chd by Wm Brockbank & Wm Steel, on Suspicion of picking his s^d Brookbank's pocket, of a Handkerchief (rem^ded yesterday for fu^r Examcon) the Handkerchief was found in the Streets & del^d to Wm Boddington; the Man who saw him – he was now will^g to go for a Soldier & was inlisted into his Majesty's 74th Regim^t commanded by Col: Irwin –he was attested likewise & was d^d.

Mr Alderman Challenor nunc.

1s.   Sarah Wager fr WC: by Josiah Doonford C. chd by him for attempting to pick him up last Night in Fleet Lane—9 o'Cl:— she was for this time (it being the first) reprimanded & d^d.

1s.   Sarah Turner fr D^oC by same C. chd by her for attempting to pick him up in Fleet Street at ½ past 9 last Night—she produced 2 Persons to her Character & it being also the 1st time of her Coming her[e], she was also reprim^ded and discharged.

P   Loveday Codner fr PC: by Chr: Leach C. chd by John Clary (on Ld Mayors Search W^t yesterday) on Suspicion of Stealing a Pint Pewter Pot, (wch was found in her Custody on s^d Search W^t in his property) Va^l 1s –the Pros^r wo^d not swear that the Pot found in her Ho: was stolen from him & there being no proof of a felony she was d^d.

1s.   Lucy Crane by Thos Bray C. chd by James Haines (on Ald^n Cokaynes W^t 10 Ap^l) for feloniously stealing a Gua & a half in Gold his monies it app^d that her Husband & the Pros^r was about to lay a Wager wth Pris^rs Husband & she took ~~on~~ the money up & kept it; there app^d no Felony – she was dischd.

     Hannah Morgan, Pre-Nom^56 Degoe bro^t } fr PC: by Eusebius Windsor C. chd by Robt Scholey (on Ald^n Challenor's W^t yesterday) on Suspicion of being concern'd ~~together~~ wth Eliz Henley (not yet taken) in feloniously stealing 10 Guas & upwards his ~~Property~~ monies – he swore to his Suspicion of her being concern'd wth the other, she was com^d to PC.

RX   Robt Scholey at Little Thorrot^57 Ess[e]x farrier   20

     Edwd Page by John Flemming C. chd by him for driving a Cart (in Aldersgate Street) with a false N^o (he having purchased ab^t 12 Mo^s ago, had never transferr'd it or ent^d it in the Office) he was directed to make Satisfac[ti]on to the Officer (the same appear^g to be thro. Ignorance.)

---

56.   'Previously named as'. See above entry with Hannah Dagoe for 10 May.
57.   Probably Little Thurrock.

Chas Toppin app^d Per M^r G's: Wheeler} sum^d ads James Kirtin an Hackney Coachman for refusing to pay him his Fare for carrying him in his Coach N° 207 on the 2^d Inst. –it app^d he carried them ab^t 14 Miles,— he was directed to pay him 9s. for fare & 1s./6d. Charges wch he did & was d^d.

P   Ann Dixon fr PC: by Abram Lacy C. chd by one Jno Nicholson (not now pres^t) wh on Suspicion of picking his pocket of 8s. – there being now no Charge ag^t her she was d^d

TC

Mr Alderman Dickinson. Wednesday 12 May 1762.
1s.   Willm Reader by Walter Pickard C. chd by Willm Smith for assaulting & bruising him & also for threatening to do him some bodily Harm, whereby he was afraid of some bodily Harm w^d be done unto him by said Reader, (on Mr J. Finley's Lincolnshire W^t 24 March, back'd by the Lord Mayor 8 May) on making an agreem^t he was d^d.

P   Eliz: Bowler by Saml Levi C. chd by Susa Pebble (on Ld Mayors W^t 10 Inst) for frequently creating Riots & Disturbances before her Door and hindering interrupting her in her Business.

1s.   Affidavit Ja^s Lewis Torer[?]

Sarah Jones, Rachel Broadbridge} fr PC: by Ben: Hughes C. chd by him for being apprehended loitering as Vagrants in the Pish of Saint Andrew Undershaft – being Vagrants were com^d to B:

Joseph Alescar by Saml Levi C. chd by Mordecai Barow & Brought upon Mr Alderman Challenor's Warr^t of the 3^d Inst for an Ass^t. On Agreem^t Disgd

George Bingham chd by Thos Starrop Ch: Wden of St Vedast alias Foster – for greatly abusing the s^d Officer, he made Oath of the Offence & was com^d to B:

1s.   Aff^t Lawrence Napier

2s.   Aff^{ts} John Smith, Thos Spencer

1s.   Isabella Watson by Wm Bomau[?] C. n Mr Ald^n Challenors W^t yesterday for an Ass^t on an Agreem^t d^d.

P   W^t ag^t Mary Chambers ads Mary Crossby Ass^t etc.

7s.   MD

Sir Charles Asgill. Thursday 13 May 1762.

1s.   Joseph Rowland fr WC: by Wm Boddington C. chd by R^d
      Chillingworth for ass^ting him in Fleet Street last Night about 11
C   o'Clock – struck him 3 times – he confess'd being in Liquor,
      and was ord^d to pay 5s. which he did & was d^d –the Ass^t was
      forgiven by the Pros^r —money sent per Const.

      John Gilmour sum^d ads Eliz: Pettifer for forcibly entering her
      Lodgings and fixing a Pad Lock on the Doors of one of her
      Rooms in Breach of the Peace – he was recom^ded willing to
      give her the Priviledges she had before & gave her 4s. for her
      Loss of time & was d^d.

1s.   W^t ag^t Ann Proudfoot & Eliz: Thompson ads Edey Cope Ass^t
      etc.

1s.   Aff^t John Sutton

      Received May 13 1762 by the Hands of Mr Boddington the
      Sum of Five Shillings for a Persons being convicted before Sir
      Charles Asgill Bart.for a Misdemeanor Per Messrs Faden
      £ 0–5–0⁵⁸

      Mary Cook, Eliz: Beaver, [illegible]} by Ja^s Parsons C. ~~chd by Eliz. Beaver for~~ fr PC charging each other with an Ass^t it app^d
      Beaver gave the first Charge who being Examin^d on Oath she
      proved the Ass^t & that Cook threatened to make the kennel
      run with her Blood which being proved likewise the Ass^t etc.
      whereon Cooke was moved to N[ewgate?]. – Cooke swore she
      woud turn second Moll Bulger & make her blood run down
      Fleet Lane kennel.

      ~~Wt agt Mary Cook ats Ann~~
CA
3

Sir Richard Glyn. Friday 14 May 1762.
      (No Attendance)

58.   This entry is a loose sheet inserted into the minute book at this point.

Mr Alderman Hart. Tuesday 28 November 1775.
> Benj: Valou, Jos^h Stallman} WC by Will: Payne C. charged by [blank] for attempting to pick pockets in Long Lane yesterday—Valou's Master app^d and promised to take care of him—he was D^d—Stallman's Father app^d –he was also D^d

1s.   Aff^t Thos Fox

Jane Davis, Martha Simms, Eiz: Urwin, Han^h Clarke} d^o C by d^o C. chd by him for severally wandering abroad and picking up Men

Ann Whitfield fr WC Thos Bennett C and Ch^d as disorderly for want of Proof D^d.

2s.   Affid^t Parkinson & Wilson

Mr Rhodes attended for Mr Nash   J.H

Mr Alderman Lee.   Wednesday 29 November 1775.
> Will. Page, Pat^k Barrett, Jas Boyden} WC by Jno Prockter C. chd by him for breaking a Lamp— they went before the Lord Mayor.

1s.   Backd a Middx W^t Per Mr Penleaze

Fra^s Simmonds D^{o}C by Joseph Angus C. chd by him for lodging in the open air Par: St Bride not giving a good Acc^t of himself

1s.   W^t ag^t Wm Stapleton ats John Strong Ass^t

1s.   D^o ag^t John Wallis ats Martha Dilly Ass^t with Intent to have Carnal knowledge of her Body ag^t her Cons^t

P   W^t ag^t John Emery ats Rachael Freem[an][59] Ass^t

D^o ag^t Edwd Jessey ats Mary Ux Assault

Mr Houstonn attended.   W. L.

---

59. Page damaged.

M[r] Alderman Smith by M[r] Alderman Kennett. Thursday 30 November 1775.

P nil   John Armstrong WC R[d] Alexander C. chd by Jos[h] Bartholomew W[h]man in Aldersgate Ward and the Constable –for making a Disturbance at the W[ch] Ho: it was an idle affair, and the W[h]man app[d] the Aggressor – the Pris[r] was d[[d]]

P   John Emery by John Woodfield C: chd by Rachel Freeman (on Ald Lee's W[t] yesterday) for assaulting beating & abusing him—d[d] —being friv[s]

Timothy Woodhead WC W[m] Payne C. and Ch[d] by Joseph Smith Vintner (Devil Tavern Temple Barr) for making a great Noise and Disturbance in his house last Night & o[r]wise misbehaving himself It app[d] he was intoxicated But on asking Pardon was reprimanded and d[d].

[blank] Barnwell app[d] by his Serv[t] sum[d] ads Tho[s] Smith a Hackney Coachman for not paying Him his Fare from the End of Cath: Str: to Copthall Court ord[d] 1/6d. fare & 2s./6d. Charges.

1s.   W[t] ag[t] Jonathan Gall ads ~~Tho[s] Smith~~ Patrick M[c]Donald.

Jos[h] Smith Tho[s] Withers C. chd by John Coverdale of Lower East Smithfield Wharfinger for driving a Cart ~~where~~ one of the Horses therein having been stolen (as was supposed) from the forest—the Horse was detained & the Man d[d] – it app[d] the man was Serv[t] ~~was~~ to M[r] Holyland a Carman who stands in Smithfield & is a Man of Credit – he was ~~d[d]~~ sum[d] to appear tomorrow.

M[r] Rhodes attended for M[r] Nash   BK.

M[r] Alderman Alsop. Friday 1 December 1775

B[60]   Marg[t] Hayes, Eliz: Hurst, Eliz: Morris, Ann Jones, Jane Roselle, Jane Melvin, Eliz: Smith[61], Mary Monk, Eliz: Ware[62], Eliz: White, Eliz: Edmonds} WC by Will: Payne C. chd by him for being severally wandering abroad—Hayes for picking up Men the end of George Alley—was notorious—Hurst—the like—Morris, was also notorious—Jones, Roselle, Melvin were

---

60. Notation of 'B' for committed to Bridewell appears in the left margin beside the all names, except Eliz: Smith and Eliz: Ware.
61. Notation of 'dd' for discharged in the left margin beside her name.
62. Notation of 'dd' for discharged in the left margin beside her name.

also Đ^d notorious—Smith (being unknown) was d^d—Monk an old Offender—Ware (being unknown) was D°—White and Edmonds were old Offenders—all (except Smith and Ware) were com^d to B. until a Court

1s.   Thos Malone, Bassam Carter} d°C by d°C. chd by each other with an Ass^t—it app^d on the Examion of sev^l witnesses—to wit Danl Wells, Saml Buggs, Mich^l Fitzgerald—Carter ~~gave~~ made the first Ass^t which was a Violent one; on Agreem^t dischd.

1s.   Aff^t Jane Ogilvie

Eliz: Wyham by Miles Hart C. chd by Will: Rowlett Chch Wden of St Magnus London Bridge for making a Disturbance before his Door—she was com.^d to B. until a Court.

nil   W^t ag^t Rob: Gyles ads Robt Bloxham Felony

Danl Morgan sum^d ads Eliz: Fairer for an Ass^t postponed 'till Tuesday next

1s.   W^t to search the Ho: of [blank] Jones on Dowgate Hill for 8 Y^{ds} of black Lace two cloth Women's Aprons & other things the property of Benja: Cooper—on his Oath

Eliz: White WC: by Will: Payne C. chd by him for keeping an Ill Governed & disorderly Ho: & Common Bawdy Ho: in Geo St Fleet Market in St Sepulchre's Parish—Per Agreem^t of the Parish officers dischd

Will: Dunbar, Edwd Langford} PC: by Thos Withers C. chd by each o^r for assaults etc. dischd

R.A.   Mr Rhodes attended for Mr Nash

Sir Charles Asgill. Monday 4 December 1775 .

3s 4d.   Will: Potter by Jos^h Gates C. chd by Will: Lyne Overseer of S^t
next   Bennett Sherehog (on Ld Mayors W^t Saturday last) for unlaw-
Sess^s   fully begetting Martha Turner Singlewoman of s^d Parish with Child which is likely to become chargeable thereto—he was bailed as below

R	Will: Potter of Hughes fields Deptford, Sawyer	£ 20
	Edwd Ferrett of Saint Paul Deptford Vict: }	Each £10
	Jno Mace of same place—Sawyer Measurer }	

pres^t Jno Moulton[63] WC by Jno Gibson C. chd by Jno Evans upon
Sessⁿ suspicion of feloniously stealing a silk handkerchief Val: 6^d his
property – on Evans Oath the Pris^r was com^d to Newgate.

R John Evans at John Woodhouse Esqr Bridewell £ 10

Thos Roberts d^oC by Chas Drummond C. chd by ~~Jno Bridges~~
Ben: Jewson for knowingly & designedly by false pretences
obtaining from him ~~Eleven~~ 14 Pieces of Sarsanet[64] Val. £10 &
upw^{ds} the property of Edwd Atkins & Jno Bridges with Intent
to cheat & defraud them thereof—John Bridges & Jewson
were sworn—on their Oaths Com^d to N.

R John Bridges of Friday Str. L. Ribbon Manufact^r for himself &
Jewson £ 20

Jno Teddy by Nathl Bowden C. chd by Jno Bennett for
assaulting him adj^d till tomorrow

1s. Aff^t Hungard Copleston

1s. Aff^t Moses Machorro

3[s]. Richd Knapp, Geo: Sant, R^d Hughes, Thos Holden} WC by
Wm Worthington Bell C. they each chd the other—Holden chd
Knapp with assaulting & knocking him down – that Hughes
said "d—n him strike him home." Thos Brearly a Watchman
also heard Hughes say so—saw Sant strike Holden—Holden
& Brearly were sworn

~~R^d Knapp of Friday S^t N° 57 Rider~~   }
~~Geo. Sant of Snow Hill Coal Merchant~~   } ~~£ 40 Each~~
~~R^d Hughes Kings Arms Holborn Bridge~~   }

~~Bail~~
~~Tho Beck N° 5 Cripplegate Buildings Haberdasher~~
~~Jno Goadby N° 10 Bridgwater Sqre L Taylor~~
Afterwards on an Agreem^t they were all 3 disch^d.

Thos Wynn WC Thos Worthington Bell C: chd by Ja^s Dunce for
stealing a Hat Va: [blank] his property, rem^ded till to morrow

Jos^h Brown PC by Fran^s Hunt chd by John Honeyball for
assaulting and abusing him, he was (Promising not to go to
his Ho: again) d^d

---

63. Appears at the Old Bailey on 6 December, where he is convicted and sentenced to be
whipped. See *OBP*, December 1775, trial of John Moulton (t17751206–35).
64. Sarsenet, a soft fabric used in linings.

~~Mary~~ Eliz: Sharp WC: Jn° Woodfield C: chd by ~~Mary~~ Eliz: Ux. Tho[s] Lightfoot, for stealing two flat Irons va[l] 1s. s[d] Tho[s] Lightfoot's property; rem[d] ed 'till to Morrow

Edw[d] Mackentear WC Jos[h] Angus C. chd by Rob[t] Baker W[h]man in Farringdon Ward Within— for abusing him on his Duty—he was also chd by the Const. for an insult.

CA   M[r] Beach attended

M[r] Alderman Bridgen by M[r] Alderman Alsop. Tuesday 5 December 1775.
Hen: Atkins, Jno Debrook} sum[d] ads Tho[s] Tuck for placing the Stages at the side of the House in Gracechurch Street, and thereby obstructing the free Passage of his Majesty's Subjects in the s[d] Street on Thursday last—they promised never to do the like in future and were thereupon forgiven

Sir C.   Will Durrell, R[d] Hitchcock, Jno Peacock, Will: Peacock}the
Asgill   Drivers of four Drays sum[d] ads Isaac Alvarez for obstructing
nunc   the free Passage in Bury Street Saint Mary Axe—by placing the s[d] Drays there—the Common Serj[t] was called in and gave it as his opinion that the Draymen were not within the Act— Dism[d]

1s.   Aff[t] Martin Cox

Eliz[th] Sharpe remanded yesterday to WC John Woodfield C. Ch[d] by Eliz[th] Ux Tho[s] Lightfoot on susp[n] of feloniously stealing 2 Flatt Irons value 1s. the Property of her s[d] Husband. For want of Evidence D[d]

Rich[d] Morgan WC John Prestage[65] C. John Botterell (Merch[ts] Watchman) for feloniously stealing a small Quantity of Tobacco of trifling value from Fresh Wharf the Property of Persons unknown He was acquitted of the Felony for want of Proof But on the Oath of Botterell Committed to B: as a Suspected Pilferer

Mary Johnson PC James Goodwin C. on Middex Warr[t] (Back't by Lord Mayor) and Ch[d] by John Lemom on Suspicion of

---

65. In another trial, Prestage identified himself as 'one of the constables belonging to the keys'. See *OBP*, January 1766, trial of William M'Cullock, William James, William Fowler (t17660116–5).

buying & receiving a Quantity of Silk knowing the same to have been Embezilled for want of Evidence disch[d]

W[m] Smith, Jane Aaron} PC by Rich[d] Brinkworth C. chd by Edw[d] Jolly a Watchman in Aldgate Ward for being found in a dark corner together in Jury S[t] under improper Circumstances & the Woman a Notorious bad Woman she was Comitted to B: & he was dischd

W[m] Hands by Nathan Veezey C. chd by Ann his Wife (on Midx W[t] Indorsed by the Lord Mayor) for assaulting & beating her—she requested to live seperate & have an Allowance which he consented to after the rate of 7s. Per

CA   M[r] Rhodes Attended for M[r] Nash.

The Right Honourable Thomas Harley. Wednesday 6 December 1775. Sir Charles Asgill[66]
    R[d] Pearce B. by Jos[h] Thompson C. chd by Jno Plumpton for feloniously stealing a gross of Pipes Val: 2s. s[d] Plumpton's Property—it app[d]: he was sent to a Customer of prosecutor's with sev[l] Gross of Pipes & he sent word that he had a Gross of Pipes short—Plumpton did not chuse to prosecute—he was d[d]

1s.   Aff[t] Jas Dashwood

1s.   Back'd a Middx W[t]

Thomas Wood by Jno Bradley C. chd by Will: Golightly (on Sir Cha[s] W[t] Yesterday) on suspicion of being concerned with other persons in defrauding him and his partner of a large sum of money –Will: Tremplett –Golightly s[d] that the Pris[r] on Saturday insured the Ticket N[o] 21481 for Monday to have a Ticket returned—that the Ticket came up—accordingly the 2[d] half hour he came to Guildhall & enquired who drew it—46407 drawn 5th Day of Drawing—654 on the 17th Day— Tremplett s[d] that Lowndes about a fortnight ago, took him to a Coffee ho: —asked him if a Ticket co[d] not be taken t̶o̶ out of the Wheel—answer'd No—gave him ½ Gua—met him 2[d] time at the Coffee House—gave him 2[d] ½ Gua—he took two Tickets out of the Wheel—kept one in his pocket, and gave it

66. Asgill's name is entered under Harley's, thus.

to Lowndes N° 21481—knows nothing of the Pris^r—has heard
Lowndes mention him—Mr Cox insisted

Grace Lowndes examined—has known the Pris^r a long time—
has never seen a Number in his Custody—at 2 Offices 20 times
each –at 79 times over 21481

Will: Stratford—Pris^r came to him about 2 O'Clock

Wood was D^d

Mr Houstonn attended. R.H.

Mr Alderman Crosby. Thursday 7 December 1775.

2s.   Affid^t Bacon, Brumwell, Pursivall, ~~West~~.

James Lawray[67] WC Wm Taylor C. chd by Jno Horton Esqr and
Thomas Bywater for feloniously stealing a linen handkerchief
Val: 1s. s^d Horton's property—the boy was only 9 Years old—
Adj^d true and committed to Newgate

RX   John Horton Esqr Tyson St^t Bethnall Green   £ 10
Thos Bywater N° 2 Addle St^t Cheesmonger   10
To prosecute & Give Evidence at the present Sess^s.

Thomas Warrell WC Joseph Angus C. and Chd by Wm Kinsley
upon suspicion of being concealed in his Dwelling House
with a felonious Intent –it app^d that the Pris^r was found in the
Chamber of Kinsley's Niece, who was Pris^{rs} Wife – there app^d
2 Witnesses here, to the Marriage – the Prisoner was thereupon
D^d

1s.   W^t ag^t Wm Askew ads Mary Ux. for an Ass^t etc.

P   D° ag^t Lawrence Connor ads Edm^d McDaniel D°

1s.   John Adams Snipes (on Mr Ald^n Alsop's Warr^t B—y[68]) WC
John Hawkins C. and Charg'd by Nicholas Simmons one of
the Overseers of St Mary Madgalen Old Fish Street London
and Arebella Todd of the Same pish Singlewoman Who on
her Examicon on Oath declar'd herself with Child and that the
s^d Child is likely to be born a Bastard & to be Chargeable to

---

67. This case seems to proceed to the Old Bailey, which was in session at the time, though the
defendant's name is different (Norrio) in the account. See *OBP*, December 1775, trial of
James Norrio (t17751206–54).
68. Bastardy.

the s^d Prsh & that s^d John Adams Snipes is the Father of the s^d Child. ~~Remanded till tomorrow~~ ag^d and Snipes was D^d

Thomas Lovejoy, Rach^l. Hill, Eliz^th Allerton}WC John Woodfield C. and Ch^d By Thos Palmer the two Women as Prostitutes attempting to pick him up last Night bet^n 11 and 12 last Night in West Smithfield and Lovejoy being apprehended

Edwd Neale WC Ja^s Forrester C. and Ch^d by him for asking Alms yesterday in the Pish of St Lawrence Jewry   It appeared that the Prisoner lately belonged to a Fishing Vessell wch had been cast away in Yarmouth Roads And the Whole Crew (consisting of 12) Except the Pris^r were drown'd. The Ch^n of the Parish where he was apprehended was recommended to take Care of him.

B.C.   7 Decr 1775   Mr Rhodes attended[69]

Mr Alderman ~~Bull~~ Townsend. Friday 8 December 1775.
(No Attendance)

Mr Beach att^d   R.H.

Mr Alderman Bull by Mr Alderman Wilkes.[70] Monday 11 December 1775.
Marg^t Richards by Wm Taylor C. chd by John Hay—Jno Perry—on Susp^n of stealing a pint Pewter Pot, wch she offered for Sale to Mr Perry – no Felony being proved the Pris^r was d^d.

Charlotte Willes WC by Jos^h Thompson C. chd by Ezekiel Varenne on susp^n of stealing some Goods out of ready furnished Lodgings – by Consent d^d

1s.   W^t ag^t Anderson Robinson ads Eliz: Boswell Ass^t. etc.

Isabella Condon WC Jno Duncastle C. chd by him for tendering in payment a piece of Counterfeit money resembling a Shilling knowing the same to be false and Counterfeit and at the time of such Tender having in her Custody one other piece of

---

69. These sign offs appear unusually in the left margin at a right angle to the main text.
70. Although John Wilkes' diary during this period makes no explicit mention of his justice room business, his dining companions frequently included other justices and aldermen. There are also brief references to him sitting as a justice during the Gordon Riots (British Library, Add. MS 30866).

Counterfeit money resembling a Shilling—ag[t] the Stat. etc. she was com[d] to WC—on Duncastle's Oath.

W[m] Bowers, Cath: Matthews} WC Jn[o] Brockholes C. chd by David Watts a W[h]man it app[d] Bowers was very drunk, & incapable of giving a rational Answer he was rem[d]ed till tomorrow— as was the Woman.

Tho[s] Kinman D[o] same C. chd by the W[h]man of Farringdon W[d] With[t] on susp[n] of stealing a piece of Timber wch he was apprehended carrying at an unseasonable hour in the Night – it app[d] to have been stolen in Middx he was ord[d] to be deliv[d] to a Midx Const.

Sam[l] Jefferys WC Tho[s] Brookes C: chd by Han[h] Smith on Susp[n] of stealing a Bacon Spare Rib of Pork Mary Ux. Ja[s] Williamson saw Pris[r] steal this Spare Rib ab[t] 8 days ago— Smith said the Pork was ab[t] 12[lbs] W[t] was worth 4½ d. per lb. therefore the value was at least 4s. –he was rem[d]ed 'till to Morrow.

M[r] Minish app[d] by his Attorney sum[d] ads Fleming for driving a narrow wheel'd Cart with 2 Horses by Permission settled.

Jn[o] Green sum[d] ads Tho[s] Meredith a Hackney Coachman for refusing to pay him for carrying him in his Coach from Chancery Lane to Walworth

Tho[s] Hayford WC by Jno Woodfield C. chd by Rob: Warford a W[ch]man of Farringdon Ward Without for taking his Lanthorn it did not appear to be done feloniously—D[d]

M[r] Beach attended   John Wilkes

M[r] Alderman Wilkes. Tuesday 12 December 1775.
Edw[d] Clement WC by R[d] Rye C. chd by Ja[s] East ~~for~~ upon suspicion of feloniously Stealing at Putney in Co: Surry 24s. his Monies – for want of Evidence Dd.

Will: Bowes, Cath: Matthews} WC by Jn[o] Brockholes C. chd by [blank]

Southam and Richmond Sworn E I S[rs][71] Sam[l] Jeffries D[o]

---

71. Possibly East India 'Soldiers' or 'Sailors'.

1s.   Affid^t Beale

Anderson Robinson Mr Aldⁿ Wilkes's Warr^t Jos^h Thompson Ch^d by Elizth Boswell per Ass^t Sett^d & d^d

Peter Murphy Mr Aldⁿ Plomers W^t Ja^s Fowler C. Ch^d by John Ward per Asst Sett^d and d^d

Alice Miller, David Rankin C. Ch^d by Sarah ux Ja^s Forrester on Suspicion of feloniously Stealing a young Fowl value 1s. her s^d husband's property. ~~remanded~~ It appeared doubtfull & being her first Offence, was reprimanded & d^d

P   Warr^t v Joseph Imbleton ads Wm Payne C. for unlawfully keeping and maintaining an ill governed & disorderly House in George St^t (within the Pish of St Sepulchre London)

P   D^o agst Ann Knowles ads Will: Payne for the same in Naked Boy Court—Par: St Martin Ludgate

Mr Rhodes attended   John Wilkes

gave 2s. to Thos White Carman sum^d ads Will: Langford for wilfully a poor Boy misbehaving himself and maliciously whipping the Horses by his Wp^s of s^d Langford and thereby damaging one of them—a ag^d Order

Sir Thomas Hallifax. Wednesday 13 December 1775.
P   Ann Connolly WC by Thos Roberts C. chd by her Husband for violently assaulting him— it app^d on the C[onstable]'s Oath that the Surgeon had declared him to be out of danger—D^d

Cath: Peterson WC by Will: Page C. chd by Will: Clifton upon suspicion of feloniously stealing several Goods of different kinds— ~~some~~ a Bed that she had pawned had been found—she was rem^ded 'till to Morrow

Ann Gadd, Ann Ringham, Cath: Calladan}WC by Ben: Holloway C. chd by [blank] Kelly a Wchman of Cheap Ward – Kelly not being present they were rem^ded 'till tomorrow

Mr Houstoun attended   TH

Sir James Esdaile by Mr Alderman Plumbe. Thursday 14 December 1775.
Ann Gadd, Ann Ringham, Cath: Calladan} WC by Ben:

Holloway C. chd by Will: Ribbitt and Ja^s Groves W^{ch}men of Cheap Ward for Severally lodging in the open Air Par: St Mildred in the Poultry not giving a good account of themselves.

Cath: Peterson d^{o}C by Will: Page C. chd by Will: Clifton upon suspicion of feloniously stealing a Bed and several other things—it app^d that the Pris^r was employed by Clifton's Wife—therefore D^d

1s.   Jno Sheppard PC by Edwd Williams C. chd by John White for defrauding him of the Insurance of two Lottery Tickets – it app^d that Sheppard was only a Servant to the Office Keeper— there did not appear the least Colour for the charge—the Pris^r was D^d

1s.   Aff^t Will: Galpin

P

Richd Jennings PC by Will: Pretty C. chd by Ann Ux: (on Ld Mayor's W^t Saturday last) for an Assault—on her Oath bailed as below – D^d –upon an Agreem^t

~~R^d Jemmings – Northumberland Alley N° 3 Cooper £ 20~~
~~Jno Cooke of Fenchurch St N° 80 Cooper~~
~~Thos W Edwd Crawford~~

Mary Ann Williamson PC by Jno Godfrey C. chd by Thos Houston Chch Warden of the Parish of Saint Helen in Bishopsgate Street for imposing upon him by obtaining money under pretence of being a Pauper—belonging to that Parish; rem^d ed 'till tomorrow

1s.   Jno Field WC by Jno Williams C. chd by Will: Miller a W^{ch}man of Castle Baynard Ward for an Ass^t—ag^d & D^d

Thos Wooldridge PC by Thos Westcott C. chd by Rob: Smith a W^{ch}man of Aldgate Ward for assaulting him—the supposed Ass^t by Wooldridge

1s.   Aff^t Ann Curron

Francis Steele PC by Thos Tuck C. chd by Nathan Cooper for abusing him and making a disturbance before his Door – it app^d by Mr Coopers shewing that on his attempting to take him into Custody he struck him— it app^d there was a kind of

Mob gathered about Mr Coopers Doors by Reason of a little Quarrell betw: a Man & his Wife ~~& the mob was collected~~ who cried stop Thief the Pris^r ask'd Pardon & was d^d

Mr Rhodes Attended SP

1s.   Aff^t Jno Harman

Mr Alderman Plumbe. Friday 15 December 1775.
        Geo: Wills by Thos Poultney C. chd by him for placing his Barrow upon the foot Pavement—rem^ded 'till Monday

        Jacob Levy, Wm Stevens} PC by R^d Brinkworth C. chd by Edm^d Kershaw for attempting to break his Shop Glass with an Intent to steal—rem^ded 'till Monday

1s.   Aff^t Peter Cramant

        Jno Townsend app^d for Messrs Davidson & Co sum^d ads Jos^h Dolphin for the Cartage of two Sacks of Beans—Ord^d paymt of 1s./6d. fare and 2s. Charges – ~~rem^ded 'till Monday~~

gave 3s. to three   Alex^r Dover app^d for Mrs Gibson sum^d ads Thos
poor Women by   Smith a hackney Coachman for his fare from Spring
his Wp's Order   Gardens to Clements Lane—Ord^d 2s. fare & 2s./6d.
                      charges

1s.   Warrant v <u>Evan Evans</u>, <u>John Hopkins</u> and <u>John Milner</u> (3 Journey men Tin Plate Workers) ads Robt Howard a Master Tin Plate Worker for unlawfully deserting his Service and Severally leaving Work unfinished which they had contracted to perform and finish

        John Moore[72] WC Thos Daniel C. and Ch^d by John Scott, Fendall Rushforth, <u>John Taylor</u> and Thos Trotman ~~for~~ on a violent Suspicion of feloniously Counterfeiting ~~the mark~~ upon a Pair of Shoe Buckles a mark Stamp & Impression in Imitation of and to resemble the mark stamp & impression of the Lyon used by the Company of Goldsmiths London to mark and Stamp wrought Plate of Silver. Adj^d true & Comm^d to WC on the Oath of Scott, Rushforth, Taylor & Trotman. ~~Sarah ux W^m Cl~~ Recog to prosecute as under

---

72. The case proceeds to the Old Bailey. See *OBP*, January 1776, trial of John Moore (t17760109-70).

RX   John Scott N° 13 Primrose St^t London Pawn B^r £ 20
Fendall Rushforth of ~~the~~ GoldSmith's Hall Assay Ma^r 20
John Taylor Beckfords Head Fleet St. Vict.   20
Thomas Trottman of the same Place Paper H[ange]r   20
    To Appear and Prosecute Ensuing Sess^s

Mr Rhodes Attended   SP[73]

Mr Alderman Kennett. Monday 18 December 1775.
    Jacob Levy, Wm Stevens} PC by Richard Brinckworth C. chd
by Edm^d Kershaw (as on Friday) —he had been searched
and the Duplicate of a Watch found upon him, wch was now
produced but sev^l friends app^g and one alledging he had worn
a Watch 12 Months & upw^{ds} & bel[ieved] that produced was
his & there being no felony com^d he was d^d

    Thos Low [blank] by Percivall Phillips C. chd by George
Smith for pawning or o^{r}wise unlawfully disposing of five pairs
of Stays of the value of £ 3—s^d Smith's property—he was by
Consent d^d

    Hugh Davis PC Edwd Daintry[74] C. charged on Susp^n of stealing
a few Hands of Tob[acc]o—was by Consent d^d

    Andrew Young PC Jas Ozeland C. chd by [blank] for being a
Vagr^t—he app^d a great Object of Charity—pass'd to Plimstock
in Devonshire

1s.   W^t ag^t Pat.^{k} Hughes (a Journeyman Leatherdresser) ads Fra^s
Botham for leaving Work which etc. –unfinished

    Philip Randall, Wm Greenwood } PC Solomon Davis C. chd
by Levy Moses for offering a Gold Watch & a Gold Seal to
Sale to him on Sat. night last under suspicious Circumstances
& wch they s^d was found in Marybone Fields—the Watch was
ordered to be advertized & they remanded 'till Friday.

1s.   Aff^t Danl Bradley

    Thos Bennett PC by Jno Prestage C. chd by John Banks for

---

73. In the manuscript, these signatures are muddled in with the previous case.
74. In another Old Bailey case Daintry (spelled Daintree) identifies himself as 'one of the
constables of the key'. These constables were building up expertise in policing this area of
London. See *OBP*, June 1785, trial of Thomas Sawyer (t17850629-8) and also the Mansion
House Justice Room minutes for 6 Dec. 1784 (LMA: CLA/004/02/002); 8 and 16 Feb. 1785
(CLA/004/02/004); 4, 7 and 9 May 1785 (LMA: CLA/004/02/007).

feloniously stealing near 2l^b W^t of Tobacco Val: 6d. the property of Will: Lee Esqr—for want of Evidence D^d

(B^{75}) Sarah Martin, (B) Mary Ellis, Eliz: Gill, Harriot Chivers, Philip Brooks} WC Wm Payne C. chd by him for picking up & inveigling Brooks into a Bawdy House in Fleet Lane— Ellis for wandering abroad and picking up Men in the Old Bailey—Chivers was chd by Ja^s Beet for making a great Noise & Disturbance in his Publick House and for assaulting him— Gill was D^d—Martin and Ellis were com^d to B

1s.   Back'd a Middx W^t per Mr Martin.

P   Geo: Palmer, Will: Hobbs} PC by Will: Smith C. chd by each other Palmer gave the 1st Charge—ag^d and D^d

1s.   W^t to search the Ho: of Watkin Jones in Mulberry Court great Bell Alley—for divers quantities of Ribbons Laces etc. the property of Jarvis Chambers and his Partner—on Chamber's Oath.

P   Jos^h Burton WC by Jno Negus C. chd by Ja^s Murray for assaulting him—he promised never again to molest Murray— D^d

P   Fred^k Hull PC by Thos Cooke C. chd by a person who is under Execution in s^d Compter– it was ag^d & D^d

Ja^s Meakin WC by Thos Amey C. chd by a Person not now present– referr'd to Ld Mayor

Mary Simmonds d^{o}C by Fra^s Phipps C. chd by Sarah White for defrauding her of upw^{ds} of £ 2– it did not appear a Fraud. D^d

Mich^l Burn d^{o}C by Ja^s Brown C. chd by Benja: Gearey for making a great noise & Disturbance in his Publick House– he ask'd pardon & was D^d

Mr Beach attended   BK

Mr Alderman Kirkman by Mr Alderman Kennett. Tuesday 19 December 1775.
Will: Greenwood, Phillip Randall} PC by Solomon Davis

75.   Indicating Bridewell for Martin and Ellis only.

C. chd by Levy Moses – Ord^d to be taken before Sir John Fielding—the Robbery having been com'd in the County of Middx, and the Information thereof being before that Magistrate

P   Ja^s Pummell by Jona: Wilkins C. chd by Mary Saunders (on Ld Mayor's W^t 15th Inst) for an Ass^t – ag^d and D^d

Jno Fuller PC by Thos Wood C. chd by Levi Solomons upon suspicion of feloniously stealing a pair of leather Shoes Val: 1s. the property of Ananias Modeighline—the Pris^r confess'd the fact at the time of apprehension but it was extorted from him –he was also charged with stealing a surtout Coat—rem^{d}ed till tomorrow

Eliz: Cable by Jos^h Tyler C. chd by Thos Wakerell Chch Warden of Allhallows London Wall—for dropping her Child within that Par: whereby it became chargeable thereto – D^d

Mr Rhodes for Mr Nash attended   BK

Mr Alderman Oliver. Wednesday 20 December 1775.
(No Attendance)

Mr Houstoun att^d RH

Sir Watkin Lewes. Thursday 21 December 1775.
(No Attendence being Saint Thomas's Day)

Rhodes Att^y attended   RH.

Mr Alderman Plomer. Friday 22 December 1775.
Patrick Hughes Journeyman Leather Dresser WC by Jno Apethorpe C. chd by Fras^s Roebotham his Master (on Ald^n Kennett's W^t 18th Inst:) for neglecting the performance of certain Work in the Manufacture of Leather wch he had undertaken to perform by permitting himself to be subsequently retained by another Master—before he had compleated the same– it app^d that he had not undertaken any new Work –& had finished all in hand– he was d^d

John Ben app^d for Mr Woodbridge who was sum^d ads Jos^h Dolphin Carman for refusing to pay Cartage for two Hogsheads of Sugar fr: Keys to Rupert Street Haymarket & back to Thames St. 13 Inst. ord^d 9s. Fare & 1s. Sum^s.

Richard Perry sum^d ads Thos Dymock for working his unlicensed Cart in this City– they withdrew & settld

Mary Wild WC by Jno Fletcher C. chd by him for lodging in
the open Air Par: St Botoph Aldersgate ~~not~~ giving no good
account of herself—passed to her Settlement.

1s.   W^t ag^t [blank] commonly called Little Bob ats Wm Butler Ass^t

1s.   Aff^t Wilkinson

1s.   W^t ag^t John Wilkins ats Eliz Hailsworth Ass^t

Mr Houston attended. W.P.

Mr Ald^n Thomas. Monday 25 December 1775.
(No Attendance being Christmas day)

Sir Walter Rawlinson. Tuesday 26 December 1775.
        Will: Speck app^d for Ann Drew sum^d ads Christopher Dobson
for driving her Cart agst Dobson's Coach and Damaging the
same– settled

nil   Wm Bolton WC by Jno Ince C. chd by Elias Grice W^{h}man
in Breadstreet Ward—for getting drunk & crying out Murder
about 12 last Night—he was d^d

Chas Priestly WC by Jno Jonas C. chd by a Mr Smith not now
present– the C certified that he forgave the Pris^r – he was D^d

And^w Johnson sum^d ads Sarah Livemore for Assaulting her–
Jane Hayes ~~and D^r McLaurin~~ Servt to Mr Johnson was examined and upon her evidence it app^d that Livemore's charge had
no foundation– Sir Walter s^d he considered it as frivolous –&
therefore dism^d the Sum^s

Rob: Taylor by Thos Goodwin C. chd by Jno Stevenson for
breaking a pane of Glass– it did not appear to have been done
wilfully– ag^d and D^d

Abram Beeharrel app^d for Mr Meads sum^d ads Saml Bridgman
Carman for the Cartage of a Load from Ralph's Key to Blooms-
bury— Ord^d 5s. fare and 4s. Charges

Mr Rhodes attended for Mr Nash.   WR

Mr Alderman Hopkins. Wednesday 27 December 1775.

Mary Harrison WC by Jonas Parker C. chd by Mary Boyd upon suspicion of feloniously stealing a black silk Cardinal Val: 5s. her property– for want of evidence—D^d

P   Jno Bacons d^{o}C by Jno Duncastle C. chd by Will: Gain and Jonathan Gain for assaulting and knocking down said Will: Gain– he agreed to make Sat^n & went back by Consent to do it—& then to be d^d.

P   Francis Harlah, Jno Hawkins} d^{o}C by Jno Sheppard C. chd by John Thompson for making a disturbance in his House– they promised not to do the like in future and were thereupon d^d

Chas Haughty WC by Jos: Thompson C. chd by Ja^s Hagarth and Ja^s Perry for feloniously stealing a piece of brass ~~Weight~~ Val: 5s. the property of s^d Ja^s Hagarth– Henry Fennel corroborated the Charge– on the Oaths of Hagarth Perry and Fennel— he was com^d to d^{o}C.

R   Ja^s Hagarth of Shoe Lane L. Brass Founder for self
and Perry   } £ 20^{76}
Henry Fennel of Peter Street Cow Cross Middx
Journeyman to s^d Ja^s Hagarth   } £ 10
Joseph Thompson &c   }

Mary Read WC same C. chd by Matthias Hamberg for feloniously stealing 26 Yards of Linen & two other pieces of Linen Val. tog^r £ 4 & upw^{ds} two Sattin Clooaks ~~six~~ 2 flannel petticoats 4 Neck Cloths 5 Gowns 6 Shirts 5 Silver Tea Spoons she was remanded 'till to Morrow

Will: Fleming app^d for himself and his Par[tne]^r sum^d ads Jno Adamson for refusing to deliver a Watch pawned with them for ½ Guinea within 2 Yrs– the principal etc. having been tender'd– postponed

1s.   Jerem^h Fagan by Jonas Parker C. chd by a person not now present– D^d

Mr Houston attended   BH.

---

76.   Possibly £10 has been superimposed.

Mr Alderman Peckham by Mr Alderman Thomas. Thursday 28 December 1775.

Sus^a Cole WC by Jos: Gates C. chd by Thos White upon suspicion of feloniously stealing a pint pewter pot Val 1s. his property– rem^{d}ed 'till tomorrow.

1s.   W^t ag^{ts} Chas Brand ads Lucy Wood for an Ass^t etc.

1s.   D^o agst [blank] Shendrick (whose Christian Name is unknown) ads Jos^a Travers & Mary Ux: D^o.

Mich^l Preston WC by Rob. Pattison C. chd by Edwd Smith for pilfering a small quantity of Coals– for want of Evidence—D^d

P   W^t agst Philip Trantam ads Cath: Sims for an Ass^t etc.

P   D^o ag^t Thos Smith ads Eliz: Kippley D^o

P   D^o agst Eliz: Steward ads Martha Quin

D^o ag^t Eliz. Knight ads [blank]

Mr Rhodes att^d for Mr Nash.
N. Thomas

Mr Alderman Hart. Friday 29 December 1775.

P   Jos^h Wheeler, Jno Wheeler} WC by Jno Apethorpe C. chd by Rob Bell for assaulting some Ladies not now present with Intent (as supposed) to rob them– for want of evidence—D^d

1s.   Mich.^{l} Poynting d^{o}C by Thos Daniel C. chd by Thos Fawconer for making a disturbance in his house– ag^d and D^d

Will: Thomas d^{o}C by [blank] Trowell C. chd by Sarah Newson & John Edwards for feloniously stealing a cloth Coat Val: 2s. s^d Edward's property– Danl Nicholas apprehended the Pris^r with the Coat.

R   Jno Edwards of Barbican L. Salesman for self & Sarah Newson} £ 10
~~Danl~~

~~Chas Griffiths d^{o}C by~~ [blank] ~~Singleton C. chd by~~

Mary Read WC Jos^h Thompson C. Ch^d by Mathias Hamberg for feloniously stealing a piece of Linen Cloth 2 pairs of Stone Shoe Buckles one pair of knee D^o a Stone hair pin 5 silver Tea

Spoons 2 linen Gowns 9 4 linen Shirts and sev^l other things Val: £5 and upwards the property of s^d Matthias Hamberg— Will: Fleming took to pawn the buckles hair pin & piece of Cloth—Ja^s Wintle & Jno Quince took sev^l other Articles to pawn from the Pris^r Adjudgd true & Committed to WC Recog to Prosecute as under

R   Mathias Hamberg N° 100 Dorset St Taylor   £ 20

Wm Fleming N° 145 Fleet St P^n Broker   10

Ja^s Wintle N° 1 Bride Passage F[leet] Street P.Broker   10

John Quince N° 33 Ludg^te Hill P^n Broker   10

    To prosecute & Give Evid.

Chas Kent by Jos: Thompson C. chd by John Boote for feloniously Stealing a piece of silk ribbon Val: 2s. & upw^ds the property of Ann Randall— John Boote was sworn and Kent com^d to WC.

R   Jos: Thompson of Bride Lane L. Const. for John Boote} £ 10

John Lipkey Thos Ward C. chd by John Holloway for loitering this day in Tower Street— was com^d to LW:

Chas Griffiths WC Saml Singleton C. chd by Job Darling for stealing a Linen Handk^f Va: 1s.– for want of evidence –D^d

Sus^a Cook WC by Jos^h Gates C. chd by Thos White for feloniously stealing a pint pewter pot Val: 9d. his property– one D^o of Edwd Richardson Val: 9d—2 D^o of John Ball– turn the other side[77]

Sus^a ~~Cook~~ Cole WC by Jos^h Gates C. chd by Thos White for feloniously stealing one pint pewter pot Val: 9^d his property– on his Oath com^d to d^oC

R   Thos White of Cateaton Street L. Vict.   £ 10

Detained on the Oath of Edwd Richardson for feloniously stealing one pint pewter pot Val: 9^d his property

R

Edwd Richardson of Billingsgate L. Vict.   £ 10

2^d time Detained on the Oath of John Ball for feloniously stealing 2 pint pewter pots Val: 1s. 6d. his property

R   John Ball N° 39 Crooked L, L, Vict.   £ 10

~~3^d time Detained on the Oath of~~

R   Jos: Gates etc.   £ 10

---

77. The page ends here and the clerk is referring to what follows.

Will: Jones, Will: Gratrex} by Jno Brockholes C. chd by Will: Holmden for being concerned together in cheating & defrauding him of the Sum of £49 ~~4s~~ and upw^(ds) ~~at~~ by cutting at Cards—the C. with Payne and Jos: Holmden heard the Pris^(rs) acknowledge the fact—on their and Will: Holmden's Oath they were com^d to WC

R   Will: Holmden of Chatham Kent Breeches Maker £ 20
Jos: Holmden of Long Acre Middx D°   }
Jno Brockholes Geo: St Fleet Mket Cons. } Ea: £ 10
Will: Payne etc.   }

Ja^s Fosset by Will: Payne C. chd by a person not now present– rem^d till tomorrow

Chas Greenwood sum^d ads Thos Smith a hackney Coachman for his fare from Bpsgate S^t to Hackney the Sum^s was dism^d

Mr Rhodes attended for Mr Nash. J. H.

Mr Alderman Lee. Monday 1 January 1776.
    Jno Alstell sum^d ads Jos: Jefferson Street Keeper for using his Cart N° 14494 in this City drawn by 2 horses the Wheels whereof not being 6 Inches broad– by Permission they withdrew & settled the Mre

Thos Cale, R^d James} WC by Will: Russell C. chd as follows Will: Cale chd Thos Cale upon suspicion of feloniously stealing a pair of men's Shoes– Cale chd James they were D^d

Marg^t Connor WC by Rob Pattison C. chd by Charles Dowling for feloniously stealing a half pint pewter Pot also a quart pewter pot– it app^d that these Pots were entrusted with the Pris^r —she was therefore D^d

Ja^s Dunlop, Will: Bennett} d°C by d°C. chd by Jos: Richardson for pilfering some Apples in Fleet Market– D^d

P   W^t ag^(st) John Holmes ads Mary Ux: for an Ass^t etc.

1s.   Rob Lee WC by Jos: Angus C. chd by Isaac Tingle for ass^(t)ing & beating him – Will: Clarke corroborated the Charge—Pris^r lives N° 110 Drury Lane– they withdrew and having ag^d Lee was D^d

1s.   David Evans by Jno Sheppard C. chd by Will: Ranson upon suspicion of feloniously steal: 2 Hats and a Bonnet– he was rem^{d}ed till tomorrow

1s.   Thos Bailey, Saml Garster} by d^{o}C chd as follows ~~Bailey~~ Garster (a W^{ch}man of Farringdon Ward without) chd ~~by~~ Bailey for ass^{t}ing him– D^d –(being frivolous)

1s.   Aff^t Buck

Mr Beach Attended   W.L.

Mr Alderman Smith. Tuesday 2 January 1776.
      David Evans, Mary Ux:} WC by Jno Sheppard Ch^d by Wm Ransonne on suspicion of feloniously stealing two Black Silk Cloaks value 15s. one Pillow Case & one Napkin value 1s. the Property of the said Wm Ransonne– For Want of Evidence d^d remanded till tomorrow for fur^r Examnon

1s.   W^t agst Thos Atterbury ads Caleb Smith for an Ass^t etc.

      Henry Hickey WC John Hawkins C. Ch^d by Catherine Downing on Suspicion of feloniously Stealing One Linnen Gown one Poplin Gown, 4 Cambrick Aprons 4 Cambrick Handkerchiefs 12 Caps one Shift, Two Petticoats, 4 Pair Worsted Stocking, Two Pair Lawn Sleeves, 4 Towels, 4 Ribbons, one Silver Tea Spoons~~-~~, one pair Stuff Shoes, one Silk Bonnet & other Things the Property of the s^d Cath: Downing– it app^d that Downing had entrusted the Pris^r with the above Things, and that he had pawned part of them– the Mre being no felony was settled— and the Pris^r was D^d

      Will: Rotheram d^{o}C by Jno Russel C. chd by Joseph Richardson for wandering abroad & lodging in the open air Par: St Bride—not giving a good acc^t of himself– rem^{d}ed 'till tomorrow, and in the meantime the Officers of Aldgate Par: were ord^d to attend

1s.   Thos Atterbury by Nathan Vezey C. chd by Gab^l Smith (on his Wp's W^t this day) for an Ass^t– ag^d & D^d

P   Jno Jury by Ja^s Tinkler C. chd by Ja^s ~~Farmen~~ Brown and Eliz: Bridges for making a disturbance in their Master's house (the Dog Tavern on Garlick Hill)—also for striking them– he made Satisfaction and was thereupon D^d

P   Back'd a Middx W^t Per Mr Wilmot

Mr Rhodes attended for Mr Nash   HS

Mr Alderman Alsop. Wednesday 3 January 1776.

    Jno Clifton, Will: Keltie[78]} WC by Jno Lambert C. chd by Edward Burghall for feloniously stealing a Ham Val: 10s. the property of said Edwd Burghall– Gab^l Johnson saw the felony com^d– they were com^d to d°C

R   Edwd Burghall of Newgate St London

Cheesemonger   }

Gab^l Johnson of Bagnio Ct Newgate S^t

Blacksmith   } Each £ 10

Jno Lambert of Warwick Lane N° 36

Constable   }

(B)Sus^a Pitt[79], (B)Eliz: Brown, (B)Han^h Smith, (B)~~Eliz: Brumage~~ Eleanor Hughes, (B)Sarah Stevens} WC by Jno Brockholes C. chd by Will: Payne for being severally loose idle & disorderly women & picking up Men– Pitt & Brown were com^d to B– all (except Hughes) were com^d to Bridewell for 14 Days– she was com^d to B. for a Month.

Marg^t Hunter by Saml Shaw C. chd by Ralph Fresilique for feloniously stealing a towel and 3 linen handkerchiefs Val: 2s. his property – for want of evidence—D^d

Thos Pawley WC by Edwd Drew C. chd by Eliz. Snook for being found concealed in her Cellar & finding upon him a Brass Cock. Jos^h Slater a person who went into the Cellar & found upon Pris^r s^d Cock & ~~Tind^r~~ Tinder Box—also an Iron Key– on the Oaths of the C., Snook, and Slater he was com^d to d°C– Valu:2s. the property of Stephen Snook

R   Jos: Slater N° 12 Lombard St White Friars Peruke Maker for self & Eliz: Ux. Step^n Snook   } £ 10

Edwd ~~Pawley~~ Drew of Essex S^t D° Const.   } £ 10

Marg^t Hunter also chd by Richd Foster for feloniously stealing 2 linen handkerchiefs his property– rem^d ed till Friday

Jno Smith by Jos^h Thompson C. chd by Will: Graves Overseer of St Bride for deserting his Wife & 2 Children whereby they are become chargeable to s^d Par: (on Sr Chas Asgills W^t 1st Inst:) referr'd to the Lord Mayor

78. This case proceeds to the Old Bailey. See *OBP*, January 1776, trial of John Clifton (t17760109–27).
79. A 'B' indicating Bridewell appears before each woman's name.

Thos Saywell PC by Jo^s Thompson C. charged by Jas McName for feloniously stealing 2 Guas in Gold and 2 Dollars—the conf[essio]n was extorted—D^d.

David Evans, Mary Ux} WC by Jno Sheppard C. chd by Sarah Ransom for feloniously stealing 2 silk Cloaks a pillow Case and a Napkin Val: 15s. the property of Will: Ransom– rem^{d}ed till friday

Will: Brotheram d^{o}C by Jno Russel C. chd by him for wandering abroad and lodging in the open air was ord^d to be sent to his Ma^r at Rotherhithe.

R.A.   Mr Houstoun attended.

Sir Charles Asgill. Thursday 4 January 1776
1s.   Aff^t Will: Marriott

Mr Rhodes attended   C A

Mr Alderman Bridgen. Friday 5 January 1776.
      (No Attendance)

Mr Beach att^d R.H.

The Right Honourable Thomas Harley. Monday 8 January 1776.
      (No Attendance)

Mr Beach att^d RH

Mr Alderman Crosby. Tuesday 9 January 1776[80]
      Reb^a Lewis WC by Isaac Gilbert C. chd by John James for embezelling 6 Oz: 10 Drams of white Bengall flat single Silk—delivered to her to wind– it app^d several of the bobbins had been changed in Order to make up the Weight delivered to her originally– the silk was nearly of the Value of 2s. an Ounce– the Mre was adj^d 'till to Morrow.

1s.   Aff^t John Dugard.

James Stewart[81] WC John Woodfield C. chd by Nich^s Tipper Snow Hill Poulterer and George Harlow on Suspicion of felo-

---

80.   Erroneously entered as 1775 in the original.
81.   The case proceeds to the Old Bailey later that week. See *OBP*, January 1776, trial of James Stewart (t17760109–71).

niously Stealing one Goose value 2s. Property of s[d] N[s] Tipper Adj[d] true and Committed to Newgate.

R   N[s] Tripper N[o] 32 Snow Hill Poulterer   £ 10
   G. Harlow N[o] 16 D[o] Ivory Turner   £ 10
     To App[r] Prosecute & Give Evidence

Sam[l] Bagnell WC John Haughton C. and Ch[d] by John Dale and [blank] who not attending He was reman[d]

Sophia Symonds PC Tho[s] Blaney C. and Ch[d] by him

David Evans, Mary Ux} WC John Sheppard C. rem[d] on Tuesday last by M[r] Ald[n] Smith for furth[r] Examion Ch[d] by W[m] Ransome on Susp[n] of feloniously Stealing 2 Silk Cloaks value 15s. & o[r] Things his Property. For want of Suff[t] Evi[d] Disch[d]

War[t] v Jacob Cardosa ads Abraham Lyons Ass[t]

W[m] Hopps W[m] Davis C. Ch[d] by Tho[s] Aldersey and Dan[l] Bishop and W[m] Lyne for violently assaulting & Beat[g] Him Adj[d] true & Committed to WC (for want of Sureties).

1s.   W[t] v John Ryder ads John Karworthy on Suspicion of Feloniously stealing Sev[l] Pieces of Silk and Cotton Stuff value £3 his Property Adjourn[d] & comm[d] to WC

1s.   Warr[t] v Marcus Polack and Jacob Polack ads Frances Marcus per Ass[t]

1s.   W[t] v W[m] Quendon ads Pierce Cummings per Ass[t]

B. C.   M[r] Rhodes Attended

M[r] Alderman Townsend. Wednesday 10 January 1776.
     (No Attendance)

     M[r] Houstoun att[d]   R H.

M[r] Alderman Bull. Thursday 11 January 1776.
     Martha West by Geo: Hatherall C. chd by Eleanor Jennings (on Ld Mayor's W[t] 9th Inst.) for an Ass[t] agreed & discharged they withdrew to settle it & did not return

     Eleanor Jennings, Ann Smith, Eilz: Smith} by Tho[s] Cooke C. chd by Martha Ux: Moses West (on Ld Mayors W[t] Yesterday) for an Ass[t] [illegible] they withdrew as above & did not return.

Jos: Fowke sum^d ads Charlotte Garwell for an Ass^t etc. agreed & dischd

Mr Rhodes Attended   F.B.

Mr Alderman Wilkes. Friday 12 January 1776.
   Mr Rhodes excused, by reason of Illness.   John Wilkes

Sir Thomas Hallifax. Monday 15 January 1776.
   Mary Clark PC by Thos Fosket C. chd by a Person not now present with picking him up in the Street, and being a Common Night Walker—she was D^d.

   Geo: Harris WC by John Woodfield C. chd by Edwd Fosset for ass^ting him– rem^ded till tomorro

   Thos Dymock Journeyman Carman by Jos: Jefferson chd by Thos Cooper his Master for embezilling his money– com^d (on Coopers Oath) to B.

   ~~Aff^t. Pearce Lapine~~

   Mr Beach did not attend.   TH Excused.

Mr Alderman Bull. Friday 15 August 1777.
   John Kennedy, Will: Graves} WC by Jno Couchman C. chd by him & Will: Gardener W^{ch}man of Cripplegate Ward with attempting to break open a House—the C[onstable] saw them trying a Shutter – Graves alledged he worked in Brick Lane – Kennedy lodges at Mr Bankes little Moorfields – Graves in Brick Lane in Rose Street at Mr Hall's – the Const was Ordered to search the Lodgings of the Prisoners.

1s.   Thos Hanforth D^oC[ompter] by D^o C. chd by him for an Ass^t; on asking pardon d^d

   Nich^s Lindsay, Fra^s Tilling} by Chas Stagg C. chd by John Loton as Yesterday – Ja^s Nelson chd Lindsay with stealing a Watch—but he co^d not recollect the Name or Number – there was no direct proof of a Felony so as to affect the Prisoners – sent on board the Tender.

1s.   Jno Edwards WC by Jno Farringdon C. chd by Peter Smith for an Ass^t—ag^d & d^d

Nich^s Nailor by Rob Wilton C. chd by Mary Ux: for assaulting her whereby she apprehends herself to go in fear & danger of bodily Harm – rem^{d}ed to WC to find Bail (at his own request).

Mr Wyatt app^d in consequence of a Sum^s – no person came to complain – d^d

Edward Smith, Mary McCoul, Eliz: Pritchel, Dorothy Brooks}
WC by Will: Morton C. chd with making a disturbance in the Old Bailey on Promising future good behaviour discharged.

1s.   Thos Coker WC by Wm Martin C. chd by Mary his Wife for Violently assaulting her – she app^d to be the Agre^r & much to blame dischd.

John Kentish Sum^d ads Thos Reynolds for a Hackney Coach Fare Ordered 11s. 6d. & no charges.

John Peters WC by Saml Thorp C. chd by Han^h Turniss & Wm Gibbs on Susp^n of Stealing nine papers of Iron Screws – he was rem^d 'till Monday

Chas Curry sum^d by Hen: Edmonds his Master to whom he is an App^r for swearing & disturbing the Peace of his Family – he promised better behaviour – d^d

P   W^t ag^t Thos Vaux ads Judith Lyon Ass^t

1s.   D^o agt Jane Wise ads Martha Cooper Ass^t

1s.   D^o agt Jno Watts ads Roger Boarder D^o

1s.   W^t agst Martha Slade for keeping and maintaining an ill governed & disorderly House & common bawdy Ho: – Par: St Sepulchre.

RX   to prosecute
Chas Stagg – Turnagain L. – Const: £ 40
RX   to give Evidence
Jno Brockholes Fleet L. – Baker   }
Will: Martin – D^o – Coffin Plate Chaver[82] } Each: £ 20

Mr Beach attended. F.B.

---

82.   Engraver of metal.

Mr Alderman Wilkes. Monday 18 August 1777.
(No Attendance)

Mr Beach attended. D.G.

Mr Alderman Sawbridge by Mr Alderman Plomer. Tuesday 19 August 1777.

1s.   Edwd Bennett WC by Chas Stagg C. chd by Ann Ward (on Ald^n Bull's W^t 14th Inst) for an Ass^t – it app^d the Pros^x was the Agressor dischd

1s.   Aff^t Wm Heathfield

1s.   Will: Falboy a hackney Coachman by Jas Goodwin C. chd by Thos Linton for plying in Bank Street – he was fined 10s. wch he p^d & 1s. Conviction

p^d 3s. to Payne for a Cart for these Women.[84]   Eliz: Parsons, Jane Thompson, Eliz: Rowe, Han^h Emerson, Ann Dove, Barbara Ruffhead, Ann Matthews, Marg^t Burne, Eliz: Stevens, Ann Brooks, Martha Jackwell, Eliz: Burnett[83]} WC by Will: Payne C. chd by him for severally wandering abroad & picking up Men – Burn, Stevens & Brooks were chd for making a disturbance – they were com^d for a Week to B– Thompson Rowe Emerson Dove and Matthews were com^d to B for 14 Days

1s.   Aff^t [illegible] Heathfield

John Peters by Saml Thorp C. chd by Hannah Farniss & Will: Gibbs & John Nicholls on Susp^n of stealing Eleven Papers Groce of Iron Screws Value 15/. s^d Gibbs's property.

Wm Gibbs N° 74 Smithfield Ironmonger for himself & John Nicholls his Appre[ntice]} £10

Mr Alderman Bull ad huc Tuesday 19 August 1777.

1s.   Will: Connor a hackney Coachman by Joseph Gates C. chd by him for plying between Freeman's Court and the West End of
p^d.   Cornhill – he was conv^d in the penalty of 10s. wch he neglected to pay, and was com^d to the London Workhouse – p^d the fine

[blank] Lamotte sum^d ads John Putterell a Hackney Coachman

---

83.   All have a check mark or a check mark and small dash beside their name.
84.   Appears in the left margin. A check mark appears beside each name and an additional '–' appears beside the names of the women committed to Bridewell.

for refusing to pay him his Fare for carrying him in his Hackney Coach from Bishopsgate Street to Bethnal Green & wait^g three hours – it appeared by the declarat^n of Mr Lamotte & an^r he waited only 2 hours 55 Minutes, complt dismissed on paying 3/6.

Mich^l Maloy, Jno Evans} WC by W Payne C. chd by him for wandering abroad – they were d^d

James Clark by Wm Payne C. chd by Eliz: Brice upon suspicion of feloniously stealing a silver Tea Spoon – there was no colour of Evidence to affect the Pris^r –d^d

nil   Bella Pearson, ~~Fra^s Beale~~, Ann Perry} by John Sheppard C. chd by Eleanor Beale (on Ald^n Plomer's W^t Yesterday) for an Ass^t – they withdrew & ag^d – d^d

Mr Nash Attended   F.B.

Sir James Esdaile. Wednesday 20 August 1777.
(No Attendance).

Mr Houstoun att^{d}ed.   D.G.

Mr Alderman Kennett. Thursday 21 August 1777.
(No Attendence).

Mr Rhodes attended.   D.G.

Mr Alderman Kirkman. Friday 22 August 1777.
(No Attendance).

Mr Nash attended.   D.G.

Mr Alderman Oliver. Monday 25 August 1777.
(No Attendance).

Mr Beach attended.   D.G.

Sir Watkin Lewes. Tuesday 26 August 1777.
(No Attendance).

Mr Nash attended.   D.G.

Mr Alderman Plomer. Wednesday 27 August 1777.
Mary Briggs, Eliz: Baker, Mary Farren, Ann Ayres, Frances

Hartshorn, Ann Stevens, Eliz: Smith, Eliz: Blackburn, Sarah Jones, Eliz: Edwards, Ann Drinkwater, Ann Thumper, Eliz: Harris, Ann Brown, Lucy Whiteman, Eliz: Evans, Mary Miller, Marg[t] Burn, E Moore, Sarah Stevens, Jane Fuller, Sarah Shibbons, Martha Jakewell[85]} WC by Will: Payne C. chd by him for being severally loose idle & disorderly Women & picking up Men in the Streets of this City – Hartshorn, Stevens, Thumper, Miller, S. Stevens & Jakewell were com[d] to B until a Court – the others were d[d]

gave a poor Woman 1s. by his Wp's Order.　Tho[s] Brown, Will: Smith, John Fadd} d[o]C by d[o]C. chd by him – the two first for attempting to pick several pockets – they were discharged—and Fadd for ~~sitting~~ begging – he was d[d].

1s.　W[t] ag[t] R[d] McFarlin ads Lydia Wheeley.

1s.　R[d] McFarlin by Jno Bradley C. chd by Lydia Wheeley (on his Wp's W[t] this day) for an Ass[t] – they withdrew & ag[d].

Will: Jones, Jos: Wells, Will: Staines} hackney Coachmen ~~chd by Jno~~ sum[d] by Will: Payne for plying oppo: S[t] Dunstan's Church – fined Ea: 5s.

Tho[s] Baker[86] WC by Jos: Thompson C. chd by Tho[s] Newell Watchman & John Bullock for feloniously stealing 2 Steel Saws ~~& the property of s~~ 8 Chissels 8 ploughing Irons and other things Val. 5s. –also 2 Steel Saws one Chissel & a Book Val. 3s. the property of James Cole – on their Oaths committed to d[o]C.

RX　John Bullock – Fleece & Son N[o] 16 Thread Needle Street Carpenter　£20
James Cole at M[r] Sherman's Black horse Alley Fleet St[t] D[o]　20
Tho[s] Newell N[o] 10 Exeter Street Strand, Watchman　20
Jos[h] Thompson N[o] 5 Bards Lane Const.　20
To appear prosecute & give Evid. next Sess[s] O[yer] &T[erminer] London

Mary Robinson WC Jonathan Wilkins C. and Ch[d] by Ellenor

85. Check marks appear beside each name, except Sarah Jones, Eliz: Harris, Ann Brown, Eliz: Evans and E. Moore, who have no marks. Hartshorn, Ann Stevens, Thumper, Miller, Sarah Stevens and Jakewell have a check mark crossed through as an 'X'; each was committed to Bridewell.
86. The case proceeds to the Old Bailey. See *OBP*, September 1777, trial of Thomas Baker (t17770910–64).

Gardiner for stealing her Cloak – she was sent back to the C[ompter].

Will: Bagnell, Will: Pollard} by Will: Stiles Jones C. chd by him for being found under suspicious circumstance in a Passage – rem^ded 'till tomorrow.

Rebecca Williams WC Wm Styles Jones C. and Ch^d by him for being a loose idle and disorderly Person and common Prostitute etc. Adj^d true and committed to B. 14 Days.

1s.   Warr^t v Eupham Ux R^d Smith ads Hannah Watts per Ass^t.

Mr Rhodes attended   WP

Mr Alderman Hart. Thursday 28 August 1777.
1s.   Will: Glover a hackney Coachman WC by Will: Payne C. chd by him for standing with his Coach opposite St Dunstan's Church – conv^d in the penalty of 5s. wch was given to Payne

1s.   James Smith d^oC by d^oC. chd by him for obstructing him in his Duty, when apprehend^g the above Pris^r – d^d.

1s.   Back'd a Middx W^t.

P   Saml Hearson WC by Jno Apethorpe C. chd by John Hunt for an Ass^t – ask'd pardon & d^d

        Will: Bagnell, Will: Pollard} who were rem^ded Yesterday & were bro^t up again – they app^d to be notorious Pickpockets – Stephen Fowkes app^d & complained ag^st Bagnell for threatening his Life – rem^ded 'till tomorrow

        Oldham Johnson app^d for Henry Perry sum^d ads Fred^k Rasch for stacking Lime in the Carriage Way – Mr Rasch was sworn to the fact – St Ann Black Friars.

1s.   Thos Richards a Hackney Coachman PC by Jno Bradley C. chd by him for plying opposite the 'Change – Bradley was sworn & he was fined 10s.

1s.   Eupam Smith by Danl Osman C. chd by Han^h Watts (on Ald^n Plomer's W^t Yesterday) for an Ass^t – they withdrew & ag^d – d^d

P   Mary Hall by Saml Thorp C. chd by Mary Joyes (on Ld Mayor's W^t Yesterday) for an Ass^t – d^d –being frivolous

Nich[s] Howard by Jno Trowell C. chd by Geo: Rawlins a W[ch]man in Cripplegate Ward for an Ass[t] – on his Oath Com[d] to WC

1s. Back'd a Middx W[t] Per M[r] Curtis.

1s. John Hall was complained against by Alice Savage for assaulting her with Intent to commit a Rape – a W[t] was granted against Hall

M[r] Rhodes attended   JH

Tho[s] Dudfield by Sam[l] Thorp C. chd by Jno Wildman his Ma[r] for wilfully misbehaving himself & leaving his Service – M[r] Wildman was sworn— and he was com[d] to B— for a Week

M[r] Alderman Peckham. Friday 29 August 1777.
Will: Bagnell, Will: Pollard} WC by Will: Stiles Jones C. chd by Stephen Fowkes Sarah Davis Eliz[th] Ux Tho[s] Brown on Susp[n] of feloniously Stealing 2 Linnen Gowns and o[r] App[l] the Property of Theophillis Brown, for Want of Evid[ce] remanded 'till tomorrow when [blank]

1s. W[t] ag[t] Chris[r] Hewson ads Hen: Bellamy

Mich[l] Clare[87] WC by Jno Apethorpe C. chd by Edw[d] Cooper upon suspicion of feloniously stealing a striped cotton Waistcoat Val: 1s. 6d. six Shirts six Stocks, two pair of Stockings one silk & the other thread— also a callico rapper – the Pris[r] lodged at a Shoemaker's facing M[r] Pullens— Islington.
RX Edw[d] Cooper Serv[t] to Rogers Iortin Chancery L Gent   £10
Jno Taylor – Bedford C[t] Covent Garden Shoem[r]   10
Mark Lyder – Serv[t] to Mr Chancy Smithy Bdings Leadenh: St. James
for Ann Collett   }
Geo: Rugeley – Swan with 2 necks [illegible]   } 10 Ea[ch]
per Ann Collett his Servant

M[r] Alderman Clarke [sic] for M[r] Alderman Peckham ad huc 29 August 1777.
R[d] Stephens W[m] Martin C. and Ch[d] by Mary Arthur ux Hugh Arthur for violently assaulting and beating her She was

87. The case proceeds to the Old Bailey. See *OBP*, September 1777, trial of Michael Clare (t17770910–70).

confirm'd in her Evidence by Mary Gerrard W°[?] adj^d true and he was committed to WC.

John Rogers, Geo. Dempson} WC ~~John Neale Cost.~~ Jos^h Gates C. and Ch^d by John Meane for throwing a Stone which struck Richard Dawes a Boy – and also for ass^{t}ing him (Meane) – they produced their Ma^r but he co^d say little to their Credit

1s.   Back'd a Middx W^t

Mr Rhodes attended   R.C.

1s.   Aff^t Will: Reynolds Highmore.

nil   Peter Dowdell by Jno Brockholes C. chd by Cath: Sheridan (on Lord Mayor's W^t 23d Inst:) for an Ass^t – Bridget Anderson confirmed the Story so far as to general Ill Usage but co^d say nothing to the particular fact – d^d

P   W^t ag^t Jas Payne ads Eliz: Worral – Ass^t etc.

Mr Alderman Hayley. Monday 1 September 1777.

1s.   Moses Willett WC by Will: Jones C. chd by Jno Rowley for an Ass^t – it app^d a trifling matter was dischd

Ann Fisher, Sarah Stephens, Eliz: Stephens, Cath: Matthews, Casaiah Evans, Mary Parker, Han^h Sparks, Ann Dean, Eliz: Burtuttle[88]} WC by Wm Payne C. chd by him for being severally loose idle & disorderly Women & Common Prostitutes – Fisher & Sarah Stephens were d^d, Eliz: Stephens & Cath: Matthews committed to B– Evans was d^d

Jno Elder sum^d ads Saml Whitten a hackney Coachman for refusing to pay him his fare from Charing Cross to Throgmorton Street – Ord^d 2s. & 2s./6d. Charges

Marg^t Butler WC by Jno Williams C. chd by Magdalen McIntire for stealing a Gown – d^d

Jere^h Rose, Geo: Bolton, Jno Chamberlain, Mary Price} WC by Will: Martin C. chd as follows – the 3 Boys by Jas Rogers for attempting to pull a Pin out of a Window— in order as supp^d to break open the House but no o^r act having been com^d they were Com^d to B: as having no visible way of living

88. Check marks appear beside each name, except Sparks and Dean.

Jno Miller the Driver of a Cart N° [blank] sum^d ads Thos Groves for obstructing the Passage in Darkhouse Lane – conv^d in 5s. penalty

~~Edwd Whitten by R^d Dawson C. chd by him for~~

P   W^t ag^t Will: Lightburne ads Ann Dawson.

P   D° agt Eliz: Furlong ads Mary Carter Ass^t

Mr Beach attended. G.H.

Mr Alderman Newnham. Tuesday 2 September 1777.
[blank] Hall sum^d ads Jos: Dolphin Carman for refusing to pay the Cartage of five Bags of Pepper from Billiter Lane to Bread Street – Ord^d the fare & 2s. Charges which was paid

Jno Fellows sum^d ads Jos: Jefferson Street Keeper for riding upon the Cart, not having a person on foot to guide the same – dism^d

1s.   John Brewett PC by Wm Hammerstone C. chd by Jos^h Richardson for not paying his fare in the Hertford Coach agreed & d^d.

1s.   Wm Lightburn [blank] by Richd Greenfield C. chd by Ann Dawson for assaulting her trifling disch^d

James Birch Junr, Thos Halyman, James Birch} by Jonas Parker C. chd by Leon^d Newbank – Grounded on the Evidence of Jas Birch the younger who had confess'd to have stole £100 Bank Note & 10 Guas in monies numbered, the note & monies of s^d Newbank – no direct Evidence app^d to fix any Charge ag^t Halyman – the Fa^r was chd as having reced the note & money but ~~with~~ it app^d the Fa^r was totally Innocent of any knowledge of this transaction & the whole resting with the Boy who bore a good Cha^r before this; was sent to the Marine Society at the request of his Father

P   W^t ag^t Mary Allen ads Ann Edger Ass^t etc.

Mr Nash attended. N.N.

Mary Smith by Chas Stag C. chd by Mary Scott for Robbing his Ready Furnished Lodgings of sundry Articles of Household Furniture – there were Promises of favour & besides, the Pris^r did the fact under the direction of her husband – d^d

Mr Alderman Lee by Mr Alderman Bull. Wednesday 3 September 1777.

Will: Roolfe Chch Wden of St John Zachary – sum^d ads Jane Stephens for relief – ord^d to be taken into the Ho:

P   Jas Lawrence sum^d ads Martha Pearce for using threats towards her whereby she apprehends herself to be in Danger – frivolous & d^d

Eliz: Crosier WC by Jno Powell C. chd by Jno Cook for stealing a pint pewter pot – rem^ded till tomorrow – com^d to B. for one Month

Lewis Smith, Will: Malone, Marcus Malone} WC by Will: Payne C. chd by him for attempting to pick sev^l Pockets – sent to the Marine Society.

Marg^t Bailey, Rach^l Hill} d^oC by d^oC. chd by him for raising a Disturbance, swearing &c.— Bailey com^d to B. till Monday & Hill for a Week

gave Payne 3s. for a Cart for these Women.   Mary Wilson, Galespa Wilson, <u>Sarah Johnson</u>, Mary Cutter, Sarah Dibdin, Mary Colman, Mary Day, Ann Day, Ann Newman, Eliz: Newman, Eliz: Hill, Sarah Brooks, Jane Thompson, Jane Ellis, Ann Shaw[89]} WC by Will: Payne C. chd by him for being severally loose idle & disorderly Women & picking up Men – all (except Mary Day, Ann Day, and Neman) were com^d to B—

Jane Fuller, Constance Christian} by Peter Ashmore C. [and] Ann Garriway, John Lumley}
by Wm Morris for being severally Idle & disorderly Persons com^d to B until Monday on Oath of Wm Morris.

P   Anthony Pollet by Edmund Strafford C. chd by Fra^s Penny for assault agreed & dis^d.

Mr Lot Mitcham Hackney Coachman convicted on Oath of Wm Cox for standing with his Coach in Fleet street on Sat^d [?] payd 5s. 6.

---

89. Check marks appear beside each name, except Johnson, Mary Day, Ann Day, Ann Newman and Ann Shaw. Eliz: Hill's check mark has been struck through once; Jane Ellis's check mark has been struck through thrice.

Mᵣ Houstoun attᵈ   F.B.

5s.8d for the Recog: Wᵗ agᵗ [blank] Nash for keeping a common ill
& discharge (the   governed and disorderly house (the Recognizance
Recogniz: was   was entered upon a piece of Paper, which is
directed not to be   mislaid)
returned, as the
Matter was settled)

Mᵣ Alderman Smith. Thursday 4 September 1777.
    James King prᵈ by Riches Reed C. charged by Richᵈ Gould for
    stealing a 200 lb wᵗ of Iron belonging to Saint Paul's Church –
    Mᵣ Pindar his Master was not willing to prosecute him he was
    ~~rep'd & dis~~ remᵈ to Produce some Person to his Chaᵣ.

1s.   Affᵗ Thoˢ Tyler

P   Wᵐ Pratt PC by Danˡ Osmond C. chd by John Pratt for
        assaulting sᵈ Jno Pratt – he Promised not to be Guilty of the
        like Offence was dischd

1s.   Wᵗ [blank] Willgoose whose Xtian name is not known ads Wᵐ
        Baker Assᵗ etc.

        Robᵗ Cooper, Jno Elsmore} by Wᵐ Payne C. chd by him & Jno
        Gibson for picking pockets in Smithfᵈ.

        Mr Howse attended   HS

Mᵣ Alderman Clark. Friday 5 September 1777.
    (No Attendance).

        Mᵣ Houstoun attᵈed.   DG

Mᵣ Alderman Wooldridge by Mᵣ Alderman Bull. Monday 8 September
    1777.
    Patᵏ McLauchlin by Jno Brockholes C. chd by Jno Wray
    [blank]

Mᵣ Alderman Bull ad huc.
    Owen Ryan by Will: Payne C. chd by him for beating his Wife
    so that her Life is in danger – she being in the Hospital –
    remᵈed.

pᵈ   Eliz: Mounsheer, Mary George, Sarah Dodd, Ann Clyde,
Payne Hester Sunderland, Alice Perry, Eliz: Harrison, Eliz: Moore,

3s. for Sarah Carter, Eliz: Croker, Ann Brooks[90]} WC by Will: Payne
a Cart C. chd by him for being severally loose idle & disorderly
Women & severally picking up Men – Croker and Brooks were
d[d] – Moore was com[d] for 14 days to B– and the others for a
Week.

Jno Thompson, Sam[l] Lemon, Peter Woodcock, Will: Cole}
d[o]C by d[o]C. chd by him for attempting to pick several Persons
pockets

Ralph Monro, Tho[s] Simpkins} fr WC by D[o] charged by him
with sleeping in the open Air last Night in Fleet Market, upon
promise of Amendm[t] discharged.

Gave a poor Man 1s. by his Wp's Order.[91]

Sam[l] Fowler WC by Jonas Parker C. chd by Tho[s] James for
picking his pocket of a handkerchief – sent to the Marine
Society.

M[r] Beach attended   F.B.

M[r] Alderman Alsop.- Tuesday 9 September 1777.
~~Jno Lane PC. by Will: Blackburn C. chd by Rob: Cocked~~

~~Rich[d] Woolley by Jno Couchman C. chd by Jas Jones[92]~~

(No Attendance)

M[r] Nash attended. D.G.

M[r] Alderman Wright. Wednesday 10 September 1777.
Jas Scott a hackney Coachman sum[d] ads John Langley for
refusing to go when required – he was conv[d] in the penalty of
10s. wch he paid.

Mary Hoff WC by Jas Polhill C. chd by Jno Till for feloniously
stealing two Shirts etc. – d[d] – the parties had entered upon a
Treaty of Compromise.

---

90. Check marks appear beside each name. The notation 'dd' appears beside Crocker and
Brooks and the number 14 beside Moore.
91. Appears in the left margin.
92. A large X appears over these two entries, which have no further details.

1s.　Rob: Wilford by Jona: Wilkins C. chd by the Churchwardens & Overseers of the Poor of the Parish of St Andrew Holborn for deserting his Wife – d^d

~~Hester Wells~~, Ann Powell, Frances Mackavoy, Eliz: Plaisto, Marg^t Smith[93]} WC by Will: Payne C. chd by him for severally wandering abroad & picking up Men

George Tucker by Saml Jones C. chd by George Harrison for stealing three Bundles of Stockings Thos Shuter an Evidence saw the Goods taken out of the Warehouse; Thos Adamson a Servant of Harrison proved the property rem^d until tomorrow.

P　John Wheatly & Ux by John Clarke C. by Mary the Wife of Thos Sutton for assault^g her on Ald^n Peckhams W^t agreed & dis^d

1s.　Wm Adderley by R^d Jones C. chd by John Jarmy for an Ass^t – d^d

Patrick Cullen WC by Will: Martin C. chd by [blank] Wray for offering some Fiat[?] to Sale d^d

P　Isaac Cambell pr^d by John Clarke C. charged by Jacob Hall a Hackney Coachman upon Suspicion of taking some things out of his Coach it appearing no charge was bro^t home dis^d.

Mr Houstoun att^d.　TW

Mr Alderman Bridgen. Thursday 11 September 1777.
　(No Attendance)

Mr Rhodes att^{d}ed　DG.

The Right Honourable Thomas Harley. Friday 12 September 1777.
　(No Attendance)

Mr Houstoun att^{d}ed　DG.

Mr Alderman Crosby. Monday 15 September 1777.
　Will: Wright WC by Jno Couchman C. chd by Thos Snelgrove for an Ass^t

---

93.　Letter 'B' appears in the margin beside Powell, Plaisto and Smith, possibly from or sent to Bridewell, with check marks beside the 'B' for Powell and Plaisto.

Ann Warren by Danl Osman C. chd by him for lodging in the open Air Par: St Dunstan

(No Attendance)

Mr Beach att^ded. DG.

Mr Alderman Townsend. Tuesday 16 September 1777.
(No Attendance)

Mr Nash att^ded   DG.

Mr Alderman Bull. Wednesday 17 September 1777.
1s.   W^t ag^t John Torriano ats John Phillips Ass^t

Thos Thomas PC by Jos: Gates C. chd by Jona: Treviso for embezilling half a Guinea – there was no evidence – d^d

Daniel Smith by Wm Payne C. charged by Anthony Leet & Richd Winbourne sent to B. 14 days on Oath of one [blank] Mullet

John Roberts by John Duncastle C. chd by [blank] upon suspicion of steal^g a Handkerchief rem^d until tomorrow

1s.   W^t ag^t Thos Nottingham ats Thos Margeram Ass^t

Saml Lambert sum^d ads Thos Smith for receiving Goods levied under an Execution – Val: £100 & upw^ds – knowing the same to have been fraudulently taken away – d^d

1s.   Ben: Thomas by Rob: Heelis C. chd by Will: Clark for an Ass^t – they withdrew & ag^d – d^d

October Sess.
3s/4d   John Torriano by Jno Bradley C. chd by John Phillips (on his Wp's W^t this day) for an Ass^t – bailed as before
RX   John Torriano of Doctors Comons Gent.   £40
    Edwd Cooper of D^o   D^o   }
    Perrot Fenton of D^o   D^o   } Ea. £20

Mary Hutt pr^d by Geo. Upton C. chd by John Case – Ann Case the Daughter appeared to make good the Charge ag^t the Pris^r wch was being found in Case's House but no appearance of any Felony com^d she was dis^d.

101

1s.   W^t ag^t Dennis McDonald ads Sarah Ux Ass^t

Ann Woodward by Levi Moses C. chd by Chas Merricain upon Suspicion of stealing three Shillings discharged no positive Proof appearing

Mr Houstoun att^d F.B.

Mr Alderman Wilkes. Thursday 18 September 1777.
~~Mary Stevens by Danl Osman C. chd by Will: Taylor~~

Sir Ja^s Esdaile   W^t ag^t John Scarlett ads Rob: Hemell for knowingly
1s.   etc. obtaining a silver Soup Ladle & 4 Silver Salts
              Val: £5 with Intent to cheat & defraud him thereof
~~Randall Sidley by Danl Osman C. chd by Thos Bramah~~

Mr Rhodes Attorney attended   D.G.

Mr Alderman Sawbridge by Mr Alderman Peckham. Friday 19 September 1777.
    Randall Sidley by Danl Osman C. chd by Thos Bramah for an Assault – the prisoner appeared to be Insane – the C. was ordered to take him to the Parish of St Clement Danes

    Mr Nash attended   RP.

Sir James Esdaile. Monday 22 September 1777.
    Margaret Keys, Charlotte Green, Margaret Keith} by Will: Moreton C. chd by a Person not now present, as idle disorderly Women – they were all d^d

    Jno DeBrooke summoned by Jno Godfrey for obstructing the free passage in Gracechurch Street with his Coach–conv^d in five Shillings fine–half to Godfrey & the rem^r to the Parish.

1s.   Jno Vine by Jno Negus C. chd by Eliz: Ux Thos Saunders (on Ald^n Bull's W^t 20th Inst.) for an Ass^t – they withdrew & were d^d

    Ann Price, Sarah Han^h Bennett, Martha Burness} by Danl Osman C. chd by Payne the Constable (who was not now present) and therefore they were d^d

    Isaac Roy, Isabella Allum, Alice Adey} by Will: Martin C. chd by Jno Kemp N° 9 in Green Arbour Court—upon suspicion of burglariously breaking open his Dwelling Ho: & stealing therein 3 silk Gown one Muslin D° 2 Linnen D° 1 Cotton D° and many other Things – for want of Evidence—dd^d

Lydia Wood, Mary Emery, Thos Aldbourn} by doC. chd by Will: Payne (who is not now present) they were d^d

P   Patrick Keene, Jno Harrison} by Chas Stagg C. chd by each other – d^d

1s.   Thos Nicholson by Rob: Wilton C. chd for an Ass^t – d^d

Jno Roach by Chas Stagg C. chd by R^d Lee for attempting to pick Pockets – d^d

Jos: Bowen a hackney Coachman sum^d by Mª Chambers for abusing her – on her Oath he was fined ten Shillings.

2s.   Richd Hand, Jos: Seabrook} PC Jos: Coleman C. chd by each other for an Ass^t – d^d upon an Agreem^t – d^d

1s.   Back'd a Middx W^t Per Mr Wilmot.

P   John Dare—by Thos Burket C. chd by Tabitha Ux: (on Lord Mayor's W^t 18th Inst.) and Chch Wdns of St Botolph Bishopsgate for leaving her chargeable to the s^d Parish – it app^d to be an irregular Charge, as the Parish should apply to the Sessions – d^d

P   George Welch from PC by Levi Moses C. charged by Matthias for assaulting him &c. Upon promise of better Behaviour in future discharged at the Request of the Complainant.

P   Susannah Downes and Robert Griffin} from PC by Robert Wilson C. chd by [blank] Proby ~~whom~~ with making a Disturbance on Saturday last, who not appearing to make good his Charge, they were discharged.

1s.   W^t against John Lander for assaulting and beating William Chitham an Infant, with a Cart Whip.

P   Warr^t agt John Gage for assaulting and beating Anne his Wife.

P   Warrant ag^t [blank] Bereuh whose first Name is unknown for assaulting and beating Michael Emanuel.

Mr Beach Attended   JE

Mr Alderman Kennett. Tuesday 23 September 1777.

Will: Court app^d for Abram Brasbridge sum^d by Thomas Cooper Carman for refusing to pay the Cartage of a Load of Sugar from the Keys to Thames Street.

1s.　Affidavit Will: Arnold.

Eliz: Shears, Eliz: Croker, Mary Miller} WC Wm Payne C. chd by him as foll^s Viz: – for severally wandering abroad and picking up Men in the Streets of this City – Shears d^d—Croker recommended to the Hospital—and Miller was also d^d

John Tomlin, Thos Fido} D°C same C. chd by him—being fo^d concealed under a Block in the Fleet Market – they were d^d

Mary Higgins WC by Will: Odell C. chd by Jno Johnson for swearing sev^l prophane Oaths—and making a disturbance – d^d

Chch Wdns of St Botolph Aldersgate sum^d by Martha Hicks for refusing her Relief—she being an Inmate and in extreme Want – the Master of the Workhouse s^d that Hicks when there, got drunk – Ord^d to be relieved

1s.　W^t ag^t Wm Upton ads James Smith Ass^t

1s.　D° ag^t Jno Rome ads Solomon Levy – D°

P　Will: Wicks by Ben: Froud C. chd by Thos Fair for making a disturbance in his House (the Silt Boat in Darkhouse Lane) – he was d^d

Mary Welch WC by Will: Martin C. chd by a Mrs Stokes of the Fleet Market (not now present) and therefore the Pris^r was d^d

Mary Short WC by Will: Stiles Jones C. chd by Edwd Cramp for bringing Gin into the Jail of Newgate – she pleaded ignorance of the penal Consequences of the Offence—and there app^d reason to believe her Story – she was d^d

1s.　W^t ag^t Thos Flin ats Alace Woolford Ass^t

Marg^t Oldrick, Ja^s Potter} WC chd ~~by~~ as follows – Potter chd Oldrick with a Felony – they were d^d

Jno Hewson doC by Will: Stiles Jones C. chd with being fo^d under suspicious Circumstances near a Ho: that was broke open on Sunday Night in Green Arbour Court – he was d^d

1s.   Uzziell Baruch by George Ellfood C. chd by Michael Emanuel
for assaulting and beating him (on Sr Ja^s Esdaile's W^t Yesterday)
– frivolous & d^d

Mr Houstoun attended   BK

Mr Alderman Kirkman. Wednesday 24 September 1777.
Will: Upton by Will: Stiles Jones C. chd by James Smith (on
Ald^n Kennett's W^t Yesterday) for an Ass^t.

(No Attendance).

Mr Rhodes attended   RH.

Mr Alderman Oliver. Thursday 25 September 1777.
1s.   W^t ag^t Jno Kelly ads Mary Mortimer Ass^t

Sarah Byegrave WC by [blank] Williams C. chd by R^d Danby
for feloniously stealing his Waistcoat Val: [blank] –there was
a doubt of the Intention – d^d

1s.   W^t to search the Apartment of [blank] Ruddock in Green
Arbour Court in the Old Bailey—ads Mary Worsley for a
Quantity of Laces stolen from her

1s.   D^o agt Thos Coffin ads Sarah Groome.

~~Ann~~ Dinah Ellis, Eliz: Cock[94]} PC by Ja^s Barker C. chd by
Danl Adams for feloniously stealing 7 Yards of Cotton Va 15s.
–s^d Adams's Property – Char^s Whincop Servt to Adams took
the Cotton upon Ellis after she had left the Shop; the o^r Woman
was in Co: with her both in the Shop & when taken, a 3^d
Woman was also in C^o at the Shop ~~but had left~~ & when taken
but made her Escape – on their Oaths com^d to D^{o}C
RX   Danl Adams of the Minories L: Linen Dra^r } ea £ 10
Chas Whincop Servt to D^o }
Ja^s Barker of Rosemary Lane L: Const.   10

P   Hannah Ames PC Levy Moses C. chd by Agness Moffatt for
stealing a Boltster and Sheet the Property of her Husband
Henry – not desiring to swear to the felony d^d.

---

94. The case proceeds to the Old Bailey. See *OBP*, October 1777, trial of Elizabeth Cock, Dinah
Ellis (t17771015–37).

1s.   W^t ag^t Emanuel Levy ads Sarah Lee Ass^t etc.

1s.   D^o ag for Eliz: Angell against Sarah Iliff Assault etc.

Alex^r Young by John Meane C. chd by Eliza: Birch Wid^o for assaulting & kicking her– R^d Woodbridge Appr: to Mrs Birch saw Young (who was a Lodger to Mrs Birch) kick her before any Ass^t was given by Mrs Birch – Wm Bridge a Const. gave an Acco^t of his threatening ab^t 12 last Night to blow any Persons Brains out who sho^d touch him – he had a Blunderbuss in his Hand wch he took fr: him & which was now drawn– app^d to be loaded with 6 small Balls or rather large Swan Shot—with a Proper proportion of Powder – this seem'd not relative to the Orig^l Assault on Mrs. Birch – on her & Woodbridge's Oaths com^d to WC:

P   W^t ag^t Jno Evans & Eliz: Powell ads Ann Plunkett – Ass^t etc.

1s.   Warr^t v John Cowper ads David Foot Ass^t.

Rhode [sic] Attend^d RO

Sir Watkin Lewes by Mr Alderman Hayley. Friday 26 September 1777.
Marg^t Simpson WC by Daniel Osman C. chd by Eliz: Wallace for assault^g and kicking her– She was confirm'd in her Evid by Ja^s Whaley a Const.

1s.   W^t v Thos Cock ads R^d Matthews per Ass^t.

P   John Lander on Sr John Esdailes W^t Jos^h Coleman C. and Ch^d by Wm Chaltham per Ass^t– Mre Sett^d and D^d

1s.   W^t v. Wm Gordon and Thos Drewrey on D^y Clk par cert they stand^g indicted at the Genl Sess^s O[yer] [&] T[erminer] for L. at Justice Hall Old Bailey for a Conspiracy and fraudulently obtain^g from Ja^s Cole 2£ 2s. by false Pretences, and (For want of App^{ce} and Plea)

1s.   Warr^t v Chas Blake ads Wm Gowdey Ass^t.

Mr Rhodes attended   JH

Mr Alderman Plomer. Monday 29 September 1777.
1s.   Back'd a Middx W^t per Mr Croft.

2s.   Maiah Coa, Jane Cook} WC by Jno Duncastle C. chd by each other –Cook charged the other with making a disturbance at her Ho: & breaking her Windows – d^d

Sarah Winn d^{o}C by Jno Meers C. chd by R^d Belcher Chch Wden of St. Bennett Pauls Wharf for abusing him – she promised better behaviour in future—d^d

Marg^t Griffiths PC by Jno Stevens C. chd by Jno Major a W^{ch}man of Aldgate Ward – com^d to B

1s.   Chas Swaine WC by Rob: Wilton C. chd by Thos Hatchman for an Ass^t – d^d

Mary Fordyce d^{o}C. by Jno Bradley C. chd by a Person not present – d^d

P   Will: Smith, Ellich Rood} PC by Solomon Davis C. chd by Thos Rosiere a W^{ch}man of Aldgate Ward for an Ass^t – d^d

Jno Scarlet PC by Jno Hawkins C. chd by Rob: Hemel for knowingly & designedly by false pretences obtaining from Will: Pepworth a silver soup Ladle & four Silver Salts Val: £5 the property of s^d Robert Hemel with Intent to cheat & defraud him the s^d R.H: thereof – upon the Oaths of s^d Hemel & Pepworth – he was com^d to d^{o}C

RX   Rob: Hemel N° 16 Foster L. Silversmith   } ea £ 10
        Will: Pepworth – D^o—Servant   }

Ja^s Smith was com^d to LW. being destitute of friends

Mr Beach attended   WP

Mr Alderman Crosby.   Wednesday 21 January 1778.
Ald^n Plomer   Grace Wallace, Sarah ~~Wallace~~ Wilson, Eliz: Rose, Ann Evans[95]} WC by Will: Payne C. chd by him for severally wandering abroad and picking up Men – Evans app^d a poor ignorant Welch Girl, just come from the Country – she was d^d – the Father of Rose app^d, to whom she was delivered – they promissed Amendment & were d^d

~~Ann Hoare by Jos: Gates C. chd by Ann Ux: Chas Tonvelle (on~~

95.   A check mark appears beside each name.

Eleanor Rigdon by Jno Edwards C. chd by John Morris with feloniously stealing a linen handkerchief – d^d

Will: Jones app^d for himself & his Partner who were sum^d to answer the Complt of John Simmonds for refusing to deliver a silver Watch – a Witness was sworn – Ord^d two Guineas by way of Satisfaction

1s.   Aff^t Will: Mervin Dillon

1s.   W^t ag^t Thos Holloman ats Mary Linsey Assault.

1s.   D^o agt John Clarke ats John Acton for searching his House for diverse Cloaths of his stolen

1s.   W^t ag^t George Featley upon Certificate of the Peace for assault^g Wm Petty – not appearing

1s.   W^t ag^t [blank] Trowell ats Eliz Kirby for assault.

Mr Alderman Plomer.   adhuc Wednesday 21 January 1778.
        Thos Priestley app^d to answer the Complt of Ja^s Parker for taking away two Loads – Will: Clapton the Driver was sworn – Ord^d to pay

1s.   W^t ag^t Eliz Taylor ats Sarah Cristy Ass^t

P.   D^o agt Thos Mason & Wm Lawrence ats Wm Brasewell Assault

        Mr Houston attended   WP

Mr Alderman Townsend by Mr Alderman Plomer. Thursday 22 January 1778.
        Chris^r Reynolds WC by Jno Bradley C. chd by Jno Hagger Overseer of Saint Alphage London Wall (on Ald^n Harley's W^t 20th Inst:) for unlawfully begetting Jane Housley Singlewoman of the s^d Parish with Child, which is likely to become chargeable thereto – rem^ded till tomorrow

1s.   Back'd a Middx W^t Per Mr Dyott

com^d as   Judith Saunders WC by Abram Solomons C. chd by Jos:
Principal   Smith, John Smith & Will: Fox upon suspicion of feloniously receiving a striped silk Sacque & Coat an iron grey coloured Gown & Petticoat and a linen Gown Val: [blank] the property of Henry Tracy, knowing the same to have been stolen

108

– Will: Robey, Jos: Smith, John Smith & Fox were sworn –
John Smith swears to the Cloaths produced being part of M^r
Tracey's property On their Oaths committed to d^{o}C.

RX   Will: Robey Bookkeeper – Saracens head Snow Hill   20

Jos: Smith   }
Jno Randall   } D^o Each 10

Jno Smith – at the Hon. Henry Tracy Portman Street   10

Will: Gill – Saracens head – for William Fox   10

Mr Alderman Wooldridge adhuc. Thursday 22 January 1778.

Jane Cox by Will: Payne C. chd by him for wandering in Fleet
Street and picking up Men – Payne said, that she confessed to
have been a Prostitute upon the Town a Week – that she said, a
Captain (Islip) had debauched her;–that about ten O'Clock last
Night she stopped several Men in Fleet Street – the Constable
was sworn—and upon his Oath—he confirmed all these Partic-
ulars

Joseph Thompson a Constable was sworn – and said, that the
Prisoner denied to him being a Prostitute. She was discharged.

1s.   John Philpot charged upon a Bastardy W^t was d^d upon Agreement

1s.   Thos Mason, Will: Lawrence } by Jno Paul C. chd by Will:
Bracewell (on Ald^n Plomer's W^t granted Yesterday) for an Ass^t
– d^d

3s.   Jno Drage, Geo: Ellis, Chas McClugh} WC by Thos Warren
C. chd by him for raising a Disturbance—& ass^{t}ing him with
a Stick – they rang at several Bells and knock'd at the Doors
in Saint Paul's Chch Yard – Drage held up the Cane at the
Constable – at half after two in the Morning Drage pushed the
C. out of the Chair – Warren was sworn—and upon his Oath
said that he followed the Pris^r up Ludgate ~~Hill~~ Street – they
were then hollowing and singing – that at or near a Woollen
Drapers Door in Saint Pauls Church Yard, the Prisoners rang at
~~the~~ a Bell – that Drage held up his Stick at him, and collared
him, that they kick'd and knocked at several other doors –
that where there were no Knockers, they kicked against the
Doors with their Heels – that this was ~~about~~ between two and
three O'Clock this Morning – that before he (the Constable)
touched any of them, he requested 'em to go about their business quietly, at which Drage brandished his Stick as with Intent
to strike him, and called out to the others – that he called out
Watch, and two or three Watchmen came to assist him, upon

which he laid hold of Mr Drage's Coat, and the W^{ch}man laid hold of the other two— that Mr Drage immediately collared him – that all the

Mr Alderman Plomer adhuc Thursday 22 January 1778.
Pris^r s were taken to the Watch House – that when in the Watch House, Mr Drage run his doubled fist twice in the Constable's Face and collared him, and said "Damme I'll do for you, I am a Lawyer, and you have got a wrong Person to deal with" – that Ellis and McClugh acknowledged in the Watch Ho: to have been riotous and noisy – that McClugh also collared him – they withdrew and ag^d – and were d^d

1s. Hannah Trowell by John Negus C. chd by Eliz: Kirby for ass^{t}ing & beating her (on his Wp's W^t yesterday for an Ass^t) d^d being friv^s.

1s. Back'd a Middx W^t Per Mr Miller

Michael Brown by Will: Stiles Jones C. chd by Jane Tully (a Middx W^t back'd by his Wp) for ass^{t}ing her & without her Consent forcibly having—carnal Knowledge of her Body – deliv^d over to a Middx [illegible] Constable

Mary Smith, Cath: Matthews, Eliz: Porch, Maria Cooper } WC by Will: Payne C. chd as foll^s Viz: Smith for picking up Men betw: 11 & 12 last Night – Matthews same time in a dark Alley – in Naked Boy Court in a dark Alley with a Man – Porch for picking up Men at Temple Bar ab^t 1– Cooper for the same both time & place – took her fr: a Man in an Alley near St. Dunstan's W^h House – Smith, Porch, & Cooper not having been known before by the Constable were d^d – Matthews being an old Offender was com^d to B.

1s. Wm Pinkston by Wm Saunders C. chd by Sarah Pinkston (on Ald^n Kennett's W^t 17 Inst) for an Ass^t – the Assault appeared to have been a violent one

1s. Francis Dunn WC by Jno Squire C. chd by him for violently assaulting & beating him – Squire was sworn – agreed & d^d

Mr Houston attended   WP

Mr Alderman Bull by Mr Alderman Pugh. Friday 23 January 1778.
Ann Bailey, Ann Draper } WC by Will: Payne C. chd by him

for severally wandering abroad & picking up Men – Draper was sent to her Friends and Bailey was d^d

1s.   Back'd a Middx W^t P

P   Thos Jones by Jos: Gates C. chd by Jos: Kirk (on a W^t) for an Ass^t – upon an Agreement – d^d

Walter Tristam sum^d ads Saml Unwin Carman for refusing to pay the Cartage of two Hogsheads of Sugar – Ord^d to pay

Joseph Cook by Will: Wilson C. chd by Will: Jones a Pawn-broker for uttering a forged Duplicate – the Mre was postponed.

1s.   W^t ag^t Will: Hobdey ads Richd Carter for an Ass^t etc.

1s.   Wm Whitaker pr. by Jos^h Coward C. chd by Ann the Wife of Peter Matthews for assault on ~~Ald.~~ Ld Mayor's W^t – Matthews gave the first Ass^t – d^d

Eleanor Keeling by Will: Smedley C. chd by Will: Bower upon suspicion of feloniously stealing a tortoise shell Snuff box – d^d (for want of proof).

Ja^s Thompson sum^d ads Thos Linton for using his unlicensed Cart for hire within this City – d^d

Sarah Franks sum^d ads Jno Laber a hackney Coachman for refusing to pay the fare from Berners Street to Castle Street – adj^d

Mary Ayres, Eleanor Atkins} by Walter Prosser C. chd by Eliz: Soames for stealing the Cloaths provided for them by the Parish of St Botolph Bishopsgate they were d^d

Paid 3s. for an Advertizement   Jno Kendal, Martha Ux:} WC by Jno Sheppard C. chd by Jno Acton upon suspicion of feloniously stealing a great Quantity of wearing Apparel his property – in consequence of a Search Warrant, a number of Articles suspected to be stolen were taken and here produced – the Pris^rs were separately interrogated about these Things and they differed – sent to d^oC until Wednesday next – the Wife was d^d – Hugh Andrew of West Smithfield Founder undertook for the Man~~'s behaviour~~.

111

Lydia Porter by Danl Osman C. chd by Saml Spencer upon suspicion of feloniously stealing two Gowns—and other things – d^d

1s.   Eliz Taylor by Nathan Lyon C. chd by Sarah Christy (on Ald^n Plomer's W^t 21st Inst) for an Ass^t – frivolous & d^d

Mr Houstoun att^d   CP

Mr Alderman Wilkes. Monday 26 January 1778.
P   Mary Green, Mary Matthews} WC: by Jos^h Coward C. chd by him for wandering & picking up Men last Night, they were both d^d.

P   Ann Evans D°C: Simon Cook C. chd by him for picking up a Man in Bow Lane she was d^d.

1s.   Thos Holliman by [blank] C. chd by Mary Lindsay for assaulting and beating her (on Ald^n Plomers W^t 21st Inst) –ag^d & d^d

1s.   Back'd a Middx W^t Per Mr Wilmot

P   Eliz: Halley, Jehonadab Donnegall} WC by ~~Jno~~ Samuel Jones C. ~~chd.~~ the Woman app^d not to be regularly charged in Custody, a W^hman alledged she was disorderly in going home at unseasonable hours with different People he c^d not say there was any Disturbances made by her she was d^d. The man was ch^d for swearing & cursing in the W^hHouse – he was d^d.

Dorothy Smith, Eliz: Beazeley} WC Jno Proctor C. chd by Walter Russell – Viz. Dor^y Smith for tendering in paym^t 24 a counterfeit Shilling knowing it to be so – having before on Tuesday 20 Inst. tend^d to him a bad Shilling
RX   Walter Russell of N° 17 Newgate Str: Callico Printer   £ 20

1s.   W^t ag^t Chas Clarke ads John Rose Ass^t

1s.   Back'd a Middx W^t Per Mr Girdler

Mr Beach attended   John Wilkes

Mr Alderman Sawbridge. Tuesday 27 January 1778.
1s.   Aff^t Henry Bunder.

2s.   Signed a poors Rate for St Leon^d Forster Lane

P   John Avery by Dav^d Ranken C. chd by Abram Gibson, for knowingly and designedly by false pretences obtaining from him 62 Ells of Silk Va: £8 with Intent to defraud him of the same – it app^d he was a W^kman who had made the silk & had obtained it fr: a Person to whom it was deliv^d to dress & said it was by Order of Mr Rob: Meyric, there was no Complaint before a Magistrate he was d^d.

John Hertford PC by Edwd Noon C. chd by Jno Fear, Rook Webster, for calling 'em in the Excise Coffee Ho: Rogues Villains &c. (this was about 11 last Night) on this he was sent to the Compter & his Coach & Horses home – there app^d no Reason for a Complaint agt the Pris^r – he was d^d.

nil   Charles Clarke by George Fleming C. chd by John Rose for assaulting him (on Mr Ald^n Wilkes's W^t 26th) it app^d to be a dispute ab^t tak^g a Horse, d^d.

Ja^s Kelly ~~sum^d~~ Carman sum^d ads Thos Carter for suffering his Horses to trot in Chancery Lane whereby great damage was done to his Coach – Rob: Hill saw the Mischief done; he was ord^d to pay 24s. Chas & 2s./6d. Costs

Mr Alderman Sawbridge, adhuc Tuesday 27 January 1778.
Mr Alderman Plomer nunc.

      Edward Jones by Wm Payne C. chd by Thos Musgrave Overseer of Walthamstow in Essex for begetting Sarah Hedge Single
3s/4d Wo: of Walthamstow ~~to~~ with Child of wch she is now pregnant (bro^t on the W^t of Peregrine Bertie Esq. C. back'd by Ld Mayor 27 Janry last)—to find Surety for his Appearance at the next
Essex Qua^r Sess^s of the Peace to be holden for s^d Co: to abide & Perform such Order or Orders as shall be made in pursuance of an Act of Parliam^t pass'd in the 18 year of 2 Eliz: concerning Bastards begotten & born out of lawful Matrimony – bailed as under
R   Edward Jones of Purple Lane Westm^r Gent^n   £ 40
      Robert Wilson White Cross St Vict^r   £ 20
      Moses Long of Walbrook London Gent^n   £ 20

John Milbourn, Houghton Batley} WC: Wm Payne C. chd by him picking the pocket of [blank] Wood ~~for pic~~ of a Linen Handkf—Va^e 1s. Wood was not now pres^t they were ord^d for fu^r Exon 'till to morrow.

Isabella Ux Geo: Gray WC same C. charged by him for stopping sev^l Gent. in Chancery Lane (being much in Liquor) &

at last picking up one Man in part[icul]ar – she alledged being insensible thro' Liquor & therefore not knowing what she did – she app^d to have behaved improperly in the W^h Ho:– disch^d.

2s.   Aff^ts John Russell, John Pitt

1s.   Aff^t Mary Harding

Geo: Aplin ~~by Wm Payne C~~: charged by Eliz: Barnard Dau[ghte]r of Mary Barnard Wid° (a Child 11 Years Old next Month) says she has slept with him sev^l times & that he has hurted her very much, her Mother slept with a Woman in ano^r Room – says he used her very ill in bed – he ask'd her if she blead – he hurted her in her Body – ~~he put~~ she told him that she did blead – says one Night when he hurt her she cryed out and was heard by the Woman in the next Room – she did not give him leave to hurt her – she bid him let her alone – he hurt her with his private parts in hers – he laid for a great while with her Mother & her but never offered any thing to her when her mother was in bed – she says after being hurt she told it to one Mrs. Hayney (who lodges in the Ho:) – she told her Mo^r who (she says) co^d not bel: it – she told her Mo^r she was hurt, & yet her Mother wo^d not look at her,—Hannah Madden Grandmother to the Child app^d with her – she ack^d to have pawned 2 Pair of the Pris^rs Breeches for 4s. with^t any Inducem^t or Order & spent the money – she says he first hurt her with his fingers & then lay upon her and hurt her – ~~it app~~. the pris^r app^d Voluntarily was not in Custody & agreed to appear on Thursday

1s.   Susannah Taylor by Wm Wilson C. chd by John Bates (on Ld Mayors W^t of 24th) for an Assault, agreed & disch^d.

Mr Nash attended WP.

Sir Thomas Hallifax. Wednesday 28 January 1778.
Marg^t Aldridge, Ann Nutt, Eliz Palmer, Mary Smith, Sarah Davis, Mary Monk[96]} WC by Will: Payne C. chd by him for severally wandering abroad & picking up Men – Aldridge & Nutt were d^d – Palmer was apprehended as a Vagrant – Smith having a Child was compassionated & d^d – Monk was com^d to B untill a Court—Sarah Akers – charged as a Vagrant

Chas Caird by d°C. chd by David Tipping for feloniously

---

96. A check mark appears beside each name, save for Palmer which has a small dash.

stealing a quart pewter pot Val: [blank] his property –Will: Tipping saw the Pot in the Pris^{rs} Custody – Mr Tipping declined a Prosecution – he was therefore d^d

Pat^k Bradey[97] by d^{o}C. chd by Jno Davenport for feloniously stealing five pieces of Beech Wood Val: 6d. his property –Will: Young a Watchman took him with the Wood upon him

RX Jno Davenport of White Friars L. Coal Merch^t }
 Will: Young – Queens Head C^t Strand – Porter } £10

1s. Will: Brown by d^{o}C. chd by Dorothy Wallace for an Ass^t – the Parties having ag^d—he was d^d

Jno Wilbank, <u>Haughton Batley</u>} by d^{o}C. chd by him for sever-ally attempting to pick pockets – Batley was chd by Benj: Wood with stealing a linen handkerchief – they were both sent to the Marine Society

1s. Aff^t Jno Baptiste Orange

Jos: Angel Driver of a Cart N° 187 produced by Jno Martin his Ma^r – sum^d ads Ben: Strange for taking more than his fare for carrying two pipes of Wine from the Custom House Key to Coventry Street – he took half a Guinea – the fare was 8s – postponed

1s. Thos Brown bro^t up on a W^t of the Lord Mayor of the 24th Inst:– chd by Thos Smith Overseer of St And^w Holborn – was d^d – the C. swore to a Compromise—and an Order from the Vestry Co^t to get the W^t d^d

nil Isaac Bacchara by Ja^s Jewster C. chd by Ja^s ~~Nixon~~ Nisbett for assaulting him – Nisbett was struck by somebody, but he co^d not speak to the Man – d^d

P W^t ag^t Joseph Milton ats Alexander Melville Ass^t

Mr Houstoun Attended TH

Mr Alderman Plumbe. Thursday 29 January 1778.
1s. Aff^t Jno Banjer

---

97. The case proceeds to the Old Bailey as a petty larceny case. See *OBP*, February 1778, trial of Patrick Brady (t17780218–57).

Mary Cooper – Wm Styles Jones C. chd by Phebe Holden – the Prosecutor not being present

P W^t ag^t Jno Wetherick ads Reb^a Cordery Ass^t etc.

1s. D^o agt Will: King ads Will: Carmon – Ass^t etc.

1s. Back'd a Middx Warrant Per Mr Dyot.

Jno Kendal who was examined on Friday—now surrendered himself according to the engagement of his Ma^r – there having been nothing transpired to discover any further Circumstances of the Robbery he was d^d & the Goods &c ordered to be restored.

Stephen Paskin[98] WC R^d Dawson C. chd by Thos King & Thos Dean for feloniously stealing a Ham Va: 10s. & upwards the Property of s^d Thos King – on their Oaths com^d to D^{o}C:

RX Thos King of Bull & Mouth St^r Cheesem^r £ 20
          for himself & Thos Dean
R^d Dawson &c.   10

Rhodes Attended   SP

Mr Alderman Kennett. Friday 30 January 1778.
Mary Davis, Mary White, Sarah Pitts, Jane Payne, Ann Farmer, Reb^a Liddell, Jane Thomas[99]} WC by Will: Payne C. chd by him for severally wandering & picking up Men – Davis picking up Men in the Temple betw^n 6 & 7 – Mary White same time in Fleet Street – Pitts the same betw: 12 & 1 – Jane Payne chd by Saml Plant W^{h}man before 12 in Bolt Court – Ann Farmer taken with Pedley below – Reb^a Liddell & J. Thomas betw 1 & 2 this Morn^g Davis, Pitts, Liddell, and Thomas were com^d to B.

1s. Aff^t John Betts.

Geo: Steventon, Jno Pedley, Will: Bean, Ja^s Denton, Geo: Wayte, Ja^s Garfitt} d^{o}C by d^{o}C. chd by him – Steventon for behaving rudely to some Women in the Street – Pedley for being fo^d with a Woman – Steventon app^d to be a Sailor on board the Sterling Castle they were d^d – Bean an Appr: to a

98. The case proceeds to the Old Bailey. See *OBP*, February 1778, trial of Stephen Pascan (t17780218–7).
99. Check marks appear beside Davis, Pitts, Liddell and Thomas, who were all sent to Bridewell.

Packer – Denton to a Bricklayer – and Geo: Wayte to a Butcher – they were d[d]

1s.   Aff[t] Will: Dean

Jno Watson sum[d] ads Jos: Dolphin Carman for refusing to pay the Cartage of ~~three~~ 2 Loads from Keys to Mincing Lane ord[d] 5s. 8d. for 2 Loads & 1s. Cha[rge][s].

Chch Wdns of Saint Michael Bassishaw sum[d] ads Ann Myatt for relief – dism[d]

Jno Bailey[100] by Tho[s] Wood C. chd by Rob: Morphet for feloniously stealing ten pairs of worsted Stockings Val 10s. his property – on his Oath com[d] to WC.

RX   Rob: Morphet of Lombard Street L. Hosier   £ 10
    Tho[s] Wood N[o] 33 Clements L. Peruke Ma[r]   10

P   Job Humphreys by Jos: Coward C. chd by him for gross abuse & refusing to pay his reckoning – d[d]

Mary Cooper WC by Will: Stiles Jones C. chd by Sus[a] Edwards for feloniously stealing a petticoat – there was no proof – d[d]

Ja[s] Scott produced the Driver of his Coach N[o] 243 sum[d] ads R[d] Banner for wilfully driving the s[d] Coach ag[st] him – Solomon Levy – Castle Street White Chapel Ord[d] to pay 17s. here on Monday

1s.   Ann Wilson by Jonas Parker C. chd by Maximinian Monge (on a Middx W[t] back'd by Ald[n] Plumbe) for assaulting Jane Lacute an Infant – dismissed – there did not appear a reason for the Complt

M[r] Beach attended BK

M[r] Alderman Kirkman. Monday 2 February 1778.
    Will: Taylor WC by Jno Prockter C. chd by Sam[l] Williams for an Ass[t]

(No Attendance)

M[r] Beach attended RH

---

100. The case proceeds to the Old Bailey. See *OBP*, February 1778, trial of John Bailey (t17780218-8).

Tho[s] Edwards[101] by John Apethorpe C. chd by Tho[s] Batlin upon suspicion of feloniously stealing 15 Yards of black silk ribbon Val: 3s. and sev[l] other pieces of Ribbon his property and also of R[d] Adams – the C. went to his Lodgings – on their Oaths com[d] to WC.

RX   Tho[s] Butlin of Wood Street L. Ribbon Weaver   £ 20
      Jno Apethorpe   }
      Jno Harper   WC.   } Each £ 10

M[r] Alderman Oliver. Tuesday 3 February 1778.

1s.   Aff[t] Stephens

       Joseph Rolls & Eleanor his Wife PC by John Dawson C. chd by him with wandring abroad & lodging in the open Air hav[g] no visible way of living on his Oath com[d] to B per W[t] till Thursday then to be passed

1s.   Aff[t] Tho[s] Wood

2s.   Aff[t] s Kinsmin & Calvert

       Eliz[h] White, Mary Fulcher} by Tho[s] Linton C. chd by him with begging this day in the Par of S[t] Michael Bassishaw. com[d] on his oath to B till Thursday

2s.   William Bolton, Solomon Hudson} WC by W[m] Steward C. chd by George Sibley with assault[g] a Person not present. reprimanded & d[d].

1s.   Aff[t] Guillimard jun[r][?]

3s.   D[o] Isiah Aaron, Solomon Zechariah, David Hart

       Tho[s] Barnwell[102] WC by W[m] Stiles Jones C. chd by ~~him~~ Samuel Edwards for fel[y] steal[g] ab[t] 40[lb] W[t] of Lead, Va: 3s. & upwards the Constable detected him & also Charles Stagg found him in the House & the Lead laying near him, he confess'd to John Brockholes & Stag to have taken him – the Lead is the Property of Sam[l] Edwards – on their Oaths com[d] to D[o]C: — Jn[o] Gaskin also was sworn

---

101. The case proceeds to the Old Bailey. See *OBP*, February 1778, trial of Thomas Edwards (t17780218–10).
102. The case proceeds to the Old Bailey. See *OBP*, February 1778, trial of Thomas Barnwell (t17780218–30).

RX   Saml Edwards of Epping in Essex Vict.   £ [blank]
       Jn° Gaskin N° 10 Fleet Lane Optician   }
       Jn° Brockholes N° 12 D° Baker   }
       Wm Styles Jones N° 40 D° Broker   } ea £10
       Chas Stagg N° 3 Turnagain Lane Peruke Maker }

Mr Alderman Oliver, Mr Alderman Plomer, adhuc Tuesday
      Saml Wallis the Owner of a Shop & House in Shoe Lane, in
      wch Shop on a Search, was found about three Quarters of a
      hundred Weight of new Copper, & also a Quantity of pewter
      melted down – he co^d not give an Account of the persons he
      bo^t this Copper of, their Worships therefore appointed him
      so to do on Tuesday the 24th day of this Instant, February in
      this Room at 12 O'Clock ~~at night~~ at Noon—& in Case such
      Persons were not then Produced by him, he wo^d be adjudged
      guilty of a Misdemeanor – ~~the Copper~~ & it was ordered that
      the Ch. Wardens of St. Bridget als Brides where this Copper
      was found do attend here and receive the Copper & advertize
      it & as the Law directs

      ~~W^t ag^t Isaac Goodburn ads~~

1s.   Ja^s Goodale [blank] Jn° Williams C. chd by Eliz: Sarah Butler
      (on Ld Mayor's W^t Yesterday) for an Ass^t – ag^d & d^d.

1s.   Aff^t Mary Ann Mercer.

      Eliz: Jones, Eliz: Brown} WC by Will: Payne C. chd by him
      for severally wandering abroad and picking up Men – were
      reprim^ded & d^d

      Nash Attended   R.O.

Mr Ald^n Plomer
1s.   W^t ag^t Hen: Grotage ads Chas Plyer Ass^t etc.

      ~~D° ag^t [blank] Smith ads~~

Sir Watkin Lewes by Mr Alderman Plomer. Wednesday 4 February
      1778.
P   Jane Rous WC by Danl Osman C. chd by Mark Witts for
      making a disturbance—at his House– she Promis'd to behave
      well in future, she was d^d.

nil   Jno Morgan d°C by d°C. chd by Will: Hull W^chman for ass^ting him & striking him with a Stick or Cane – said, that Mr Morgan pushed him – the Ald^n said, there was no Charge – d^d

Saml Cherry sum^d by Sarah his Wife for ass^{t}ing her – ag^d to allow her 3s. a Week – and to separate

Geo. Parsons pr. by John Edwards C. chd by Philip Lowen pastry Cook in Red[cross] Street, for stealing a 3^{dy} [three-penny] Cheese Cake he was a Boy ab^t 13 years old & being willing to go to Sea, was sent back to be carried to the Marine Society.

Geo: Landon Baynham WC by Jno Allen C. chd by Abram Lialto for refusing to pay him the Money due for his fare for carrying him in his hackney Coach from Ludgate Hill to Leman Street Goodman's Fields

George Freeman sum^d ads Urbanus Beachfield to produce the Driver of his Cart N° 5751 for permitting the Night Soil to run out of the s^d Cart in Jewry Street – adj^d till tomorrow

p^d 3s. for an Advertizem^t of this Linen	Eliz: Brooks, Sarah Edwards} WC by R^d Dawson C. chd by Wm Ja^s Burrows upon suspicion of feloniously stealing a Quantity of Linen—wch Brooks offered to ~~Brooks~~ Burrows to pawn – remanded until Monday – A.I.—21 Y^{ds}.

1s.   Jane Randel, John Watson} by Richd Dawson C. –they charged each other with an Ass^t – d^d

Mr Alderman Plomer for Sr Watkin Lewes.   ad huc Wednesday 4 February 1778.
        Thos Lovegrove ~~Thomas~~, Edward Beedle} WC by Will: Payne C. chd by him – Thomas for assaulting him—& swearing 5 prophane Oaths – Parish of Saint Bride – rem^{d}ed till tomorrow – Beedle was chd with singing Ballads in St Paul's Chch Yard – d^d

Mr Houston attended   WP

Mr Alderman Plomer. Thursday 5 February 1778.
        Joseph Mitten WC Wm Payne C. and Ch^d by John Javine for assaulting and beating him – rem^d & d^d

3s.   Affid^t Hooper, D^o Miller, D^o Dangerfield

Mary Smith, Sarah Withers, Eliz: Drummond, Elizth Wright, Elizth Phillips, Ann Gardner, Elizth Carpenter, Martha Holdsworth, Elizth Wood, Mary Baker, Myre Gordon[103]} WC Wm Payne C. and Charg'd by him for being loose idle and disorderly Women and Common Prostitutes Severally picking up Men last – Smith was taken in Fleet Street—but not being known—d^d – Gordon was apprehended in the Temple – she was d^d – Port Road Island – Gardiner, Carpenter, Holdsworth & Drummond com^d to B – the others d^d

W^t ag^t Thos Knight ads Cath: Harrod – Ass^t

Eleanor Andrews[104] by Jos: Thompson C. chd by Saml Kempson for feloniously stealing four Yards of printed Cotton Val: 10s.—his property – on the Oaths of Kempson & the Constable com^d to WC.

RX   Saml Kempson of Fleet Street L. Linen Draper   } £
      Jos: Thompson – Bride's Passage – Watch Maker   } 10

Moses Leater produced the Driver of his hackney Coach N° 225 – Jno Meter – sum^d ads Samuel Fenning for refusing to go when required—on the 30th January last – adjourned till tomorrow but afterw^{ds} the Complt was withdrawn.

Mary Walmsley chd by Will: Payne for lodging in the open Air – Parish of St. Catharine Cree Church – Ord^d to go to her Parish

Mr Rhodes attended   WP

Mr Alderman Thomas. Friday 6 February 1778.
Jane Mandy by Thos Linton C. chd by him for begging – granted a pass to Abingdon

1s.   Aff^t House

1s.   W^t ag^t Hannah Faries[?] ads Mary Powell Ass^t etc.

P   Enoch Mason WC by Jno Prockter C. chd by Ja^s Clarke for feloniously stealing a piece of Cheese – there was some doubt of the Intent as he had taken the Cheese off the Window and

103. A check mark appears beside each name, and that beside Elizabeth Wood has been made an 'X'.
104. The case proceeds to the Old Bailey. See *OBP*, February 1778, trial of Eleanor Andrews (t17780218–56).

carried it into the Shop & then took it out again – he was disch^d.

Jno Brown sum^d by Jno Fleming Street Keeper for using his Cart in this City – not being licensed – ag^d

1s.   Thos Knight by Moses Orme C. chd by Cath: Harrod (on Ald^n Plomer's W^t Yesterday) for an Ass^t – it app^d friv^s – the W^t was d^d.

1s.   W^t ag^t John Cotton ads Reb^a Ansty Ass^t on And^w Richardson.

Mr Nash attended   N Thomas

~~Mr Aldn. Peckham~~ Mr Alderman Hayley. Monday 9 February 1778. Sarah Edwards[105] [blank] by Richd Dawson C. chd by Will: Ja^s Burrows upon suspicion of feloniously stealing a piece of Linen—wch she offered to pawn with Burrows – Thos Pitt Stead app^d & owned the Linen – the prisoner, after much hesitation, confess'd to have received from Mr Stead's Servant, Rob: Williams, this Linen – Bern^d Stead's property – on the Oaths of Stead & Barrow – committed to WC.

RX   Thos Pitt Stead – Friday Street Lo Linen Draper £ 20
       W. J. Burrows – Barbican Pawnbroker   20

nil   David Wilson, Tabitha Kemp } WC by Will: Payne C. chd by Eliz: Milner – there was no regular Compl^t – d^d

1s.   Jno Dover, Sus^a Cooper} d^oC by d^oC. chd by him – being taken together in an indecent Situation in a Court – they were reprim^ded & d^d

Sarah Borke d^oC by d^oC. chd by him for picking up Men – she had not been here lately, though formerly an old Offender – d^d

Ann Davis, Jane Morgan} d^oC by d^oC. chd by him for the like Offence – they were not known – d^d

Reb^a Cecil by d^oC. chd by him for wandering abroad & lodging in the open Air

Abram Wooller d^oC by d^oC. chd by him for picking Pockets

---

105. The case proceeds to the Old Bailey. See *OBP*, February 1778, trial of Robert Williams, Sarah Edwards (t17780218–6).

last Night – seven handkerchief (several mark'd) were fo^d upon him – rem^{d}ed till tomorrow

Richd Davis, Jno Stumel, Jno Wigmore} WC by Will: Payne C. chd by him for attempting to pick several Pockets – the Father of Davis app^d and took him away by the Alderman's permission – the other two were rem^{d}ed till tomorrow

Jno Crozier, Thomas Dennis, Samuel Blakey} by d^{o}C. chd as the last above – two handkerchiefs were fo^d upon Dennis – they were rem^{d}ed

P Optmy Wadsworth WC by Will: Owen C. chd by Eliz: Dickens for grossly insulting her – he ask'd Pardon – d^d

Jno Squires d^{o}C by Richd Dawson C. chd by Isaac Hyams & Will: ~~Weell~~ Wing for assaulting ~~him~~ s^d Hyam & damaging his Goods – Jacob Levi was sworn an Interpreter, as Hyams co^d not speak English – the prisoner was com^d to d^{o}C.

1s. Mary Heath by R^d Gusson C. chd by Jno Flude for making a disturbance—in his House – rem^{d}ed 'till tomorrow

Jos: Innis, Will: Fuller 667, Jno Elborough, Alex^r Harris, Thos Snow} hackney Coachmen – sum^d by Will: Payne for severally plying between Freeman's Court & the West End of Cornhill – ~~Innis~~ Payne could not speak to the Driver – d^d – Fuller was spoken positively to by Payne – Fuller was conv^d in the penalty of 10s.—wch he paid – Harris was sworn to, for plying on the 29th January last – conv^d in the like fine – p^d

Mary Dowland, Bridget Dowling} charged by Will: Wright Chch Wden of Saint Bridget for working in the House & taking the Money – d^d

Mr Beach attended GeH.

Mr Alderman Newnham. Tuesday 10 February 1778.
~~Eliz Sutton~~

Abram Wooller, Jno Stummel, Jno Wigmore, Jno Crozier[106]} WC by Will: Payne C. chd by him for severally attempting to pick Pockets—on Sunday Night – seven handkerchiefs – one

---

106. Check marks appear beside Stummel, Wigmore and Crozier's names, but the latter two checks are crossed through as 'X'.

RX   silk & 6 Linen – were fo^d upon Wooller who was com^d to D^{o}C
for stealing these handkerchiefs Val: 3s. property unknown
RX   Will: Payne &c.   £ 10

Eliz: Wilson, Eliz: Lee, Mary Green} d^{o}C by d^{o}C. chd by him
for severally wandering abroad & picking up Men – they were
all upon promises of Amendment d^d

P   Mary Wilks WC by Stephen Pyle C. chd by William Everard
Vict^r for being very abusive in his House & throw^g the Pot
thro the Window & assault^g some Persons in his House, reprimanded & d^d

nil   Samuel Thomas WC Robt Wilton C. chd by Francis Aspinal
for wilfully break[in]g his Windows & assault^g him, they app^d
both in fault d^d

Sarah Hancock[107] WC by R^d Greenfield C. chd by ~~Thos~~ Jno
Scanderett, for feloniously stealing 4 quart pewter 4 pint Do
Pots Val: [illegible] s. his property – a prosecution was declined
at first— but afterw^{ds} the prisoner was com^d to d^{o}C –on the
Oaths of Scanderett, Martha Fielde & Geo: Sandey – she was
com^d to WC
RX   Jno Scanderett of Fetter L. Vict: for self & Fields   £ 20
RX   She was detained for stealing 3 Quart, 3 pint & ½ pint Val: 4s.
Sandey's property
Geo: Sandey – Fetter L. Vict: £ 10

Mary Beachman by Jno Sheppard C. chd by Jno Acton for
feloniously stealing a flat Iron Val: 10d. his property – she had
a Child at her breast – she was d^d

P   Jno Bowden PC by Will: Blackmore C. chd by Will: Worgent
for making a disturbance in his Public House – d^d

1s.   Aff^t Harper

Thos Brown sum^d ads. Ja^s Hartfield a hackney Coachman for
refusing to pay him his fare for being in his Service upwards
of an hour – adjourn'd

1s.   Jos: Jones by Jno Brown C. chd by Elias Lazarus (on Ald^n
Plomer's W^t 7th Inst:) for an Ass^t – the W^t was d^d

107. The case proceeds to the Old Bailey. See *OBP*, February 1778, trial of Sarah Hancock
(t17780218–9).

Hugh Hart, Ann Ux:} PC by Ja^s Munday C. chd by Mary Pentelow upon suspicion of feloniously stealing sev^l things – rem^{d}ed 'till tomorrow

Geo: Palmer by Jno Fleming Street Keeper C. chd by him for driving a Cart without Name or Number – they withdrew and agreed – d^d

Han^h Chapman WC by Stephen Pine C. chd by a Person not now present – she was d^d

P   Ja^s Welch by Thos Linton C. chd by Ebenezer Brathwaite Overseer of Saint Vedast Foster Lane (on Ld Mayor's W^t Yesterday) for unlawfully begetting Mary Welch, single woman of that Parish with Child wch is likely to become chargeable thereto – bailed as below.

RX   James Welch N° 3 Kings Head C^t Gutter L. Lab: £ 40
       Arthur Samuels of Bambridge S^t – Lab: }
       Ja^s Debin of Long Lane N° 62 L—Cook   } 20

[blank] Buefoy sum^d ads Will: Smith Carman for refusing to pay the Cartage of a Load from Smart's Key to Cupers Bridge – Ord^d the fare & Charges.

Mr Nash attended   NN

Mr Alderman Lee by Mr Alderman Plomer. Wednesday 11 February 1778.
       Sarah Martin WC by Jno Prockter C. chd by him for making a disturbance in Saint Pauls Church Yard at one this Morning – d^d

Thos Asbury app^d for Mr Finch sum^d ads Thos Witenor a hackney Coachman for refusing to pay the fare from Moorgate to the Turnpike on the City Road—and back to Bazinghall Street the Gro^d is to be measured

Thos Bagley, Thos Hadley} WC by Samuel Mabbeley C. chd by ~~him~~ Carey Stafford upon suspicion of feloniously stealing several Iron Hoops the property of said Carey Stafford

Hugh Hart, Ann Ux:} WC by Ja^s Munday C. chd by Mary Pentelow as Yesterday – there was no proof – d^d

Ann Harding WC: Rob: Croft C. chd by Eleanor Greenhow, for feloniously stealing a black Sattin Cloak Va [blank] her

125

Property & a Shift Va [blank] the P[ro]perty of Eliz: Jones & a pair of black worsted Stockings va [blank] the Property of [blank] she did not chuse to ~~purchase~~ prosecute – d[d]

1s.   W[t] ag[t] Jno Eldridge ads Peirson Whelan Ass[t]

M[r] Rhodes attended   WP

1s.   D[o] ag[t] Tho[s] Nash & Cha[s] Moore ads Robert Boston for unlaw-fully embezzilling Monies reced

M[r] Alderman Wooldridge. Thursday 12 February 1778.

Ald[n] Wright   Fra[s] Franklin sum[d] ads Jno Fleming Street Keeper for using his narrow wheeled Cart in this City – they with-drew & settled

gave a poor   Tho[s] Bagley, Tho[s] Hadley} chd as Yesterday by Carey
Woman 1s.   Stafford – the former was sent to Sea & the other d[d]

gave a poor
Man also 1s.

gave also 2s.   Mary King, Ann King} WC by Will: Payne C. chd by
more to a   him for severally wandering abroad and picking up Men
poor Woman

P[s108]   W[t] ag[t] Tho[s] Patey ads Eliz: Ux: Will: Kitchen –Ass[t]

Mary Hummerstone by Will: Hummerstone C. chd by him, for no Offence – d[d] – but afterw[ds] passed

M[r] Rhodes attended.   TW

M[r] Alderman Hart. Friday 13 February 1778.

Jos[h] Moore, John Paul C. and Ch[d] by Geo Griffin for making a Noise and Disturbance in his house last Night and wilfully breaking his Windows, Black Swan S[t] Paul's C. Yard Adj[d] frivolous and D[d].

James Startupt Rob[t] Lee C. and Ch[d] by Robert Haskins for assaulting and Wounding him ~~with~~ on his Neck with a Knife or some other offensive Weapon remanded 'till Monday for further E[xamination]

---

108. It is possible that 1s. was entered initially.

Rob[t] White Jos[h] Jefferson C. and Ch[d] by W[m] Press his late Ma[r] for wilfully misbehaving himself in his Service and imbezling his Money   White undertook to pay his Ma[r] by Installm[ts] and was D[d].

2s.   Aff[t] Impey and ano[r]

1s.   D[o] Comerford

Abram Evans [blank] Jno Williams C. chd by Joseph Cookson for feloniously stealing a flitch of Bacon Val: [blank] his property – in regard to a most excellent Character—d[d]

Sarah Hayley, Cath: Ashley, Mary Cloud, Eliz: Taylor, Eliz: Parsons, Eliz: Edwards, Mary Giles, Mary Dodson, Mary Simpson, Ann George, Charity Sharp, Mary Tidsell, Ann McDaniel[109]} WC by Will: Payne C. chd by him for severally wandering abroad & picking up Men – Hayley was disch[d] upon her promise of Amendment – Cloud & Taylor were not known and therefore d[d] – Parsons and Edwards app[d] to be old Offenders and were com[d] to B – Giles, Dodson & Simpson were apprehended together, making a disturbance – George, Sharp & Tidsell were d[d] – McDaniel, Parsons & Edwards were afterw[ds] d[d]

Tho[s] Pating WC by d[o]C. chd by Eliz Ux: Will: Kitching (on Ald[n] Wooldridge's W[t]) for an Ass[t]

Jacob Sibley d[o]C by d[o]C. chd by him for lodging in the open Air ~~sent to the Parish~~ He desir'd to be sent to Sea and was accordingly recom[d] to the Marine Society

Eliz[th] Whitworth, John Sheppard C. and Charg'd by Mary May for knowingly and designedly by false Pretences obtaining from her 5s. 6d. with intent to defraud the s[d] Mary May thereof

1s.   Warr[t] ag[t] Tho[s] Startup ads Marg[t] Strong per Ass[t]

1s.   Warr[t] v John Driver ads George Craig per Ass[t]

M[r] Rhodes attended   J H

P   W[t] ag[t] Esias Israel ads R[d] Cockle for steal[g] half a Gua

---

109. A check mark appears beside each name except McDaniel. The checks beside Parsons and Edwards have been crossed through as 'X'.

Mr Alderman Wright. Monday 16 February 1778.

    Jno Heyliger WC by Jno Paul C. chd by him for wandering abroad & lodging in the open Air – Par: St Mary Magdalen Old Fish Street – Ord^d (being a Foreigner) to be taken to that Parish, to be provided for

    Mary McDaniel d^{o}C by Harman Smith C. chd by David Davis upon suspicion of feloniously stealing a guinea in gold – on his Oath committed to d^{o}C.

RX   David Davis – Mutton C^t Maiden L. Wood S^t
    Shoemaker   £ 10

P   Ja^s Startup WC by Rob: Lee C. chd by Rob: Haskins for assaulting & wounding him in the Neck – the Father of Haskins offered to release him upon asking Pardon – d^d

1s.   Thos Startup by Rob: Wilton C. chd by Marg^t Strong (on Ald^n Hart's W^t 13th Inst.) for an ag & d^d [sic] Assault– Sarah Roberts saw an assault com^d by Startup, who had hold of Strong's Head – they ag^d.

    Rose Beaumont WC Wm Payne C. chd by him for wandering and picking up Men last Night in the Temple

    Jno Burn by d^{o}C. chd by him for making a disturbance in the Street – he was d^d

1s.   W^t ag^t Morris Savage ads Ja^s Smith a hackney Coachman for refusing to pay 2s. –his fare – there having been 3 Sum^s

2s.   Francis Manning, John Aked} by Jonas Parker C. chd by ~~him~~ each other for an Ass^t – d^d

    Geo: Sullivan PC by Jno Meredith C. chd by Tim^y Callaghan for ass^{t}ing & falsely imprisoning him – d^d

P   Thos Baker, Eliz: Haycock} d^{o}C by d^{o}C. chd as follows – Baker gave the 1st Charge – for making a disturbance – they ag^d & d^d

1s.   Will: Thomas, by R^d Arnold C. chd by Sarah Bilham (on Ld Mayor's W^t) for an Ass^t – d^d

    Marg^t Supple d^{o}C by Ja^s Newland C. chd by him for an Ass^t – Eliz: Winter charged her improperly – d^d

P   Jos: Barnsley PC by Levi Moses C. chd by Jno Ja^s Barber for ass^ting him – d^d.

Chas Mitchell Do D^oC: same C. chd by Bazil Righton & Hannah Dixon for feloniously stealing a Ham – rem^ded till tomorrow

Mary Hand by Wm Cockman C. chd by Saml Acton, for knowingly and designedly pawning or unlawfully disposing of 2 Shirts, seven pairs of Stockings & o^r Things his property – d^d

Mr Beach Attended   Thos Wright

Mr Alderman Wooldridge by Mr Alderman Pugh. Friday 26 February 1779.

gave a poor   Eliz Moses PC by Adam Shackle C. chd by him for
Woman 1s.   picking up Men – d^d

Eliz Baker d^oC. by d^oC. chd by him for lodging in the open Air – d^d

Jacob Jonas PC by Thos Burket C. chd by Thos Jones and Thos Holbrook for feloniously stealing a silk Gown, a linen Napkin, a quilted Petticoat, a muslin Apron and sundry other things – rem^ded till Tuesday.

Geo: Medler WC by Rob: Roe C. chd by Will: Bowker for stealing a Shirt, two pair of Stockings his property – he consented to go for a Soldier

1s.   Chris^r Robson by Will: Martin C. chd by him for ass^ting him – d^d

Marg^t Flinn WC by Jos: Coward C. chd by him on suspicion of feloniously stealing twelve copper half pence – d^d

Mary Holmes d^oC by R^d Greenfield C. chd by Sarah Kirke for unlawfully disposing of some Linen entrusted with her to work up – being an old Woman d^d

Middx   Thos Murphy by Will: Payne C. chd by Jos: Tomlins ~~for~~ on a violent Suspicion of stealing ~~one~~ two pieces of Irish Linen Value £7 & upw^{ds} the property of Peter Fair – com^d to d^oC.

RX   Peter Fair Lambeth Wash Tambour Worker   } £ 10
     Joseph Tomlins – his Servt   }

1s.   Mary Jones WC by Geo: Frost C. chd by him for picking up Men – d^d

W^t agst Eliz: Whitmore ads Sarah Ransom – Ass^t

Back'd a Middx W^t per Sir John Fielding

Mary Neale by Ja^s Oseland C. chd by a Baker with stealing some bread – granted a pass to Bristol.

W^t ag^t A: Sanguinetti ads Mendes de Costa.

Mr Beach att^ded   EP

Mr Alderman Wright. Monday 1 March 1779.

    Richard James[110] WC by John Couchman C. chd by Rob: Haynes for stealing 3^{lb} W^t of Snuff Val: 10s. his ~~the~~ property – com^d to d°C.

RX   Rob: Haynes of Aldersgate St Tobacconist }
    John Couchman – D° – Taylor   } Ea. £10

1s.   Aff^t R^d Eyles

1s.   W^t agst Thos Jordan ads. Eliz: Lloyd Newton Ass^t

Edwd Stewart, Eliz: Bidmate} by Chris^r Manning C. chd by Mary Brown for being concealed in a Closet in her Room with intent to commit felony – there was no proof agst either of them – d^d

1s.   John Hopkins by Jno Edwards C. chd by John Burbidge ~~for~~ an Officer of Excise for obstructing him in the execution of his Duty, in seizing six Casks of Molasses Spirits – he asked pardon – d^d

Geo: Conway d°C by d°C. chd by Jno Sheppard as a disorderly Person – ag^d to go to Sea

Ann Taylor d°C by John Meers C. chd by Ja^s Suffolk for making a disturbance in his House – she was a Pauper of St Mary Magdalen Old Fish Street – d^d

---

110. The case proceeds to the Old Bailey. See *OBP*, April 1779, trial of Richard James (t17790404–12).

gave this   Joyce Golding d°C by Geo: Frost C. chd by him for
Woman 1s.   picking up Men – d^d
by Order

1s.   Aff^t Geo: Fickel

Thos Jennings [blank] by Jno Hunt C. chd by Chas Allen for
desertion from the Northamptonshire Militia. A Certif[icate]
from the Commanding Officer was produc'd that he was
allowed leave of Absence – d^d

Sarah Holt d°C by Will: Hawkins C. chd by Will: Swansborough & Rob: Welch for stealing 14 Yds of printed Cotton Val:
40s. s^d S[wansborough]'s property – rem^ded till tomorrow

Abraham Sanguinetti by Jos: Gates charged by Mendes de
Costa (on Ald^n Plomer's W^t 26th Febr^y) on suspicion of feloniously stealing a Banker's Note drawn by John Hollingworth,
for £20 – the Mre was settled by the Minister of the Synagogue

1s.   W^t ag^st Thos Trip ads John Green – Ass^t etc.

2s.   Will: Gravel, Will: Lee} WC by Jno Squire C. chd by a Person
not now present – d^d

David Morgan by Jno Davis C. chd by him as an idle, disorderly person – referred to the Comm^rs

Rebecca Tinley by Wm Strongatarms C. chd by Will: Long for
ass^ting several persons in Field Lane – d^d

1s.   Peace W^t agst. Adrienne Julie Roux Devin ads Nich^s Pierre her
Husband.

Geo: Venables by R^d Streetin C. chd by Anth^y Westray for
feloniously stealing a Box of Lace – rem^ded till tomorrow

Magdalen Shays by Will: Martin C. chd by Thos Flude for
stealing a Tea board Val: 1s. his property – d^d

P   John Grant by Thos Ponsonby C. chd by Jno Joyce for
attempting to commit a rape – the Woman not being present –
d^d.

Mr Beach Att^d   TW   Thomas Wright

131

Mr Alderman Pugh. Tuesday 2 March 1779.

Eliz: Bidmate by Chris^r Manning C. chd by Mary Brown & Eliz: Collins on suspicion of feloniously stealing a few pewter Plates – the felony (if any) was com^d, 18 Months ago – d^d

1s. John Rawson WC by [blank] Silk C. chd by James Priestland for an Ass^t – d^d

1s. Benj: Barton by Will: Payne C. chd by Marg^t Newnham for an Ass^t – agreed & d^d

1s. Ind^d a W^t Middx from Justice Croft

Moses Hyams WC by Ja^s Taylor C. chd by Thos Herring for violently ass^ting him & wounding him in his hand – referred to the Comm^{rs}.

2s. Aff^t Marg^t Thomas bis.

+ nil W^t ag^t Mary Eyres ads Ann Bryant for pawning a Shirt entrusted her to make up.

Theophilus Bellas WC by Will: Payne C. chd by him as an idle disorderly person, fit to serve his Majesty.

1s. Aff^t Mary Wilson

Samuel Taylor, Will: Bryant} d^oC by d^oC. chd by him for attempting to pick Pockets – referred to the Comm^{rs} on Thursday

1s. Stephen Jennings by Wm Govan C. chd by Edwd Wright (on a W^t) for an Ass^t – ag^d & d^d

Jno Barlow, Edwd Goldsmith}PC by Hen: Cohen C. chd by him as idle & disorderly Persons & common Gamblers – referred to the Comm^{rs}.

Jacob Jonas[111] by Thos Burket C. chd by Thos Holbrook & Thos Jones for stealing a silk Gown, a Napkin, a quilted Petticoat & a muslin Apron & sundry other things Val: 40s. s^d Holbrooks property

111. Jonas was removed from the Poultry Compter to Newgate prison on 9 April. See Poultry Compter Calendar (April 1779), LMA: CLA/047/LJ/01/1077. The case proceeds to the Old Bailey. See *OBP*, April 1779, trial of Jacob Jonas (t17790404–11).

RX   Thos Holbrook – Old Bedlam Peruke Ma^r } £10
      Thos Jones – White hart C^t Bpsgate S^t }

      Geo: Venables WC by R^d Streetin C. chd by Anth^y Westray for
      feloniously stealing a Box of Lace – ag^d to go to Sea

1s.   John Fester by Joseph Gates C. chd by John Honeyball (on
      Ald^n Wright's W^t Yesterday) for an Ass^t – it was a dispute
      about the right to some Labour – d^d

      Sarah Holt by Will: Hawkins C. chd by Wm Swanborough &
      Rob: Welch for feloniously stealing 14 Y^{ds} of printed Cotton
      Val: 40s. s^d Swanborough's property – d^d

P   Saml Mee by Will: Payne C. chd by him for obstructing him
      in his Duty – d^d

      Jas Burgis by Jos: Gates C. chd by him for plying with his
      hackney Coach between Freeman's Court & the West End of
      Cornhill

nil   Richard Paget by Will: Payne C. chd by him for ass^{t}ing &
      knocking down a Lad in his presence d^d

      Ben: Fitter, Jno Mowett, R^d Jones} WC by Will: Payne C. chd
      by him as idle & disorderly persons & fit to serve the King –
      Ord^d to the Comm^{rs}.

      Mr Nash attended   EP

1s.   W^t ag^t Garrack Fitzpatrick ads. Mary Taylor

Mr Alderman Alsop by Mr Alderman Pugh. Wednesday 3 March 1779.
1s.   W^t v. Wm Knighburne[?] ats Stephen Folkes[?].

1s.   Search W^t for Richd Sprags House of Jarvis in little Britain for
      a Tea Chest.

1s.   Affidavit Cochild[?]

      Geo: Jennings, John Baker} by Wm Stronger being Idle Boys
      sent to Compter for tomorrow.

1s.   Aff^t Abraham Poupard

P   Agnus Vaines by Wm Payne C. by Marg^t Willis on Ald^n Sains-
       bury W^t for ass^t – frivolous & d^d

1s.   Aff^t Downes.

       Will: Hawkins sum^d by Thos Plant hackney Coachman for
       refusing to pay him for damage done to his Coach Glass –
       Ord^d to pay 4s. & 2s./6d. charges.

       Eliz: Waters by Will: Martin C. chd by Thos Wood on suspi-
       cion of stealing a Watch – for want of Evidence d^d

       John Stevens by Will: Arnold C. chd by him – being insane &
       wandering abroad – rem^{d}ed

       John Bowler by Walter Newbon C. chd by him as a fit person
       to serve the King – he app^d to be an Appr: – d^d.

       Mary Greenwood, Mary Gay} rem^{d}ed on Thursday were this
       day bro^t up – Fairbank did not appear – d^d

1s.   John Bunn by Elias Aaron C. chd by Thos Bunn (on Ald^n
       Plomer's W^t) for an Ass^t – frivolous & d^d

       Will: Hill by Will: Payne C. chd by him as a fit person to serve
       the King – it app^d that he constantly followed a young Lady
       (a Miss Gray) to the Meeting – that he ass^{t}ed her – he was a
       Married Man – referred to the Comm^{rs}.

1s.   Back'd a Middx W^t per Mr Justice Blackborow

1s.   W^t ag^t Henry Bench ads Joseph Samuel

       Mr Housetown attended   EP

Mr Alderman Bridgen by Mr Alderman Plomer. Thursday 4 March
       1779.
       Geo. Jennings, John Baker} Bro^t and Charg'd Yesterday by
       Wm Stronger C. for being idle Boys and Suspected Pilferers
       &c. rem^{d}ed 'till to Day.

       Jane Winbold by Will: Bruff C. chd by Thos James for feloni-
       ously stealing a quart pewter Pot his property – in pity to her
       Family, James declined a prosecution – d^d

       Chas Jarvis by Will: Payne C. chd by Richd Sprags (on a Search

W^t granted to search Jarvis's House for a Tea Chest, which was fo^d) but there was no reason to suppose Jarvis to be criminal – d^d

P   Danl McNaughton WC by Will: Martin C. chd by Jno Griffiths for an Ass^t – d^d

Mr Rhodes attended   WP

The Right Honourable Thomas Harley. Friday 5 March 1779. (No Attendance)

Mr Nash att^{d}ed

Mr Alderman ~~Bull~~ Townsend by Mr Alderman Plomer. Monday 8 March 1779.
Ann Overy WC by Jno Cruse C. chd by him for making a great Noise and Disturbance – she was a miserable Woman & promised to behave better in future – d^d.

P   Thos Baker [blank] by Jno Couchman C. chd by John Coulson (on Ald^n Pugh's W^t) for an Ass^t – d^d.

Will: Stevens WC by Isaac Gilbert C. chd by Walter Strong for stealing a linen handkerchief, sent on board the Tender

1s.   Sus^a Clifford by Will: Martin C. chd by Dinah Matthews (on Ald^n Pugh's W^t 6th Instant) for an Ass^t – ag^d & d^d

1s.   Back'd a Middlesex W^t per Mr Durden.

Eliz: Chandler, Eliz Wilson[112]} WC by Thos Croom C. chd by Rob: Whitby on suspicion of stealing his silver Watch Val: 40s. – com^d to d^{o}C.
RX Rob: Whitby – Charles St Berkeley Square £ 20

1s.   W^t against Mary Dye ads Jane Curry – Ass^t

1s.   D^o against Eliz: Armstrong ads Eliz: East D^o

Mr Beach att^{d}ed WP

---

112. The case proceeds to the Old Bailey. See *OBP*, April 1779, trial of Elisabeth Chandler, Elisabeth Wilson (t17790404–39).

P   Will: Haddell by Fra^s Witherick C. chd by Hump^y Jones for making a disturbance in the Street – d^d.

Mr Alderman Bull by Mr Alderman Plomer. Tuesday 9 March 1779.
Eliz: Armstrong by John Cruse C. chd by Eliz: East (on Ald^n Plomer's W^t) for an Ass^t – being frivolous & d^d.

Mary Penn[113], Ann Ware, Mary Wilson, Eliz: Jones, Mary Alsop, Mary Smith, Marg^t Roach, Cath: Johnson} WC by Ja^s Taylor C. chd by him for severally wandering abroad and picking up Men – they had already suffered by Confinement three days – they were all d^d

Thos Ellis, Thos Ayres, Ja^s Hicks} d^{o}C by Jno Negus C. chd by him as idle & disorderly Persons & fit persons to serve the King – Hicks was d^d – Ellis & Ayres were rem^{d}ed to be taken before the Com^{rs}.

David Brown, Will: Cambrook, Peter Paul} by Will: Hunt C. chd by Fra^s Best for making a great Noise & disturbance in his House – the Antigallican Coffee House – Paul was chd by James Esdaile for ass^{t}ing him and tearing his Coat – two Witnesses proved this Ass^t – referred to Mr Ald^n Clark

2s.   Aff^{ts} Stamp & Butt

Edwd Baker sum^d by Frances Hewsden for fraudulently selling her a Bedstead for and as Mahogany, whereas in fact, it was partly of an inferior Wood – ag^d to refer the dispute to Mr Rayner

1s.   W^t agst Martin Byland ads Thos Chambers – Ass^t

1s.   Eliz: Allen by Will: Sargeson C. chd by Eliz Bristow (on Ald^n Plomer's W^t) for an Ass[ault] – ag^d & d^d

Henry Parmiter, Will: King} by Rob: Green C. chd by Ja^s Betts on suspicion of stealing a quantity of Malt – rem^{d}ed till tomorrow

Mary Collier by Caleb Harden C. chd by Mary Williams for stealing a fillet of Veal

Mr Nash attended   WP

---

113. A check mark appears beside her name in the left margin.

Mr Alderman Wilkes. Wednesday 10 March 1779.
(No Attendance)

Rhodes Att^y attended   RH

Mr Alderman Sawbridge. Thursday 11 March 1779.
Aaron Davis by Will: Payne C. chd by him as a fit person to
serve the King – d^d

Walter Brown WC by d^{o}C. chd by Will: Pinsent on suspicion
of burglariously breaking & entering his dwelling House, and
feloniously stealing seven Crown pieces, two half Crown
pieces, five Shillings, two six pences, a silver pepper Caster, 5
silver table Spoons, 3 silver tea D^o – and sundry other things
– Val: £20 his property – Pinsent was sworn – the pris^r was
rem^{d}ed

Thos Wheatley by Jos: Thompson C. chd by Will: Wiggins for
stealing a parcel containing a piece of Beef, a towel &C.

Charlotte Waters, Ann Smith, Robt Fiers} d^{o}C by Rob Trotter
C. chd by him for no Offence – they were d^d

Nathl Whitehead, Ja^s Taylor C. Ch^d by Benjn Sutton on Suspicion of receiving a Bath Surtout Coat d^d

Chris^r Ogleby sum^d by Richd Beezley for unlawfully permitting
Journeymen to game in his Public House – he saw persons on
Saturday and Monday playing at Cards – John Negus & John
Trowel were sworn – they saw several Persons who appeared
to be Journeymen and Labourers playing at Cards in Ogleby's
House – he was convicted in the penalty of 40s. – he promised
to bring the Money tomorrow

Ellis Greenhow summoned personally by Thos Linton ads
Walter Newbon – for knowingly permiting Journeymen
Labourers and Apprentices to game and play at Cards &c. ag^t
Stat. – Adj^d true and convicted penalty 40 shgs

Henry Parmenter, Robt Green C. and Charg'd by James Roberts
for knowingly and designedly by false Pretences obtaining
from him 3 Q[uarter]^n malt value £4 with Intent to Cheat and
defraud him of the same. The malt having been Stopt on Susp^n
It was restor'd and P^r disch^d.

Mr Rhodes attended   JS

137

Sir Thomas Hallifax. Friday 12 March 1779.

> Marg[t] Roberts, Mary Webber} WC by Matt[w] Mead C. chd by him for being idle and disorderly Persons and common Prostitutes sev[lly] picking up Men last Night on Ludg[te] hill They Promis'd Amdendm[t], rep[d] and Disch[d].

John Collison d[o]C by d[o]C. chd by [blank]

Rach[l] Darby d[o]C. by Rob: Roe C. chd by him for Wandring abroad and lodging in the open Air having no Visible way of living. It appear'd on her Examination that ~~her R[t] of Sett[t] is in S[t] Geos [illegible] in the East~~ She was bound an App[ce] by Prish of S[t] Mary White Chapel to an Inhabitant S[t] Geo[s] in the East and that in Consequence of her Ma[r] having severely beat her ~~and~~ She deserted his Service and ran away. The Const was order'd to return the Girl back to her Ma[r]

M[r] Rhodes attended   TH

M[r] Alderman Kennett by M[r] Alderman Thomas. Monday 15 March 1779.

1s.   John Burke WC by Percival Phillips C. chd by Cath: Sheridan (on Ld Mayor's W[t]) for an Ass[t] – ag[d] & d[d]

1s. P   W[t] ag[t] John Webb ads Will: Stephenson Ass[t]

1s.   D[o] ag[t] Mary Weyland ads Cath: Boswell D[o].

1s.   Martin Byland by Jno Carpenter C. chd by Tho[s] Cham-
took a bad   bers (on Ald[n] Plomer's W[t]) for an Ass[t] — Pros[r] app[g] to
Shilling   have been the Aggressor the Pris[r] was d[d].
   M[r] Berch[114] att[d]   N Thomas

M[r] Alderman Kirkman by M[r] Alderman Plomer. Tuesday 16 March 1779.

1s.   Aff[t] Rob: Daniel.

Eliz: Pullen PC by Will: Payne C. chd by him for obstructing the Passage at the Royal Exchange, by selling Fruit there – she was d[d]

Tho[s] Winsett, Porter to Mess[rs] Warne & Hawconer, Haberdashers in Newgate Street sum[d] ads Dan[l] Rush, for an Ass[t] & damaging 600 Eggs – it was not wilfully done – d[d]

---

114. Most probably Beach, but the handwriting is unclear.

Ja^s Lyon WC by John Trowel C. chd by Eliz: Ux: (on Ld Mayor's W^t) for an Ass^t – she was sworn and he was com^d to d^{o}C

Wm Cambrook, Hugh Pollett, Peter Paul, Saml Shaw, Wm Hunt} 4 of the Constables of the Ward of Broadstreet, sum^d ads Francis Best, for unlawfully assembling at the Antigallican Coffee House on the 6 Inst. & there making an Affray in Disturbance of his Majesty's Peace – they were chd for a 2^d Offence of the like Nature on the 8th Inst. ag^d to ask Pardon in the Coffee Room on Thursday

Joseph Davis PC by Thos Parrott C. chd by him as a fit person to serve the King

Peter Paul (one of the Const^s above) was chd by James Esten for ass^{t}ing him and tearing his Cloaths

Jane Smith by Matt^w Mead C. chd by Jane Peach on suspicion of feloniously stealing two Yds of thread Lace Val: 1s. – disch^d.

1s.   Saml Noble by Jno Dale C. chd by Marg^t Dibing (on Ld Mayor's W^t) for an Ass^t – being friv^s d^d.

1s.   Aff^t John Wilmot

Thos Smith WC Wm Hawkins C. chd by Paul Smith, for picking his pocket of a Linen Handkerchief Val: 1s. s^d Paul Smith's Property – rem^{d}ed 'till to morrow.

P   Danl Langing [blank] same C: bro^t by him to give an Acc^t of himself, being apprehended talking to some Girls of the Town ab^t 9 last night the bottom of Holborn Hill – his Ma^r app^d to his Cha^r he was d^d.

Wm Thompson WC Saml Roberts C. chd by Mary ux Robt Burgess –for burglariously breaking and entering the Dwelling ho: of s^d Rob: in the Night time with Intent to commit felony therein, rem^{d}ed 'till to morrow.

Angel Simons, PC Geo: Fleming C. chd by a Person not now pres^t for picking a pocket, rem^{d}ed & Const ord^d to attend to Morrow.

Jacob Levy by Will: Payne C. chd by him for obstructing him in his Duty – d^d

139

Thos Heath PC by Jno Barber C. chd by him under the New
Act – referred to the Commrs

John Dennison WC by John Bindley C. chd by Margt Dodd for
taking her Cloak – dd.

Mary Bates by Edwd Thompson C. chd by John Hasslap for
knowingly etc. obtaining from John Robinson a Quartern of
Flower, a quartern Loaf

Mr Nash attended   WP.

Mr Alderman Sainsbury. Wednesday 17 March 1779.
John Jones WC by John Hart C. chd by [blank]

Henry Washington C. gave an Account of several suspicious
Circumstances respecting a Fire in the House of Thos Hillyer
in Bird in hand Court, Cheapside – Also Rob: Mills a Wchman,
Henry Atkins Junr – Mr Atkins about half past 12 heard an
Alarm of fire – he dressed, was inform'd it was at Hilliard's
– he went there, met a Wchman on the Stairs – he saw three
Women in the Room – Mrs Hilliard, a Mrs Curry (a Lodger)
and Hilliard's Maid – a bucket with Combustibles was fod in a
Closet in Hilliard's Room
      Mrs Curry—went to bed about twelve—dropt asleep in
about a Quarter of an hour – was awaked by Mr Hilliard – she
heard him tell the Maid in a low Voice that the House was on
fire – Curry told her Husband to get up
      She thought by the Sound she heard Hillyard open the Closet
where the fire was – some little time afterwards she heard the
Key turn again to lock the Door, and she thinks she heard the
Key draw out
      She said last Night to Hillyard "You went out last Night to
the Closet Mr H[illiard]" "No (he answered) I did not, but to
the Kitchen"
      Geo: Curry Husband of the last Witness—saw a smoke
when he got out of his own Room—but he would not be positive to any other Circumstance
      Mary Gravell, Servant to Hillyard was next examined – In
the Closet wherein the combustibles were found, the Earthen
Ware stood – this Witness cleared the Closet of every thing
Yesterday – Except last Night, she never remembers the Key
to be taken out of the Door – She was ordered very unusually
to bed, before her Master and Mistress – She never was before
      Thos Hillyard was called in and said that after Supper last
Night he went down into the Kitchen and the Cellar –he was

going into bed when he smelt the fire – he then pushed into the Maid's Room, and also knock'd against the Wainstcoat – he shoved the Maid's Room open, & said "Molly have you any Light here, or is your Candle safe, for I believe the House is on Fire" He thought the Shavings were in a blaze – he passed the Closet where they lay, but did not examine it nor did he smell to the key hole – he said, he co^d not give a reason for not looking to the Shavings

Mrs Hillyard – Her Husband alarmed her by saying, that there was a fire – He run for the Engine – He pointed to the light arising from the Closet, and said there it is – but told her not to open the Door as the fire wo^d burst out

Mr Houstoun attended.   TS

Sir Watkin Lewes. Thursday 18 March 1779.
John Jones pr by John Hart C. charged by [blank]

(No Attendance)

Mr Houstoun att^ded.

Mr Alderman Plomer. Friday 19 March 1779.
John Jones WC by John Hart C. chd by a Person not now present—as an idle, disorderly Person – his Mother took him away & promised to take Care of him.

Will: Calledine, Will: Brown, Thos Grove[115]} d^oC by John Duncastle C. chd by John Collier on suspicion of burglariously breaking & entering his dwelling House & stealing therein a silver Watch & a Quantity of Linen & other things remanded till Tuesday.

Mary Smith d^oC by Rob: Wilton C. chd by [blank]

Eleanor Mahony d^oC by Will: Martin C. chd by Alice Ux: (on his Wp's W^t) for an Ass^t – ag^d & d^d

Eliz: Little, Sarah Rice, Han^h Arnold} d^oC by Walter Newbon C. chd by him for severally wandering abroad & picking up Men – they were d^d – Arnold was chd with making a disturbance

115. A check mark appears beside his name.

1s.   Aff^t John Clark

John Smith d^{o}C by Will: Hawkins C. chd by [blank]

Will: Adams, Mary Walker} d^{o}C by Simon Cook C. chd by Will: Payne – being fo^d together in a House of ill fame

Will: Thompson[116] d^{o}C by Saml Roberts C. chd by Mary Ux: Rob: Burge for burglariously breaking & entering the dwelling House of the said Roberts in the Night time with Intent to commit Felony therein

RX   Robert Burge & ux^r } N° 32 Cork Lane Snowhill – Glass & China Man   20

John Penny, Will: Blunt, John Phillips, John Rice, Stacey Sabey[117]} WC by Henry Oxley C. chd by him as idle, disorderly Persons and fit to serve the King – Penny produced his Ma^r & Landlord – he was d^d – Blunt app^d to be a Man of good Character & in Employ – d^d – Phillips's father app^d – Rice was d^d – Sabey was d^d

Joseph Coleman d^{o}C by Will: Payne C. chd by Edmund Monk for ass^{t}ing him with Intent to commit the detestable Crime of Buggery – Mr Dep^y Nixon gave him the Character of an honest, sober Man – the fact app^d indisputable, & being confirm'd by W: Payne & Rob: Croft he was com^d to D^{o}C:

RX   Edm^d Monk Salisbury Crt Jeweller to Prosecute £ 10

Joseph Wilson WC by Will: Payne C. chd by him for plying with his hackney Coach between Freeman's Court & the West End of Cornhill – Payne & Jos: Gates were sworn – conv^d in the penalty of 10s.

Jane Adams PC by Will: Martin C. chd by John Allen for making a disturbance in his House – she was a Lodger – ag^d to quit on Thursday next – d^d

~~Will: Thompson~~ Willm Walker by Edward Thompson C. chd by John Hesley for committing a riot & disturbance in s^d Hesley's house.

1s.   Peace W^t for Thos Gall ats Wm Thompson

---

116. This case proceeds to the Old Bailey. See *OBP*, April 1779, trial of William Thompson (t17790404-48).
117. A check mark appears beside each name.

Marg^t Crife, Eliz: Davesis, Marg^t Knight, Ann Galent, Sarah Smith, Eliz: Rolston, John Tuckie[118]} WC by Will: Payne C. chd by him for severally wandering abroad & picking up Men – Crife and Davis were taken together com^d to B – Knight & Tuckie were also fo^d together– Davis & Smith were com^d to B untill a Court

R^d Palmer sum^d ads John Robinson for an Ass^t & breaking a 3 foot Bath Stove – damage to it 9s. – dis

Mr Houston attended   WP

Mr Alderman Peckham by Mr Alderman Sainsbury. Monday 22 March 1779.

1s.   Henry Marriott by Ja^s Dell C. chd by Roger Mason for assaulting him – d^d

P   Mary Davis WC Chas Moody C. chd by Thos Weald at the Cock in the Corner Ludgate Hill, for breaking his Windows – d^d

Thos Wood by Zachariah Holmes C. chd by him for making a disturbance in the Street

Thos Hilliard[119] was this Day brought from PC and his Confession read to him, and he was asked if he would sign the same – He answered he was not willing—that he was not in his right Mind on Saturday when he uttered the purport.

Rebecca Lee, Singlewoman, Servant to Mr Wenham in the Poultry was sworn and examined – Says, that Hilliard was at her Master's House on the 4th March – she gave him a Tub with some kitchen Stuff in it to sell for her – she looked at the Tub now produced, which was taken out of the Closet in Hilliard's House – she does not know it is the same – it is about the Size – he took it over the Way and in less than half an hour brought her 1s./6d. and the Cloth – Hilliard did not bring the Tub, and this Witness took no Notice about it.

There was no particular Mark on the Tub containing the Kitchen Stuff whereby she can know it again – She told him, that the Tub would serve very well to light fires with, and it

---

118. A check mark appears beside each name, but those beside Davis and Smith have been crossed as X.
119. Hilliard was removed from the Poultry Compter to Newgate prison on 9 April. See Poultry Compter Calendar (April 1779), LMA: CLA/047/LJ/01/1077. This case proceeds to the Old Bailey. See *OBP*, April 1779, trial of Thomas Hilliard (t17790404–36).

was not worth any thing, meaning, that he might keep it, or bring it back.

Thos Kirby to Mrs Mary Hoffman Wid^o a Tallow Chandler in the Old Jewry was the next Witness – Says, that he knows the Pris^r, who used to deal as a Customer to Mrs Hoffman – Hilliard came some little time about a fortnight or three Weeks ago to her Shop, and brought a little Tub with some kitchen Stuff in it – he desired the Stuff might be weighed, and he would call for the Money – that the Tub brought by Hilliard was about the Size of a common Oyster Barrel – He cannot pretend to say the Tub produced is the same

Edwd Pitcher & Henry Washington were also sworn & examined – Pitcher confirmed in part the Evidence of Kirby – co^d not speak to the Tub produced

Washington said, that on Tuesday Night last, Hilliard came seemingly in a great Fright to the Watch house, and desired Assistance to get out the Engine, for that he believed his ~~fire~~ house was on fire, or that it was on fire; (which of the Expressions Hilliard used, Informant cannot say) Hilliard after he spoke quitted the Watch House immediately – Informant went to Hilliard's House—went up Stairs & there he saw two Women, one of whom said, it proceeded from a Chimney that was repaired in the next House

Rebecca Wife of Geo: Currie was next examined – heard Hilliard go very frequently into the Closet – but upon the whole, perceived nothing particular in his behaviour on that Evening

A little after 12, she was awaked by Hilliard calling to his Maid "Molly, Molly, this House is on fire, get up" in a much lower Voice than he usually spoke in – She called repeatedly to her Husband to rise – She called also to Hilliard "What is the Matter, where about is the fire" and such as that – she was going down Stairs, & on the Landing Place she felt a heat from the Closet & perceived a Light – she told the Watchmen to go no further, for there was the fire – there was a Cry for the Key, and the Maid said, her Master had got it – that after she was in bed, she heard the Lock of the Closet Door turn'd with the Key, and after staying some little time, she heard the Key turn again as lock't – and the key drawn softly out – and afterwards she heard the Chamber ~~Room~~ Door of Hilliard open

Mr Alderman Hayley. Tuesday 23 March 1779.
Ald^n Sainsbury nunc
RX   Rebecca Lee Servant to Mr John Wenham, Lottery Office Keeper – Poultry   £ 20

Thos Hilliard was again bro^t up & Hen: Washington proceeded in his Evidence and was previously sworn.

Henry Atkins Junr was next examined – he swore, that between 12 & 1 on Wednesday Morning, he heard somebody, whom he took to be Hilliard, call out that there was a fire in Hilliard's House – he went to the House & saw a great Smoke and a Flame – he made Enquiry for the Key

to prosecute   Hilliard was committed to PC.

RX   Dep^y John Smith of Bucklersbury Druggist   £40
RX   Edward Pitcher} Servants to Mrs. Mary Hoffman }
       Thos Kirby   } of the Old Jewry Tallow Chandler } Each 20
       Will: Payne etc.   }
RX   Geo: Currie of Bird in hand Court for <u>Reb^a Ux</u> }
       Henry Atkins Junr Bird in hand C^t Serj^t at Mace }
       Henry Washington N° 4 Walbrook Warehouseman }
       Ja^s Wallis Street of Bucklersbury L. Stationer }
          Edward Lane his Servt   }
       for unlawfully & maliciously setting fire to his Dwelling House – ag^t the Statute &c.

John James, Walter Geary} by Jos: Tidmarsh C. chd by Amos Vogler for making a disturbance d^d

Eliz: Whitmore by Jno Edwards C. chd by Sarah Ransom (on Ald^n Pugh's W^t 26th Febry last) for an Ass^t.

Mr Nash attended. TS

1s.   John Webb by Jno Guise C. chd by Wm Stephenson (on Ald^n Thomas's W^t 15th Inst:) for an Ass^t – it being frivolous d^d

Mr Alderman Newnham. Wednesday 24 March 1779.
       Mary ~~Jokay~~ Junque, Mary Smith, Eliz Dickenson[120]} WC by Will: Payne C. chd by Benj: Leethorp for feloniously assaulting him in putting him in fear in a House in black-boy Alley & ~~feloniously stealing~~ taking from his Person a guinea, half a Guinea, two half Crown Pieces, two shillings & 3d. ½ —on his Oath committed to d^oC.

120. Check marks appear beside Junque and Smith's names. The case proceeds to the Old Bailey. See *OBP*, April 1779, trial of Mary Junque, Mary Smith (t17790404–40).

R   Will: Box – Doctors Commons Apothecary for
Leethorp   } £ 10
Will: Payne &c.   }

Edwd Price WC by Will: Bailey C. chd by Ben: Stennett for
feloniously stealing five Cups, six Saucers, and a Tea Pot of
small Value – d^d.

[blank] Smith sum^d by John Smith a hackney Coachman for
refusing to pay him his fare for carrying him in his hackney
Coach from Fleet Market to the Minories.

nil   James Debaufre, Thos Wild} Saml Shaw C. chging ea other –
Debaufre gave the 1st Charge for forcibly entering his dwelling
House last Night – the o^r charged Debraufre with an Ass^t – it
app^d a troublesome litigious Mre & both sides appg to blame
– they were d^d the Magistrate not [blank]

1s.   Eliz Buck by [blank] C. chd by Eliz: Stevens for assaulting her
etc. (on Ald^n Plomer's W^t 23d. Inst.) being friv^s d^d.

1s.   W^t ag^t Thos Flight ads Tho: Bateman

Marg^t Turner by John Duncastle C. chd by John Bell, & John
Duncastle for paying a counterfeit Shilling to him on the 17
Inst & tendering ano^r bad Shilling on the 19 & on being stopt
sev^l good six pences were found upon her & ~~she [illegible]~~ 1s.
& 10d. ½ in half pence were found up on her, & she wanted
change on buying a Penny Article.
R   Jno Duncastle – Old Change for self & Bell.

Thos Groves WC by Jno Duncastle C. chd by Jno Collier on
suspicion of burglariously breaking & entering his Dwelling
House & stealing therein a silver pepper Castor, a silver Watch
& other things sent to Captain Stirling

1s.   W^t ag^t Thos Edwards ads Mary Vernon Ass^t

P   D^o agt Thos Gough ads Jos: Chapman – D^o

Mr Ald. Sainsbury. Mr Houstoun att^d   TS

Mr Alderman Lee by Sir Thomas Hallifax. Thursday 25 March 1779.
Ald^n Townsend   Peace W^t ag^st John Norris ads Rob: Smith

gave a poor family 1s.	Tim^y Alden B. by Thos Holt C. chd by Rob Edwards on suspicion of feloniously stealing a bridle – there was no proof – d^d

John Berkeley, John Palliney} PC by Thos Gates C. chd by him as Vagrants – playing on a drum in the Street – d^d.

Will: Cooke by Jos: Thompson C. chd by Mary Ux: (on Ald^n Pugh's W^t) for an Ass^t – ord^d to the Comm^{rs} by the M^r [blank]

Will: Lowers WC by Jos: Thompson C. chd by him as a Vagrant, wandering abroad & lodging in the open Air – d^d.

1s. Affidavit Rein Tipkes Moolenaur and Interpreter

Will: Sheppard, Ralph Lemon} by Thos Fosset C. chd by R^d Wells as fit persons to serve the King – referred to the Comm^{rs}

Mr Rhodes attended TH

Mr Alderman Clark. Friday 26 March 1779.

1s. W^t ag^t Hannah Salter and Sarah Mortimer ads Eliz: Hart

Abraham Dawson [blank] by Jno Edwards C. chd by Geo: Rouse (on suspicion of picking his Pocket) sent on board the Tender

1s. W^t against John Bevitt ads Ann Flindell Ass^t

Nathl Stagg, John Williams} WC by Thos Wittenom C. chd by him as fit Persons to serve the King – d^d

P Will: Kelly WC by Thos Croome C. chd by Will: Page for an Ass^t – d^d

Martin Finday by Matt^w Mead C. chd by him on suspicion of stealing a piece of lead of very trifling Value – rem^{d}ed till Monday.

Will: Mitchell sum^d by Sarah Hughes for an Ass^t – dism^d

Thos Groves WC by John Duncastle C. chd by Jno Collier on suspicion of burglariously breaking & entering his dwelling House & stealing therein – rem^{d}ed till Monday

1s. W^t ag^t Thos Hine ads Thos Butterfield Ass^t etc.

1s.   Back'd a Middx W[t] per M[r] Blackborow.

P   W[t] ag[t] John Gahagan ads Sarah Ux: – Ass[t] etc.

    M[r] Beach attended   RC

nil   Peace W[t] ag[t] Joseph Barow ads Will: Payne.

M[r] Alderman Hart. Monday 29 March 1779.
    Will: Giffley WC by Tho[s] Burket C. chd by him as a fit Person
to serve the King – referred to the Comm[rs]

1s.   Sarah Tracey by Will: Martin C. chd by Eleanor Solomon (on
Ald[n] Clark's W[t]) for an Ass[t] – they withdrew & ag[d]

~~Lawrence Mahon by~~

    Benj: Harmon by d°C. chd by John Catlin Overseer of the
Parish of S[t] Sepulchre (on Ald[n] Pugh's W[t]) for unlawfully
begetting Mary Jones with Child – going to be married

    Sarah Ann Holt, Sarah Atkinson, Reb[a] Finley, Ann Evans} by
Walter Newbon C. chd by him for severally wandering abroad
& picking up Men – they were d[d].

    ~~John~~ Robert Dallas sum[d] by Will: Denham for assaulting him
– ~~Will Draper~~ d[d].

2s.   Henry Railton, ~~Sam'l Hart,~~ John Thomas} WC by Will: Brock-
well C. chd by[121] for an Ass[t] – they were discharged – no proof
appearing of the Ass[t].

    Tho[s] Groves d°C by John Duncastle C. chd by John Collier on
suspicion burglary & robbing him of a silver pepper Castor, a
~~silver~~ metal Watch – com[d] to B.

P   Emanuel Fonseca by Rich[d] Brinkworth C. chd by Eliz: Rose
(on Ald[n] Plomer's W[t] 26th March) for an Ass[t] – ag[d] & d[d]

    Geo: Wharton by Tho[s] Edwards C. chd by a Person not present
with felony – they were d[d]

---

121. The prosecutor in this case is not clearly stated. It may be Thomas and the clerk made an
error in listing the defendants.

P   Will: Newell by John Negus C. chd by Mary Collis for making a disturbance – d^d

Jos: Tason, R^d Shoemaker} by Will: Payne C. chd by him for picking Pockets – com^d to B as idle & disorderly persons

Ann Benner by David Ranken C. chd by Eliz Sinfield on suspicion of stealing two Ounces of Tea – d^d

Mr Beach attended   JH

Mr Alderman Wright. Tuesday 30 March 1779.
     Han^h Atkins, Eliz: Babbridge, Mary Webb ~~Han^h Wesley~~} WC by Matt^w Mead C. chd by him as idle & disorderly Persons – they were d^d and the C. seemed to have acted rather improperly

1s.   Affidavit Chas Bureau

2s.   Alex^r Stewart, Henry Brewster} WC by Wm Cromwell C. chd by John Lokes a Toll Collector on Black Friars Bridge – they withdrew & ag^d d^d.

Eliz: Ferne by Geo: Frost C. chd by him for picking up Men – d^d

P   Mary Selby pr by Walter Newborn C. chd by Sarah Lee on L^d M^{rs} W^t for assault – d^d

P   Eliz King, Eliz Markes} by Walter Newborne C. chd by Ann Strong – for assault – d^d

Eliz. Brady pr, Ja^s Smith —} by Thos Polton C. chd as follows – Brady as a Common Prostitute – d^d

John Barlow by Hen: Cohen C. chd by him as a fit Person to serve the King – d^d

Jos: Winterflood PC by Luke Pollard C. chd by Saml Durham on suspicion of feloniously stealing Wines – d^d.

Mr Houston Att   TW

Mr Alderman Pugh. Wednesday 31 March 1779.
1s.   Aff^t Rob: Farrah.

~~Howell~~ Abram Wilkinson sum^d by Jos: Dolphin Carman, for refusing to pay the Cartage of five Bags of Wool – Ord^d to pay

Mary Morgan WC by John Squire C. chd by him for being a disorderly Woman – d^d

Eliz: Snowball d^oC by Will: Hawkins C. chd by him as a Vagrant – rem^ded

~~Rob: Lee sum^d by~~

Eliz: Hassell by Will: Hawkins C. chd by Will: Wallis for making a disturbance – d^d

John Quilter by Saml Roberts C. chd by him ~~for~~ as a fit Person to serve the King – they withdrew

Mr Houstoun att^ded   EP

Mr Alderman Alsop. Thursday 1 April 1779.
Eliz: Powell WC by Rob: Trotter C. chd by [blank] Spiddell on suspicion of stealing a silk handkerchief – For Want of Proof she was D^d.

Cath. Thompson, Sarah Wills, Han^h Reeves, Mary Hammel, Alice Cole, Han^h Smith, Sophia Owen, Ann Bennett, Ann Cox^122} WC by Will: Payne C. chd by him for being severally loose, idle, & disorderly Women d^d

Eliz^th Baker WC Thos Croome C. and Ch^d by Stephen Joyce a Watchman for being idle and disorderly &c For want of Suff^t Proof, She was disch^d.

Ann Hill WC John Bennett C. and Ch^d by Ann Wills W^o for feloniously stealing a Pewter Quart Pot Value 1s. Property Woodward Archer Harlow at the Marquis of Granbys head
RX   Confirm'd Mrs. Wills's ~~Evid.~~ in her Evidence Fleet M^t   10
Ann Wills Hole in the Wall Fleet St W^o Vict^r   £ 20

Adj^d true and Comm^d to WC To prosecute & give Evidence next Sess^s O.T. in & for London

1s.   Affid^t Showell, Arden

---

122. The letter 'B' appears beside Thompson and Hammel. The notation 'Dd' appears beside Wills, Reeves, Cole, Bennett and Cox. The notation 'pass'd' appears beside Owen.

1s.   Warr[t] v. John Ellis ad[s] Dorothy Hollingshead per Ass[t].

Rhodes Att[y] attended   R.A.

M[r] Alderman Bridgen. Friday 2 April 1779.
    (No Attendance being Good Friday)

M[r] Alderman Crosby. Monday 3 April 1779.
    (No Attendance)
    M[r] Beach att[d]ed

M[r] Alderman Townsend. Tuesday 6 April 1779.
    Cath: Matthews, Ann Cadman, Ann Harrington, Ann Bailey,
    Alice Perry, Mary Cutter} WC by Geo: Frost C. chd by him
    for severally wandering abroad & picking up Men.

(No Attendance).

M[r] Alderman Bull by M[r] Alderman Pugh. Wednesday 7 April 1779.
1s.   Ja[s] Parker WC by Rob: Wilton C. chd by Edw[d] Gardiner for
    being fo[d] secreted under his Servant's Bed—it app[d] a Court-
    ship between him & the Maid—d[d].

Cath: Matthews, Ann Cadman, Ann Harington, Ann Bailey,
Alice Perry, Mary Cutter, Joyce Golding[123]} d[o]C by Geo: Frost
C. chd by him for severally wandering abroad & picking up
Men—Perry to be pass'd tomorrow to S[t] Mary Lambeth—
Cutter who was pass'd to Chelsea, sent there with the C.—the
others were d[d].

Mary Wellington, Ann Parsons, Sarah Roney, Reb[a] Goodwin,
Mary Walker, Mary Martin} d[o]C by Will: Payne C. chd as the
others—d[d]

Eliz. Morris, Eliz: Bradley, Cath. Bird, Eliz: Wyer, Eliz:
Lorrison} WC by Will: Payne C. chd as the before mentioned
Women viz: with picking up Men—d[d]

P   Charlotte Rood d[o]C by Tho[s] Pitney C. chd by a W[ch]man (not
    present)—d[d]

Joseph Daniel d[o]C by Rob: Trotter C. chd by him as a fit person
to serve the King—he app[d] to be a Man no ways an Object of
the Act

123. A check mark appears beside each name except Golding.

2s.   Thos Thornton, Luke Paris} d°C—by d°C. chd by him for being loose & disorderly & fit to serve the King—d^d.

Mary Kief d°C by d°C. chd by him for wandering abroad & picking up Men—d^d

Richd Hayward d°C by Thos Wittenom C. chd by him—but a Watchman apprehended him— sent to the Marine Society.

Will:^{m} Hewell d°C by d°C. chd by Benjn ~~Harper~~ Archer for making a disturbance and breaking his Windows he app^d to be insane

Mary Jenkins d°C by Matt^w Mead C. chd by him for picking up Men—d^d

John Weston d°C by Will: Payne C. chd by Rob: Croft for ass^{t}ing him with Intent to commit Buggery. Croft, Payne were sworn—c om^d to d°C.

R   Rob: Croft etc. }
         Will: Payne etc. } Each £ 10

Thos Fletcher d°C by John Prockter C. chd by Philip Stevens for embezilling some Money – ag^d to go to Sea

Cath: Webb by Jno Godfrey C. chd by Richd Hallier for feloniously stealing 11 Y^{ds} of silk Ribbon Val. 5^s his property— rem'ed till tomorrow.

4s.   John Harding, Will: Harding, Will: Kitting, Thos Thwaits} WC by Geo: Frost C. chd by John Bradley for ass^{t}ing his Wife— they acknowledged the fault—d^d.

Sarah Jacobs by Fra^s Witherick C. chd by him for picking up Men—d^d

Ja^s Doring by Henry Washington C. chd by him for begging— d^d

Will:^{m} Smith by Aaron Coates C. chd by Stephen Church on suspicion of stealing two silver pint Mugs rem^{d}ed till tomorrow

Philip Trant Will: Birdwood C. chd by Will:^{m} Oxlade for feloniously stealing two bushels of Coals Value 2s. his Property. remanded till tom^{ow}

John Mente PC Thos Ponsonby C. Ch^d by Eliz^h ~~Kent~~ Ux and Eliz^th Kent per Ass^t Mre Sett^d & D^d.

Wm Gray, Marg^t Ward} PC John Godfrey C. and Ch^d by him

Eliz^th Smith WC Saml Preston C. and Ch^d by Ann Garratt for pawning or o^rWise unlawfully disposing of a Copper Sauce Pan a Tin Boiler a Bolster and other Goods her Property wch had [blank]

1s.   John Ellis by John Bradley C. chd by Dorothy Hollingshead (on a W^t) for an Ass^t d^d.

John Maskall WC Peter Larydale C. chd by him, for getting in Liquor & misbehaving—he app^d to be weak in his Intellects— d^d

nil   Jer: Sheen John Couchman C: chd by Richd Foster for ~~susp^n of steali~~ taking a Note of hand off a file, it was for 7s. –the note was restored d^d

Walter Corvell, Ann Cole, Mary Cavenagh} WC Jno Squire C: chd by him—on Susp^n of being pick pockets—on being search'd, Cavenagh had 2 Tea Spoons found upon her—she alledged her fr^ds were gone on a Supposition that no ~~other~~ Magistrate w^d attend this day—they were rem^ded 'till to Morrow.

Martha Ployer Wm Hawkins C: chd as a Vagr^t ord^d to the Parish Work house 'till better.

Mary Cochran Ja^s Barker C: chd by Bridget Simmonds (on Ald^n Plomer's W^t 7 Inst) for an Ass^t d^d—friv^s.

nil   W^t ag^t Stephen Sargo ads Chris: Manning Ass^t etc.

1s.   D^o ag^t Wm Hagley ads Geo: Sweet Ass^t etc.

Rhodes Att^y attended   EP

Mr Alderman Wilkes by Mr Alderman Pugh. Thursday 8 April 1779.
Jane Morris, Jane Thompson} WC by Geo: Frost C. chd by him for severally wandering & picking up Men last Night – d^d.

Henry Fountain, Will: Sanxey} d^oC by Rob: Roe C. chd by Henry Hart for stealing a handkerchief –they ag^d to Sea

Cath: Webb by John Godfrey C. chd by Richd Hallier for feloniously stealing 11 Yards of silk Ribbon—com^d to B.

1s.   Mary Ann Orion by Hen: Westley C. chd by Martha Baldwell for making a disturbance—she was d^d

Mary Collins by Matt^w Mead C. chd by Jos: Cookson for feloniously stealing a piece of Pork of trifling Value—d^d

Ann Thomas WC Wm Martin C. and Ch^d by Stephen Joyce a Watchman for Wandring abroad & Lodging in the open Air Last Night Prsh St Sepulchres having no visible Way of living or Place of Sett^t She appearing dis tressd & contaminated, The Ald^n recom^d her to the Hospital for the [week?].

1s.   John Cash (Ald^n Plomers W^t) Wm Cook C. Ch^d by Thos Parrott per Ass^t Mre Sett^d and D^d

1s.   Sarah Holt WC Thos Whittaker C. chd by Elizth Evans per Ass^t Adj^d frivolous and D^d

Walter Cowell, Ann Cole & Mary Cavenagh} rem^d yesterday and Ch^d by John Squire a Const. as suspected Pick Pockets Adj^d true and Comm^d to B. 14 Days

Philip Tranter rem^d yesterday for fur^r Examnion Wm Birdwood C. Ch^d by Wm Oxlade a Coalm[erchan]^t for feloniously Stealing 2 Bushels of Coals Value 2^s. his Property. <u>Geo. Bates</u> and <u>Timothy Weldon</u> 2 Watchmen of Castle Baynard Ward provd the Charge & on their Evid he Was Committed to WC he confessed, that the Horse Keeper (for his Assistance) told him he might take the Sweepings on their Oath com^d to B.

John Jones WC John Squire C. Ch^d by him for Wand^g Abroad and lodging in the open Air last Night having no Visible way of living &c.

1s.   Mary Sealey by Thos Parrott C. chd by Ann Mann (on Ald^n Plomer's W^t) for an Ass^t –being frivolous was d^d

John Swaine by Will: Payne C. chd by a Person not now present – d^d

1s.   Warr^t v Mich^l Martin ads Ja^s Homan per Ass^t

P   D^o ag^t Jane Vickers ads Mary Griffiths.

Mr Rhodes attended   John Wilkes.

Mr Alderman Sawbridge. Friday 9 April 1779.
Ann Simpson WC Jos^h Fields C. and Ch^d by Wm Moore on Suspicion of feloniously Stealing 6 Gas his Property

Wm Shephard WC Wm Greenwood C. and Ch^d by him on Susp^n of being an idle and disorderly Person having no Visible Way of living. A Ma^r Perukem^r app^d on his Behalf declared that he had Employ^d him 4 Months in his s^d Trade at 14s. per Week and Was a Steady Sober Man & a good Workman. He was thereon disch^d.

1s.   Affid^t Bautz.

1s.   Mich^l Martin by Will: Govin C. chd by Ja^s Homan (on Ald^n Wilkes's W^t Yesterday) for an Ass^t —frivolous & d^d

Will. Hewins by Saml Roberts C. chd by Richd Hughes for making a disturbance in his Yard of the Kings Arms Inn Leadenhall Street d^d

Will. Sankey who was Yesterday ord^d to the Tender was d^d –he was unfit

1s.   Aff^t John Meriton

nil   John Lokes, John Salt and Geo: Eggleston—Collectors of the Toll on Black Friars Bridge—were sworn

Mr Rhodes attended   J. Sawbridge.

Sir James Esdaile. Monday 12 April 1779.
Eliz: Goodenough, Sarah Alder, Eliz: Alder, Ann Holder, Sus^a Stewart} WC by Matt^w Mead C – chd by him [blank]

John Bristow by Will: Martin C. chd by Thos East

(No Attendance)

Mr Beach attended   RH

Mr Alderman Kennett. Tuesday 13 April 1779.
1s.   Aff^t Jos^h Amici

1s.   W^t v. Eliz Smith ats Ann Kaget Ass^t.

Eliz: Goodenough, Sarah Alder, Eliz: Alder, Ann Holder, ~~Sarah~~
Sus^a Stewart} WC: Matthew Mead C. chd by him for severally
lodging in the open Air par: St Bridget,—Goodenough was
sent to the Hospital, the 2 Alders ord^d a pair of Shoes ea:–
Holder ord^d to go to St Thomas's & Stewart sent to St Lukes
Old Str.

1s.   Back't W^t [blank]

Thos Day Carman sum^d ads R^d Starrap ano^r Carman for ~~not~~
taking a Load out of Turn

Eliz. Lorrison, Mary Jones, Eliz: Wyre} WC: Hen. Westley C.
chd by him for loitering past 12 in Fleet Street— they were d^d.

John Tibbell WC Chas Moody C. chd by him for loitering ab^t
12 in an Alley near blackfriars – d^d.

Mary Wyld D^oC same C: chd by him for picking up Men in
Fleet Street, d^d.

P   R^d Carter WC Thos Groom C: chd by Frances Moseley, for an
Ass^t –it was a trifling Mre d^d.

1s.   Aff^t Ezekiel Delight

Isabella Lexton pr by Francis Lee C. charged by Agnes Baynes
upon Susp^n of stealing divers things her property dis^d at the
request of the prosecutor.

1s.   W^t v. Sarah Smith ats Lucy Edwards Ass^t

1s.   W^t v. Sus^n Appleton ats John Charge upon Sus^n of stealing a p^r
of Sheets out of ~~her~~ his Lodgings

1s.   D^o v. Ann Kneed ats Eliz Penn Ass^t

P^r124   W^t v. Wm Simms ats Sarah Drexley for stealing a few Half
pence and a Check Apron.

P   W^t v [blank] Lewis ats Saml Wiseham upon Sus^n of stealing
divers Goods in his house

124. Probably 'produced', referring to the apron.

P   W^t v. James Newman & ~~Ja^s~~ Matthew King ats Eliz King—Ass^t

Mr Houston Attended   BK

Mr Alderman Kirkman by Mr Alderman Plomer. Wednesday 14 April 1779.

P   Patrick Appleby WC by John Hunt C. chd by him for insulting him –d^d

1s.   Mary Duncombe by Jno Trowel C. chd by Sarah Kinsey (on his Wp's W^t) for an Ass^t—ag^d & d^d

1s.   Sarah the Wife of Thos Smith by George Frost C. chd by Lucy Edwards on Ald^n Kennet's W^t 13 Inst. for assault^g her – ag^d & d^d

Catherine Matthews pr by George Tiern[?] as a Vagrant—sent to the Parish of Saint Faith

Wm Simms, Thos ~~Ellietis~~ Elliotis & <u>John Williams</u> by Richd Beasley C. charged by Sarah the Wife of John Drexley for stealing a Check Apron and 14 copper half pence (on Ald^n Kennets W^t 13th Inst.) the property of the s^d Jno Drexley.

RX   John Drexley Crown Alley Moorfields Paper Stainer for Sarah his Wife} £ 10

Richd Legoe chd Simms with stealing a Quilt, a Pillow, and a Bed, a copper Tea Kettle, a copper Sausepan and other things, rem^ded until Monday.

Geo: Morrison chd him with purloining some leather Stuff to make Shoes with

2s.   Matthew Newman, Ja^s Newman} by Walter Newbon C. chd by Eliz: King (on Ald^n Kennett's W^t) for an Ass^t—ag^d & d^d

2.^s   Aff^ts Langhorn and ano^r

John Kelly bro^t by the Church Wardens of Saint Michael Crooked Lane for running away from his Wife and leaving her chargeable to s^d parish – the Woman sent to the Workhouse & the Man discharged

P   Matthew Newman, James Newman} by Paul Newball C. chd by Eliz King for assault on Ald^n Kennets W^t 13 Inst^t discharged being frivolous.

Mr Houston attended   WP

Mr Alderman Sainsbury. Thursday 15 April 1779.
    [blank] Williams sum^d by Jos: Dolphins Carman for refusing
    to pay the Cartage of three Loads, settled.

    Will: Jones WC by Edwd King C. chd by John Scott (not now
    present) – the C. also chd him as an idle, disorderly person –
    d^d.

    Thos Magrave, Will: Sanderson} sum^d to show Cause why
    they should not be ordered to receive & entertain Thos Poole
    their Apprentice – the Cause of discharge not appearing suff^t
    – discharged

    Ben: Filter WC by Jos: Thompson C. chd by Ben: Roberts for
    feloniously stealing a linen handkerchief Va 1s. on his Oath
    com^d to N:

RX   Benj Roberts of Maiden Lane Wood street Coachman   10
    Jos^h Thompson [blank]

    Danl Ragan WC same C: chd by Silvanus Hall for breaking a
    Square of Glass in a new Building near black friars Bridge –
    reprim^ded & d^d

gave a poor   John Loader WC John Procter C. Richard Ewin his Ma^r
Woman 2s.   to whom he is an Apprentice, on suspicion of stealing
    three Cards of thread Lace, rem^ded till tomorrow

    Mess^r Derby's sum^d ads John Flemming Str: Keeper for owing
    their Carriage in this City—not having their Name & Number
    places thereon—adjudged not to be Within the Act

    Moses Hyam WC Wm Hawkins C. chd by him for being along
    with Women & being a person of an indifferent Cha^r was
    apprehended as a person fit & proper to serve the King—d^d

    Will: Smith sum^d by Fleming for using his narrow Wheel Cart
    in this City

P   Search W^t for Richd Ewin for sev^l peices of Lace his property
    – the House of Mary Lauder in Kings head Court St Paul's
    Church Yard.

P   W^t per Wm Hunt ats Mary Ux. Ass^t

Mr Houstoun att^d

Danl Harding, Jeremiah Steel} pr by Nathan Brown C. charged by John Kilpack upon Sus^n of Stealing a Great Coat rem^{d}ed till to Morrow.

1s.   W^t v. Henry Collet ats Hannah Collet Ass^t.

TS   Mr Houstoun attended

Sir Watkin Lewes. Friday 16 April 1779.
No attendance.

Mr Houstoun att^d RH

Mr Alderman Thomas by Mr Alderman Kennett. Monday 19 April 1779.
Eliz: Rigby, Marg Strutton} WC by Ja^s Taylor C. chd by him for asking him to treat them – they did no more; d^d

Zach^h Hockley by Brian Chandler C. chd by [blank] Crawshaw Overseer of the Parish of Saint Giles Cripplegate, for unlawfully begetting Mary Franklin, singlewoman of the said Parish with Child, chargeable thereto – he app^d to be a Seaman – d^d

R^d Wilcox Driver of a Cart N^o [blank] produced by His Ma^r Will: Staines, sum^d by Matthew Hagstone for driving the s^d Cart agst his Coach – Ord^d to pay 6^s.

Diana Sinclair sum^d by Will: Bishop a hackney coachman for his fare – Ord^d 2s./6d. fare & 5^s Charges

John Kelly by Geo: Wolf C. chd by Philip Tacey for feloniously stealing a linen handkerchief Val. 4d. his property ag^d to go to Sea—N° 77 Queen Street, the place of Tacey's residence.

Middx   Richard Crouch,[125] Saml Allen} WC by Thos Fox C. chd by Will: Phillips & Will: Hawkins on suspicion of feloniously
next   stealing a 36 ℔ flats [illegible] of Butter Val: 18s. in a Waggon
Sess^s near Acton —Thos Atkins & Hawkins were sworn– also 5 silver Watches Val: £ 5 & upw^{ds} – Phillips's property

---

125. The case proceeds to the Old Bailey. See *OBP*, May 1779, trial of Richard Crouch (t17790519-36).

RX   Will. Phillips Bicester in Oxfordshire Carrier   £ 10

Will Hawkins— his Servt 10

Thos Atkins Servt to Thos Bennett Buckingham   10

P   Jos: Clarke by Walter Newbon C. chd by Eliz: Clarke (on Ald^n Plomer's W^t 17th Inst.) for an Ass^t – d^d

Sarah Davis, Sarah Parker, Ann Bailey, Alice Perry} WC by Geo: Frost C. chd by him for severally wandering abroad & picking up Men – Parker was chd by the C. for making a disturbance—she was d^d

Wm Sims WC R^d Briton C. chd by ~~George Morrison~~ R^d Legoe & Mary Ux for feloniously stealing out of his ready furnish'd Lodgings a Feather Bed, Bolster, Cover lid, copper Tea Kettle small Copper Saucepan, a Flat Iron, & a small Iron Candle-stick Val 40s. s^d Legoe's Property – com^d on his Oath to D^{o}C

RX   R^d Legoe of Petticoat Lane L: Cordwainer for himself & Wife £ 10

Alice Pike D^{o}C: Hen: Oxley C. chd by Geo: Bates for feloniously stealing two pewter Dishes 6 pewter plates 1 Holland Shirt 1 Sheet 1 Handkf 2 pillow Cases 2 pair of Stockings 1 Gown 1 Shift, 1 Apron, —d^d

Thos Weldon, Mary Barnes} WC by Jno Squire C. chd by him for being together in an indecent Situation—they were d^d

Lydia Thorpe, Geo: Gardiner} d^{o}C by d^{o}C. chd by him for begging in the Parish of St Faith – d^d

Sarah Jackson, Eliz: Lock} chd by Squire for severally wandering abroad & picking up Men—d^d

Danl Harding by Nathan Brown C. chd by John Kilpack on suspicion of stealing a great Coat Val: 2s. 6d., Ord^d to Sea

Geo: Clark WC by Will: Martin C. chd by him for making a disturbance—before the Watch House –d^d

1s.   W^t ag^t Ann Green ~~ads~~ & [blank] Gibson ads Eliz: ~~Murphy~~ Macway

P   D^o ag^t Moses Holloway ads Ann Jameson

P   D^o ag^t Thos Bramwell ads Cath: Ux: Ass^t

1s.   D° ag¹ Eliz: Anderson ads Wᵐ Redrick

M' Beach Attended   BK

M' Alderman Peckham. Tuesday 20 April 1779.
1s.   Thoˢ Beeby by Rob: Roe C. chd by Sarah Richardson (on Aldⁿ
        Plomer's W¹) for an Assᵗ – frivolous & dᵈ

        Will: Johnson WC by Mattʷ Mead C. chd by Thoˢ Wells &
        Sarah Ux: Giles Herring on Suspicion of feloniously stealing
        5s. in Silver, monies numbered, the Monies of the sᵈ Giles
        Herring – in consideration of his family he was dᵈ.

1s.   W¹ ag¹ Eliz: Fowler ads Jane Frost—Assᵗ

2s.   Affᵗ Will: Buncomb & John King

1s.   Isaac Noah DeCosta by Thoˢ Emery C. chd by Will: Veck (on
        the Lord Mayor's W¹ 19ᵗʰ Inst.) for an Assᵗ—agᵈ & dᵈ

        Will: Cherry PC by Jno Carpenter C. chd by Michˡ Clark on
        suspicion of stealing six Coats nine Waistcoats & four pairs of
        breeches Val: [blank] his property – Cherry remanded until to
        morrow.

        Rebecca Linley appeared but no Evidence appeared ag¹ her
        discharged, but to be forthwith coming when required

        T̶h̶o̶ˢ Jaˢ Kennedy[126] by Rob: Best C. chd by Fraˢ Bradford &
        Thoˢ Ramell for stealing 12ˡᵇ of pepper Va: 18s. privately in
        the Shop of sᵈ Bradford.
R   John Lepard of Newgate Street Sta[tione]ʳ   10
        Robert Best of paternoster Row peruke Maker. Prosʳ 10
        Jno Bradford of Newgate Street Grocer   20
        Thoˢ Ramel Sᵗ Mildreds Court Poultry   10

        Henry Greenshaw by Robᵗ Row pr charged by John Hogg upon
        Suspⁿ Stealing some things in a parcel remᵈ until to morrow

1s.   Back'd a W¹ per M' Girdler

nil   Samˡ Green pr by Farrel Currin C. charged by him for being an
        Idle & disorderly person— he did nothing, nor was there any
        Groᵈ for apprehending him—dᵈ.

126. This case proceeds to the Old Bailey. See *OBP*, May 1779, trial of James Kennedy
    (t17790519–13).

Dorothy Barber by Will: Martin C. chd by him for begging in the Parish of St Sepulchre, whereto she belongs—sent there.

P   Rob: Spencer, Ann Bailey, Ann Harrington} by Farrel Currin C. chd by him for making a disturbance they were all drinking Gin together—d^d

1s.   Eliz: Anderson by Thos Tallard C. chd by Will: Redrick (on Ald^n Kennett's W^t Yesterday) for an Ass^t d^d

Sarah Crag pr by John Squire C. chd by him for begging— Ord^d a Pass

Mr Houstoun attening   EP

P   W^t ag^t Eliz: Evans ads John Dunn Ass^t

P   D^o ag^t Wm Wild ads Jane Ux:— D^o

Mr Alderman Hayley by Mr Alderman Pugh. Wednesday 21 April 1779.
Will: Harley WC by John Duncastle C. chd by him on suspicion of stealing sev^l handkerchiefs rem^{d}ed for the Commissioners in order to serve the King

Will: Crichton, Fra^s Pope, Ja^s Balam} d^{o}C by Will: Payne C. chd by him for attempting to pick several Pockets—seven handkerchiefs were taken from Balam – he and Pope ag^d to serve the King—they were all taken for that purpose to the C.

1s.   Elias Israel by Jno Goodwin C. chd by Isaac Isaacs (on Ald^n Plomer's W^t) for an Ass^t—ag^d & d^d

Walter Patmore WC by Thos Fox C. chd by a person not now present—he ag^d to go to Sea

Lydia Taylor by Will Martin C. chd by Mary Hyland for feloniously stealing a red Cardinal   d^d–it being very doubtful who told Truth.

Will: Cherry PC by Jno Carpenter C. chd by Mich^l Clark on suspicion of stealing six Coats nine Waistcoats & four pairs of breeches—he was d^d –sev^l persons gave him an excellent Character

Henry Greenshaw by Rob: Roe C. chd by John Hogg on suspicion of stealing some things in a Parcel rem^{d}ed til to Morrow.

162

Sam¹ King pr by Jos: Gates C. plying with his Coach ~~on~~ by Freeman's Court Cornhill—fined 5s. which he paid on the Oath of Gates

Jane Huggard by Will: Payne C. chd by him for begging in the Hall—dᵈ.

1s. Wᵗ agᵗ [blank] Radley ads Amey Adley—Assᵗ etc.

Jaˢ Hodge by Jaˢ Cowpas C. chd by Mark Smith on suspicion of stealing six squares of Glass

Mark Smith of Jewry Street Minories Glazier
Thoˢ Goldbury of Battle Bridge Grays Inn Lane Carp.

1s. Wᵗ v. Rich Smith & Wᵐ Brown ats Samuel Abrahams Assᵗ

Middx ~~John Lo~~ Jaˢ Hodge by Jaˢ Copous C. chd by Will: Harrison, Thoˢ Charles & Mark Smith for stealing five six light Sashes Val. £6 & upwᵈˢ the property of the sᵈ Will: Harrison – he was comᵈ to dᵒC.

RX Will: Harrison Nᵒ 37 Lambs Conduit Sᵗ Gent }
Thoˢ Charles Nᵒ 14 Dorset Sᵗ Carpenter } 10
Mark Smith Nᵒ 5 Jewry Sᵗ Glazier }
Jaˢ Copous Wormwood Sᵗ Nᵒ 32   10

Mʳ Houstoun attᵈ. EP

Mʳ Alderman Newnham. Thursday 22 April 1779.

P Mary Radley by Walter Prosser C. chd by Amey Adley (on Aldⁿ Plomer's Wᵗ) for an Assᵗ—they withdrew & agᵈ –dᵈ

P Hen: Halsey, Eliz: Ux:} by Will: Martin C. chd by Thoˢ Cox for an Assᵗ—there was no Assᵗ comᵈ—dᵈ

Amey Hadley by dᵒC chd by Eliz: Cox (on Aldⁿ Plomer's Wᵗ) for an Assᵗ—dᵈ

Will: Brown WC Timʸ Jones PC} by Will: Selby C. chd by Jaˢ Beabey a Watchman in the Ward of Farringdon without for taking his Lanthorn they withdrew & agᵈ –dᵈ

Peter Madan sumᵈ by Rob: Best for selling Beer without Licence—convᵈ in 40s. penalty.

Francis Taylor WC John Squire C. Chᵈ by John Jones Church-

Warden of St Michael le Quern for refusing to Contribute any
Thing towards the Maintenance and Support of his Wife, who
is insane and now become Chargeable to s^d Pish & therefore
he urg'd that Taylor was an Object within the Meaning of the
impressing Act—but the Ald^n said, he thought he was not the
Object —d^d

Jane Buckley WC by Will: Martin C. chd by Chris^r Brown for
making a disturbance—and assaulting his Wife—d^d

Chch Wdns of St Michael WoodStreet sum^d by Eliz: Phillips
for relief – d^d

P   W^t ag^t Mary Griffiths ads Eliz: Lowe Assault etc.

Rhodes Att^y att^d NN

Mr Alderman Lee. Friday 23 April 1779.
      Mary Knight, Ann Smart} by Matthew Mead C. chd by [blank]

(No Attendance)

Mr Alderman Wooldridge. Monday 26 April 1779.
      ~~Sarah Aldwright by John Edwards C.-chd by John Page~~

      ~~Mary Knight, Ann Baker, Marg^t Owen, Cath: Matthews}WC
      by Geo: Frost C.~~

      ~~Will. Hawkins John Fenley by Will: Hawkins C.-chd by Mich^l
      Bannister on suspicion of feloniously stealing an iron Shovel
      =there was no felony com^d =d^d~~

      ~~Rob: Loader WC-by John Proctor C.-chd by Mary Risen~~

(No Attendance) Mr Beach att^{d}ed.

Mr Alderman Hart. Tuesday 27 April 1779.
Ald^n Pugh nunc. Mich^l Warren WC by Chas Drummond C. chd by
1s.   Marg^t Dunn for throwing down her Apples—he was
               d^d on making Satisfaction

      Mary Knight, Ann Baker, Marg^t Owens, Cath Matthews} pr by
      Geo. Frost C. for being severally Idle & disorderly Persons &
      lodging in the open Air—rem^{d}ed to be pass'd

      Sarah Aldwright WC by Jno Edwards C. chd by John Page

for feloniously stealing two pint pewter Pots & a Knife Val: 2s. his property – Elizabeth Humphries saw the Pris^r drop the Pots –on Page's Oath—com^d to B, until a Court.

Ann Downes pr by Wm Payne C. for being an infamous pick pocket Payne charged that she acknowledge a Fact of that Nature

Henry Grimshaw pr by Robt Row C. charged by John Hogg for fraudulently obtaining a parcel from Mr Handforth containing some Meat

1s.   Eliz: Cort, ~~Will Lutwych~~} by Will: Payne C. chd by Marg^t Thatcher (on the Lord Mayor's W^t Yesterday) for an Ass^t – frivolous & d^d

1s.   Aff^t Hugh Keeffe

1s.   Aff^t Fra^s Lavell

Peter Madan sum^d by Rob: Best for selling Beer without Licence in the Ward of Farringdon with~~out~~ in – allowed a fort-night to purchase

Isaac Bacharah by Will: Cooke C. chd by him as a fit person (under the Impressing Act) to serve the King – he was adjudged not to be within the meaning of the Act – d^d.

P   Mary Griffiths by Jno Trowel C. chd by Eliz: Lowe (on Ald^n Newnham's W^t 22^d Inst:) for an Ass^t— frivolous & d^d.

P   Saml Barber by Will: Martin C. chd by Thos Goodwin Chch Wden of St Sepulchre (on the Lord Mayor's W^t) for deserting his Wife, who is become chargeable to the s^d Parish –it app^d there was no desertion—d^d

Marg^t Norton by Jno Beale C. chd by Thos Sommering for feloniously ass^{t}ing him in the Kings Highway, putting him in fear & taking from his person a pair of silver knee buckles, a pair of Mocoa Stone sleeve buttons & a cambrick Stock—rem^{d}ed

Will: Marks PC by Rob: Green C. chd by Thos Pearson for feloniously stealing a quantity of Rosin – ord^d to Sea

gave 1s.to a   Will: Shaw by Ja⁵ Barker C. chd by him as a fit person
poor Woman   to serve the King—dᵈ.

> Will Dormer chd by Ja⁵ Andrews for attempting to pick his
> Pocket—sent to the Marine Society

1s.   Wᵗ agᵗ [blank] Okeley v. John Inedon for assᵗ

> Mʳ Houstoun attᵈ   TH

Mʳ Alderman Wright. Wednesday 28 April 1779.
1s.   Ja⁵ Field by Geo: Frost C. chd by Ja⁵ Fortescue for wilfully
       breaking a looking Glass—Priscilla Dixey swore to an Assᵗ—
       they withdrew & agᵈ – dᵈ.

> ~~Mary~~ Eliz: Weldon, Mary Jones, Eliz: Dyer, Lucy Johnson,
> Ann Burton} WC by Rob: Trotter C. chd by him for severally
> wandering abroad & picking up Men— they made a distur-
> bance & abused the Watchman Rob: Walker who was sworn—
> comᵈ to B.

> Rebᵃ Little, Jane Drandle, Susᵃ Johnson} dᵒC by dᵒC. chd by
> him for severally wandering abroad & picking up Men—dᵈ

> Susᵃ Morgan, Sarah Jones}WC by Hen: Oxley C. chd by him
> for abusing him—Jones appᵈ to be concerned in a robbery—
> Morgan dᵈ so was Jones & Norton

> ~~Amey~~ Ann Bailey, Lydia Wood, Eliz Rigby} pr by Peter
> Ashmore C. chd by Amey Dawson Bailey upon Suspⁿ of
> stealing a pʳ of Silver pʳ Buckel the sᵈ Wood & Rigby of
> stealing an apron

> Eliz Wood pr by John Shephard C. chd by Ann Tisdel for
> stealing an two Aprons & Black Callimancoe petty coat
> discharged it appearing the prisʳ had boᵗ the Goods.

> Philip Gregory WC by Will: Payne C. chd by him for begging
> in the Parish of Sᵗ Ann Black friars—dᵈ.

> Messʳ Gifford Mitchel Evans & Hammond sumᵈ appeared by
> Richᵈ Meers a Drayman on Complaint of Joseph Gates for
> standing with his Dray—dᵈ.

> Sarah Nunn pr by Wᵐ Hawkins C. charged by Thoˢ Bingham
> upon Suspicion of stealing some Silver, discharged for want of
> Evidence

166

Wm Elliot, John Gibbs} pr by Wm Hawkins C. Elliot rem^d for tomorrow & to go to Sea being an Idle & disorderly Boy the other dis.

P   Saml Taylor by Will: Hawkins C. chd by Jos: Coward for making a disturbance—d^d.

Wardoff Thompson sum^d by James Foorbyttle for using threats whereby he is in danger—d^d

1s.   W^t v. Wm Asdel ats Ann Cope Ass^t

Mr Houstoun att^d   TW

Mr Alderman Pugh by Mr Alderman Crosby. Thursday 29 April 1779.
Ann Hill by Matt^w Mead C. chd by Alex^r Clagg for stealing a pint pewter Pot Val: 10d. his property—rem^ded till tomorrow

1s.   Aff^t John Robson

Rob: Loader by John Procter C. chd by Mary Ux: Ja^s Risen for burglariously breaking & entering the dwelling House of the s^d Mary Risen & feloniously stealing a silver Table Spoon, a pair of silver shoe Buckles –rem^ded till Monday

1s.   John July by Matt^w Mead C. chd by Rob: Hall for an Ass^t— ag^d & d^d

B.C.   Mr Rhodes attended

Mr Alderman Alsop. Friday 30 April 1779.
Willm Warren, Dennis Murray[127], Ja^s Jacobs} WC by Will: Payne C. chd by him for wandering abroad & begging – they all promised to keep out of the City – d^d

1s.   Backd a Middx W^t per Mr Wright

Ann Hill WC by Matt^w Mead C. chd by Alex^r Clagg & Will: Rose for feloniously stealing a pint pewter Pot Val: 10d. his property—com^d to B. untill a Court.

Mary Evans, WC Thos Whittenham C. and Ch^d by Jane Daker her Mistress for pawning or otherwise unlawfully disposing

---

127. Check marks appear beside Warren and Murray's names.

of a black Mode Cloak trim'd with Crape Value 20 Shill^{gs} her Property – Thos ~~Johnson~~ Clarke produced a black mode Cloak of Daker's – For Want of Evidence—D^d

Richd Evans by John Duncastle C. chd by Chas Rayley his Ma^r for embezilling his Money – intrusted to pay for certain Things, which he got on his Master's Credit, he forgave him – d^d

P   James Pomwell WC Wm Martin C. and Ch^d by Mary Saunders for an Ass^t –d^d.

nil   Jane Cordinay WC Same C. Ch^d by John Remington and Saml Small for no Offence—d^d

Catherine Brett WC Mr Ald^n Plomer W^t Saml Roberts C. and Ch^d by him and Thos Goodwin ChurchW^n of St Sepulchre London for leaving her Infant Female Child aged 10 Weeks at the Door of the s^d Roberts within the said Prsh whereby s^d Child is become Chargeable &c—com^d on his Oath.

RX   Thos Goodwin N° 2 Hosier Lane Gold beater   £ 10
Saml Roberts N° 4 Lock Lane Snow Hill Beadle   10

Nunc Sir Thomas Hallifax for Mr Alderman Alsop, ad huc Friday 30 April 1779.
Thos Buckney Sum.^{d} by Edward Lee for loading Timber 23.^{d} instant in your unlicenced Carriage within this City, and carrying Same for Hire to Gravel Lane Hounsditch –ag^d.

Rhodes att^y attended   Tho Hallifax

The Right Honourable Thomas Harley. Monday 3 May 1779.
(No Attendance)

Mr Beach att^{d}ed

Mr Alderman Crosby. Tuesday 4 May 1779.
1s.   Danl Murphy by John Squire C. chd by ~~him~~ Jos: Fowler for ass^{t}ing him & knocking him down—d^d

Mary Grainger, Han^h Jones} WC by d^{o}C. chd by him for begging in the Parish of Christ Church—rem^{d}ed

Thos Walton by Thos Parrott C. chd by Ann Walton (on Ald^n Plomer's W^t) for an Ass^t— ag^d & d^d

168

Robert Lowder[128] pr. by John Procter C. chd by Mary Rison for fel stealing a p[r] of Silver Buckles and a Table Spoon value 20s.

Charles Paxton

RX ~~Re Mary the Wife of~~ James Rison at the Bell in Warwick Lane ~~Bishopgate Street~~ Tappster[?] for Mary Ux: £ 20
Cha[s] Paxton at M[r] Davidson's Southwark 10
Jos: Neale N[o] 3 Lumley C[t] Strand Serj[t] 10

Jane Cardiney pr. by W[m] Martin C. for taking an Infant out of Fleet Market rem[d] till to morrow.

Low Bates an apprentice to M[r] Joseph Gaunt for being an Idle & disorderly Apprentice discharged before Ald[n] Plomer & his Wsp

~~W[t] v. Rich[d] Gill ats~~

B.C. M[r] Houston attended.

M[r] Alderman Townsend by M[r] Alderman Crosby. Wednesday 5 May 1779.
Mary Stevens, Ann Richards, Charlotte Gibbs, Mary Dunn[129]}
WC by Will: Payne C. chd by him for severally wandering abroad & picking up Men

John White, Geo: Bolton} d[o]C by d[o]C. chd by him as fit Persons to serve the King—d[d]

Sarah Davis, Eliz: Roper, Mary Smith} d[o]C by d[o]C. chd by him for singing Ballads in S[t] Pauls Chch Yard – they had Children—d[d] on their promise to keep out of the Street

B.C. M[r] Rhodes attended.

M[r] Alderman Bull. Thursday 6 May 1779.
Martin Robinson app[d] for Mess[rs] Parton and Haynes sum[d] by Joseph Dolphin, Carman, for the Cartage of half a Load from Bileter Lane to Aldersgate Street – paid

P
W[t] ag[t] Rob: Club ads Benj: Tunnacle Ass[t] etc.

---

128. The case proceeds to the Old Bailey. See *OBP*, May 1779, trial of Robert Lawdon (t17790519–4).
129. A check mark appears beside each name.

Rach[l] Farey, Mary Bell} WC Matt[w] Mead C. and Ch[d] by Barbarah Adams for robbing her ready furnished Lodgings of a bolster, a pillow, a brass Candlestick, a copper Sausepan, a Quilt, ~~a bedstead~~, three blankets & a pair of Sheets Va: 20s. & upw[ds] her property.

John Strangeway & Sarah Ux: R[d] Bond—d[d]

1s.   Aff[t] Rob: Clarke

1s.   Back'd a Middx W[t] per M[r] Querrill

John Foster app[d] for John & Peter Calvert complained ag[st] by John Fleming, for not having a Number to their Dray – the Driver was produced

Rebecca Wilmot, Eliz: Bonser, Rose Caroy} WC by Will: Payne C. chd by him for wandering abroad & picking up Men – Will: Beake keeps the House

Tho[s] Groves by Will: Payne C. chd by him on suspicion of Felony – d[d]

Jane Cordelier WC by Will: Martin C. chd by John Remington for following a Child to Strip her – com[d] to B.

Rhodes Att[y] attended   F.B.

M[r] Alderman Wilkes. Friday 7 May 1779.
    Will: Smith[130] WC by Will: Brockwell C. chd by Will: Orme & Ja[s] Bowker for feloniously stealing a bath beaver Surtout Coat Value 15s s[d] Orme's property – on their Oaths com[d] to d[o]C.

RX Will: Orme N[o] 36 Old Change London Cutler	10
~~Reb[a] Davis d[o]C by Zach[h] Hardman C.~~	10
Ja[s] Bowker N[o] 36 D[o] Publican	10
Will. Brockwell Purse C[t] N[o] 4 Old Change Silversmith	10

1s.   W[t] ag[t] John Holford ads Tho[s] Holmes Ass[t]

Rebecca Davis WC Zachariah Hardman C. chd By Ann Worgan for assaulting her and o[r]wise wilfully misbehaving herself last Night etc. M[rs] Worgan (on her asking Pardon) Consented to her being discharg[d].

---

130. The case proceeds to the Old Bailey. See *OBP*, May 1779, trial of William Smith (t17790519–12).

Sam[l] Alchorn W[m] Harris C. and Ch[d] by Prudence Alchorn
his Wife for assaulting and beating her (on M[r] Ald[n] Plomer's
Warr[t]) Adjudg[d] true and Comm[d] to WC for Want of Bail

Bernard Henry, John Bingley C. and Ch[d] by Anthony Andrews
and Tho[s] Searl his Apprentice, and George Carter on Suspicion
of feloniously Stealing a Guinea Property of s[d] Anth[y] Andrews,
For Want of Proof he Was disch[d].

3s.   Aff[t] Diederick Van Holsten, Peter Nilsen, Jenes Erickson.

M[r] Rhodes attended   WP

M[r] Alderman Clark. Wednesday 6 O'Clock 28 June 1780.
    George Staples[131] charged by Jno Williams & John Flitchett
for being concerned in a riotous & tumultuous Assembly of
Persons unknown—and there being present at and feloniously
& traitorously assisting in demolishing the House, Goods &
Furniture of Ja[s] Malo—He was standing Oppo[te] M[r] Malo's at
the time the House &c. were consumed—Saw the pris[r] up one
pair of Stairs, throwing furniture into the Street, where other
Goods were burnt—Saw him drink out of a Bottle & take off
his Wig & huzza'd—then he fell to Work again, tearing down
part of the Wainscotting—then drank out of another Bottle –
com[d] to WC (on their Oaths.)

RX   John Williams – Bridgewater Gardens L. Porter   £20
    John Flitchett – Par: St Giles Cripplegate Carver   20
    John Smily – White Cross Street L. Glazier   20

    John Smily – saw the Pris[r] present, whilst M[r] Malo's House
was pulling down – he saw the pris[r] put his hands to the Rails
as if endeavouring to pull them down

Ald[n] Plomer   Will: Clarke Appr[e]: to Ja[s] Ramsden Cit: & Butcher
    complain'd ag[st] for deserting his Service – he acknowl-
    edged the Charge to be true – Ord[d] to be d[d]

    Isaac Robins, George Coleman} charged by Jonathan Smith
on suspicion of being concerned in a riotous & tumultuous
Assembly of Persons unknown, at the House of Tho[s] Langdale,
situate at Holborn Bridge—and there being present at & feloniously & traitorously assisting in demolish[g] the said House—
Smith never saw the Pris[r] s before – he was defective in Sight

---

131. The case proceeds to the Old Bailey. See *OBP*, June 1780, trial of George Staples
    (t17800628–37).

of one Eye – there was the fullest proof, that Smith was entirely mistaken—Edwd Bradley, Shoe Lane, Currier, proved the pris^rs to be at Work at the time Smith offer'd to swear they were at Langdale's – d^d.

1s. Charlotte Pugh – chd by Jane Evans (on Ald^n Plomer's W^t) for an Ass^t – d^d

1s. Aff^t John Owen

1s. Hen: Weed, PC charged by John Rogers (not now present) for an Ass^t – d^d.

R.C.

Mr Alderman Wooldridge. Thursday 29 June 1780.
Geo: James Saunderson (an App^ce) WC John Cruse C. Ch^d by Wm Lukes his Ma^r for running away and absenting himself from his s^d Ma^rs Service with^t his knowledge or Consent. Adj^d true and by mutual Consent the Apprentice was disch^d by Judgm^t in the Mayors C^t & Sent on Board the Mermaid Privateer Comm^d by Captain Fielding

1s. Warr^t ads Joseph Dixon ag^t John Metcalf per Ass^t

P Warr^t v. Frances Brazier ads Mary Foster per Ass^t

1s. Affid^t Parker

Mary Sanders WC Matt^w Stimpson C. Ch^d by Robert Trotter with being a loose idle & disorderly Person & a common Prostitute – Adjudg'd true & comm^d to Bridewell till a Court

Wm Weldron & John Townsend} WC Robt Trotter C. & Ch^d by Wm Wood N° 91 Fleet for distributing inflamitory Hand Bills and for Encouraging the Rioters at the late Fire in Moorf^ld by calling out No Popery &c. They app^d to be stout healthy Boys & fit for his Majestys Ser^e. They were at their own Request sent on Board a Tender &c. By R^t Trotter Const.

Gave the prisoner 1s. Per Order	Wm Stokes PC Robt Trotter C. and Ch^d by Wm Wood N° 91 Fleet St^t for Encouraging the Late Rioters at the demolishing of the Romish Chapel in Moorf^d on Wednesday 7th Inst. by join^g the general Cry of (No Popery &c.) He app^d on examicon to be a private Sold^r in a Marching Regiment & to be absent on Furlow &c.

    & being in an ill State of Health & having offended through Ignorance, He was reprimanded & D^d.

P   Warr^t v. John Kissel ads Jane ux per Ass^t

    Mr Rhodes Attended.   TW.

Mr Alderman Hart. Friday 30 June 1780.

1s.   Thos Sears PC John Smith C. Ch^d by Thos Beswick Vict^r for greatly misbehaving himself last Night at Mr Beswicks & ref^g to quit his house at a late hour after having been requested so to do He made Submission ^Was reprimanded & Dd.

1s.   Warr^t v. Asher Simons ads Jacob Nathan Poland per Ass^t

P   D^o agt Wm Wyburn & Mary Ellis ads Eliz^th Salmon per D^o

    Thos Wilson WC Saml Roberts C. Ch^d by Jos^h Hemens Serj^t of the green Regim^t of the City Militia for wandring abroad & lodging in the open Air having no visible way of living, rem^d for fur^r Examicion

    ~~Wm Battersby & Ann his Wife} WC John Scandrett Const. & Ch'd by him~~

1s.   Frances Brazier (on Mr Ald^n Wooldridge's Warr^t) Thos Withers C., Ch^d by Mary Foster Per Ass^t. She made Satisf^h and was d^d.

2s.   Rebecca Davis & Sarah Davis} (on Mr Ald^n Plomers War^t) Thos Parrott C. & Ch^d by Hannah Levy Per Ass^t. Mre Sett^d & D^d

4s.   Affid^t Foster & an^r D^o Williams, D^o Mitchell & Hart

P   Ja^s Purcell by Ja^s Ives C. chd by Thos James Lawrance (on a peace W^t) for using threats whereby &c. – d^d

next Sess^s   Ja^s Purcell the Leaping Barr Coff House Christ C.

    Surry   £40

R   Edward Pugh N° 9 New George St^t Christ Church

    Shoem^r   £20

    Wm Greedey s^d Parish Christ Church Farrier   £20

    To app^r & ans^r next Sess^s in & for London

    Wm Goodchild[132] PC Aaron Coates C. Ch^d by Jos^h Travers a

---

132. This case proceeds to the Old Bailey. See *OBP*, June 1780, trial of William Goodchild (t17800628–105).

Grocer for feloniously Stealing 4^{lb} W^t black Pepper Value 5s. Property Saml Smith, Wm Smith, Jos^h Nash, Francis Kemble & Jos^h Travers, grocers and Copartners in Trade. Wm Hewitt (Warehouse Man) confirm'd Mr Travers in his Evidence Adj^d true & com^d to W.C.

RX   Joseph Travers N° 80 Cannon Street Grocer   £20
Wm Hewitt Warehouseman to Smith & Co. Grocers
& Partners   £10
Aaron Coates N° 27 Little East Cheap Oilman & Const   £10
    To Prosecute & give Evidence at Sess^s now holding in & for London.

Thos Flanagan, Thos Stone & Edwd Williams} PC Saml How C. and ch^d by Jos^h Travers on Suspicion of feloniously Stealing a Quantity of Nutmegs Value [blank] the Property of s^d Smith & Co. Grocers & Partners   For Want of Proof D^d

Attended Mr Rhodes   JH

Mr Alderman Sainsbury. Monday 3 July 1780.
1s.   Aff^t Magnus Johnson

1s.   D^o Ja^s Waters

p

    Mary ~~Hacket~~ Andrews by Geo: ~~Andrews~~ Hacket C. chd by William Charlton for abusing him – d^d

    Timothy Green, Mary Somers} by Will: Wilson C. chd each other – Green chd Somers with defrauding him of six Pence – he gave her the Money – d^d

1s.   Attested Lewis Richard

    Hen: Croucher, Ann Croucher, Eliz: Sharp} by Boyse May C. chd by Will: Drew on suspicion of feloniously stealing a Parcel of China—Ann the Dau[ghte]r was the principal & the others reced the Goods—Mr Drew declined a Prosecution – d^d.

    John Freeman, Mary Williams} PC by Will: Cooke C. chd by Thos Ross a Watchman – being fo^d together, going to a bad House – there was no Indecency, nor disturbance – the C. was reprim^{d}ed – and the pris^{rs} were d^d.

1s.   John Gilchrist, Marg^t Mann} by doC. chd by him – being fo^d together in a bye Passage at an unseasonable Hour – d^d.

Ann Hockwell, Ann Cummings} PC by Will: Cooke C. chd by him for making a disturbance in the Street & collecting a Mob – they app^d to be Women of the Town, but promising better behaviour in future—they were d^d.

Eliz: Sharp by Boyse May C. chd by Elizabeth Topham for feloniously stealing one Yard and a half of long Lawn & a Child's Robe—Susanna Turner pawned the Robe in Shoe Lane – the Lawn & three Clouts[133] at Mr Brooks, in Fleet Market – rem^{d}ed 'till Wednesday, when the pawnbrokers are to appear.

Mary Sainsbury ~~Saunderson~~ by Matt^w Stinson C. chd by Will: Sewell for feloniously stealing a Sieve of Cherries – d^d by desire of Mr Sewell

Mich^l Carney PC by Rob: Green C. chd by John Lawrence & Deliverance Hawkins for feloniously stealing a bundle, ~~containing a Suit of Cloaths~~ the felonious taking appeared somewhat doubtful and the man being willing to go to Sea (he was a sailor) the Pris^r was rem^{d}ed untill an Officer sho^d call, & take him on board a Ship.

Mary McCarty WC by Chas Allen C. chd by Will: Butts for selling Cherries by short Weight – d^d.

Mary Chambers PC by Matt^w Fisher C. chd by Mary Randall on suspicion of stealing a Gua in Gold, a Crown Piece, & 2s. in Silver, monies numbered – the Monies of the s^d Mary Randall – for want of Evid^{ce} the Pris^r was d^d.

1s.   Eliz: Crowe by Luke Hanwood C. chd by Jane Robertson (on Ald^n Plomer's W^t 1st Instant) for assaulting & beating her, Prosx appg originally the aggressor – d^d.

P   ~~W^t. ag.t Cha. Hassey ads~~
W^t ag^t Ann Fray ads Sarah Wilson Ass^t etc.

1s.   W^t ag^t Chas Pearson ads Darby Kelroy Ass^t etc.

not   ~~D^o ag^t George Walsham ads James Hudson his Appr: Ass^t etc.~~
issued

Mr Beach attended   TS

133. A patch of cloth.

Mʳ Alderman Kitchin. Tuesday 4 July 1780.

Geo: Gibson, Jaˢ Jagar} WC by Thoˢ Gates C. chd by him as suspicious Characters – being apprehended in Petticoat Lane at an unseasonable hour – Jagar was remᵈed to produce Persons to his Character – Gibson appᵈ to be a Deserter from the Conquestadore— remᵈed. (22 Geo: 2 C.33 S.40)

1s.   Affᵗ Rᵈ Grace.

Edwᵈ Cuffley charged by Will: Dorrill, Inspector of the pavements within this City, for assaulting him in the Execution of that Office – Cuffley collared Dorrill – Thoˢ Shute was sworn & saw him collared – Dorrill was also sworn – convᵈ in the penalty of 5s. which Mʳ Hall took to pay into the Chamber.

1s.   Affᵗ Rob: Wilks

Eliz: ~~Brown~~ Ux Wᵐ Smith WC by John Duncastle C. chd by Edwᵈ Penny on suspicion of feloniously stealing ~~four~~ three pair of leather Gloves Val: 4s. his property – Will: Charlton saw the fact comᵈ – remᵈed untill tomorrow

Will: Dorrill, Inspector appᵈ to answer the Complt. of Geo: Smith for presenting something like a Pistol, and swearing he'd blow his brains out if he touch'd a Hamper – he said, he was at that time in fear of his Life – Thoˢ Ellis was present – also Jarvis Adamson – it appᵈ by the Evidence of Geo: Stanfield an Officer of Excise, that he was obstructed by Smith, whereupon Dorrill interfered as a Constable – dᵈ

Henry Jones by Stephen Flindal C. chd by Samˡ Marshal Esqʳ for feloniously stealing a cloth Jacket and Waistcoat, & two pair of breeches, Val: [blank] Maria Hall saw the Prisʳ take the things away – dᵈ.

1s.   John Mico by Timothy Placo C. chd by Samˡ Betts (on Aldⁿ Plomer's Wᵗ) for an Assᵗ – dᵈ Prosʳ appᵍ the Aggressor

1s.   Wᵗ agᵗ Joshᵏ Phillips ads Mary Frosle[?]Assᵗ etc.

P   Dᵒ agt Hector McCoy ads Mary Ux – Dᵒ.

Mʳ Nash attended. HK

Mʳ Alderman Alsop by Mʳ Alderman Kitchin. Wednesday 5 July 1780.

1s.   Wᵗ v. John Hol~~denms~~,Wᵐ Evans & Thoˢ Waller ats Wᵐ ~~Do~~ Bolt.

Eliz Sharp pr by Boys May C. charged by Eliz ux Jon^a Topham
for steal^g –3 Clouts a Child's Robe & a Yard and half of Long
Lawn Va 6s. 1d. Jon^a Topham – John Cargill Servt to Jno Brooks
P^{n}broker Fleet Markett, took to pawn, a piece of long Lawn &
3 Clouts fr: Sus^a Turner, (who was present & acknowl^d to have
pawned 'em by Pris^{rs} Consent), they were pawn'd in the name
of Sarah Rôch, Geo: Stables Servant to Thos Cotterell P^{n}broker
Shoe Lane took fr: Turner a Child's Robe in the Name of Sarah
Roach – d^d for want of sufficient Proof – d^d.

Eliz: Ux: Will: Smith WC by Jno Duncastle C. chd by Edwd
Penny (as Yesterday) and by his desire – d^d

Geo: Gibson, Ja^s Jagar} charged by Thos Gates – being apprehended at an unseasonable Hour in the Street – Gibson app^d
to be a Deserter from the Conquestadore – Jagar gave a good
Account of himself and was d^d – Gibson's Master app^d & gave
him a Character for Industry – d^d

~~Geo. Gibson pr by Thos Gates for being a Deserter on board
the Conquest at the Nore~~

~~Wt v.~~ Eliz Leonard pr by Joseph Thompson C. charged by
Wm Grey as a Vagrant – she was so ill as not to be able to be
brought up – Ord^d to remain

Luke Holden complained agst by Rob: Rivers – for an Ass^t –
ag^d

Mr Houstoun attended.
HK

The Right Honourable Thomas Harley. Thursday 6 July 1780.
~~Chas Jones by Ja^s Ashmore C. chd by~~

~~Mary Riley WC by John Hart C. chd by Manly~~

~~Sarah Armstrong & Sarah Atkins C by Benjamin Church C.
charged by John Small for making a Noise – d~~

Mr Houstoun att^d (No Attendance)

Mr Alderman Crosby by Mr Alderman Clark. Friday 7 July 1780.
    John Bailey pr by John Tilberry Williams C. charged by him
    – but Williams did not appear – d^d

Saml Miller pr by John Couchman charged by Saml Cheesewright for leaving Work unfinished on the Ld Mayor's W^t 7 6 Inst – he ag^d to return & finish the Work – d^d.

John Bollen, Giles Bollen} by Luke Herod C. chd by John Downes – apprehended at an unseasonable Hour in the Minories – Giles app^d to have been a Seaman & produced his discharge Mr Simpson knew 'em to be painters in Employ – d^d

Sarah Snowball by Ja^s Prior C. chd by Sarah Gardner her Mistress for assaulting & pulling her down – com^d to WC.

1s. Amos ~~Dibbidgh~~ Biddulph pr by Robt Green C. chd by Thos Jenkins on Ald^n Plomer's W^t for Ass^t dis^d.

Thos Pratt by Will: Sumner C. chd by Will: Evans for threatening to set his House on Fire – rem^{d}ed to enquire whether he deserted from the Queen's Regiment.

1s. Ja^s Tyner by John Proctor C. chd by Jno Evans a hackney Coachman for bilking him of his fare – ag^d & d^d

1s. Hester Jewell by Ja^s Munday C. chd by Mary Horton for an Ass^t – d^d

Mary Watson by Will: Sumner C. chd by a Person (not now present) as a Vagrant – she belongs to Westerton in Suffolk – rem^{d}ed to be pass'd

P Jane Armstrong, Sarah Atkins} WC by Benj: Church C. chd by John Small a Watchman for making a Disturbance – d^d.

Mary Smith doC by Boyse May C. chd by him for lodging in the open Air – recommended to St Bartholomew's Hospital

Mr Houston attended R.C.

Mr Alderman Townsend. Monday 10 July 1780.
  (No Attendance) Mr Beach att^{d}ed

Mr Alderman Bull. Tuesday 11 July 1780.
  Thos Pratt WC by Will: Sumner C. chd by Will: Evans (not now present) as on Friday last – ag^d to enter into the Navy

  Mary Watson doC chd with lodging in the open Air – recommended to the Hospital to be cured of the foul Distemper

Saml Parsons doC by Bryan Chandler C. chd by John Richardson – being apprehended as a suspicious Character – d^d

1s. W^t ag^t Thos Entry ads Saml Lewis Ass^t etc.

1s. Back'd an Essex W^t per Mr Cuthbert

John Lloyd by Saml Shaw C. chd by Thos Figgis, a Publican for refusing to pay a Bill of 4s./8d. for Meat and Liquor – Ord^d to pay it

P Mary Basset WC by Thos Emery C. chd by Sarah Dudley for Abuse – d^d

1s. W^t ag^t Chas Surrs ads Ann Newman Ass^t etc.

Eliz: Somers, Sarah King} WC by John Cruse C. chd ~~by~~ as follows – King charg'd Somers with an Ass^t – they app^d to be loose Characters d^d.

Geo: Walshaw sum^d by Ja^s Hudson his Appr: for assaulting & beating him – ag^d to be d^d on Tuesday by two Magistrates

Eliz: Godfrey an Appr: charged by Patience Denham her Mistress (to whom she was bound by the Trustees of St Ann Aldersgate Charity School) for running away – she app^d to be obstinate and wo^d not answer a Question – rem^{d}ed

Mr Nash Attended F.B.

Mr Alderman Wilkes. Wednesday 12 July 1780.
1s. W^t v. Sarah Clarke ats Mary Tolks Ass^t

Robert Belcher an Apprentice pr by Thos Emery C. chd by John Robinson his Master for being an Idle & disorderly Apprentice & absenting himself from his said Master's Service & Justice Addington's W^t 5 Inst back't by Ald^n Kitchins – referr'd to a Middx Justice, Robinson being resident in the County.

P Jane Williams by Will: Sargeson C. chd by Mary Satch (on Ald^n Plomer's W^t) for an Ass^t – they withdrew & d^d

1s. Aff^t John Toyne

Richard Smith ~~Eliz: Coleman Wild~~} WC by Rob: Trotter C. chd by ~~him for~~ Eliz: Wild for violently assaulting and beating

179

her – a loaded Pistol was taken upon him – rem^ded to enquire if he has escaped from New Prison – and so was Wild

Hannah Loney d^oC by Will: Wilson C. chd by Ann Cummings (on the Lord Mayor's W^t) for an Ass^t – they withdrew & d^d.

1s.   Back'd a Middx W^t Per Mr Croft.

P   Mary Coker B—by Thos Holt C. chd by Ann Young (on the Lord Mayor's W^t) for an Ass^t – ag^d & d^d.

1s.   John Metcalf by John Grose C. chd by Joseph Dixon (on Ald^n Wooldridge's W^t) for an Ass^t – ag^d & d^d

Sarah Clark by John Flindal C. chd by Mary Tolks (on Ald^n Hart's W^t) for an Ass^t – it app^d they fought together – d^d

Jane Mcgee by Luke Herod C. chd by Lawrence Lee for abusing him & making a disturbance – d^d

Mr Houstoun attended   John Wilkes

1s.   Seth Williams by John Guyse C. chd by Hollingsworth, a Publican, for an Assault – d^d

1s.   W^t ag^t John Malcin, John Green & Jos: Smith ads John Holyland on suspicion of stealing a Sack of Coals.

Ann Frankdown by Thos Fenner C. chd by him for lodging in the Parish of St Lawrence Jewry in the open Air – rem^ded to be pass'd

Mr Alderman Sawbridge. Thursday 13 July 1780.
    (No Attendance)
    Rhodes Att^y attended

Sir Thomas Hallifax. Friday 14 July 1780.
P   Eliz: Wild WC by Rob: Trotter C. chd by him for making a great Noise and Disturbance – she was d^d.

Eliz: Norris d^oC. by John Couchman C. chd by Joshua Highway on suspicion of feloniously stealing a silver Watch – she confess'd under a Promise of favour—and there was no other Evidence – d^d.

Will: Paid d^oC by John Ballard C. chd by Will: Price for attempting to pick his Pocket – he was d^d

Will: Long[134] ~~Thorp~~ WC by Will: Matthews C. chd by Geo: Lynam ~~John Langham~~ & Will: Jonathan Eade on Suspicion of feloniously stealing ~~a Parcel of Nails, of~~ 1000 Princes Metal Nails Val: 7s./~~6d~~ the property of Thos Shrimpton, Jno Russel and Will: Ewster – com^d to d^{o}C – Saml Fowler

RX Geo: Lynam for self and Eade and Fowler   £ 10
~~Will. Jonathan Eade Saml Russel Fowler for self~~
~~and Eade~~   ~~£ 10~~

P   Mary Fellows by Walter Prosser C. chd by Susanna Hewson (on the Lord Mayor's W^t) for an Ass^t – the complaint was a trifling one – the Pris^r was d^d

John Green, Jos: Smith} by John Guyse C. chd by John Holyland (on a W^t Per Ald^n Wilkes) on suspicion of feloniously stealing a Sack of Coals, his property – rem^{d}ed 'till Monday to have another Witness.

Thos Minors WC Ben: Church C. chd by James Bunford for that he was apprehended the 20 ~~Inst.~~ult as a Vagrant, he had been kept ever since in the Compter to find out his Settlement but not being able to do it, he was ord^d to the Parish where he was apprehended.

Edwd Dowling PC by Jos: Sheppard C. chd by Isaac Forster for stealing a Trowel – d^d for want of Proof

P   Cath: Brian, Mary Rowland} by Luke Herod C. chd by Cath: Clifford (on the Lord Mayor's W^t) for an Ass^t – frivolous & d^d.

P   Cath: Clifford, Rose Glover} by d^{o}C. chd by Cath: O'Brien (on Ald^n Plomer's W^t) for an Ass^t – friv^s and d^d

1s. Sarah Cootes, John Davis} by Joseph Keen C. chd by Hannah Phillips (on the Lord Mayor's W^t) for wilfully breaking her Windows – there was no Evidence to support the Charge – d^d.

1s. Ann Mitchell by Thos Parrott C. chd by Mary Aarons (on Ald^n Plomer's W^t) for an Ass^t – d^d (being friv^s)

1s. Millament Blow by d^{o}C. chd by Ann Barnett (on Ald^n Plomer's W^t) for an Ass^t – d^d.

---

134. The case proceeds to the Old Bailey. See *OBP*, September 1780, trial of William Long (t17800913–32).

P   Sarah Clark by John Flindal C. chd by Matt^w Dutton for an Assault –d^d.

Thos Phillips by Jos: Keen C. chd by John Davis (on a W^t) for using threats whereby &c. d^d (being friv^s)

Mr Beech attended   TH

Sir James Esdaile by Mr Alderman Plomer. Monday 17 July 1780.

1s.   Cath: Taylor by Will: Wilson C. chd by Mary Huntsmull (on Alderman Thomas's W^t) for an Ass^t – the Parties withdrew & ag^d – d^d

Mary Bowtell by Will: Martin C. chd by Fra^s Hambleton – being found in a House of ill fame in Long Lane – d^d.

1s.   Affidavit Saml Coal

Marg^t Adair WC by Matt^w Stimson C. chd by him and another Person not present, on suspicion of felony – d^d.

Eliz: Clark d^{o}C. by John Bush C. chd by John Lee N° 9 Cock Court for feloniously stealing a linen handkerchief – Val: 3d his property – com^d to B.

John Green, Jos: Smith } chd by John Holyland (on Mr Ald^n Wilkes's W^t) on Suspicion of feloniously stealing a Sack of Coals, his property –Will: Spurr saw three Men (but co^d not speak to either of the Pris^{rs}) aside in a field out of the Road—with the Cart – John Watkins

   Green said, that about three Miles from Tyburn Turnpike, a Sack of Coals was dropt at a public House – but he declared himself ignorant of the Sign, says that he and the other prisoner had no hand in taking these Coals nor had either of them any money for 'em, not been sharing with Malyn (who was the 3^d Carman & who drove the Waggon) the money given ~~for~~ them by Mr Allnut

Saml Blakey ~~by~~ brought up & said by two ~~of~~ Const^s of Middlesex Attending on Justice Blackborow to be accused by an Accomplice before s^d Magistrate of stealing Comon Prayer Books & a variety of other Things from Lady Huntingdon's Chapel (late the Pantheon) was ord^d to be deliv^d over to ~~a Midd~~ these Const^s –to be [~~illegible~~] carried before a Middx Justice

1s.   W^t ag^t Jas M^{c}mical ads Saml Sharwood Overseer of the Par:

of St Ann Aldersgate for running away & deserting his Wife & family whereby &c.

John Radcliffe sum^d by Hen: Brind, Overseer of Saint Olave, Silver Street, for refusing to pay his Proportion of the Poor's Rate of the said Parish – referr'd to a Vestry

Mr Beach attended   WP

Mr Alderman Plumbe. Tuesday 18 July 1780

P   Eliz: Onington by John Clements C. chd by Elias Clark (on a W^t) for an Ass^t – Clark com^d the 1st Ass^t – d^d

1s.   Juda Jacobs by Abram Solomons C. chd by Jno Levy (on Ald^n Plomer's W^t) for an Ass^t – they withdrew & agreed d^d.

1s.   Back'd a Middx W^t Per Mr Wright

       Sus^a Evely by Edwd Thompson C. chd by Ja^s Bundle, a Watchman for making a disturbance – d^d.

       Edwd Carman WC by Paul Postan C. chd by ~~Thomas~~ Anne Richards with assaulting her & striking her with a drawn Bayonet, he asked pardon & was d^d.

1s.   ~~Eliz^h Bradley~~ Thos Heath WC by Boyse May C. chd by Eliz^h Bradley with assault^g her and knocking her down – Bradley was known here as a Common Prostitute—but it app^d she was ill used – She forgave him and he was d^d.

1s.   Back'd a Middx W^t

P   Cath: Taylor WC by Will: Wilson C. chd by Mary Huntsmull (on a W^t) for an Ass^t – they withdrew & ag^d – d^d.

1s.   Back'd a Middx W^t Per Mr Blackborow

       John Everall, ~~John Snape~~} WC by Edwd Thompson C. chd as follows – Snape gave the 1st Charge agst Everall for collaring him & accusing him of being concerned in picking his Pocket – it app^d to be a Mistake of Everall – Everall was affected in his Brain – d^d

       Ambrose Ward by Saml Roberts C. chd by Stephen Joyce a Watchman – rem^{d}ed 'till tomorrow

~~Sarah Clark by Jos: Penn C.~~

Mr Nash attended

Mr Alderman Kirkman. Wednesday 19 July 1780
~~Ald^n Wilkes~~ ~~W^t ag^t Jonathan Brown ads Isaac Pearce –Ass^t etc.~~

~~Benj: Fetters WC by Rob: Trotter C. chd by –~~

~~Ambrose Ward d^{o}C by Saml Roberts C.~~

Ald^n Wilkes   Daniel Read PC charged by Robert Holden, Major of
P   the White Regiment of Militia – being appreh^d as a
               suspicious Character – d^d.

Mr Houstoun att^d

Sir Watkin Lewes. Thursday 20 July 1780.
Mr Ald^n Hart.
         Ann Anderson[135] WC by John Scandret C. chd by Thos Grif-
         fiths for feloniously stealing 9s. in Silver, one cotton Gown,
         one stuff quilted Petticoat, two linen Aprons, one muslin
         handkerchief, one silk Bonnet, one pair of plated buckles, one
         Shift, and one pair of Cotton Gloves Val: 40s. the Property of
         Eliz: Smither – also one Suit of orange coloured Cloth, Suit of
         Cloaths, a pair of Women's Shoes and a cotton handkerchief
         Val: 40s. and upwards the property of the said Thos Griffiths
         – Adjudg'd true on Informon of said Thos Griffiths & Elizth
         Smith, which were severally taken in Writing and on Oath –
         com^d to d^{o}C
RX   Thos Griffiths Fish Street Hill, London Peruke Maker   £10
       Will: Smither of Leadenhall Mket, Butcher for
       <u>Eliz Smither</u>   } 10
       John Scandret – Fetter L. Victualler   }

2s.   Aff^{ts} Thos Longman, John Bew

1s.   Joseph Roberts PC Wm Godfrey C. Ch^d by Geo Darant, Joseph
       Bisson, Moses Tilley (Serj^t of the Hampshire Militia) and
       Barth^w Parkman (a Sentinal on Duty) for making a great Noise
       & Disturbance last Night &c.— he was in Liquor & had com^d
       no breach of the Peace reprim^d & d^d.

135. The case proceeds to the Old Bailey. See *OBP*, September 1780, trial of Ann Anderson
(t17800913-99).

1s   Backt Justice Addingtons Warr^t

~~Jos: Nicholson by Boyse May C. chd by Ja^s Hoar~~

~~Eliz: Hunter by John Couchman C. chd by~~

John Worsley PC John Fenner C. Ch^d by Wm Frost & John Frost on suspicion of feloniously stealing £40 Property of the s^d Wm Frost For Want of Evidence was d^d.

Mary Taunton WC by Benj: Scott C. chd by Jos: Andrews of the Cloysters, Mercer, for feloniously stealing 31 Yards of black silk Lace Val 30s. & upw^ds his Property – no Proof – d^d.

1s.   Mark Leoni by Char^s Delagal C. chd by Timothy Sullivan (on a Middx W^t back'd) for an Ass^t –d^d.

Rhodes Att^y attended

Mr Alderman Plomer. Friday 21 July 1780.
2s.   Affidavits Rob: Mendham, David Meredith

Mark Leoni—charged by Timothy Solomons for an Ass^t – com^d in Middx – referr'd

1s.   W^t ag^t Ja^s Sheridan ads Tim^y Solomons Ass^t

Ambrose Ward – charged by Stephen Joyce a W^chman for making a disturbance – sent to the Marine Society

P   Cath: Smith by Will: Wilson C. chd by Eliz: Carter (on a W^t) for an Ass^t – d^d.

1s.   Jos: Nicholson WC by Boyse May C. chd by Ja^s Hoar for an Ass^t – ag^d and d^d

1s.   a Person charged with Ass^t – ag^d and d^d

Eliz: Wicks by John Fleet—C. chd by John Hickson on suspicion of feloniously stealing a Suit of Cloaths, a mode Cloak, 2 Cotton Gowns, for want of Evidence – d^d

Richd Ivey sum^d for assaulting & beating Chas Silverwood – d^d.

Mr Houston attended GeH

Mr Alderman Thomas. Monday 24 July, 1780.
 Geo: Watts enlisted into Colonel Harcourt's Light Horse – paid 20s. Smart – and was d^d

1s. John Micoe by Moses Orme C. chd by Saml Hogg (on a W^t) for an Ass^t – friv^s and d^d.

  Sarah Hill by Matt^w Stimson C. chd by Wm Purdue on Suspicion of feloniously stealing a pair of Shoes, a gold Ring – it app^d that Purdue's Son had robb'd him, and that there was a Connection between the Son & the Pris^r – d^d.

  Eliz: Barnett apprehended on a Search W^t of Mr Ald^n Plomer – d^d – her Son being the House Keeper

1s. John Livingstone, Jane Picket} WC by Jno Berry C. chd by Will: Straker – being found together in a House of ill fame in Union Court, Holborn – Pickett com^d to B.– the Man d^d.

  Will: Brown a hackney Coachman sum^d by Thos Fortune for taking more than his fare for carrying him in his hackney Coach from Holborn to Bishopsgate Street – Jos: Richardson, Measurer, was sworn – s^d the Ground was 1 Mile and half, & 19 Yards – d^d. (being 19 Yards more than the distance) of one Mile & half.

1s. John Mason by Will: Sumner C. chd by Ann Carey for an Ass^t – d^d

  Mr Beach att^d N Thomas

nil Thos Walsh by Chas Delagal C. chd by Mary Wood for an Ass^t – they withdrew and d^d.

  Sarah Painter by Nathan Brown C. chd by him for lodging in the open Air – recommended to St Bartholomew's Hospital (being foul)

Mr Alderman Peckham. Tuesday 25 July 1780.
Ald^n Townsend
nil John Burney by Will: Wilson C. chd by John Cleeve for an Assault – d^d

3s. Aff^t Fran^s Garman, Thos Taylor, John Miller

  Will: Procter, Thos Readshaw} by Will: Martin C. chd by John Richardson, Thos Bennett and Thos Snow—being apprehended in an indecent Situation – the privities of Readshaw were exposed – Readshaw said, he was an Undertaker in Wardour Street Soho – Procter is a Grocer at Hatton Wall N° 12— Procter, Richardson, Bennett & Snow were sworn – Procter declared he had assaulted him with Intent to commit Buggery Mr Miller keeps the House in Wardour Street – by his own desire, Readshaw rem^{d}ed untill tomorrow

Mary Graves, Eliz: Wright } by Will: Sumner C.

Richd Cass Driver of a hackney Coach N° 843 – sum^d by R^d Grindall Esqr for taking more than his fare for carrying more than him in his said Coach – fined 10s. of which the D^r reced 5s.

1s. Mary Kelly by Rob: Trotter C. chd by Judith Read (on Ald^n Plomer's W^t) for an Ass^t – ag^d and d^d.

W^t ag^t John Weston ads Jno Shank for knowingly & designedly by false pretences obtaining from him the Sum of £28.13s.4d with Intent to cheat & defraud him thereof

Ald^n Wooldridge Thos Gobbey [blank] by Jos: Thompson C. chd by Judith Ux: (on Ald^n Hayley's W^t) for an Ass^t – on oath of his Wife com^d to WC.

Eliz Morrison by Will: Payne C

P Emanuel Levy by [blank] C. chd by Jane Levy (on Ald^n Plomer's W^t) for an Ass^t – d^d

Jane Darland, Mary Lee, Rosetta Webber} WC by Jos: Thompson C. chd by him for picking up Men – Webber's Mother app^d and took her away

Will: Hall—chd by Stephen Joyce a Watchman as a suspicious Character – he had com^d no Offence – d^d – his father app^d & took him home

1s. W^t ag^t Emanuel Levy ads Eliz^h Hart Assault &c

1s. John Price WC by Jno Squire C. chd by his Wife (not now present) for an Ass^t – ag^d & d^d

Mary Graves, Eliz: Wright} d^{o}C by Will: Sumner C. chd by Stephen Hunt for no Offence – d^d.

Mr Nash attended   TW

2s.   Back'd two Middx W^ts Per Mr Staples & Mr Hyde

Mr Alderman Hayley. Wednesday 26 July 1780.

Ald^n Wooldridge Thos Readshaw rem^ded to WC Yesterday; was now bro^t up, and charged by Will: James Procter, Jno Richardson, Thos Bennett and Thos Snow for assaulting the s^d Will: Procter with Intent to commit the detestable Crime of Buggery – Richardson apprehended them – Snow said, that Readshaw & Procter were close together – Richardson said, that Procter at the time seemed in much Confusion, and he consider'd both equally criminal – Readshaw said "that he overtook Procter on Monday Night between 11 and 12— He said, that if the Pris^r would let him[136] have hold of his Arm, he'd be much oblig'd to him, as he was much in Liquor—He (Procter) took away a Lanthorn & run away with it – he went off with another Man's Lanthorn – the W^chman wo^d have beat Procter, had not Readshaw prevailed on him to desist

That going down Snow Hill, Procter said "What do you think of a good Prick" Readshaw said "I don't know what you mean" Procter said "I don't do much in that Way, but when I do, I have 5 Guineas, but as I have taken a liking to you, I'll oblige for two".

They walk'd together to the place where apprehended.

Ja^s Bunford Watchman – s^d that Procter or some person took away his Lanthorn on Monday Night – Procter was much in Liquor and had the Lanthorn – Geo: Pearce another Watchman—s^d that Readshaw & Procter pass'd him – Procter took his Lanthorn, & Pearce re-took it – Procter app^d to be much in Liquor

Saml Williams N° 104 Blackman St Southwark, Cutler – Says, that he lodged in his House – had a good Character from Mr Dyer, Curate of Saint George – Richard Farrer Mercer in the Cloysters never heard of such a Charge ag^st Readshaw – Chas Molloy N° 113 Portland Street, painter always consider'd him as a family Man – knows he lived happy with his Wife Readshaw was d^d.

---

136. The account is split at this point over two pages in the original.

Thos Reeve WC by Will: Payne C. chd by him for distributing Bills, which he sold for one penny each – d^d.

Will: Law by d^{o}C. chd by Thos Pratt on suspicion of feloniously stealing two gold Watches – there was not the least Proof – d^d.

P   Mary Borous by Ja^s Barker C. chd by George Burton (on Ald^n Plomer's W^t Yesterday) for an Ass^t – d^d

John Holden by Will: Payne C. chd by him & Powell for attempting to pick his Pocket – sent to Sea

a Child was brought by Jos: Thompson C. Says his father is Isaac Carey of King Street Golden Square – two pair of Stairs

Reb^a Rix WC by Will: Wilson C. chd by Eliz: Woodhouse for feloniously stealing a Sheet, & sundry other things – d^d.

1s.   W^t ag^t Ann Jones & Eliz: Jones ads Eliz: Lovegrove Ass^t etc.

2s.   Affi^t Geo: Scott bis.

Mr Rhodes attended Ge H.

Mr Alderman Hayley. Monday 28 August 1780.
Susanna Sargent, Sarah Harris} WC by Boyse May C. chd by him for severally wandering abroad and picking up Men – they promised Amendment – d^d

John Etherton PC by R^d Jutson C. chd by John Miller, Thos Francis and Rob: Sibthorp for feloniously stealing a Sack and half of Corn – for want of Proof d^d

John Elliott sum^d by Thos Bland for detaining a cloth Waistcoat – dism^d

Mr Beach attended   GeH

John Wood by John Prockter C. chd by Thos Musgrave for driving a Coach over a Boy of eleven Years old – rem^{d}ed for further Examon on the Oath of Mr Musgrave who saw the Fact (wch M^r M believes, was accidental and not wilful) com^d

1s.   Affidavit John Robson.

Mr Alderman Newnham. Tuesday 29 August 1780.

1s.   Rob: Rice by John Collinson C. chd by John Latcomb for abusing him – he made a Sumission and was d^d.

1s.   Geo: Cook WC by John Larkin C. chd by John Parker for making a disturbance in his Shop – d^d

Thos Sherman d^{o}C by John Fleet C. chd by Will: Ja^s Burrows on suspicion of feloniously stealing a silver tea Spoon, which he offered to pawn – ag^d to go to Sea.

Richd Habgood by Will: Stiles Jones C. chd by Francis Ward for ass^{t}ing her with Intent to have carnal Knowledge of her Body—against her consent – last Night he got into bed when she was asleep – he was upon her, which awaked her

Han^h Sewell, Mary Knight, Eliz: Lewis, Sarah Brown} WC by John Fleet C. chd by him for severally wandering abroad & picking up Men – d^d

John Wood d^{o}C by John Prockter C. chd by Thos Musgrave for driving a Coach over a Boy 11 Years old – rem^{d}ed 'till tomorrow.

Will: Waites by Tim^y Plaw C. chd by Nathaniel Harris for feloniously stealing ~~four~~ two Quartern Loaves Value 1s. the Property of Walter Newbon – d^d.

2s.   Moses Joshua, Lydia Joshua} by Aaron Aaron C. chd by Joseph Joseph (on a W^t) for an Assault – friv^s and d^d.

to prosecute   Richd Habgood – charged by Ja^s May for an Ass^t with Intent to commit the detestable Crime of Buggery – on his Oath com^d to d^{o}C for want of Sureties.

RX   Ja^s May – white Swan Snow Hill – Painter   £ 20

Thos Davis, John Daniel, Philip LeGrand} WC by Hen: Wesley C. chd by him for lodging in the open Air, in Fleet Market – rem^{d}ed 'till tomorrow to be pass'd.

Mr Nash attended   NN

Mr Alderman Burnell by Mr Alderman Wooldridge. Wednesday 30 August 1780.

Mary Wilkinson WC by Jno Couchman C. chd by Will:

Cockman for robbing her ready furnished Lodgings of a pair of Sheets, a copper Tea Kettle – the things being restored – d^d

P   Mary Oliphant charged by Ann Tunstal for an Assault.

John Wood WC by John Prockter C. chd by Thos Musgrave for driving a Stage Coach over a Boy – d^d – John Rymer is the Master.

P   Mary Carpenter pr. by John Croose C. chd by him for making a riot & disturbance in Drs Commons dis^d.

P   W^t v Mary Phillips Mary Fareman & Samuel Fareman ats Mary Hubbard asst.

~~W^t v Ann Day ats Ja~~

1s.   W^t peace v. Edwd Sutton Phillip Newell & Eliz Edwards ats Jo^s Stafford.

1s.   W^t [blank] Riley & John Reed ats Jos^h Stafford the like offence.

Mr Houston attended   T.W.

Mr Alderman Clark. Thursday 31 August 1780.
    ~~Thos Davis WC by Hen: Wesley C. charged by~~

~~Sarah Short, Mary Lattimore} d°C by Jos: Thompson C. ch'd by~~

~~Ann Munday, Ann Bailey, Marg^t Davis} d°C by Matt^w Stimson C. ch'd by~~

~~Ja^s Kelly WC by Will Sargeson C. ch'd by~~

~~Thos Watkins d°C by [blank] Phipps C. ch'd by~~

~~Thos Inwood doC by [blank] Finch C. ch'd by~~

~~John Gorman, Ja^s Cave, Danl Sullivan} doC by John Scandret C. chd~~

(No Attendance.)

Mr Houstoun att^ded.

Mr Alderman Wooldridge. Friday 1 September 1780.
~~Ann Munday, Ann Bailey, Marg^t Davis } WC by Matt^w Stimson C. ch'd by~~

Gave poor Woman 1s.

1s.   W^t ag^t Hen: Crooke ads. Ann Pavior

Thos Watkins by Fra^s Phipps C. chd by John Butcher his Ma^r to whom he is an Appr: for disorderly Behaviour – ag^d to go to Sea

Will: Day d^oC by Jno Collinton C. chd by Eliz: Tipscoe on Suspicion of feloniously stealing a Shilling – d^d.

RX   Edwd Sutton Ashen Tree C^t White Friars for self
       & P Newey[137]   £ 40
       Edwd Read – D^o — Clerk   40

bo^d to answer Jos: Stafford (on a Peace W^t)

1s.   John Garman, Jos^h Cape, Daniel Sulliman} by Richd Stritton C. chd by Robert Morris Servt to Mr Langdale upon Susp^n of steal^g Lead – for want of Evidence dis^d – Gorman enlisted

1s.   Affidavit Will: Hughes

Mr Houston attended. T.W.

Mr Alderman Hart by Mr Alderman Plomer. Monday 4 September 1780.
Charlotte Waters, Eliz: Wilson, Sarah Smith, Mary Moore, Ann Fox, Mary Parker, Eliz: Cooper, Mary King, Sarah Lambert, Ann Smith[138]} WC by Will: Payne C. chd by him for being severally apprehended picking up Men in the Streets of this City—and being loose idle and disorderly Women and Common Night Walkers – Waters and Wilson were taken together sitting quietly in a House – the Ald^n s^d he thought their apprehension improper – they were d^d and so were the others, having in the Opinion of the Alderman suffered by Imprisonment & promising to keep out of the Streets.

Ja^s Crick, Thos Wale, Richd Jobson} d^oC by Jos: Thompson C. chd by him with lodging in the open Air Crick deliv^d to his Mother

137. Probably a misheard Newell. See earlier warrant for this matter above..
138 Check marks appear beside Waters, Wilson, Smith, Moore and Fox.

~~John Harding, Thos Simpson} d°C by [blank] Spratley C. chd by~~

P   W^t ag^t John London ads Sarah Ux: Ass^t etc.

P   Mary Smith, Lucy Warner} d°C by Benj: Church C. chd by him, as disorderly Women – they made a Disturbance – d^d

1s.   Mary Whitehead by Chas Delagal C. chd by Jane Ryland (on a W^t) for an Ass^t – d^d

1s.   Back'd a Warwickshire W^t

        Mr Beach did attend   WP

Mr Alderman Sainsbury. Tuesday 5 September 1780.
        Sarah Langing, Mary Johnson, Mary Floyd, Mary Turner, Bridget Thompson, Marg^t Hunt, Mary Hunt, Mary King, Eliz^h Robins, Fra^s Morgan, Mary Myers[139]} WC by Wm Payne C. chd by him for severally wandering abroad in the Streets of this City and there acting as Common Prostitutes by picking up Men – Floyd being an old Offender, was com^d to B.– Turner produced a person to her Character and was d^d – So did Marg^t Hunt & Mary Hunt – they were d^d – King was here Yesterday & forgiven for a similar Offence – com^d to B – the others were ~~com~~ d^d

~~Ann Bailey WC by Rob Trotter C. ch'd by Ellis~~

        Ann Newell d°C by Saml Stephens C. chd by Aaron Wood for feloniously stealing five earthen Welch Dishes Val: 5d. the property of William Bacchus – for want of Proof—d^d

Ald^n Wilkes   Geo: Priault an Apprentice sum^d by John Silk his Ma^r for laying out of his House & refusing to obey his lawful Commands – he promised to reclaim & the Ma^r ag^d to try him again

        Isaac Sakey by Thos Parrott C. chd by Reb^a Levy (on a W^t Per Ald^n Plomer) on suspicion of feloniously stealing one Guinea in Gold & 4s. in Silver – Abram Levy saw the Pris^r pick up the Money and run away – a Prosecution was declined – d^d.

139. All of the names have check marks beside them, but Floyd and King have their marks altered to an 'X'.

~~Thoˢ Micom~~, Eliz: Micom} by dᵒC chd by Jane Hitherley (on a Wᵗ) for an Assᵗ – they withdrew but coᵈ not agree – adjourned 'till tomorrow.

Thoˢ Simpson, John Harding} by Thoˢ Spratley C. chd by Mary the Wife of Edward York for feloniously stealing a pair of Men's leather Breeches—of the value of 5s. the propʸ of the sᵈ Edwᵈ York – comᵈ to WC.

RX　　Jaˢ Plowman Nº 66 Fore Street L. Press Master for
　　　self & York　　　　　　　　　　　　 } £ 20
　　　Thoˢ Spratley Nº 100 Fore Sᵗ Broker　　 10

Arnold Broom WC by John Cruse C. chd by Tyrrell Wilcox & John Whiteaws[?] for picking the Pockets of some Person unknown in Bartholomew Fair – his father appᵈ and promised to send him to Sea

1s.　　John London by John Edwards C. chd by Mary Ux: (on a Wᵗ) for an Assᵗ – dᵈ.

1s.　　Wᵗ agᵗ Thoˢ Phillips ads Mary Ux: Assᵗ.

Mʳ Nash attended　TS

Mʳ Alderman Kitchin.　Wednesday 6 September 1780.
　　　(No Attendance).

Mʳ Houstoun attended　　RH

Mʳ Alderman Alsop.　Thursday 7 September 1780.
the Aldⁿ woᵈ　~~Backt Justice Staples Midsex Warrᵗ~~
not back it.
~~1s.~~

Ann Bailey WC Robᵗ Trotter C. Charged by Ann Ellis & Mary Jones with feloniously stealing a Gown – Bailey appᵈ to be innocent – dᵈ.

Eleanor White, Martha Brown, Jane Pike, Mary Dennis, Mary Brown, Miney Rollinson, Alice Watkins, Cath: Vernon, Eliz Robins, Mary Davis, Ann Smith[140]} WC by Will: Payne C. chd by him for severally wandering abroad & picking up Men – Brown and Pike were sitting in a door-way in Fleet Street – they were dᵈ – Dennis & Mary Brown were lodging in the

---

140. A check mark appears beside each name, except for White.

open Air – they were d^d – Vernon not known and d^d – Robins com^d to B – the others were d^d.

John Blake, Fra^s Lapworth, Will: Rosseau, [blank] Gough, Thos Allen, Richd How, Will: Armstrong, Thos Harrison, Richd Siddell, John Davis, Will: Forrest} summoned by Saml Nash, Overseer of the Poor of the Parish of Saint Ann in Black Friars—for refusing to pay their Proportion of the Poor's Rate of the said Parish – Blake s^d he was exempt being Beadle of Scotch Hall, a Charitable Foundation – adj^d 'till a Meeting of the Committee – the others were ord^d to pay, and Warr^{ts} of Distress, otherwise ordered.

1s.   Thos Jackson Driver of a Dray N° 6734 sum^d by Fra^s Jackson for driving the s^d Dray agst him wilfully and injuring him & his Wife – conv^d in the Penalty of ten Shillings which he p^d – half was given to Jackson – the other half to be paid the Overseer of Saint Sepulchre

John Lumbley by Saml Roberts C. chd by a Person (not now present) for stealing a Watch – a Sum^s ord^d & Pris^r rem^ded

Thos Nichols by Will: Thomas C. chd by Eliz: Pollard for throwing a Child (4 Years old) down and thereby breaking his Thigh – it being doubtful whether the Child was out of danger – rem^ded

Danl Read Duewick by Percival Phillips C. chd by John Merriman his Ma^r to whom he is an Apprentice for absenting himself from his Service, without his Consent – referred to the Chamberlain

1s.   Hyam Jacobs by Thos Parrott C. chd by Ann Emanuel (on a W^t) for an Ass^t – ag^d & d^d

P   Susanna Williams by Jos: Thompson C. chd by Eliz: Cotham per Assault Sett^d and disch^d.

Hyam Jacobs (on Aldⁿ Plomers W^t) David Marks C. Ch^d by Ann Emanuel per Ass^t Adjudg'd true on her Oath & Bail put in He was Permitted to make Satisfⁿ & was d^d.

P   W^t v. James Riley ads. Sarah ux Per Ass^t

John Dunn PC Thos Parrott C. Ch^d by Christian Schaun on suspicion of feloniously assaulting him, putting him in fear & robbing him of his Watch & handkerchief

1s.   Warr^t v Elizth ux Jonathan Stephenson She standing indicted at the Genl Sess^s Peace at Guildhall Monday 13th Septr. 19th Geo 3^d for assaulting John Holford as per Cert Clk P[eace].

Rhodes Att^y attended   R.A.

The Right Honourable Thomas Harley. Friday 8 September 1780.
(No Alderman).

Mr Alderman Crosby. Monday 11 September 1780.
Ald^n Wilkes   Ja^s Emmerton, ~~William Armstrong~~} WC by Will:
1s.   Wilson C. chd by Will: ~~Robinson~~ Armstrong for making a Disturbance – ag^d and d^d

Mr Alderman Townsend by Mr Alderman Wilkes. Tuesday 12 September 1780.
Octo^r Sess^s.   Thos Bredell otherwise Thos Bredall com^d 2^d August for
RX   not appearing to an Indictment preferr'd & found for wilful and corrupt Perjury – bailed to plead

4s./4d.   Thos Bredall Maddox Street Apothecary   £ 100
Francis Bredall D^o D^o £ 50
Chas Edward Bredall   D^o Gent.   £ 50

Joseph Bureau at John Rowe's Esq^e Norfolk Street – consented on the part of Rob. Crowe Esq^e – the Prosecutor – Mr Kirby was sworn to the Consent of Mr Chaloner, Clerk to Mr Lindsay

1s.   Isaac Miller WC by R^d Hart C. chd by Frances Henley for assaulting her – the C. said the Injury was trifling, if any – d^d

John Lumbley by Saml Roberts C. chd by a Person not now present – on Suspicion of stealing a Watch – no felony com^d

Mary Thompson by Will: Wilson C. chd by Elmsley (not now present) on Suspicion of stealing a quart pewter Pot – d^d

Mr Nash attended   John Wilkes

1s.   W^t to search the House of John Dovey N° 4 New Street Square – on the Oath of Patrick Rork for Gold & Silver Watches, Diamond Rings &c.

Mr Alderman Bull. Wednesday 13 September 1780.
(No Attendance).

Mr Houstoun att^{d}ed   RH

Mr Alderman Wilkes. Thursday 14 September 1780.
     Mr Rhodes attended   RH.   (No Attendance)
     Genl E[?] Middx.

Mr Alderman Sawbridge. Friday 15 September 1780.
     (No Attendance).

Mr Nash attended.

Sir Thomas Hallifax. Monday 18 September 1780.
     (No Attendance).

Mr Beach att^{d}ed.

Sir James Esdaile by Alderman Hart. Tuesday 19 September 1780.
P   Will: Rivers by Jos: Gates C. chd by Mary Saunders (on a W^t
       by the Lord Mayor) for an Ass^t – they withdrew & he ask'd
       Pardon – d^d

       Mary Jones WC by Richd Tilcock C. chd by [blank] Keys on
       suspicion of stealing six knives & forks – Mr Jenkins, Watch
       Maker in Aldersgate Street can give her (she says) a Character.

P   Mary Knight by Jno Squire C. chd by Isaac Page a Watchman,
       for wandering abroad at an unseasonable Hour, and swearing
       – d^d

1s.   W^t ag^t Will: Edmonton (a Journeyman Weaver) ads Ja^s Pilgrim
       for purloining some Silk deliv^d to him, to make into Handker-
       chiefs

       Mr Nash att^{d}ed

Mr Alderman Plumbe by Mr Alderman Hart. Wednesday 20 September
     1780.
     (No Attendance).

Mr Rhodes attended   RH.

Mr Alderman Kitchin. Thursday 21 September 1780.
     Mary Jones by R^d Tilcock C. chd by Thos Keys for feloniously
     stealing ten Knives & six Forks – Val: 2s. his property – d^d

197

John Cooper by Jno Larkin C. chd by Jno Mills on Suspicion of feloniously stealing four pair of Sheets, a pint silver Mug & other things – he said he lived Clerk in Dublin & came by the Liverpool Coach to the Swan with two Necks Inn – went to Oxford thence came to the Cross Keys Inn – rem^ded and the Property ord^d to be advertized

Thos Nicholls was d^d it appearing that the Child was out of Danger – d^d

Will: Edmonton by James Munday C. chd by Ja^s Pilgrim for purloining or embezzling some part of a Quantity of Silk, entrusted to make into Handkerchiefs – Pilgrim was not the Master – the Prisoner was therefore disch^d on his undertaking to appear again if and when requir'd

1s.   W^t against Nathan Nathan & Ralph Barnet Ass^t etc.

Wm Burbridge[141] & Edward Fisher} WC (Mr Ald^n Plomers Warr^t) Richard Jutson C. Ch^d by Richd Mortimer for assaulting him. Mary Gee & Hester Gordon both Conf^d Mortimers Evidence & fur^r Declar'd that They were Severally assaulted by the Prisoner. Bail put in as over Leaf.

Nunc Mr Ald^n Newnham. Ad huc Thursday 21 September 1780.
1s.   Warr^t v Wm Henry Curtis ads Wm Hillier Per Ass^t.

3 / 4	Wm Burbridge N° 74 Aldgate Butcher	£40
RX	Ann Powell Same Place Widow Vict.	20
	Aaron Aaron Shoem^r Row Butcher	20

To app and ans^r next Sess^s in & for London for assaulting Richard Mortimer.

3 / 4	Edward Fisher N° 74 Aldgate Butcher	40
RX	Ann Powell } Same as above	20
	& Aaron Aarons }	20

To app & ans^r next Sess^s London for assaulting Richd Mortimer

Mr Alderman Kitchin (now)

John Pullen WC John Hescott C. Ch^d by Eliz^th Oakes per assault – Was confirm'd in her Evidence by Dianna Blackburn. Mre adjourn'd until tomorrow one O'Clock

---

141. This case, the recognizances that follow and the warrant against William Henry Curtis all appear to have been heard by Alderman Newnham.

1s.   Arthur Goff WC Richd Farmer C. Ch^d by Edwd Berry per Ass^t Confirm'd in his Evidence by the Const and Martin Harrison a Serj^t in the Yellow Regim^t.

1s.   John Aked Warr^t ag^t him for assaulting Charity his Wife.

P   Warr^t v John Pugh ads. Elizth Hayes per Ass^t.

Rhodes Att^y att^d. HK

Sir Watkin Lewes by Mr Alderman Kitchin. Friday 22 September 1780.
John Pullen WC (remanded yesterday for Want of Bail) John Hescott C. Ch^d by Elizth Oakes per Assault Adj^d true on Oaths of s^d Oakes & Dianna Blackburn.
John Pullen N° 78 in Long Lane West Smithfield.

1s.   W^t ag^t Jno King ats Jacob DeMoses Rey ads Ja^s Allen Ass etc.

1s.   Danl Richier by Will: Payne C. chd by John Deacon, Overseer of the Poor of the Parish of St Dunstan in the West (on a W^t) for unlawfully begetting Mary Pledge, Singlewoman with Child, which is likely to become chargeable thereto – ag^d to marry – d^d (by consent of Mr Deacon)

Peter Walker WC by Will: Wilson C. chd by Ja^s Fownes for deserting from the Westminster Battalion of Middlesex Militia – there was no proof of Desertion – d^d.

Will: Daniel, Saml Stevenson, Ja^s Thomas} by Thos Green C. chd by Rob: Gray, and Richd Harper for feloniously stealing a deal box, containing sundry things – rem^ded 'till Monday next for further Examination

Eliz: Pointer by d^oC. chd by Will: Sellard on suspicion of being concerned with a Person unknown in stealing a great Coat.

Sir Watkin Lewes (Nunc)

1s.   John Andrews (on Ld Mayors Warr^t) Wm Emmery C. and Ch^d by Wm Wilkinson per Assault. For want of Proof W^t disch^d.

Thos Davis WC Wm Spaughton C. Ch^d by Henry Stokes on Suspicion of feloniously Stealing two Bobings of Bengal Single Silk Value 5s. Property John James and Henry Stokes Weavers & Cottoners— Benjⁿ Hathaway & Martin Mason (two Journeymen Weavers) Declar'd that 18 Bobings of Silk were delivered out to the Pris^r this Morn^g ab^t 7 OClock in order to manufacture into Handkerchiefs & ab^t an hour afterw^{ds} two of the 18 Bobings were Missing. For Want of Sufficient Proof He was Disch^d.

Jane Chapman WC Saml Roberts C. Ch^d by Geo Summerley on Suspicion of feloniously Stealing a Bank Note Value £10 his Property For Want of Proof D^d.

Robt Johnson WC Richd Beazley C. Ch^d by John Clarke on Susp^n of feloniously Stealing 3^{lb} W^t Pickled Pork value 1s. his Property. For Want of Proof D^d.

1s. Elizth Phipps (on Ld Mayors W^t) Richd Conion C. Ch^d by Catherine Wyatt perAssault etc.

1s. Jos^h Johnson WC Wm Payne C. Ch^d by Edmund ~~Robert~~ Roebuck – d^d.

Rhodes Att^y attended   WL

Mr Alderman Plomer. Monday 25 September 1780.
   Hannah Brent, Mary Bark, Jane Dellemore, Sus^a Liddell, Sarah Cooper, Mary Summers, Hannah Salter, Mary Wild, Sarah Davis, Sarah Baldwin, Sarah Lee, Eliz: Collins, Mary White, Mary Duck, Mary French, Marg^t Hughes[142]} WC by Will: Payne C. chd by him for severally wandering abroad & picking up Men – Brent & Bark were taken in Fleet Street – Dellemore was talking with a Man – She also was d^d – those mark'd X com^d to B.

   Susanna Lynn, Ann Herring, Sarah Catchpole, Sus^a ~~Hull~~ Serjeant} WC by Will: Payne C. chd by him with the like Offence – not being notorious & promising Amendment – d^d

nil W^t ag^t John Holslow ads Will: Rodd C., for ass^{t}ing him on his Duty.

   Griffith Humphreys WC Thos Linton C. chd by David Povah, the White Bear in Aldersgate Street; for abusing him in his Ho: & in Co: with two others not here, eating & drinking to the am^t of 7½d. – d^d upon Agreem^t.

142. A check mark appears beside each name except for French and Hughes. 'X' appears beside Dellemore, Liddell, Salter, Wild, Davis and Duck.

John Cooper by John Larkin C. chd by John Mills (as on Thursday last) on suspicion of feloniously stealing 4 pair of Sheets, a pint silver Mug & other things – a Shirt was produced, fo^d on the back of the Prisoner, which was stolen from the Inn, and the property of Thos Reed of Feversham – rem^{d}ed until Thursday

Will: Daniel, Saml Stevenson, Ja^s Thomas[143]} WC by Thos Green C. chd by Rob: Gray & Richd Harper for feloniously stealing a Deal Box, a bill of Exchange drawn by Thos Pipon, & payable to Peter Simonet or his Order, for the Sum of £40 – also two pieces of Muslin, two Cards of Lace, one silk Watch String, 4 pair of paste Shoe Buckles, 4 large fish skin Cases, one Shirt, a pair of worsted Stockings, one leather Portmanteau Val: £10 and upw^{ds} the property of Andrew Collier – com^d to WC.

RX   Rob: Gray Bell Savage Inn Book Keeper to Prosecutor   20
Richd Harper of Grays Inn Lane, Middx Saw Maker }
Ja^s Harrison – N° 85 Watling Street Shopman to   }
Mr Jennings   } each 10
Joseph Adams N° 10 Kings Street Jeweller   }
Thos Green N° 47 Fleet Market Victr   }

1s.   Mary McCarty [blank] by Matthew Stinson C. chd by Eliz: Bambridge (on the Ald^n's W^t 23d Inst) for an Asst etc. d^d. prosx app^d the Aggressor d^d.

3s./4d.   Supersedeas for John King of Popes Head Alley Warehouseman – for ass^{t}ing Ja^s Allen – £40
RX   Bail
         Thos Lucas of Ray Street Clerkenwell Broker   20
         Abram Demattos of Leadenhall Street Broker   20
         a Supersedeas was signed.

1s.   Back'd a Middx W^t per McGirdler.

Wm Chatham, John Bailey} WC by Rob: Best C. chd by Jno Jennaway, as follows Viz: for coming into Mr Lidiard's Shop in S. Pauls Ch: Yard & Chatham drawing Jennaway's attention to the selling a p^r of Buttons at one part of the Shop, whilst Bailey attempted to steal a Gold Watch out of the shew Glass – he happen'd to be mistaken in the Glass for instead of lifting up as such Glass as usually do, the Top was fastened out down

---

143. The case proceeds to the Old Bailey. See *OBP*, October 1780, trial of William Daniels (t17801018–37).

& the Thing were drawn out sideways & he attempting to life the Flap up, broke one of the Squares of Glass – but no part of the Things in the shew Glass was removed – they were rem^ded for further Exon – 'till Wednesday.

Ja^s Bass [blank] by Thos Linton C. chd by Eliz: Evans for assaulting her (on Ld Mayor's W^t 25 Inst to day) for an Ass^t – ag^d to be rem^ded for Bail

Mary Bass ats Hurst [blank] by Thos Linton C. chd by Thos Nabbs (on Mr Girdler's Middx W^t this day back'd by Ld Mayor) for stealing out of her ready furnish'd Lodgings 2 Sheets two Pillows one Blankett & other Things s^d Nabb's Property – the Pris^r Alledged the Things supposed to be stolen were now in the Lodgings – d^d – (the prosecutor with prisoner went to see if it was true)

Rob: Johnson by R^d Beazeley C. chd on Suspⁿ of stealing 3lb W^t of Bacon, a Hatters Hat Iron was found upon him, & he not giving any Acco^t of himself & being a suspected pilferer was com^d to B. on Const^s Oath.

Ja^s Carr WC John Cruse C. chd by Thos Bennett on Suspⁿ of stealing monies plate & wearing Apparel Table linen Shirts a Bk Note of £10 to the Amount of £30 & upw^{ds} – this was supposed to be done in Decem^r last.

Mary Ux: Wm Brown saw Ja^s Carr take a Box contain^g Mrs Bennett's Wearing Apparel & carry it to a Hay loft belonging to Carr's Fa^r— & that these things were bro^t to the next day into her Room & some of Mrs Bennett's Linen being wet was taken out to dry – says she saw some of Mrs Bennett's Shirts in the Box – also Table Linen, she bel^d there were two Boxes and a large Bundle all taken by Carr, the Pris^r. She saw 2 Boxes open'd, besides Mrs Bennetts Cloaths wch she knew she saw either one or 2 of Mr Bennett's Shirts some Table Linen & Sheets – there was great Doubt whether there was any felony – the Mre was adj^d to next Monday & Mr Bennett desired to bring his Wife

P   Eliz: Monk [blank] by Chas Delagall C. chd by a Mr Ogle not now pres^t (for stealing a handkf) no Person appear^g ag^t her she was d^d.

P   Mary Knight WC Boyce May C. chd by a W^hman who was not now present d^d

Mr Beach attended   WP

1s.   Ann Head WC by Martin Platts C. chd by John Mallet for an Ass^t – ag^d & d^d.

Mr Alderman Thomas. Tuesday 26 September 1780.
        Jos:Holford, Reb^a Robins} WC by John Couchman C. chd by Jno Jefferies for assaulting him and his Wife—and for making a Disturbance in his Public House – they withdrew & ag^d – d^d

Ann Ross d^oC by John Bush C. chd by Robert Walker with being a Common Prostitute

1s.   W^t ag^t Rob: Bassam ads Frances Williams – Ass^t etc.

1s.   Lawrence Mann by Richd Tilcock C. chd by Rachael Branning (on a W^t per Aldⁿ Plomer) for an Ass^t – d^d

John Bonner, Hugh Bonner} PC by Luke Herod C. chd by Will: Taylor for assaulting and beating him – two Witnesses proved Mr Taylor to have interfered improperly in the first Instance, and that he committed the first Assault upon the Prisoners – d^d.

John Holslow by John Francis C. chd by Will: Rodd, Constable, for assaulting him on his Duty – the C. saw the Pris^r strike Rodd – John How of Blacksmiths Hall saw the prisoner obstructing Rodd – they were permitted to withdraw – ag^d & d^d

Sarah Hill WC by Thos Bull C. chd by Joseph Coward & Saml Singleton for charging s^d Coward and his Wife with being the Cause of demolishing Mr Langdale's House – d^d.

Will: Bell [blank] by Hen: Hesketh C. chd by Robt Rusted with feloniously steal^g a Picture val 6s. his property, for want of evidence d^d.

Eliz^h Margery sum^d ads Wm Bishop Overseer of St Barth^w the Great for refus^g to pay 18/9 Poors Rate.

Ann Speren[?] sum^d ads D^o for 9s. D^o.

Mary Edgerton sum^d ads D^o for 7/6 d^o proposed pay^g 8d. a Week wch was accepted.

Jacob Harshman sum^d ads D^o for 9s. d^o – referr'd to the Comm[itt]ee

Peter Earle sum^d by John Fleming Street-keeper for using his narrow wheeled Cart in this City, drawn by two horses – a Case of necessity – d^d.

Richard Avery sum^d by Thos Griffin, for working his unlicensed Cart for hire within this City – Ord^d (on his own Confession) to pay 20s.

Mr Nash attended   N Thomas

1s.   W^t ag^t John Jones ads Jos: Clark – Ass^t etc.

1s.   D^o agt Archer Riley ads Sus^a Greenslade Ass^t etc.

P   D^o agt Peter Dowdle ads Cath: Sheridan – D^o

Mr Alderman Peckham. Wednesday 27 September 1780.
       Will: Chatham, John Bailey} WC by Rob: Best C. chd by John Jennaway (as on Monday last) – Mr Freshfield N° 19 Smithfield informed the Aldⁿ that he had received Information of a Robbery com^d at Gravesend of two Watches, and that he believed the pris^{rs} to be the persons, by their Description – rem^ded for further Examination on Monday

       Will: Edmonton by Ja^s Munday C. chd by John Remington, a Weaver his Master, (on a W^t) for purloining or embezzling some part of a Quantity of Silk entrusted with him to make into handkerchiefs there was no Witness to prove a deficiency – the pris^r was therefore d^d.

       John Taylor by Jos: Thompson C. chd by Thos Joachim (on a W^t per Aldⁿ Plomer) on suspicion of feloniously stealing a quantity of Nutmegs, Mace, Cloves, Cinnamon and other Goods – about two Pound of Mace was found in his Lodgings – he said he bo^t it on board the Dutch Ship at Blackwall – there was a felony in Middx wherein the Pris^r was concerned, and his Brother being in Custody for the same Offence—rem^ded to be examined by Mr Justice Wright – the Charge made by Mr Joachim was not substantiated

P   Rob: Bassam by Will: Pretty C. chd by Frances Williams (on a W^t) for an Ass^t – ag^d & d^d

1s.   Will: Smith by Thos Parrott C. chd by Simon Cohen (on a W^t) for an Ass^t – ag^d to go with the Const.

1s.   Archer Riley by Matt^w Stimson C. chd by Sus^a Greenslade (on a W^t) for an Ass^t – d^d

nil   Geo: Linsell by Jno Edwards C. chd by Joseph French for seizing a Cask of British Brandy, and assaulting him – it app^d that Linsell is an Officer of Excise – that he took the Cask after the permit was shewn him – the Remedy being by Action – d^d.

        Will: Yarrington by Thos Linton C. chd by Will: Buckland,
3s./4d. Overseer of Saint George in Botolph Lane (on a W^t) for unlaw-fully begetting Mary Campey Singlewoman, of the said Parish with Child, which is likely to become chargeable thereto – bailed
RX   William Yarrington at Mr Weston's   £ 40
        Thos Weston – lower Thames Street Salter   £ 40

        Ann Baldwin WC by Will: Sargeson C. chd by Eliz: Smith ~~(on a W^t) for an Assault~~ – for robbing her ready furnished Lodg-ings – she was married & lived in these Lodgings with her Husband ~~d^d~~ rem^{d}ed

P   Ja^s Bass com^d for assaulting Eliz Evans on her Oath (Vide Yesterday) d^d.

        Mr Houstoun att^d RP

P   Patrick Dunn by John Fleming Street Keeper, for riding upon his Dray, & having no Person on foot to guide or conduct the same – d^d (being lame).

1s.   W^t ag^t Mary Henly & Rachel Caton ads Lawrence Mahn Ass^t

Mr Alderman Hayley. Thursday 28 September 1780.
Ald^n Plomer   Saml Herod app^d for his Master Isaac Nasso, sum^d by Edwd Fisher a hackney Coachman for refusing to pay him his fare for carrying Mr Nasso in his Coach from Friday Street to Charles Street—Middlesex Hospital – Ord^d 2s. Fare & 2s./6d. Charges

        Will: Jenkins[144] WC by Jno Edwards C. chd by Edm^d Newson with feloniously stealing one piece of Irish Linen Val: 20s. and

144. The case proceeds to the Old Bailey. See *OBP*, October 1780, trial of William Jenkins (t17801018–7).

upw^{ds} his property – Mary Lamb & Richd Bubb were sworn – com^d to d^oC

RX   Edm^d Newson – Barbican Salesman   £ 20
Mary Lamb – his Servant   10
Richd Bubb – Cooper's Alley White X St Brush Ma^r   10

1s.   Ann Wood by Will: Martin C. chd by Mary Clarke (on a W^t) for an Ass^t – they withdrew and ag^d – the Warrant was d^d.

P   Mary Monk, Joseph Knight} by Saml Roberts C. chd by him for being in Company together – d^d

Will: Haslegrove charged by Thos Joachim on suspicion of being concerned with John Taylor examined Yesterday, in feloniously stealing Tea, Cinnamon, Mace &c. – the only Proof was, that the prisoner had an Order from Taylor to fetch a Quantity of Tea at a public House in Chandos Street – he ag^d to appear on Wednesday before Justice Wright

P   Edwd Jones by Thos Parrott C. chd by Elizabeth Dowland (on a W^t) for an Ass^t – they withdrew & ag^d – d^d

Mary Knight by Rob: Wheelwright C. chd by Thos Butler, Watchman of Cornhill Ward for sitting at a door in Cornhill – com^d to B. for seven days.

nil   John Hollingsworth, Hester Ux:} by Ja^s Jewster C. chd by Mark Smith for assaulting his Wife & making a Disturbance – d^d

Mr Houstoun attended GeH

Mr Alderman Newnham, Mr Alderman Wright. Friday 29 September 1780.
Mr Whitebreads Servt appr^d for the Drivers of 2 drays N°s 3540 & 3541 chd by Jno Flemming for severally riding on the s^d drays 27 Inst. not having each a person on foot to guide & conduct the same – the Parties were permitted to withdrew and ag^d.

P   Jas Drummond sum^d ads Jno Oram for assaulting him – it app^d very trifling the Mre was dismiss'd.

P   Eliz: Williams Wm Payne C. chd by him for singing Ballads, was reprimanded & d^d.

Jeremiah Williams, Morris Roberts}

Eliz: Moon WC by Will: Martin C. chd by Eliz: King for abusing her, and assisting a Man in injuring her Daughter, but it app^d the Girl was not injured – d^d.

Ann Smith, Eliz: Love, Sophia Cook} by Jno Jones C. chd by Jno George on suspicion of feloniously stealing 42 yds. of Mode – rem^{d}ed 'till Monday

Mr Houston attended   NN

John Rofey by R^d Dawson C. chd by John Meyrick for charging him with a felony – d^d.

Mr Alderman Burnell. Monday 2 October 1780.

Ald^n Pugh. Will: Bennett the Driver of a Cart N° 483 – produced by Benj: Kennett – sum^d by Hen: Hall, for driving the s^d Cart upon the Foot Pavement – d^d

1s. Back'd a Middx W^t per Mr Hatsell.

1s. Thos Humphries WC by John Bush C. chd by Martha Ux: for an Ass^t – d^d.

Walter Jones by Will: Beaton C. chd by John Banks his Ma^r on Suspicion of feloniously stealing about 3 Gallons and half of Brandy – it appeared not to be a felony – d^d.

P Ann Griffiths WC by Thos Bull C. chd by Will: Judd for an Ass^t – d^d

W^t agt John Gibbard ads Thos Morris Ass^t etc.

Jos: Dobley PC by John Brown C. chd by Thos Goldey his Ma^r on Suspicion of feloniously stealing a Shilling – d^d.

Will: Chatham rem^{d}ed on Wednesday—was again rem^{d}ed – he afterw^{ds} ag^d to go to Sea.

Ann Cadman by Jos: Thompson C. chd by Chas Lecount on suspicion of stealing a pair of Gloves – rem^{d}ed to enquire whether she is a Convict

Ja^s Clayton by John Duncastle C. chd by Jno Sullivan for carrying Side Arms—he not being a Soldier – discharged it appearing to be a frolic without design for Mischief

Mary Brown by Will: Payne C. chd by him for picking up a Man – not known & d^d.

Ann Baldwin by Will: Sargeson C. chd by Eliz: Smith for robbing her ready furnished Lodgings of a pair of Sheets, and other things – she was married & lived at the time with her husband – d^d.

Eliz: Saunders by Will: Payne C. chd by him for accosting him in the Street – d^d

Ann Grind, Eliz: Davis} by d^{o}C. chd by him—chd by him for picking up Men – d^d.

Thos Beach Esq attended   CP

Mr Alderman Hayley. Tuesday 2 January 1781.
Ald^n W^t ag^t Richd Hickman ads Jno Cullen Ass^t etc.
Wooldridge
1s.

2s.   Thos Kennedy, Jos: Noton} by Boyse May C they chd each
           other with an Assault having ag^d they were d^d
1s.   W^t ag^t Mary Tustin ads Marg^t Bluntash Ass^t

Ald^n
Wooldridge   Mary Bishop by Chas Delegal C. chd by Jno Boxey with
              feloniously ~~stealing~~ assault^g him & putt^g him in fear &
              tak^g from his Person one Bank Note of the value of £10,
              one Bill of Exchange ~~drawn by for~~ accepted value ten
              pounds & nine Guineas in Gold monies number'd his
              property – com^d to WC for a Capital Crime as ment^d
              above
RX   John Boxey of Folkestone in the Co^y of Kent Butcher
              £ 20

           Sarah Purdue WC by Wm Wilson C. chd by Mary Petrie on
           susp^n of fel^y stealg a great quantity of Apparel, remanded.

P   John Williams by Will: Sumner C. chd by Mary Ux (on a W^t)
           for an Ass^t – d^d

Ald^n Wm Johnson WC by Saml Roberts C. chd by Ja^s Fee
Wooldridge   for feloniously stealing a deal box Value 2s (as on
              Wednesday last) com^d to d^{o}C.

RX   James Fee Servt to Wm Whittakers of New Castle Street Dealer in Potatoes £10

Mr Alderman Woldridge nunc Mr Ald. Hayley.

~~William Tranter~~ John Parker by Will. Sargeson C. chd by Thos Wing, a Watchman of Cripplegate Ward on suspicion of being a felon – (as on Monday last) there was no proof of any felony. He was chd by Gabriel Heath for ass^ting & threatening him, whereby he goes in danger of his Life—com^d to WC for want of Sureties

Will. Tranter chd by John Wing on Suspicion of being the Companion of Parker, and snapping a Pistol at him—rem^ded to produce persons to his Character

Eliz: Sharp. by Thos Bull C. chd Wm Swanborough for feloniously stealing six Yards of printed Cotton Va^l [blank] his property. Mr Swanborough being desireous to make an Enquiry about the Pris^r rem^ded 'till tomorrow

Mr Nash attended
GeH.

Mr Alderman Newnham. Wednesday 3 January 1781.

~~Mary Tustin by Thos Warren C. chd by Marg^t Bluntash (on a W^t) for an Ass^t d^d~~

~~Eliz Sharp by Thos Bull C. chd by Will. Swansborough for feloniously stealing six Yards of printed Cotton Val:~~ [blank] ~~his property~~

~~Ann Smith, Cath: Stokes } WC by Martin Platts C. chd by Tyler~~

(No Attendance)

Mr Alderman Clark by Mr Alderman Hart. Thursday 4 January 1781.

P   Jere^h Letts by John Cruse C. chd by Helen Thompson (on a W^t) for an Ass^t ag^d & d^d

Will: Isherwood a hackney Coachman sum^d by Jacob Henry Suwe for refusing to carry him, when required so to do, upon the Stand in Bpsgate Street ag^d

Sarah Brown WC by Jno Bailey C. chd by Geo: Eward her Landlord for [illegible] making a disturbance. It app^d that

Eward had without any ~~Inquiry~~ Authority, taken the pris[r] into Custody- d[d].

Uziel Barah sum[d] by John Fleming Street Keeper for using a Cart in this City with a false Number. Barah claimed the Cart—said he bought it of two Labourers unknown—adj[d] 'till Monday next – there was great doubt whether the Cart was Bara [sic].

Mich[l] Green WC Jos[h] Thompson C. Ch[d] by Thomas Fenner on Suspicion of feloniously Stealing a Deal Box cont[g] black & White Thread Laces Value £26 his Property. M[r] Fenner was Called but not appearing, was ordered by the Ald[n] to be Summ[d] for Monday next to give Evidence in a Case of F.[elon]y until which Time Pris[r] was remanded 12 °Clock. N.B. Mich[l] Green declar'd that he's by Trade a Watch Case maker and now & for 18 Months past has lodgd at M[r] W[m] Peters's opposite Crown Alehouse in College Street Lambeth, Watch Case M[rs].

1s.   Warr[t] v John Abney ad[s] W[m] Wood per Ass[t]

Tho[s] Owen by Tho[s] Emery C. chd by Sam[l] Pierson (on a W[t]) for an Ass[t] –Adj[d] true on his & the Evid of John Armstrong & Recog to app etc. as under

3s./4d. Tho[s] Owen N.[o] 13 Silver Street London Vict[r].   20

       Edward Morton N.[o] 5 Redlyon C[t] D[o] Serj[t] at Mace   20

RX   Tho[s] Clark N[o] 1 Bar Yard D[o] Wire Drawer   20

       To app & ans[r] next Sess[s] Peace in & for L.

P   Warr.[t] v John Daniel ads Mary Fordham per Ass[t]

M[r] Rhodes attended   JH

M[r] Alderman Wooldridge. Friday 5 January 1781.

    M[r] [blank] Jordain sum[d] ads Ja[s] Harrison Hackney Coachman for refus[g] to pay him his Fare from the top of the Haymarket to S[t] Tho[s] Apostles. Ord[d] to pay 2s. & the Charges

Tho[s] Lucas, Ann Ross} WC by Sam[l] Roberts C. chd by John Hollingworth she ~~woman~~ for being an Idle disorderly Woman & a Common Prostitute on his & Roberts Oaths Com[d] to B— he was rep[d] & dischd

Eliz: Woollan by Joseph Batten C. chd by Ann M[c]Kenzie & Will: Johnson on Susp[n] of Stealing a quantity of different

Wearing Aparrel—it app^d she had confess'd under promises she was ~~dischd~~.

P   W^t ag^t Edwd Harvey ads Mary Ann Ux^r

Wm Smith Sum^d ads Thos Cooper Carman for taking a Load out of turn on Saturday last Henry White the driver Swore to the Fact Ord^d to be Settled

John Playle by Will Wilson C. chd by George Blow on Susp^n of ~~George Blow~~ Stealing a Metal Watch & two Gold Seals was rem^d & the Watch Ord^d to be advertiz'd

P   W^t ag^t Frances Stokes & Sarah Pryor ads Bridget Anderson Ass^t

Wm Ambrose by Jos: Gates C. chd by Wm Pottinger Overseer of Cavesham Oxon (on a W^t Per S: Freeman & back'd by ~~the Lord Mayor~~ Ald^n Pugh) –for running away & leaving his Wife & family chargeable to s^d parish

1s.   ~~W^t~~ Back'd J Girdlers W^t

2s.   D^o 2 Per W Blackborow

gave a poor woman 1s.   Sarah Mortimer, Sus^a Ferris} by W Payne C. chd by him for making a riot & disturbance at six OClock in the Morning & for being common pros^{tes} were rep^d & dischd

Mr Nash attended   TW

Mr Alderman Hart by Mr Alderman Kitchin. Monday 8 January 1781.
1s.   John Bowden by John Larkin C. chd by him for making a disturbance – d^d

Uziel Barah sum^d by John Fleming Street Keeper for using his Cart without a Number in this City—Chas Halliday Foreman to Mr Gardner in Wormwood Street s^d he had seen the Cart & it was the same to which he put a pair of Wheels—Saml Chapman wrote the Advertizement Ord^d the Cart to be restored.

Thos Hermitage sum^d to produce the Driver of his Cart N° 9456 to answer the Complt of Jno Fleming, Street Keeper, for riding upon his Cart – they withdrew & settled.

P   W^t ag^t Ann Plunket & Mary Plunket ads Sarah Ux Jno Stevens, Ass^t etc.

Will Tranter by Will: Sargison C. chd by Jno Wing on Suspicion of being the Companion of one Parker, who was driving a Cart suspected to be employed in committing felony—there was no fact to charge him with—d^d.

Thos Hambleton, Ja^s Bacon} PC by Thos Ashby C. chd by Will: Crompton a W^{ch}man of Broad Street Ward, for being found in a Cellar concealed—Hambleton app^d to be a W^{k}man belonging to Mr Wix Bricklayer, and of good Character—Bacon produced his Landlady—There was no Intent to steal, except to drink porter in the Cellar—d^d.

Jos: Newman D^{o}C. same C. chd by John Bossenade for stealing a linen handkerchief—he app^d to be a Man of bad Character—there was no Evidence—rem^{d}ed to go to Sea

Cornelius Dempsey PC by Jos: Sheppard C. chd by David Burney and Will Morris for defrauding [blank] Dixon of £70 & upw^{ds} –Dempsey rec^d the Money & undertook for 11 Seamen going on board the Heart of Oak—Mr Burney having taken Dempsey's Security to answer, it app^d their was no fraud – d^d

P   Edward Hervey by Thos Parrott C. chd by Mary Ann Hervey (on a W^t) for an Assault—d^d.

HK   Mr Beach att^{d}ed

Mr Alderman Wright. Tuesday 9 January 1781.
        Simon Solomans[145] by Will: Govan C. chd by Thos Plummer for feloniously stealing a hamper & 24 glass Bottles val 5s his property, on his Oath & the
        Oaths of James Gibson & Wm Browne com^d to P.C.
RX   Thomas Plummer of Lime Street London Merch^t for himself & James
        Gibson & Wm Browne   } £20
        William Browne of Priests Alley Tower Street   £10

        Cath: Dix by Thos Withers C. chd by Elean^r Wallather for personating the Sister of her Husband thereby procuring

---

145. The case proceeds to the Old Bailey. See *OBP*, January 1781, trial of Simon Solomons (t17810110–10).

Letters of Administration, and obtaining £16—rem^ded untill Thursday to Produce a power to receive the Money

Ann Courtney WC by Chas Delagal C. chd by Edwd Smith for soliciting him to go with her—d^d

1s. John Moss WC by John Carter C. chd by Wm Crowther for embezzling 20 pair of silver Bow Scissors entrusted with him to polish....he desired to inlist for a Soldier which was granted & he was attested.

P Frances Stokes, Sarah Pryer} by Jere. Thompson C. chd by Bridget Anderson (on Mr Ald^n Wooldridge's W^t 5th inst^t) for an Ass^t— Anderson app^d to be drunk at the time—d^d

Wm Mathewson[146] by Wm Martin C. chd by John Parker for feloniously stealing a Deal Box and a Cord of the value 1s./6d. s^d Parkers Property on his Oath com^d to WC
RX   John Parker of Iver in Buckinghamshire Waggoner   £10
Wm Martin of N° 3 Elliot St. Old Bailey Const.   10

David Phillips by Saml Roberts C. chd by Will Newman Overseer of the Parish of St Sepulchre (on a W^t) for unlawfully begetting Mary Morris, Singlewoman of the s^d Parish with which Child, which is become chargeable thereto – rem^ded his Ma^r undertook to pay 2 Guas if he didn't marry the Woman & thereupon by Consent of the Parish he was d^d.

1s. Jerrett Keene PC by Will: Blackburn C. chd by Ralph Harris for feloniously stealing six pair of buckskin Gloves Val: [blank] his property—rem^ded, as it app^d a Servt of Mr Harris was concerned—but by desire of Mr Harris d^d & a W^t granted ag^st Saml Cheddington.

Thos Jenkins WC by Will: Catchpole C. chd by him being stopt with a bundle, containing four Table Cloths at an unseasonable Hour—d^d as it was proved the Cloths were his own

Will Geo: Fox WC by Will: Catchpole C. chd by Ja^s Money Watchman of St Sepulchre, for getting over a Wall, as supposed, for some bad purpose—Ord^d to the Kings Head, Tower Hill, as it was said the Pris^r had entered [blank]

---

146. The case proceeds to the Old Bailey. See *OBP*, January 1781, trial of William Mathews (t17810110–22).

3s.   Saml Page, Will: Kemm, John Darnton} by Ja^s Warnett C. chd
        by Jos: Hall for an Ass^t—settled and d^d.

        Eliz Jones, Geo: Fawcett} by Thos Wall C. chd by Thos
        Holleyoak & Jos: Holleyoak for an Ass^t—it app^d a trifling
        Affair d^d.

1s.   Aff^t Rebecca Dixon

        John Banks app^d for Messrs King & Co. for refusing to pay the
        Cartage of a two H[ogs]he[ads] of Sugar from Smarts Key to
        X [Cross] Lane Queen S^t — Banks alledged he had paid him
        his demand & the Carman denied it. That he only p^d 2s. the
        Fare was 2s./9d. he paid 2s./9d. & Charges on the oath of ~~John~~
        the Carman of John Aberdeen

        John Unien[?][147] sum^d ads John Fleming for using his Cart not
        hav^g any Name or Number thereon the Mre was dismissed

        John Bond sum^d ads James Outon for the Cartage of eleven
        Firkins of Butter from the Custom House Key to Westm^r
        Bridge Surry side—p^d 4s./6d. & 2s. Charges.

        Mr Nash attended.   T.W

Mr Alderman Pugh.   Wednesday 10 January 1781.
2s.   Affts Stephen Munden, Robert Trueman

1s.   ~~W^t ag^t Chas Ratwall ads~~
        back'd a Middx W^t Per Mr Wilmot

1s.   Warr^t v Wm Harpur ads Wm Lewis Per Ass^t

        Patrick Mahon, Wm Payne C. & Ch^d by him for asking Alms
        this Day in the Pish of St Mich^l Bassishaw London ag^t Stat.
        –he said that his Settlement is in the County of Sligo, in the
        Kingdom of Ireland, com^d to B.

        John Playle by Will: Wilson C. chd by Geo: Blow on Suspicion
        of feloniously stealing a metal Watch and two gold Seals—he
        lodges at Mrs Jones's in Fleur de Luce Court, Grays Inn Lane

147. Possibly Urien.

1s.   Wm Brittell WC Wm Catchpole C. Ch^d by Thos Gill for assaulting him—they withdrew & ag^d –d^d.

1s.   W^t ag^t. one of the Drivers of the Putney Stage belonging to Chas Rix, commonly called happy ~~King ads~~ Dick, for stealing a Rug etc. the property of Will: Bisby

1s.   Richd Lambert PC by Marcus Levi C. chd by Geo: Wade a Watchman of Portsoken Ward for an Ass^t –they withdrew & ag^d –d^d.

1s.   Attested Ja^s Grant E. I. S.[148]

      Rhodes Att^y attended   EP

Mr Alderman Kitchin. Thursday 11 January 1781.
      ~~Cath^ne Dix rem^d on Tuesday last to WC for fur^r Examicon this Day, Thos Withers Const. Ch^d. by Eleanor Wallather~~

1s.   Wm Harper WC John Fleming C. (on Mr Ald^n Pughs W^t) Ch^d by Wm Lewis per Ass^t. Mre Sett^d & D^d.

      Rhodes Att^y attended   HK

Mr Alderman Burnell. Friday 12 January 1781.
      Ann Head by Thos Parrott C. chd by Ja^s Debighty a W^chman for swearing & making a disturbance the C. said she was in liquor—com^d to B.

      Richd Wadman the Driver of a Cart sum^d ads Chas Cowell, Street Keeper, for riding upon the same, having no person on foot to guide or conduct the Horses thereof—Cowell having no Witness—the Complt. was d^d

next ~~Mary~~ Sarah Ux: Hen: Jones WC by Thos Warren C. chd by
Sess^s Will: Tilsley & R^d Floyer for feloniously stealing 4 Yds ¼ of printed Cotton Val: 7s. & upw^ds his property – ~~on their Oaths com^d to d^oC.~~ d^d.
RX   ~~Will: Tilsley of Newgate Street L. Linen Draper for self & Floyer   £20~~

      Chch Wdns of St Giles Cripplegate sum^d by Ja^s Wilkes & Mary Ux: — he had a pension wch he insisted to retain—ag^d to

148. Probably East India Service.

allow him 1s./6d. a Week out of the pension—Ord^d relief on Cond[iti]on of allowing the difference

2s.   Aff^ts Will: Ward and Saml Smith

Rhodes Att^y attended   John Burnell

Mr Alderman Alsop. Monday 15 January 1781.
        Cath: Dix by Thos Withers C. chd by Elean^r Wallather for obtaining the Wages of a deceased Seaman, by representing herself to be his Sister & thereby procuring Letters of Administration. Rem^ded 'till tomorrow at one O'Clock, to give her an Opportunity of producing a power from the dece[ase]d & also a Witness.

        Sarah Harvey WC by Will: Catchpole C. chd by Edwd Doyle a Watchman of the Ward of Farringdon without and Mary Williams for stealing a black silk Hat—Williams was drunk & incapable of telling any of the Circumstances d^d.

2s.   John Cogar, Thos Bailey} by Thos Emery C. chd by John Vaughan (on L.M's W^t 13. Jan) for an Ass^t –on an Agreem^t they were d^d.

        Will: Yeo app^d for John Ayearst sum^d by Jno Fleming Street Keeper, for driving his Cart N° 14643—the s^d Number being false—they withdrew & ag^d –d^d.

        Frances Goad, Hannah Green, Sarah Mortimer, Marg^t Thompson, Ann ~~Endel~~ Hindel, Sus^a Cooper^149} WC by Thos Land C. chd ~~by~~ as follows—Goad was chd by the C. with making a disturbance in the W^chhouse – Ja^s Duncomb, a W^chman chd Green with the same, & swearing Mortimer was not regularly charg'd—Thompson had com^d no Offence—Hindle had done nothing—Cooper was chd by the C. with threatening to cut off his head—they were all d^d.

1s.   W^t ag^t Thos Evans ads Thos Newman Ass^t on Eliz: Ux:

R. A.   Mr Beach attended.

---

149. A check mark appears beside each name except for Hindel and Cooper.

The Right Honourable Thomas Harley by Mr Alderman Wooldridge.
Tuesday 16 January 1781.

    Cath: Dix WC by Thos Withers C. chd by Elean^r Wallather
& [blank] Hooper for obtaining the Wages of a deceased
Seaman, by personating his Sister & thereby procuring Letters
of Administration to be granted rem^{d}ed 'till Friday next—the
papers are at Mrs Burnitt's, a little House at the back of Greenwich

    Edwd Ellis app^d for Messrs Watlington & Co sum^d by John
Fleming, Street Keeper, for using a Dray N° 1277—drawn by
two horses, the Wheels whereof not being six Inches broad—
they withdrew & ag^d —d^d

    Lilly Spraggs by R^d Conen C. chd by him for damning him &
making a disturbance in the Watch House—d^d

    Mr Nash attended

Mr Alderman Crosby. Wednesday 17 January 1781.

    Thos Evans by Jos: Thompson C. chd by Thos Newman (on
Ald^n Alsop's W^t 15th Inst.) for assaulting Eliz: Ux:

(No Attendance)

    Mr Houstoun att^{d}ed

1s.   ~~W^t ag^t Marg Hammond ads Ann Collins Ass^t~~
~~Ald^n Wilkes~~

Mr Alderman Townsend. Thursday 18 January 1781.

Ald^n Wooldridge John Pearson app^d for Messrs Pott and C^o sum^d by
    John Fleming, Street Keeper, for using a narrow
    wheeled Cart in this City—ag^d.

Mr Alderman Bull. Friday 19 January 1781.

Ald^n Pugh   Chch Wdns of Saint Antholin sum^d by Thos Howell
    for relief—was sworn—said, he served his Apprentice-
    ship—Ord^d relief

1s.   W^t ag^t [blank] Kinsey ads W: Jos: Williams Assault etc.

    Cath: ~~Dix~~ Dicks WC by Thos Withers C. chd by Eleanor
Wallather & Edwd Hooper for willingly & knowingly personating or falsely assuming the Name or Character of Cath: Dicks

the natural & lawful Sister & next of Kin of R^d Wallister, ~~with Intent~~ in order to receive his Wages – there was no Proof of Dicks taking out Adm[inistrati]on—rem^ded & Sum^s issued

P   Sarah Samuel by Jos: Gates C. chd by Frances Hart (on Ald^n Pugh's W^t Yesterday) for an Ass^t –d^d.

2s.   Sign'd Rate Book of St Ann Aldersgate

nil   Aff^t– Jos: Barnes

Ja^s Scott the Driver of a hackney Coach N° 143 sum^d by Rawson Aislabie for taking more than his fare—confess'd the fact—forgave him on Condition of paying 5s.

Alwood Broome by Jno Fleet C. chd by him for stealing a linen handkerchief—sent to the Marine Society

1s.   Ellis Jones by Thos Waugh C. chd by Thurston John Caton (on a W^t per Lord Mayor 6th Inst:) for an Ass^t –Jane Wiblow did not see the beginning of the Affray – Hen: Shires saw Caton seize Jones & hold him some time by the Collar—then Jones struck Caton & not before—d^d.

Josiah Kinsey by Hen Hesketh C. chd by. Wm Jos^h Williams (on his Wps W^t this day) for assaulting & beating him, the Pros^r app^d the Aggressor he was d^d.

1s.   Jos^h Clark by Saml Roberts C. chd by Fran^s Hamilton one of the Overseers of St Sepulchre for begetting Eliz: Mann single-woman of s^d parish with Child (on Ald^n Peckham's W^t 20 ~~Inst~~ Novr last)—ag^d and d^d.

1s.   W^t ag^t John Hanson ads Isaac Lucas Ass^t etc.

Saml Overill by Will: Cambrook C. chd by John Spurrier for pilfering Candle Meat & other things—d^d

Mr Houston att^d.   Evan Pugh

Mr Alderman Wilkes. Monday 22 January 1781.
     (No Attendance)

     Mr Beach att^ded

Mr Alderman Sawbridge. Tuesday 23 January 1781.

1s.   W^t ag^t Danl Abel, John Hoppe & John Battell Journeymen Lamplighters ads Geo: Rogers

Mr Nash attended.

Sir Thomas Hallifax. Wednesday 24 January 1781.

Ald^n Plomer   Cath: Dicks WC by Thos Withers C. chd by Eleanor Wallather & Edward Hooper for willingly & knowingly personating or falsely assuming the Name or Character of Cath: Dicks, the natural & lawful Sister & next of Kin of Richd Wallister, in order to receive his Wages—rem^{d}ed till tomorrow

Eliz: Weeks, Cath: Evans } WC by John Fleet C. chd by him for accosting him in Aldersgate Street & asking him to go with them—d^d.

1s.   Thos Yoell sworn a Letter Carrier

Mr Alderman Plomer. Adhuc Wednesday 24 January 1781.

Patrick Norton[150] WC by R^d Reeves C. chd by John Cocker, Benj: White, & Ja^s Cole for feloniously Stealing 2 lbs 12 ^{oz} W^t of sewing Silk Val: 3^s/6^d £3 the property of s^d John Cocker—com^d to d^{o}C.

RX   John Cocker of upper Thames Street Dyer for self, White & Cole   } £ 20
R^d Reeves Garlick Hill Baker   £ 10

Mr Houstoun co^d not attend being Ill.

Sir James Esdaile by Mr Alderman Plomer. Thursday 25 January 1781.

Cath: Dicks[151] WC by Thos Withers C. chd by Eleanor Wallather and Edwd Hooper for willingly and knowingly personating or falsely assuming the Name or Character of Cath: Dicks, the natural & lawful Sister & next of Kin of R^d Wallister, in order to receive his Wages—Mr Hooper produced the Adm[inistrati]on, which was given by the pris^r to procure the Wages, & the same were paid to her—com^d to d^{o}C.

RX   Eleanor Wallather Bell Alley Petticoat Lane Widow } £20

---

150. The case proceeds to the Old Bailey. See *OBP*, February 1781, trial of Patrick Norris (t17810222–51).

151. The case proceeds to the Old Bailey. See *OBP*, February 1781, trial of Catharine Dicks (t17810222–31).

Edwd Hooper of Seething Lane Gent. } Each £20
Roger Copeney 3 Tun Alley Wingfield Street }
Weaver

John Harper, Will: Dunn} by Will: Pretty C. chd by John Murphy (on Ald^n Plomer's W^t 12th Inst.) on suspicion of feloniously stealing a Quantity of silk Handkerchiefs Value £8 his property—there was no Evidence—d^d

P   Thos Young WC by Hen: Hesketh C. chd by Thos Baker, Watchman of the Ward of Queenhith for sauntering about at an unseasonable hour—there was no Charge—d^d.

3s.   Cath: Low, Mary Baldwill, Sarah Baldwill} by Reeve Martin C. chd by Cath: Taylor (on Ald^n Plomer's W^t 24th Inst.) for an Ass^t –they withdrew, made Satisfaction & were d^d.

Benjn Partridge[152] WC Wm Catchpole C. Ch^d by Peter Dobey Journeyman Carter on Suspicon of felon^ly stealing a Wooden Flatt (Mark A.B. N° 4) Cont^g 46^lbs of Butter Value £ 1.18^s. Property of Thos Garfield

RX   Thos Garfield N° 24 RedLyon St Clerken Well Salesman of Butter   } £20
Peter Dobey Servt to Thos Jewers N° 110 Tichf^d St^t Oxford M^t   } 20
To appear Prosecute & give Evidence Next Sess^s in and for London.

Wm Catch Pole [illegible] in to give Evid^e on Trial £10

Mr Rhodes attended   WP

Mr Alderman Plumbe. Friday 26 January 1781.
Ald^n Crosby   Dinah Abrahams by Thos Parrott C. chd by Alice
1s.   Midway (on a W^t of Mr Ald^n Plomer Yesterday) for an Ass^t –ag^d & d^d

1s.   W^t ag^t Alice Dorman ads Sarah Davis Ass^t

Ald^n Plomer   John Housman by Jos: Thompson C. chd by Geo: Blow for feloniously stealing two Plated Table Spoons, which were found upon him in the Compter—the C. said he came from the Hulk—rem^ded 'till tomorrow.

---

152. The case proceeds to the Old Bailey. See *OBP*, February 1781, trial of Benjamin Partridge (t17810222–18).

220

Jos: Hill of Bow Lane app^d to claim a Trunk and Wearing Apparel stolen from him & found per Search W^t at the Bull and Mouth Inn—he was sworn to his marriage & the Landlord sum^d for Monday next.

Mr Alderman Kennett. Monday 29 January 1781.

~~Hester Walden WC by Thos Williams C. chd by Eliz: Jones on Suspicion of feloniously stealing a Box containing wearing Apparel~~

~~Alice Dorman d°C by Richd Spratley C. chd by Sarah Davis (on Ald^n Crosby's W^t 26th Inst) for an Ass^t~~

Mr Beach att^ded   (No Attendance)

Mr Alderman Plomer. Tuesday 30 January 1781.

1s.   John Wise, a Journeyman Buckle Maker by Jos: Thompson C. chd by Thos Nash his Ma^r for wilfully damaging & destroying certain Tools of his said Ma^r –they withdrew & ag^d –d^d.

1s.   Eliz: Smith by Saml Roberts C. chd by Jane Smith (on Ald^n Pugh's W^t 24th Inst.) for an Ass^t –they withdrew & ag^d –d^d.

Hester Waldon WC by Thos Williams C. chd by Eliz: Jones feloniously stealing a box containing sundry Articles of wearing Apparel—rem^ded 'till Thursday.

1s.   Aff^t Edwd Robinson

Sarah Aldridge[153] WC by Will. Catchpole C. chd by John Winstanley for feloniously stealing a quart pewter pot Val: 1s./4d. his property—com^d to d°C

RX   John Winstanley Long L. Vict: £ 10
      Will: Catchpole Smithfield Peruke Ma^r   £ 10

1s.   W^t ag^t Jno Steel ads Saml Thomas—Ass^t etc.

John Jones & Mary his Wife} by John Clarke C. chd by David Ogilby for fel^y steal^g two quart & one Pint Pewter Pots of the value 4/ his property– ~~upon~~ by the Consent of the Pros^r Jones was inlisted ~~for~~ a Soldier

---

153. The case proceeds to the Old Bailey. See *OBP*, February 1781, trial of Sarah Aldridge (t17810222–19).

1s.   W^t ag^t Thos Dray, Mary Dawson, Thos Barnesley Simon Jacobs
      ads Alice Medway—Ass^t etc.

      John Housman by Jos: Thompson C. chd by Geo: Blow (as on
      Friday last)—there was no Proof—d^d

1s.   John Steel by Jos: Gates C. chd by Saml Thomas (on a W^t) for
      an Ass^t—d^d.

1s.   W^t ag^t Chas Young ads Lemon Abrahams Ass^t etc.

~~1s~~ nil W^t to search the Lodging of John Spratt in the House of [blank]
      in George Court Snowhill for three India Bonds of the value
      of £100 each— a red silk Gown & other Wearing Apparel the
      property of Mary Fish.

1s.   W^t ag^t Mary Matthews ads Ruth Wright Ass^t

      Mr Nash attended   WP

Mr Alderman Thomas. Wednesday 31 January 1781.
1s.   John Allen by Will. Blackburn C. chd by Mary Linley (on a
      W^t per Aldⁿ Plomer Yesterday) for an Ass^t – they withdrew &
      ag^d – d^d.

      Ann Price by Will. Payne C. chd by Will. Minns for an Ass^t –
      com^d (for want of Sureties) to WC on Minn's and the C's Oath

      Edwd ~~Joy~~ Ivey, Mich^l Houghton} sum^d ads Saml Sherrington
      for unlawfully detaining a Box containing £100 & upwards in
      Money, 8 Shirts and other Articles, his property—Sherrington
      said he packed up the Money etc. on Monday Morning last at
      Maidstone—the Matter not coming properly before the Magis-
      trate—d^d.

1s.   W^t ag^t Nathl Smith ads Jos^h Pring his Master for deserting his
      Service before the Term of his Contract was expired.

      Francis Guley by Will:^m Payne C. chd by Clement Meymott
      (on a Middx W^t back'd by the Lord Mayor) on suspicion of
      feloniously stealing a wainscot Table & six Chairs—referr'd
      to a Middx Justice

      Timothy Harley by Wm Payne C. C^d by William Kelly for
      deserting his Regiment as a Soldier—com^d to the Savoy

Eleanor Crawford by d°C—chd by Edwd Reynolds for wilfully breaking a pane of Glass at Goldsmiths Hall—she promis'd not to go again—d^d.

Will: Beckford the Driver of a hackney Coach N° 597 sum^d by David Stiff for driving him to Holborn instead of Poplar—fined 20s. wch he p^d half rece'd by Stiff

3s./4d.	John Read by John Colliton C. chd by Danl Jones for standing Indicted last Sessions for assaulting him—to which Indictment he has neither app^d nor pleaded—bailed	

RX   John Read Castle Str: Oxford Mket Carpenter } £20
       Will. Daft—Noble Street L. Vict: }
       Rob: Hodgson of Queen Street 7 Dials Painter } Each 10
       and Glazier

3s./4d. Chas Lucas bailed for the same
RX   Chas Lucas N° 3 Oat Lane L.   £20
       Rob: Hodgson super   10
       Fra^s Leicester Ilford Essex Gent   10

1s.   Aff^t Geo: Benington

P   W^t ag^t Jno Williams ads Mary Ux:—Ass^t etc.

Middx
3s./4d. John Barton by Jno Marwick C. chd by Thos Poole, Overseer of St James Clerkenwell (on a Middx W^t back'd by Ald^n Plomer) for unlawfully begetting Mary Beniworth, Singlewoman, of the said Parish with Child, which is likely to be born a Bastard and to become chargeable thereto—bailed
R   John Barton of Cheapside L. Coffeeman   £ 40
       Jos: Thorpe—Bow Lane Vict.   20
       Chas Rowley of Great Sutton Street Clerkenwell
       Iron Plate Worker   20

Mr Houstoun attend^d N Thomas

Mr Alderman Peckham. Thursday 1 February 1781.
Ald^n Hart
    Ja^s Springmore sum^d. by John Fleming Street Keeper, for using his narrow wheeled Cart in this City—with two horses—they withdrew and ag^d—disch^d

    William Spaughton, C., sum^d by Ann Pearson, for unlawfully discharging a Person apprehended by him, without bringing him before a Magistrate—there was no proper Charge—the Sum^s was d^d.

Ald^n Peckham Hester Waldon WC by Thos Williams C. chd by Eliz: Jones on suspicion of stealing a box containing sundry Articles of wearing Apparel—rem^{d}ed untill Monday in order that the Porter who took away the Box by prisoner's Order, should attend.

1s. Warr.^{t} v Alexander Lemmon ad^s Henry Laycock Ass^t

Ja^s Gray sum^d by Deborah Dove for an Ass^t—d^d.

1s. Aff^t –Deputy Wilson

P John Williams by Fra^s Phipps C. chd by Mary Ux: (on Ald^n Thomas's W^t Yesterday) for an Ass^t the Wife not appearing— d^d

4s. Peter Ward, John Pearson, John Simpson, Will: Pashby} Aff^{ts}

paid the C. Ann Smith, Jane Davis, Harriot Hooper, Sarah Nunn[154]}
1^s for a WC Joseph Thompson C. & Ch^d by him for being idle &
Coach to disorderly Women & Common Prostitutes Sevlly picking
Bridewell up men bet^n 12 & one last Night in the Ward of Farm-ingdon wit^t –Nunn d^d the others being old Offenders—they were com^d to B.

Ann Ux: Edwd Price com^d Yesterday, was by Consent d^d.

~~Eliz Davis~~

Mr Rhodes atten^d RP

Mr Alderman Hayley. Friday 2 February 1781.
John Roberts WC by Will: Blackburn C. chd by Will: Callogill on suspicion of burglariously breaking & entering the dwelling House of [blank] Ross with Intent to commit felony therein—a Person who apprehended the Pris^r not being present—rem^{d}ed 'till Monday

Sophia Leadham, Eliz: Anderson, Mary Wilson, Eliz: Davis, Mary Bunn, Eliz: Keene, Sarah Swain, Sarah Jones, Sarah

154. A check mark appears beside each name.

Haynes[155]} d^{o}C by Jos: Thompson C. chd by him for severally wandering abroad in the Streets of this City and picking up Men—Leadham was apprehended in the Old Bailey between 1 & 2—d^d—Anderson not known—d^d.— Wilson promised to amend—d^d.—Davis taken on Ludgate Hill—d^d.—Bunn was chd by George Stafford (not present) with stealing a handkerchief—rem^{d}ed till Monday—Jones was fighting in the Fleet Market— she was d^d

Rob: Drury WC by William Catchpole C. chd by Saml Small for defrauding him of about 20^s by tossing with a counterfeit halfpenny, which had two heads—Thos Liversuch saw the halfpenny—there was no Proof of Drury being in Possession of it—d^d.

~~Thos Jackson d^{o}C by Will: Payne C. chd by~~

Ald^n Pugh	Rob. Weatherhead sum^d by Eliz: Nourse for wilfully driving his Cart against a certain other Cart, whereby damage was done to the Windows of the said Eliz:—settled.
1s.	Aff^t Rowland Page
1s.	Alex^r Leman by Walter Prosser C. chd by Hen: Laycock (on Ald^n Peckham's W^t Yesterday) for an Ass^t—Laycock was the Aggressor—d^d
gave a poor Woman 1s.	Will: Lightburne by Will: Catchpole C. chd by Sarah Ellis (on a W^t per Ald^n Plomer) for an Ass^t –Com^d (on her Oath) to WC for want of Sureties
1s.	Backd a Middx W^t
1s.	D^o –D^o

Mr Nash attended.   GeH

Mr Alderman Newnham. Monday 5 February 1781.
    Mary Bunn by Jos: Thompson C. chd by George Stafford for feloniously stealing a silk handkerchief. d^d

Ald^n Hayley	Thos Allcock, Carman, sum^d by Will: Parker for taking two Loads out of Turn in Budge Row—Jos: Pearce was Sworn &

155. A check mark appears beside each name.

225

said, that he believed the Wines were not the property of Mr Prettyman—Ord^d [blank]

Hester Coose produced Jos: Faulkner the Driver of a hackney Coachman N° 128 sum^d by Mr Sheriff Crichton for driving the said Coach wilfully agst the Chariot of the said Sheriff & damaging the same – in the Poultry—Thos Taylor was sworn— s^d that the Accident happened thro' the Sheriff's Coachman stopping on a sudden, whereby the pole run into the panel—the Sum^s was d^d.

Mr Beach attended   GeH

Mr Alderman Clark. Tuesday 6 February 1781.
    John Roberts WC by Will: Blackburn C. chd by Will: Calogill on suspicion of burglariously breaking & entering the dwelling House of [blank] Ross with Intent to commit felony therein— Calogill co^d not speak to the Person of the Pris^r –d^d

    Hester Waldon d^oC by Thos Williams C. chd by Eliz: Jones on suspicion of stealing a box containing wearing Apparel— rem^ded 'till Thursday

2s.   Sign'd Certif: St Giles Cripplegate

    Thos Bass WC by R^d Conen C. chd by Stephen Reynolds his Ma^r upon suspⁿ of fel^y steal^g a deal Box of the value of 1s his property. No Evidence—d^d

1s.   Edwd Bassett, Ann Beale, Jos: Clark, Eliz: Warren} d^oC by Ja^s Drummond C. chd by Rob Walker W^{ch}man of Farringdon Ward without— being found together doing nothing—Clark & Warren were in a Coach in an indecent Situation Warren and the others were d^d

    Sus^a Greenslade d^oC by R^d Mardell C. chd by him for being in the Street drunk—d^d

P   Mary Sanders in the W^t named Mary Barnes by Jos^h Thompson C. chd by Joseph Kaye (on Mr Aldⁿ Hart's W^t 5th inst^t) for assault^g & beat^g him—d^d

1s.   W^t ag^t Sarah Landy the Younger ads Thos Jenkins Ass^t etc.

1s.   Jos: Hopwood by Thos Parrott C. chd by John Moore (on Mr Aldⁿ Plomer's W^t) for an Ass^t d^d on Agreement

P   W^t ag^t John Emory ads Eliz^h his Wife Ass^t etc.

Mr Nash attended.   R.C.

Mr Alderman Wooldridge by Mr Alderman Kitchin. Wednesday 7
February 1781.
Ann Jenkins WC John Newman C. Ch^d by Mary McDonald on
Suspicion of feloniously Stealing a dark Printed Cotton Gown
– there was no Proof – d^d

1s.   Aff^t Thos Baker

P   Martha Baldwell on Mr Ald^n Plomer's Warrant Joseph
Thompson C. Ch^d by Alice Carter Per Ass^t [156]– d^d as it app^d
Carter gave the 1st Ass^t.

Alice Carter (on Mr Ald^n Harts Warr^t) Jos^h Thompson C. Ch^d
by Martha Baldwell per Ass^t – Cath: Lowe & Jane Wright
proved the Ass^t & confirmed Baldwill in her Story – they withdrew.

1s.   Francis Penrose WC Martin Platts C. Ch^d by Dudley Adams
for assaulting him. Alexander Catmer confirm^d. They withdrew & ag^d –d^d.

Dudley Adams's Evidence, Thos White spoke to the same
Effect –d^d.

Gave a poor Woman by his Wps Order 1s.[157]

Hugh Davidson sum^d by Eliz: Davis for refusing to deliver a
Child's frock—pawned within two Years for 1s. dism^d.

Rhodes Att^y attended   H K

Mr Alderman Hart. Thursday 8 ~~January~~ February 1781.
1s.   Hester Walden WC Thos Williams C. Ch^d by Elizth Jones (as
on Tuesday last) ~~rem^{d}ed~~ Sett^d & D^d

Frances Burgess, Catherine Jenkins } WC Joseph Patten C. &
Ch^d by Martha ux George Owen a Vict. in Newgate Market on
Suspicion of feloniously stealing 6 Gas the Property of the said

---

156. An unintelligible mark appears following Assault, not transcribed here.
157. Appears in the left margin.

George Owen. There was no Proof to affect the Prisoners who were therefore d^d.

John Laird sum^d by Elias Whitecot, a hackney Coachman for refusing to pay him his fare for being in his Service upwards of seven hours—Ord^d 7/6d. fare & 3s. Charges.

~~John Davis WC John Roberts Const. Ch^d by~~ A Man (who refused to tell his Name) was bro^t by Will: Howard C. & chd by Saml Sadler for feloniously stealing a Quartern Loaf of Bread Value 6d the property of John May—rem^{d}ed 'till tomorrow.

Hannah Smith WC Wm Crompton C. Ch^d by him for asking Alms of the Churchwarden of the Parish whereto she belongs – d^d

Henry Jones[158], John Hickman, Sarah Walker, Ann Smith & Mary Bunn } d^{o}C. by John Blandy C. chd by Saml Reddenhurst – Jones with stealing a brown cloth Woman's Cloak Val: 4s his property – Mary Smith saw the Pris^r drop it – com^d (on their Oaths) to d^{o}C.

RX	Saml Reddenhurst N° 108 Shoe L. Cl:	}	Ea
	Mary Smith N° 4 Carolina Court, Saffron Hill	}	£ 20
	John Blandy N° 40 Ludgate Hill Hatter		10

Hickman was chd with abusing the C[onstable] – he was d^d – Bunn chd Walker & Smith with an Ass^t – com^d to d^{o}C – for want of Sureties

James Pullum, Jos^h Thompson C. Ch^d by Peter Cossart ~~on suspicion~~ N° 1, Bell Court Mincing Lane Merch^t on Suspicion of feloniously Stealing a foreign Bill of Exchange Value £39.15s.10d. Will: Warren Chancery L[ane] Chinaman—Rob: Mason D^o Grocer, ag^d to answer for the Prisoner's Appearance, when the person (who deliv^d him the Bill) was taken

P Ann Wise WC Wm Sporten[?] C. Ch^d by Mary Bailey her Mistress for assaulting her & otherwise greatly misbehaving herself—She askt Pardon & was d^d.

1s. Thos Boston on Mr Ald^n Wrights W^t Wm Fagan C. Ch^d by Wm Winchurch for assaulting him. He made Satisf^n & was d^d

---

158. The case proceeds to the Old Bailey. See *OBP*, February 1781, trial of Henry Jones (t17810222–52).

John Davis on Mr Ald^n Pughs W^t Saml Roberts C. and Ch^d by Church W^{ns} & Overseers of St Sepulchre London for deserting his Wife & Child whereby they are become chargeable to the s^d Prish – com^d to B.

Sam. Matthews, Edwd Gee, Jos: Scales, John Godman[159] } sum^d by John Chamberlain for exercising their resp[ect]ive Trades on Sunday last—they promised to desist in future – d^d

1s.   ~~Cath~~ W^t ag^t Chas Hart ads Ja^s Kerwick – Ass^t etc.

Rhodes Att^y att^d.   J.H.

Mr Alderman Wright. Friday 9 February 1781.
David Cooper Sum^d ads Nathl Fell for causing or Permitting a Quantity of Filth to be laid & deposited in Botolph Lane on Wednesday 7th Inst^t ag^t Statute Adjudg^d true & convicted in Penalty 5s.— wch was p^d into the Chamber

P   Joseph Taylor WC Thos Cordell C. Ch^d by Wm Elliott for making a Noise and disturbance last Night in St Paul's Church Y^d & otherwise misbehaving himself etc. He was reprimanded & D^d

The Man who Yesterday refused to tell his Name, was again bro^t up & now refused – rem^{d}ed 'till Monday

Mr Rhodes Att^d TW

Mr Alderman Pugh. Monday 12 February 1781.
1s.   Warrant ag^t Robert Gordon for assaulting Francis Perry.

1s.   The like ag^t Samuel Fall for assaulting Mary Fowle.

Mary Brown WC by Reeve Martin C. chd by a Person not now present – d^d

P   John Craft by Joseph Gates C. chd by him for ill treating a Bullock & beating it with a large Stick – he promised never to do so again – d^d

Ja^s Gray by Jos: Pybus C. chd by John Millan Overseer of the poor of the Par: of St Bartholomew the Great (on a W^t) for

159. A check mark appears beside each name.

unlawfully begetting Eliz: Wright, Singlewoman of s^d Parish with Child, which is likely to become chargeable thereto – ag^d to go back in order to settle with the Officers.

1s.   Aff^t Rob: Jackson

1s.   Ja^s Newson charged by Jos: Railton, who upon Cond[iti]on of the Prisoner's going to Sea, declined to prosecute his Charge – he enlisted in the Chatham Division of Marines & was attested

Chas Kirk sum^d by Will: Applebee, Carman for refusing to employ his Cart in Cross Lane on the 29th day of January last, adj^d 'till tomorrow, to prove that Applebee was absent from the Cart

The Man chd with stealing a Quartern Loaf was bro^t up – he app^d to be an Ideot [sic]– d^d

1s.   Aff^t John Dod

Ann Wilson by Chas Delegal C. chd by Fra^s Phillips & Mary Ux: for feloniously stealing an Ounce of white thread, two balls of Worsted – some Sugar & other trifling Articles – rem^ded 'till tomorrow as she was in liquor

Mr Beach attending.   E.P.

Mr Alderman Kitchin. Tuesday 13 February 1781.
Ann Wilson by Chas Delagal C. chd by Francis Phillips & Mary Ux for feloniously stealing an Ounce of white thread, two balls of worsted & sundry trifling Articles – Mr Phillips declined a Prosecution, the Value being so trifling.

John Godin, Ja^s Nicklin, Jos: Freeman} summoned by Nathaniel Fenn for laying or causing to be laid a Quantity of Filth in the Street – it was ag^d to have the Dispute heard by the Commissioners of Sewers

1s.   Sam. Fall by Will: Bailey C. chd by Mary Fowle (on a W^t) for an Ass^t – ag^d & d^d

Eliz: Mcginnis by Saml Roberts C. chd by Will: Newman Overseer of St Sepulchre for abusing him – d^d

Jos: Hoare sum^d by John Marshal for contemptuously refusing to appear before him & other Rulers of the Waterman's

Company, to answer a Complaint for placing his great Boat at Black Friars Bridge Stairs to the Obstruction of Landing— Marshal saw the Fact com^d – he was sworn – conv^d in & paid the Penalty of 9s./6d. including 1s. for the Sum^s.

nil   W^t ag^t Thomas Shenton ads Finney Sindefield for unlawfully paw[nin]g certain Muslin intrust^d with him to Tambour

Mr Nash attended   HK

Mr Alderman Burnell. Wednesday 14 February 1781.

1s.   W^t to search the Apartments of Sarah Moore in Purse Court, Old Change for Bonds, Bills & or Securities Val: £500 stolen from Hen: Thrale Esq^e – on Oath of John Perkins

Will. Ives by John Prockter C. chd by Thos Letts for violently assaulting him in company with two other Persons unknown, & wounding him – com^d to WC for want of Sureties (on Letts's Oath)

1s.   Aff^t Thos Lansdown

Ben: Beadle by Saml Roberts C. chd by Edwd Wright Whit-comb Churchwarden of St Sepulchre (on a W^t) for deserting his Wife, whereby she is become chargeable to the s^d Parish – he agreed to allow her 2s./6 a Week, & was upon that Promise d^d

Will: Craig WC by R^d Finch C. chd by Will: Churchill a hackney Coachman for bilking him of his Fare – from Lime-house to Temple Bar – the C. went with the Pris^r to obtain the Money.

1s.   Back'd a Middx W^t

Chris^r Burnitt app^d & produced Ja^s Pitt the Driver of his Waggon sum^d by Will: Parker, Carman for wilfully driving the Waggon ag^st s^d Parker's Cart & thereby damaging the Horse – Moses Orme was present

P   Warrant against Ann Strutt ads Margaret Dunnage Ass^t

Mr Houstoun att^d.   John Burnell.

Mr Alderman Alsop. Thursday 15 February 1781.

Chch Wdns of St Lawrence Jewry sum^d by Sarah Smith for relief – Ord^d to relieve her

P   W^t ag^t Jere^h Emlin ads Mary Hewitt Ass^t etc.

1s.   Timothy Ryordan WC by Will Howard C. chd by Ja^s Jefferies for assaulting him, & wilfully breaking his Windows – they withdrew & ag^d

Will: Craig WC by R^d Finch C. chd by Will: Churchill (as Yesterday) – Churchill did not appear & the Pris^r appeared to be insane – d^d

1s.   Aff^t Thos Allen

Ann Price[160] Jno Edwards C. chd by Maynard Brown and Jos^a Richmond for feloniously stealing a pint pewter pot Va:[blank] s^d Richmond's Property, and also a Quart pewter pot Va: [blank] s^d Brown's P[ro]perty – Sarah ~~Bailly~~ Bailey in Richmonds Ho: saw prisoner ~~past~~ take the pint pot now Produced, & also saw the Quart pewter pot under her Arm

RX   Maynard Brown of Jewin Street Vict. for his Wife & Bailey £20

Mr Houstoun attended.   R.A.

The Right Honourable Thomas Harley by Mr Alderman Plomer. Friday 16 February 1781.
Henry Jefferies WC by Jno Prockter C. chd by Thos Letts for violently Ass^t ing & wounding him – com^d to d^{o}C for want of Sureties (on Letts Oath)

Ja^s Nicklin sum^d by Ben: Fenn for laying or causing to be laid a Quantity of Filth in Botolph Lane on the 10th Inst. John White saw Mr Nicklin's Servant on Saturday last about 3 O'Clock throw some Filth into the kennel – he was sworn – he did not see Mr Nicklin at this time – the Ald^n declared his Opinion, that Mr Nicklin was not liable to answer, but his Servant.

Mary Graves by Jno Collinton C. chd by Mary Marsh on suspicion of stealing a Shirt & Apron – there was no Proof – d^d.

Mr Houston attended.   WP

Mr Alderman Crosby. Monday 19 February 1781.
1s.   W^t ag^t Ann Handy ads Cath: Martin – Ass^t etc.

---

160. The case proceeds to the Old Bailey. See *OBP*, February 1781, trial of Ann Price (t17810222-53).

Judah Saunders PC by Hugh Pollatt C. chd by Tho[s] Townsend on suspicion of stealing two pieces of Calimanco – rem[d]ed till tomorrow

Tho[s] Slime by John Clark C. chd by Fra[s] Taylor (on a W[t]) for an Assault – Tho[s] Hurst saw the Pris[r] strike Taylor four times – on their Oaths bailed

RX   Tho[s] Slime of the Quest Ho: Cripplegate – Serj[t] £ 20
Ben: Archer White Street – Ship Vict.   }
Mich Garment Angel Alley Bpsgate Street Vict } Each £ 10
3 Jolly Weavers   }

Ann Ireland by Rob: Sedgwick C. chd by Will: Killingley, Churchwarden of the Parish of Saint Stephen in Coleman Street, for assaulting him – M[r] K. ag[d] to procure her Passage to Scarborough

1s.   W[t] ag[t] Rich[d] Coverley a Journeyman Shoemaker ads Will: Russel a Shoemaker his Ma[r] for embezziling 5 pairs of shoe top – pieces

Jos[h] Wood PC W[m] Ginn C. chd by a Person not now present on Susp[n] of stealing 2 Iron Bars in the Steel Yard, no Person app[g] now he was remanded 'till tomorrow

1s.   W[t] ag[t] Mich[l] Welch & Eleanor Ux ads Mary Hawkins – Ass[t]

1s.   Sarah Lewis by Tho[s] Emery C. chd by Ann Ux Tho[s] Kellett (on a W[t] Per Ald[n] Plomer) for an Ass[t] – ag[d] & d[d]

Ja[s] Fee WC by Sam[l] Roberts C. chd by Will: Whittaker his Ma[r] for defrauding him of Money – taken of Customers to whom the Pris[r] sold Potatoes – there was a doubt if a felony was com[d] – d[d].

Ann Handy by Will: Bailey C. chd by Cath: Martin (on his Wp's W[t] this day) for an Ass[t] – Handy ag[d] to settle, or to be bro[t] again tomorrow

R[d] Coverley a Journeyman Shoemaker by Tho[s] Parrott C. chd by Will: Russel his Ma[r] (on his Wp's W[t]) for embezzilling 5 pairs of Men's Shoe – ~~Pots~~ top pieces

1s.   Will: Williams by Ja[s] Barker C. chd by Will: Hartin (on Ald[n] Plomer's W[t]) for an Ass[t] – they withdrew & co[d] not agree – d[d]

3/4

RX

Ja[s] Wright Merryweather by Tho[s] Goodwin C. chd by Sebastian Lima (on a W[t]) for an Ass[t] – on their Oaths he was ord[d] to give Bail or be com[d]

Ja[s] Wright Merriweather of the Bull's head Aleho: St Catherines, } 40
Gentleman Midshipman under Lieut. Scott }
John Scott of Burr Street St. Catherines Par S[t] Bot. Aldgate Middx Gent } 40

Evan Thomas from PC by Miles Hart C. charged by James Taddy for feloniously stealing about 4 lb. Weight of Tobacco, Val: 4s. the property of himself, Geo: Cooper & Fra[s] Garratt his partners in Trade – on his Oath & also of Tho[s] Nott com[d] to d°C – afterw[ds] d[d]

William Barratt PC by Edw[d] Daintree C. chd by John Jordan for feloniously stealing 3 lbs. Weight of Tobacco Val: 3s. the Property of Persons unknown

W[m] Bolton, John Low } WC W[m] Payne C. chd by him & ano[r] Person not now present as foll[s] Viz: Bolton for stealing a Bridle Val: [blank] the property of [blank] Matthews (who is not now present) & Low for receiving it knowing the same to be stolen – rem[d] 'till to morrow

M[r] Beach attended. B.C.

M[r] Alderman Townsend. Tuesday 20 February 1781.

Ald[n] Pugh   Sarah Ux Hen: Simpson[161] WC by Will: Blackburn C. chd by Isaac Smith for feloniously stealing eight Negligee Silk Handkerchiefs Val: 20s & upw[ds] his Property – Will: Carnell saw the Fact com[d] – on their Oaths committed to d°C

R   Isaac Smith of Cheapside L. Linen Draper for self & Carnell   £ 20
Will: Blackburn of N° 41 Old Change L. Watchmaker   £ 10

Ald[n]   Rich[d] Coverley a Journeyman Shoemaker by Tho[s] Parrott
Townsend   C. chd by Will: Russel, a Shoemaker, his Ma[r] (on a W[t]) for
Pugh   embezzilling Material he was entrusted to put upon Shoes [illegible] Sam[l] Shoell deliv[d] out the Leather – com[d] to B. for 14 days

---

161. The case proceeds to the Old Bailey. See *OBP*, February 1781, trial of Sarah, the wife of Henry Simpson, Henry Simpson (t17810222–20).

Judah Saunders WC by Hugh Pollett C. chd by Thos Townsend on suspicion of feloniously stealing two pieces of Callimanco – there was no Proof – d^d

1s.   Rob: Wood a Journeyman Tinman by Thos Parrott C. chd by Thos Smith a Tinman his Ma^r (on Ald^n Plomer's W^t 17th Inst) for unlawfully departing from his Service & leaving certain Tin Work unfinished which he had undertaken to perform – the parties agreed & the W^t was d^d

Edwd Lloyd by Jos: Gates C. chd by Geo: Will: Cartwright (on Ald^n Pugh's W^t of this day) for an Ass^t – d^d & Cartwright was left to his Indictm^t

John Wheeler summoned by Richd Hawe one of the Rulers of the Waterman's Company for refusing to attend and answer a Compl[ain]t for placing his Tilt Boat athwart the Stairs at Billingsgate – Hawe was sworn – he was conv^d

Mr Nash attended. JT

Mr Alderman Wilkes. Thursday 22 February 1781.
Martha Inglestone WC by Jno Prockter C. chd by a Person not now present with felony – there was no Charge – d^d

Will: Barratt PC by Edwd Daintree C. chd by a Person not now present, with stealing 3lb W^t of Tobacco Val: 3s. the property of Persons unknown – d^d

Philip Carnan by Major Williams C. chd by Will: Lane for feloniously stealing eight silver Table Spoons, two silver Salts, a pair of silver shoe Buckles, a silver pint Mug, 12 silver tea Spoons, a pair of silver tea Tongs, a black silk Cardinal, two pair of Sheets and several other things, Val: [blank] the property of the s^d Will: Lane – Ann Gardner s^d that Lane's Wife desired the things to be sold – rem^{d}ed to produce the Plate tomorrow

Hen: Ducker d^{o}C by Jno Edwards C. chd by Philip Matsell on suspicion of feloniously stealing three Tires & a Piece of Iron – by desire of his Ma^r, d^d

1s.   Edwd Bennett by R^d Conan C. chd by Matt^w Good (on Ald^n Crosby's W^t 10th Inst.) for an Ass^t – ag^d & d^d

Sarah Robinson by David Ranken C. chd by him for lying

in the open Air, in the Parish of St Mildred in the Poultry –
remanded to be pass'd to her Parish

Jos: Wood PC by Will: Ginn C. chd by Will: Holmer Junr for
feloniously stealing two iron barrs Val: [blank] – John Stubley
apprehended the Pris^r with the Iron under his Coat – for want
of Evidence – d^d

Pat^k McKaran Kaon WC by Jona: Prior C. chd by Geo: Sked-
ding for feloniously stealing four pair of Shoes, & three pair
of Soles & six wooden Lasts Val: 6s. & upw^{ds} the property of
s^d Geo: Skidding – Richd Mound heard him confess – com^d to
d^{o}C.

RX   Geo: Skidden blue hart C^t Coleman St. Cordwainer   }
      Richd Mound – London Wall   D^o } £10
      Jonathan Prior – N° 3 Evans C^t Bazinghall S^t D^o }

1s.   Aff^t Ann Jackman

Will: Molton, John Lowe} by Will: Payne C. chd by him –
Molton for stealing & Lowe for receiving a leather Bridle Val
3s. – Molton ord^d to the Marine Society on acc^t of his Youth

Mary Cheeseman PC by Will Martin C. chd by Patience
Harslam for feloniously stealing three pair of silk Stockings
etc. – it having been in part heard at the Mansion Ho: – d^d.

Sus^a Davis WC by Jos: Thompson C. chd by Ja^s Pitticlew on
Suspicion of stealing half a Gua & 7s. – d^d

Fra^s Appleton sum^d by Thos Griffin, Carman for refusing to
pay the Cartage of sundry Loads of Goods – he agreed to pay
2 Guas this Week

Mr Rhodes attended.   John Wilkes.

Mr Alderman Sawbridge.   Friday 23 February 1781.
nil   [blank] Ross by Reeve Martin C. chd by him for ass^t ing him
       – d^d

Gerard Thos South sum^d by John Wheatland – Churchwarden
of the Parish of Saint Peter in Cheapside, for refusing to repay
£ 3.10. – being Rewards paid on account of a Fire in your
Chimney

Philip Carnan by Major Williams C. chd by Will: Lane for

feloniously stealing 8 silver Table Spoons, 2 silver Salts, a pair of silver shoe buckles, a silver pint Mug, 12 silver tea Spoons, a pair of silver Tea Tongs, a black silk Cardinal & several other things Value £5 & upw^{ds} – Lane said, he had no Charge to make – d^d

Eliz: Kelly by John Newman C. chd by Edwd Archer for feloniously stealing one Guinea, three half Guas in Gold & 10s. in Silver, monies numbered, the Monies of the s^d Edwd Archer – rem^{d}ed 'till tomorrow

1s.   Mary Cook by Jona: Prior C. chd by John Cook her Husband (on a Peace W^t Per Ald^n Plomer) for using threats whereby &c. – d^d

Thos Flathers by Chas Staples C. chd by Jane Ux: Thos Layton for going into her Cellar with Intent to commit felony – rem^{d}ed to have other Witnesses

Eliz Griffiths by John Edwards C. chd by John Wilkinson on suspicion of stealing 26 Yards of Scotch Carpet Val. £3.10. Will: Leadman & Wilkins were sworn – com^d to WC.

RX   ~~Will.~~ Ja^s Ford St Martins leGrand Auctioneer } £ 20
John Edwards for self Wilkins & Leadman }

2s.   Aff^{ts} John Rolanson & Chas Fountain

Mr Beach attended   J Sawbridge.

Sir Thomas Hallifax. Monday 26 February 1781.
Ald^n Plomer

    John Lloyd WC by John Prockter C. chd by Geo: Priestley for feloniously stealing 24lb W^t of Butter Val: [blank] – rem^{d}ed to be sent on board the Tender, the Evidence not being compleat and the Pris^r being a disorderly Person.

1s.   Aff^t John Straton

Thos Flathers by Chas Staples C. chd by Jane Ux: Thos Layton for burglariously breaking & entering the dwelling House of the s^d Thos, with Intent to commit felony therein – he ag^d to enlist

~~Thomas~~ Roger Jones, John Williams } WC by Will: Catchpole C. chd by Mary Teasdale for making a disturbance in her

237

Publick House – the C. charged Jones with ass[t] ing him – they withdrew and ag[d]

P   Eliz: Kenny by R[d] Streetin C. chd by Rob[t] Muffatt for wilfully breaking her Windows – d[d]

Charles Batchelor from WC by Thomas Henley C. chd by John Crowley

David Slocomb by Joseph Gates C. charged by John Crowley for assaulting him, for Want of the Compl[ainan]ts Appearing, discharged.

Ambrose Ward from PC by John Stephens C. charged by a Person not present with picking his Pocket last night of a Linen Hankerchief who not appearing ~~to support his Charge the s[d] Ward was discharged~~, the matter was postponed till tomorrow.

1s.   Warrant ag[t] Samuel Mason ats Bibid for assaulting Elijah Davis, and Samuel Meeh

M[r] Beach attended   WP

~~George Cass~~ Margaret Wright by George Cass C. charged by Anne Monro with feloniously stealing two Linen Shirts her Property Yesterday from the Woolwich Stage, Value 8d[?] rem[d]ed till to Morrow.

Sir James Esdaile. Tuesday 27 February 1781.
M[r] Ald[n]   Marg[t] Wright by Geo: Cass C. chd by Ann Morris for
Wooldridge   feloniously stealing two Shirts two Stocks & other ~~things~~ wearing Apparel, the Pros[r] having prom[d] not to prosecute if she wo[d] redeem them out of Pawn, she was d[d]

Eliz[h] Bambridge by W[m] Catchpole C. chd by Mary Thompson (on M[r] Ald[n] Plomer's W[t] 26th) for assault[g] & beat[g] her & tak[g] from her 3/9 in half pence her property disch[d]

1s.   Back'd a Middx W[t]

nil   John Sketchley WC by Edwin Daniel C. chd by John Chambers with assault[g] him & tak[g] his Watchmans Staff from him – it app[g] friv[s] discharged

Ambrose Ward rem^ded Yesterday – the Waiter did not appear
– Ord^d to the Marine Society

Mr Alderman Wooldridge. Adhuc Tuesday 27 February 1781.

gave a	Thomas Flathers WC by Chas Staples C. chd by Jane
Woman 1s.	the Wife of Thos Layton with burglariously break^g &
gave a poor	ent^g the Dwell^g House of s^d Thos with intent to commit
Man 1s.	Felony therein – he was remanded yesterday – no
	Evidence of Burglary app^g he was com^d to B p^r W^t as
	an idle & disorderly Person

P   Peace W^t ag^t John Wilkes ads Martha his Wife

P   Mary Mckenzie by Will: Ginn C. chd by Ann Mascal (on Ald^n
       Pugh's W^t Yesterday) for an Ass^t – friv^s & d^d

Thos Jackson bro^t from WC – having been in Custody since
the 30th Janry last, chd with a Fraud – no person appearing ag^t
him – d^d

1s.   Affirmation Jos: Bailey

Ja^s Wheeler a Journeyman Weaver by Thos Emery C. chd by
John Tilford for embezzling 3 lb W^t of Silk, entrusted with
him to make into handkerchiefs – rem^ded untill tomorrow –
afterw^ds referr'd to a Middx Justice

Mr Nash attended   T.W.

Mr Alderman Plumbe [by?] Alderman Plomer. Wednesday 28 February
       1781.

1s.   Back'd a Middx Bench W^t

John Godin sum^d by John Lyness for laying or causing to be
laid in Botolph Lane, a Quantity of Filth on the 23^d Inst. –
Lyness s^d the Servant threw out the Filth – he was sworn – but
Mr Godin promising never to do so again, the Penalty was not
insisted on

nil   Will: Goodall, Ja^s Mason} by Will: Howard C. chd by Geo:e
       Cass for ass^ting him – Cass app^d from several Witnesses, to
       have com^d the Assault – that he was in liquor, and collared the
       Prisoners 1st – d^d

Rob: Adams the Driver of a Cart N° 394 produced by Rob:
Park sum^d by Ja^s Scott – adj^d 'till tomorrow

Harry Powell sum^d to produce the Driver of a hackney Coach N° 321 – to answer the Complaint of John Marriott for driving the said Coach ag^st him and doing him great personal Injury – settled.

P   W^t ag^t R^d Phillips ads ~~Hughes~~ Ruth Ux: Ass^t etc.

Mr Houston attended   WP

Mr Alderman Kennett. Thursday 1 March 1781.
Ald^n Wilkes

Frances Hart sum^d by Will: Machin a hackney Coachman for refusing to pay him his Fare for carrying her in his hackney Coach from Catherine Street to St Paul's – the C. was sworn & s^d that the same Shilling he received from Mrs. Hart, he believed to be bad, and he bent it with his Teeth – Ord^d 1s. Fare & 2s./6d. Charges, wch were p^d.

Mr Alderman Plomer. Friday 2 March 1781.
1s.   W^t ag^t Will:Pearson ads Mary Ux: John Penstone for an Ass^t with Intent to commit a rape

John Lloyd WC by Jno Prockter C. chd by Geo: Priestley for feloniously stealing a wicker flat & 24^lb W^t of fresh Butter Val: [blank] – remanded on Tuesday next to have the flat identified

1s.   W^t ag^t Sarah Purdue ads Sus^a Lyland Ass^t etc.

John Hart sum^d ads Henry White Deputy of the Ward of Cripplegate within for not keeping his Times of Watch & Ward – he begged the Deput^s pardon prom^d not to offend again & was dism[isse]^d

Susanna May [blank] by [blank] Linton[162] C. chd by Elizabeth White for assaulting her & slapping her Face – their Ma^r app^d to whom it was referred to settle the Mre betw^t them

1s.   Henry Green WC by John Collington C. chd by John Marsh a Vict^r with refusing to pay his Reckoning & abus^g him, he prom^d to pay, begged pardon & was d^d

1s.   Eliz^h Crowther by Ja^s Drummond C. chd by Sarah Shepherd (on L M^s W^t 28th Feb^y) for an Ass^t agreed d^d

---

162. Probably Thomas Linton.

Sarah Tomkins, Alice Watkins } WC by Chas Moody C. chd by Jos^h Cook for feloniously steal^g two Guin^s his prop^y – they applied to him to take them in a Hackney Coach to the Exchange— wch he did, but not being able to prove they took it they were d^d

1s. W^t ag^t Jonathan Anderson for wilful & corrupt Perjury upon the Cert. of the Clk of the Sess^s of Oyer & Terminer

1s. Samuel Noton, Ann Rose} WC by Ja^s Drummond C. chd by John Trimbey a Watchman for being found in a Passage in an indecent posture – reprimanded & d^d

Richd Phillips WC by Wm Catchpole C. chd by Ruth his Wife (on Mr Ald^n Plomers W^t 28 Feb^y) for an Assault, com^d for want of Sureties p^r W^t.

P Mary Williams, Mary Jones} PC by Wm Govin C. chd by Charles Campbell with assaulting him & Mary Eliz^h his Wife for assaultg last Night, they asked pardon – d^d.

Mr Nash attended WP

Mr Alderman Wooldridge. Monday 5 March 1781.
Benj: Cole sum^d to produce the Driver Thos Perry of his hackney Coach N° 274 –to answer the Complaint of R^d Potter for driving the s^d Coach agst his Cart, and damaging a Quantity of Meat – Thos King saw the Coach go agst the Cart & overturn it, as he believes wilfully – Cole was sworn – Thos Williams app^d to be the driver– settled

1s. Aff^t John Chaldecott

1s. D^o John Russel

Mary Gallen, Ruth Hale} by Will: Catchpole C. chd by each other – Hale gave the 1st Charge for stealing 1s.—and Gallen chd Hale with an Ass^t – the Parties having settled – d^d

Will: Wright by Rob: Jones C. chd by Will: Brander (not now present) for refusing to take five persons in his Coach – d^d.

R^d Sparkes by John Feakins C. chd by Jos: Finch (on the Lord Mayor's W^t) for pawning or otherwise unlawfully disposing of a silver Watch – there was no Proof – d^d.

1s.   Chas Rice by Jno Dale C. chd by Mary Ux for an Ass^t – she forgave him & therefore he was d^d

~~Eliz Barlow WC by Jos: Barlow C. chd by Wm Miller~~

Sarah Howse by John Dove C. chd by John Clarke for feloniously stealing a silver shoe buckle Val: 5s. & upw^{ds} – d^d.

Mr Beach attended. T.W.

Mr Alderman Peckham. Tuesday 6 March 1781.
~~Mary Patrick by Jno Prockter C. chd by~~ [blank]

1s.   W^t ag^t Ja^s Fisher ads John Chapman – Ass^t etc.

Ald^n Pugh

3s./4d. Saml Morris, Will: Whiteley} WC by Jno Edwards C. chd by Will: Bryant for assaulting & falsely imprisoning him – Bryant was sworn – Whiteley was com^d to d^{o}C & Morris bailed as below

RX   Saml Morris N° 60 Cow Cross Middx Gent   £ 40

Richd Rowley   D^o Baker   20

Rob: Morris N° 2 Church Y^d C^t Inner Temple Gent   20

1s.   Back'd a Middx W^t Per Mr Addington

1s.   John Allford WC by Thos Massey C. chd by Mary Meredith for assaulting & beating her – they withdrew & ag^d – d^d.

3s.   Edwd Eaton, Ja^s William, Jno Kendrick } by Reeve Martin C. chd by Barnard Briggs a Publican on Ludgate Hill for ass^{t}ing him – Mary Walker saw the Ass^t com^d – ag^d & d^d

1s.   John Wood by Thos Fenner C. chd by Edwd Williamson (on Ald^n Wooldridge's W^t) for an Ass^t – John Lloyd was sworn & s^d that Williamson struck first – d^d.

1s.

    Edwd Williamson by d^{o}C. chd by John Lloyd (on the Lord Mayor's W^t of this day) for an Ass^t – d^d.

1s.   W^t ag^t Marg^t Dunn ads John Fitzgerald Assault etc.

2s.   John Dewes, Will: Hews, Will: Cox} by John Collison C. chd by Will: Beesom (on Ald^n Wooldridge's W^t Yesterday) for an Ass^t—d^d

P   Han^h Cooper charged by Mr Deputy Thorpe for making a disturbance – she was forgiven – d^d

~~John Whitlin chd by Ann Grub for ass^ting her Son~~

John Lloyd WC by Jno Prockter C. chd by George Priestley for feloniously stealing a wicker flatt and 24^lb W^t of fresh Butter Val: 10s & upw^ds his property – Geo: Watlinton saw him take it – com^d

RX   Geo: Priestley Newgate Mket Butter Merchant   £ 20
      Geo: Watlinton   D^o   Butcher   10

Mr Nash att^ded

Mr Alderman Peckman. Adhuc Wednesday[sic][163] 6 March 1781.
    Sarah Parker by John Procter C. charged by Mr Ald^n p Woolridge as a disorderly person at his Worship's request discharged.

Mr Houstoun att^d. RP.

Mr Alderman Hayley. Wednesday 7 March 1781.
Ald^n Pugh.   Back'd a Middx W^t Per Mr Wright.
1s.

P   W^t ag^t Rob: Smith ads Alexander Speance for knowingly &c. obtaining £1.9.- with Intent to cheat & defraud him thereof

Mr Ald^n Hayley Nunc
    Edwd Robinson[164] PC by John Godfrey C. chd by John Harden & John Fairbank for feloniously stealing a leather trunk, a claret coloured great Coat, a pair of worsted Stockings, three linen Shirts, 3 Stocks, a linen handkerchief, a pair of mocoa Shidds set in Silver, a pair of Boots, a razor in a tortoise-shell Case & a silk Purse Val: 40s & upw^ds the property of the said John Fairbank – rem^ded (a number of duplicates being fo[un]^d upon him) to enquire at the different Pawn Brokers nam'd in s^d Duplicates for the particular Goods pledg'd by the Pris^r for the Purpose of having the Properties ascertain'd &c.
RX   Jno Fairfax Bury St Edmunds, Suffolk Carrier   £ 20
      Phil Philpot Bpsgate Street L. Innholder   }
                                    } Each £ 10
      John Godfrey – Suttons C^t Bsgate St Const.   }

163. A different clerk's hand from the previous entries on this date. Probably an error by the clerk. Peckham's name is misspelled and the date should be Tuesday, 6 March.
164. The case proceeds to the Old Bailey. See *OBP*, April 1781, trial of Edward Robinson (t17810425-53).

1s.   Aff^t Jno Pinkett

3s./4d. Mich^l Lyshir by Saml Roberts C. chd by Francis Hamilton Overseer of the Poor of the Parish of St Sepulchre London (on Ald^n Pugh's W^t of the 2^d Inst.) for unlawfully begetting Eliz: Clark, Singlewoman of the s^d Parish with Child, which is become chargeable thereto – bailed

RX   Mich^l ~~Lyshir~~ Lashar – at the Falcon Gravel L.
Southwark Glass blower   } £
Danl Cox   D^o D^o Glass maker } 20

Thos Jones WC by John Mean C. chd by Thos Reading for feloniously stealing a cloak bag – he was sent to the Marine Society – the Fact being com^d in the County of Middx – he was referr'd to Bow Street

1s.   W^t ag^t John Griffiths ads David Williams Ass^t etc.

1s.   W^t to search the Apartm^{ts} of Hen: Drury in Jewin Street for a Counterpane – on Oath of Richd Pitt.

Eliz: Barlow WC by Jos: Thompson C. chd by Will: Miller for feloniously stealing 5 silk Watch ~~Chains~~ Strings & 2 silk Cane Strings – rem^{d}ed till Monday next, as the Prisoner's dau[ghte]^r was not in Custody

1s.   Ja^s Fisher by Thos Parrott C. chd by John Chapman (on Ald^n Peckham's W^t Yesterday) for ass^{t}ing & kicking him – they withdrew and ag^d – d^d.

1s.   W^t ag^t Martha Whittaker ads Geo: Gardener for leaving Work unfinished in the Furrier branch—wch she contracted to perform

nil   Mary Jolly [blank] by Jno Fenner C. chd by Will: Bensfield (on Justice Kettilby's W^t back'd) for pawning fourteen pair of breeches entrusted with her – referr'd to a Surry Justice

Mary Jones WC by Will: Compton C. chd by Ja^s Roberts for feloniously stealing a copper Cover – rem^{d}ed to make Inquiry of her Character

John Matthews by Will: Payne C. chd by John Dearburgh on suspicion of stealing a Quantity of Sugar – rem^{d}ed for Mr Bell to appear

Mr Rhodes attended   GH.

Mr Alderman Newnham. Thursday 8 March 1781.
     ~~Edward Robinson rem^d yesterday to PC for fur^r Examion John Godfrey Const. Ch^d by~~

John Matthews W. Payne C. Ch^d by James Bell and John Dearburgh (his Clk) on Suspicion of feloniously stealing a large Quantity of Sugar – d^d.

Mary Jones rem^d yesterday to WC for fur^r Examicon Wm Compton C. Ch^d by Ja^s Roberts for feloniously stealing a Copper Cover Value 2s. his Property – Directions given Pl[ainti]^f to inquire into her Character She was reprim^d & D^d.

1s.   Martha Whittaker bro^t by Wm Catchpole C. on Mr Aldⁿ Hayleys Warr^t Ch^d by Geo. Gardiner her Ma^r for leaving certain Work unfinish'd in the Furriery Branch, Wch she by Contract had undertaken to perform, ag^t the Stat. Mre heard before Mr Aldⁿ Newnham & the Chamberlain Who and[sic] direct'd that the Woman sh^d return & offer to finish her Work of Wch she readily agreeing to Comply with, she was d^d.

John Moor WC. Chas Delegall C. Ch^d by James Newland on Suspicion of attempting to pick his Pockett rem^d till tomorr. when Moor is to produce Evidence to his Char^r

Richd Jutsum a Butcher Sum^d ads Deodatus Dean Overseer of Poor of St Botolph Aldgate for exercising his said Trade in s^d Parish on Sunday last in the Time of Divine Service ag^t the Stat. For Want of Proof, D^d.

Rec^d at the same time this Penalty for the use of the Poor of ye said Parish ~~Rec'd the same time~~. R. Young Oversire.

Saml Matthews a Butcher Sum^d ads D^o for the like Offence Adj^d true and Convicted in Penalty 5s.

Edward Gee Sum^d ads Deodatus Dean (Overseer as af^d) for exercising his Trade of a Butcher on Sunday last as before. For Want of Proof he was D^d.

Joseph Scales Sum^d ads Deodatus Dean Overseer &c For the like Offence, For want of Proof D^d

Edwd Cock a Butcher Sum^d ads D^o For the like Offence For Want of Evidence he was d^d

John Ryder a B[utche]ʳ Sumᵈ ads Ditto. For the like Offence
For want of Evid He was Dᵈ

1s.   Benjᵃ Petersom (on Mʳ Aldⁿ Wooldridges Warᵗ) Henry Hosketh
C. Chd by Richᵈ Powell for assault[in]g Jane ux & Mary his
Daughter, For Want of Proof he was discharg'd

Mʳ [blank] White Sumᵈ ads Robᵗ Josling a Hackney Coach man
for refusing to pay him his Fare for carrying him yesterday
in his Coach from the West End of Sᵗ Pauls Church Yard to
Charing Cross & from thence to Sᵗ James Street   The Magistrate Adjudg'd paymᵗ of 2s. for the Fare with 2s.6d. the Costs
accrew'd

Geo Carey Wᵐ Howard C. Chᵈ by Bryant Wormall for breaking
a Square of Glass in his Shop Window with Intent to commit
Felony therein, remᵈ till tomorrow for fuʳ Examicon

1s.   Wᵐ Stately Samˡ Corp C. Chᵈ by Jaˢ Loppingwell a Sheriffs
Officer for assaulting him in the execution of his Office, Adjᵈ
true But upon his agreeing to make reasonable Satisfaction for
the Damᵉ Sustain'd He was reprimanded & discharg'd.

1s.   Wᵐ Whitely ads Wᵐ Bryant per Asst Dᵈ by Consent

Mʳ Rhodes attended. NN

Mʳ Alderman Clark. Friday 9 March 1781.
     ~~Robt~~ Edward Mann sumᵈ ads. Nathaniel Fenn for laying or
Causing to be laid a Quantity of Filth in Botolph Lane on the
6ᵗʰ Instᵗ John White Servᵗ to Mʳ Fenn Swore to the Fact. Mʳ
Mann was Convicted in Penalty 5s. – paid into the Chamber

John Crane Sumᵈ ads Dᵒ for the like Offence John Taylor anoʳ
Servᵗ to Mʳ Fenn depos'd to the Fact & he was convicted in
Penalty 5s. – pᵈ into the Chamber.

1s.   John Griffiths WC John Edwards C. (on Mʳ Aldⁿ Hayleys Warrᵗ)
Chᵈ by David Williams Per Assᵗ Maria Hitchins confirm'd Mʳ
Williams in his Evidence. He made Satisfⁿ & was Dᵈ.

John Smith WC Major Williams C. Chᵈ by George Faulkner for
assaulting him with Intent feloniously to Commit the detestable Sin of Buggery on his Body, agᵗ the Order of Nature &c.
– Faulkner sᵈ he believed the Prisʳ entered his Body – remᵈed
'till Monday, for the Landlord to attend

John Moore by Chas Delagal C. chd by Ja^s Newland for putting his hand into his pocket with Intent to commit Felony – d^d.

1s. Affid^t Weatherhead

1s. D^o Will: Holland

Geo: Cary by Willm Howard C. chd by Bryant Wormall for breaking a shew Glass with Intent to commit Felony – he ag^d to go to Sea

Ja^s Fennell by Jos: Thompson C. chd by Sam. Wiltshire for feloniously stealing a pair of black sattin Breeches – no Proof – d^d

1s. Marg^t Stokes by Willm: Catchpole C. chd by Elizth Davis (on the Lord Mayor's W^t of the 7th Inst) for an Ass^t – Wm How was present & confirm'd Davis's Evid. Mre Sett^d and d^d

2s. John Davis, Elizth Davis} by Ja^s Drummond C. chd by Marg^t Churchill (on Ald^n Plomer's W^t Yesterday) for an Ass^t – Adj^d frivolous & D^d.

1s. Warr^t v Henry Rennie ads Wm Wimpory per Ass^t

1s. War^t to Search House & Premises of Thos Pratt in Church Yard C^t Fetter Lane ads. Robt Wickham of N° 66 Fleet St^t Vict. for Goods and Apparel Lately Stolen from his sd Premises

Mr Rhodes attended RC

Mr Alderman Wright. Thursday 17 May 1781.
Chas Pearce sum^d by Thos Gibbs a hackney Coachman for refusing to pay him his Fare for being in his Service upwards of four hours – he was sworn & ord^d the Fare & 2s./6d. Charges.

1s. Aff^t Ben: Brooks, D^o Adams, D^o Scanlon (a Coal Merch^t)

John Shipman WC Thos Massey C. Ch^d by Wm Perrin a Watchman of the Ward of Farringdon within ~~on Suspicion~~ being apprehended by him last Night bet^n 12 and one loitering about in s^d Ward under very suspicious Circumstances. There was nothing Criminal prov'd and his Fa[the]r and sev^l others appearing & giving him a good Character, He was reprim^d and disch^d.

1s.   Warr^t v John Griffiths ads Mary Higgins per Ass^t

Thos Biggs PC Jos^h Ellis C. Ch^d by Saml Austin on susp^n of feloniously Stealing 4 oz. of Silk Twist value 6s. 6d. the Property of Saml Austin— remanded for fur^r Examicon till Monday

1s.   Warr^t v Henry Knobley ads Rach^l Solomon per Ass^t

Chas Brown was again bro^t up for Examination – David Smith was sworn – Eliz Park was sworn they said they never saw any Tammies[165] in their Master's Houses – they never knew Clewes to leave Tammies – Brown was sworn – he said that Clewes and he went together to Handfield's House – that a Man with an Apron, whom he don't know, gave him the Tammies up Stairs – that he had a Glass of Brandy given him by this Stranger – that Handfield persuaded him to abscond – Mr Milward engaged for Handfields Appearance

P   Thos Marshal by Ja^s Barker C. chd by Eliz Reed (on a W^t by his Wp) for an Ass^t – he ask'd Pardon and was d^d.

P   Ann Sidebothom by Will: Catchpole C. chd by Marg^t Willey (on Ald^n Wooldridges W^t on Tuesday) for an Ass^t – they withdrew & ag^d – d^d

3s.   Nich^s Jersen, Nielson Hansen } Aff^{ts} – & an Interpreter

1s.   Eliz Coulson, John Inston} by John Guise C. chd by each other Inston 1st charged Coulson with making a Disturbance— and throwing rotten Apples at him – and Coulson chd Inston with ass^{t}ing her – Saml Titcomb proved that Inston struck her with a Cane – it app^d that Inston had acted very improperly – he was ord^d to make her Satisfaction – they withdrew & ag^d – d^d

1s.   Warr^t v. Judath Bouitibole ads ~~Rich~~ Rach^l Levy Ass^t

Rhodes Att^y attended   TW

Mr Alderman Pugh. Friday 18 May 1781.
1s.   Back'd a Middx W^t Per Mr Hyde

1s.   Aff^t Will: Osbaldiston

---

165. Probably a tammy, a fine worsted cloth, often with a glazed finish (*OED*).

2s.   D° Will: Still and Sam¹ Chapman

P   Wᵗ agᵗ John Church ads Eliz: Ux: Assᵗ etc.

Jos: Hand sumᵈ by John Rose Carman for refusing to pay the Cartage of ten Bags of Wool – Ordᵈ the Fare & 2s. Charges.

Thoˢ Qeresole WC chd by Will: Rogers for feloniously stealing a linen handkerchief – several other Handkerchiefs were found upon him – remᵈed 'till tomorrow.

Mʳ Beach attending.   EP

Alderman Plomer.[166]

Levy Simons, Hyam Joseph, Usher Alexander } sumᵈ by Jos: Nicholson Overseer of the poor of the Parish of Saint James Dukes Place, for refusing to pay their several Proportions of the Poor's Rate – Simons & Joseph allowed a Month – Alexander to pay one Quarter immediately & allowed a Quarter to pay the remʳ.

Patᵏ Kendlen[167] PC by Will: Crank C. chd by Sims Scarff & Thoˢ ~~Flight~~ Bright for feloniously stealing a wooden Porter ~~Hogshead~~ Cask Val: 10s & upwards the property of Felix Calvert ~~Esqᵉ~~ Rᵈ Ladbroke and Will: Whitmore Esqᵉˢ – on the Oaths of Scarff and Bright – comᵈ to d°C.

RX   Sims Scarff of Cosen Lane L. Cooper   } Each
        Thoˢ Bright of Queen Street – East Merchᵗ   } £ 10
        Will: Cragg – N° 5 Kennett Wharf Fruiterer }

1s.   Wᵗ agᵗ Thoˢ Johnson ads Sam¹ Solomon Asᵗ etc.

nil   D° agᵗ John Pearce ads Griffith Buckley for unlawfully disposing of 6 Silver spoons & a pʳ of Silver Tea Tongs – delivered to him to engrave.

Mʳ Alderman Kitchin. Monday 21 May 1781.

Jaˢ Clayton appᵈ for [blank] Season sumᵈ ads Jaˢ Whitley a hackney Coachman for not paying him his Fare for carrying him fr: Gracechurch Street to Fenchurch Street thence to the Strand – ordᵈ 1ss/6ds Fare & 2ss/6ds Charges

---

166. Plomer seems to take over here but does not sign off at the end of the day as usual.
167. The case proceeds to the Old Bailey under the name Kendler. See *OBP*, May 1781, trial of Patrick Kendler (t17810530–19).

1s. W^t ag^t Mary Ansell ~~Mrs.~~ [blank] Lack & [blank] Dowell two women whose Surnames are unknown ads Thos Ginn for an Assault on him & Sarah Ux.

Humph: Haycock WC John Casbolt C. chd by Jno Webster, for assaulting and wounding him in the Belly with some sharp Instrument – on his Oath committed to d^{o}C for want of Sureties

1s. W^t ag^t Will: Smith a Journeyman Tobacco Pipe Maker ads Rob: Phipps his Ma^r for leaving Work unfinished

P Eliz: Lewis WC by Reeve Martin C. chd by Edwd Lewis her Husband for an Ass^t – he app^d to be much in liquor – d^d.

Thos Biggs PC by Jos: Ellis C. chd by Sam: Austin for feloniously stealing 4 Ozs of silk Twist – Val: 6s.6d. his property – by desire of Mr Austin – d^d

P Sus^a Clifford by Saml Roberts C. chd by Will: Crowder & Crusella Ux for assaulting the said Crusella – they withdrew and ag^d – they promised to quit on Saturday – d^d

nil W^t ag^t Geo: Will: Chaloner ads John Leage for pawning a silver Watch entrusted to mend

Mr Beach att^{d}ed. HK

Mr Alderman Burnell by Mr Alderman Pugh. Tuesday 22 May 1781.
1s. Aff^t Mary Bell

Jos: Stokes by Rob: Astock C. chd by Ja^s Davies Overseer of the Poor of the Parish of St Andrew Holborn, London for unlawfully begetting [blank] Jenkins Singlewoman with Child, chargeable to the said Parish – he ag^d to marry the Woman & was thereupon d^d (by Consent)

Jasper Burr the Driver of a Cart N° 16565 produced by [blank] Green – sum^d by John Fleming Street Keeper for riding upon the s^d Cart – they withdrew and ag^d

Dan Bourne WC by Will: Liddle C. chd by Mary Cartwright for ass^{t}ing her – rem^d 'till tomorrow (being in liquor)

Geo: Witcher, Mary Ux:} d^{o}C by Will: Payne C. chd by him for begging – rem^{d}ed to be pass'd

250

1s. W^t ag^t Jordan Wane ads Sophia Ux: – Ass^t

John Gregory by Jos: Sheppard C. chd by Thos Cooper, Carman his Ma^r for embezzilling 5s./6d. allowed to pay the Money to his Master

P W^t ag^t John Bowman ads Eliz: Robertson, Ass^t

Mr Nash att^{d}ed. Mr Nash attended. T.W.[168]

Mr Alderman Alsop. Wednesday 23 May 1781.
Will: Storey sum^d by John Chester a hackney Coachman for refusing to pay him his Fare for carrying him from the Minories to Wapping – thence to Lombard Street – Mr Storey was left to consider whether to pay or to have the Ground measured.

Jordan Wane by Thos Emery C. chd by Sophia Ux: (on a W^t Per Mr Ald^n Wooldridge Yesterday) for an Ass^t – they withdrew and ag^d to seperate and d^d

P Humphry Haycock com^d Yesterday – d^d

Dan. Bourne WC by Will: Liddle C. chd by Mary Cartwright for ass^{t}ing her – they withdrew and ag^d= Cartwright's Husband insisting upon a Guinea and half – the Ald^n thought it an Imposition – d^d

P Peter Bath by Danl Wells C. chd by Geo: Cass, Patrole of Cripplegate Ward without for ass^{t}ing him – d^d

P W^t ag^t Mary Davis ads Jos: Hardisty Ass^t etc.

P Mich^l Buckley by Will: Martin C. chd by Ann Stiles (on Ald^n Wooldridge's W^t Yesterday) for an Ass^t – d^d

1s. W^t ag^t Saml Johnson & Saml Adams ads Joshua Isaacs Ass^t etc.

1s. D^o ag^t Solomon Emanuel ads Moses Jacobs D^o

1s. D^o ag^t Laazer Tetestu De Somsem[?] ads Eliz: Ux, Ass^t etc.

---

168. Appears to have been signed once by the clerk and a second time by another hand, possibly that of Mr Nash. The initials T.W. probably stand for Thomas Wooldridge, who may have stepped into the chair, unrecorded by the clerk.

3   M[r] Houstoun attended. R.A.
h[?][169]

Right Honourable Thomas Harley by M[r] Alderman Plomer. Thursday
          24 May 1781.
1s.   War[t] v [blank] Howard (Xtian Name unknown) ads W[m] Battle
          Per Ass[t]

6s./8d.   John Shapcot & Jos[h] Ingleston} WC W[m] Cromwell C. Ch[d]
          by Sam[l] Lee one of the Toll Coll[rs] on Black Fryers Bridge for
          assaulting him yesterday when upon his Duty, John Fell one
          of Watchman confirm'd M[r] Lee in his Evidence as did John
          Evans, Adjudg[d] true & disch[d] on Bail as under
RX   John Shapcott N[o] 2 Mincing Lane Porter   £40
          Tho[s] Green of the Red Lyon Fenchurch Street Vict   20
          Howel Powell of Water Lane Black Friars Vict   20
                    To app and ans[r] next Sess[s] London
RX   The above persons gave Bail a 2[d] time for an Ass[t] on John Fell.
          To app & answer as Last above.

          Benj[n] Braithwaite sum[d] ads John Fleming Street Keeper for
          using his Cart N[o] 1550 within this City on the 21st Inst drawn
          by two Horses the Wheels thereof not being 6 Inches broad – it
          app[d] an Act of necessity a Neighbours Cart having broke down
          & he lent the Cart—the Compl[t] was dismiss'd.

          Joseph Ingleston WC by John Allen C. chd by him for
          assaulting him on his Duty; Allen referred to one Mich[l] Grif-
          fith, who appearing declared he did not see Ingleston strike
          him – the pris[r] was cautioned to behave well in future he was
          d[d].

          Stephenson Lidlie, W[m] Lidlie} WC W[m] Smedley C. chd by
          John Bethell for assaulting one Tho[s] Hillam a Coachman
          to Tho[s] Saltonstall Chapel Str[t] Bedford Row Rich[d] Meers a
          W[h]man saw Pris[r] assault Hillam the Fact was s[d] by Bethell to
          be done at the End of Creed Lane, that the Coachman cried
          hallo' – to the Gent, as they were crossing the End of Creed
          Lane, – upon wch one of the Gent. turn'd about and cried out
          damn you will you ride over us – the mre was adj[d] to Tuesday
          at 12

---

169. Unintelligible mark here: possibly 's h', '3/4' or '3/s.'.

Hamilton Queen Street Westm[r] undertook for the Appearance of the Pris[rs]

W[m] Long WC Solomon Stott C. chd by Geo: Lucas for stealing a pair of Sheets, [blank]

Ann Hall WC (on Lord Mayors War[t]) W[m] Martin C. Charg'd by Hannah Tucker for assaulting her For Want of Proof she was disch[d].

Warr[t] v John Metcalf ads James Kelly Per Ass[t]

M[r] Rhodes attended   WP

M[r] Alderman Crosby by M[r] Alderman Plomer. Friday 25 May 1781.
    Ann Jones[170] WC by Bryan Chandler C. chd by Tho[s] Townraw Mary Ux: and Hen: Freeth for feloniously stealing a cloth Coat, 3 Cloth Waistcoats and a pair of breeches a ~~mahogany tea Chest~~ black silk Hat, and Bonnet Val: 40s & upw[ds] the property of s[d] Tho[s] Townraw – on their Oaths com[d] to d[o]C.

RX   Tho[s] Townraw – Dolphin C[t] Noble   }
        Hen: Freeth &c   } £10
        Bryan Chandler N[o] 34 Noble Street Bricklayer   }

John Saunders d[o]C by Tho[s] Douglas C. chd by John Butcher his Ma[r] for ass[t]ing Frances his Wife – She was sworn – com[d] to d[o]C

1s.   John Metcalf by Will: Bailey C. chd by Ja[s] Kelly (on his Wp's W[t] Yesterday) for an Ass[t] – they withdrew and ag[d] – d[d]

Rich[d] Clewes by Sam. Yardley C. chd by John Storey (on Ald[n] Wooldridge's W[t] 15[th] Inst.) on suspicion of feloniously stealing 75 Pieces of Tammies – Val: £50 & upw[ds] the property of the s[d] John Storey and Chris[r] Alderson his Partner – rem[d]ed 'till tomorrow, the Witnesses not being now present.

1s.   W[t] ag[t] Ann Jenkins ads Ann Paver Ass[t] etc.

M[r] Nash attended   WP

M[r] Alderman Townsend. Monday 28 May 1781.
    Rich[d] Clewes WC by Sam[l] Yardley C. chd by [blank]

---

170. The case proceeds to the Old Bailey. See *OBP*, May 1781, trial of Ann Jones (t17810530–33).

Aldⁿ Geo: Will: Chalmers by John Negus C. chd by John Leage (on
Pugh   a W^t Per Aldⁿ Kitchin the 17th Inst.) for knowingly & design-
edly pawning, or otherwise unlawfully disposing of a silver
Watch – ag^d & d^d

John Sanders com^d on Friday – d^d

Mr Alderman Bull. Tuesday 29 May 1781.
1s.   W^t ag^t Sus^a Hicks ads Cath: Atkinson Ass^t et.

Mary Keefe, Mary Walker} WC by Richd Coverley C. chd
by Mary Madan for stealing an Apron – it was a Question
between them, and no felony – d^d

Aldⁿ   Henry Leman WC by Solomon Stott C. chd by a Person
Wooldridge not now present with picking his Pocket – rem^ded to be
(Nunc)   deliv^d to his Mother.

Will: Long d^oC by d^oC. chd by Geo: Lucas (not now present)
for stealing a Pair of Sheets – no proof appearing – he was d^d

Thos Cotterell sum^d by Ann McGinnis for refusing to deliver to
her sundry Articles of bed furniture, Glass and China pawned
with him within two Years – it app^d that several of the things
were not pawned with Mr Cotterell – the Sum^s was therefore
d^d

not granted   W^t ag^t Deborah Costar ads Ann Veline Ass^t etc.

Richd Clewes by Saml Yardley C. chd by Chris^r Alderson (on
his Wp's W^t 15th Inst.) on suspicion of feloniously stealing
75 Pieces of Tammies Val: £50 & upw^{ds} – the property of the
s^d Chris^r Alderson and John Storey his Partner – rem^ded 'till
tomorrow

P   Mary Coxe by Will: Catchpole C. chd by ~~Will:~~ Hannah Gilpin
(on Mr Aldⁿ Wooldridge's W^t) for an Ass^t – friv^s and d^d.

Mr Alderman Wooldridge for Mr Alderman Bull, ad huc.
Eliz:Bainbridge by Will: Catchpole C. chd by Jno Teasdale
for feloniously stealing a Coverlid – no Proof of the felony
appearing – com^d to B as a loose idle and disorderly Person.

Mr Nash attended   TW.

Mʳ Alderman Wilkes by Mʳ Alderman Wooldridge. Wednesday 30 May 1781.

1s. Wᵗ to search the House of Edwᵈ Clark in Golden Lane, for Cottons, Linens & silk Handkerchiefs – on Oath of Samˡ Peticary.

1s. Affidᵗ Weatherall

Wᵐ Allen sumᵈ ads John Fleming Street Kʳ for using his Cart Nᵒ 16607 within this City on Friday last drawn by two Horses the Wheels thereof not being of the full Breath of Six Inches as the Law directs – withdrew & settled

Thoˢ Fairfax Sumᵈ ads Wᵐ Dorrill ~~for~~ to produce Driver of his Coach Nᵒ 855 he standing Chᵈ with wilfully misbehaving himself on 24ᵗʰ instᵗ by driving the sᵈ Coach upon the Foot Pavemᵗ in Jewin Street. Adjᵈ true & fin'd 5s.

1s. Backt Justice Levys Wᵗ

William Lightbourn on Justice Blackboroughs Wᵗ backt by Mʳ Aldⁿ Pugh Wᵐ Catchpole C. Chᵈ by Sarah Ellis Per assᵗ. He made Satisfaction and was Dᵈ.

Richᵈ Clewes was broᵗ up for further Examon and charged by Messʳˢ Story and Alderson on suspicion of feloniously stealing 75 Pieces of Tammies – Brown said, that he and the Prisʳ went together to the House of Handfield, and he (the Witness) went up one pair of Stairs & took seven pieces of Tammies to dye – Brown was sworn – he sᵈ that the seven Pairs he carried to Matthews, he received in the House of Handfield – he was remᵈed for farther Examination until Friday

P Wᵗ agᵗ [blank] Thomas ads Welcome Vincent Assᵗ etc.

1s. Susᵃ Hicks by Rob: Aston C. chd by Cath: Atkinson (on Aldⁿ Bull's Wᵗ Yesterday) for an Assᵗ – agᵈ and dᵈ.

gave a poor Woman 2s.[171] Zachariah Holmes, Street Keeper, complained agᵗ for receiving 2s./6d. to compromise an Offence, by a Carman riding upon his Cart – he acknowledged the Fact, and was reprimᵈed

---

171. Appears in the left margin.

1s.   W^t ag^t Isaac Fernandez ads Jacob Solomons Ass^t etc.

Mr Rhodes attended   T.W.

Mr Alderman Sawbridge by Mr Alderman Wilkes. Thursday 31 May
    1781.
    Thos Lamb sum^d ads Fra^s Murden a Carman for ref^g to pay him
    his Fare for Cartage of 2 Loads of Liquors from Brewers Key
    to your Warehouse in Cannon St^r on 11th March last & also
    for one other Load on the 13th of s^d Month & also for Waiting
    Persuant to the Order of Sess^s

    Thos Lamb Sum^d 30th May 1781 ads Fr^s Murden Carman
    for refusing to pay the Cartage of 3 Loads from the Keys to
    Cannon St^t And also for Wait^g on or ab^t 12th April last Persuant
    to the Order of Sess^s.

    Henry Parker, Mary Young} WC John Fleet C. Ch^d by Joshua
    Humphreys for stealing a gold Watch & sundry Articles of Plate
    – rem^{d}ed 'till tomorrow in order to bring further Witnesses.

1s.   Cecilia Brown WC by Robt Aston C. chd by Roger Nott for an
    Ass^t – she promised not to do the like – d^d

1s.   W^t ag^t Frances Hughes ads Eliz AilsworthAss^t etc.

Mr Rhodes attended   John Wilkes

Sir Thomas Hallifax. Friday 1 June 1781.
1s.   Affid^t Hopper

    Henry Parker & Mary Young} remanded yesterday to WC John
    Fleet C. Ch^d by Joshua Humphrys for feloniously Stealing in
    the Dwelling house of the s^d Joshua in the County of Midsex
    One Gold repeating Watch Value [blank] One Silver Punch
    Bowl value [blank] One Silver Tankard Value [blank] and
    sundry other Articles of Plate & other Goods the Property
    of the s^d Joshua Humphrys – rem^{d}ed 'till Monday next to be
    heard by the Chamberlain before whom the Matter first came
    on.

    Josiah Groves, Ja^s Smith[172]} by John Edwards C. chd by Phebe
    Grindley for feloniously stealing sundry Articles, viz. – two

---

172. The case proceeds to the Old Bailey. See *OBP*, July 1781, trial of Josiah Groves, James
    Smith (t17810711–18).

linen Shifts 2 Shirts, Val: [blank] her Property – com^d to WC on their Oaths.

RX Phebe Grindley No 11 Red Cross Street L. Widow }
Ann Ireland Bull Yard Aldersgate Street – Widow }
Ja^s Goodson – N° 11 Red Cross Street – Labourer } £10
Will: Allen – Half Moon Alley Moorfields – Labourer } Each
John Edwards – Barbican Breeches Maker }

not W^t ag^t Hen: Spotsford an Appr[entice] ads Thos Saunders
granted Assault etc.

Richd Clewes was further examined – chd by John Story and Chris^r Alderson on suspicion of feloniously stealing seven Pieces of Tammies value £5 their property – Thos Handfield was sworn & said, that he was in the Room where the Tammies were taken out of at 2 O'Clock on that day – that the Goods were not then in the Room – he does not know who bro^t the Goods there, and suspects no particular Person – For want of suff^t Proof the Warr^t was disch^d.

Jane Whittington (a Pauper) WC Wm Compton C. Ch^d by Wm Bishop Overseer & Thos Fenton Church Wⁿ Prsh S^t B[artholome]w the great for making a great Noise & Disturbance yesterday before the Church W^{ns} House, calling him ~~by~~ sev^l Opprobrious Names & otherwise misbehaving herself – rem^ded 'till tomorrow

Thos Jones by Will: Wood C. chd by Will: Gough and Sam. Hill, for feloniously stealing a Shirt & a pair of Stockings, and other things – Hill lives at Acton Wells.

P ~~John Marriott by~~ Eliz: Thomas by Jno Marriott C. chd by Welcome Vincent (on a W^t Per Aldⁿ Wooldridge) for an Ass^t – frivo^s and d^d.

Eliz: Trantum WC by Jos: Thompson C. chd by him for lodging in the open Air

Mr Rhodes attended TH

Sir James Esdaile. Monday 4 June 1781.
(Mr Beach attended) (No Attendance)

Mr Alderman Plumbe by Mr Alderman Wooldridge. Tuesday 5 June 1781.
P W^t ag^t John Crofts and Sarah Rimes ads Ann Kelly Ass^t

Mary Hooker by Rob: Jones C. chd by John Ashburner for making a disturbance – the Alderman said, there was no breach of Peace – d^d

nil   W^t ag^t [blank] Branscomb ads Mary Ux: Wm Hooker Ass^t

Edwd Reynolds WC by Jno Newman C. chd by him for ass^{t}ing & beating him – com^d to WC for want of Sureties (on Newman's Oath)

Thos Hall –chd by Hannah Baker on suspicion of feloniously stealing four Chests & one bag of Tea, Val: £100 & upwards, her property – he was sworn, and said, that his Brother (Mrs B's Servt) delivered the Tea in Petticoat Lane & Rosemary Lane – a Wt was granted agst rem^{d}ed to obtain a W^t in Middlesex to search two Houses

Alice Dormer WC by John Newman C. chd by John Singleton, a W^{ch}man for an Ass^t – recommended to the Hospital.

Hannah Cooper WC by Wm Hunt C. chd by Maria Thomas for assaulting her, being a Pauper was sent to St Brides Workhouse

1s.   Will: Lightburn charged by Sarah Ellis for an Ass^t – (on the Lord Mayor's W^t of Saturday last) – d^d.

Mary Roberts WC by Wm Rogers C. chd by Robert Lemon on suspicion of feloniously stealing a pair of Sheets – ag^d to redeem the Sheets – d^d.

Mr Nash attended.   T.W.

Mr Alderman Kennett. Wednesday 6 June 1781.

Henry Parker, Mary Young } WC by John Fleet C. chd by Joshua Humphreys for feloniously stealing in his dwelling House in the Co: of Middx, one gold repeating Watch, one silver Punch Bowl, one silver Tankard, and sundry other Articles of Plate Val: £50 & upwards, the property of the said Joshua Humphreys

John Crofts, Sarah Rimes} by John Negus C. chd by Ann Kelly (on Aldn Wooldridge's Wt Yesterday) for an Ass^t

Mary Burgess WC by John Colliton C. chd by Ja^s Priest, Churchwarden of the Parish of Christ Church Newgate Street, for an Ass^t and making a great Noise and Disturbance

(No Attendance.)
(Mr Houstoun att^ded)

Mr Alderman Plomer. Thursday 7 June 1781.
(No Attendance)

(Mr Houstoun att^ded)

Mr Alderman Gill. Friday 8 June 1781.
Middx ~~Hen: Parker~~ Chas Thompson, Mary Young[173]} WC by John
Fleet C. chd by Joshua Humphreys for feloniously stealing
in the dwelling House of the s^d Joshua Humphreys, sit[uate]
in the County of Middx, one gold repeating Watch, one silver
Punch Bowl one silver Tankard, two silver Salts, one silver
pint Mug, 3 silver table Spoons, 9 silver tea Spoons, a silver
milk Pot, and other things Val: £20[174] & upw^ds his property –
Lucretia Ux: Will:Green saw Thompson go out with a Bundle
– on the Oaths of Humphreys, Green & Simon Spicer com^d to
WC.

RX   Joshua Humphreys – Bear Y^d Drury L. for self & Green } £10
      Simon Spicer of Little Britain L.   }

1s.   Aff^t Walter Powell

      Will: Scott sum^d by Rob: Bromley a hackney Coachman for
      refusing to pay him his Fare for being in his Service with
      the hackney Coach from a Quarter past eight 'till two in the
      Morning – the Coachman & R^d Price were sworn – that he
      waited and was not asleep – Ord^d the Fare & 4s. Charges

1s.   Francis Copeland [blank] by [blank] C. chd by John Clinton
      Overseer of the Poor of the Parish of Saint Botolph without
      Aldersgate (on a W^t Per Mr Ald^n Wright 7th Inst.) for unlaw-
      fully begetting Eliz: Sturtle, Singlewoman of the s^d Parish with
      Child, born in & chargeable to the same – d^d

Mr Alderman Peckham. Monday 11 June 1781.
      Eliz: Bradley WC by Hen: Hancock C. chd by Ja^s Lewis for
      an Assault – com^d to B as a loose, idle & disorderly Woman

      Reb^a Tinley d^oC by Will: Martin C. chd by Ja^s Williamson for
      picking up Men in Chick Lane – d^d.

173. The case proceeds to the Old Bailey. See *OBP*, July 1781, trial of Charles Thompson, Mary
     Young (t17810711–7).
174. The 2 has been overwritten by a 1 or a 4.

1s.   Aff^t W: H: Deacon

P   W^t ag^t John Calloway ads Jane Ux: Ass^t etc.

P   D^o agt Marg^t Churchill ads Ann Townsend D^o.

        Mr Beach attended   RP.

Mr Alderman Hayley by Mr Alderman Pugh. Tuesday 12 June 1781.
P   Henry Nobley by Thos Walker C. chd by Simon Solomon (on
        Ald^n Wright's W^t 17th May.) for an Ass^t – ag^d & d^d

1s.   Aff^t Tim^y Jordan

1s.   W^t ag^t Thos Thornton ads Mordecai Henriques. Ass^t

        John Stevens by Ja^s Prior C. chd by Will: Gardner and Mark
        Riggs for feloniously stealing a Quartern Loaf Val: 7½d. the
        property of [blank] Knight – Mr Knight ag^d to forgive him – d^d.

1s.   Back'd a Middx W^t Per Justice Penleaze

1s.   Geo: Gill WC by Fra^s Phipps C. chd by Geo: Seddon and Peter
        Parnell with feloniously stealing 2000 brass Nails Val: 11s. his
        Property – he was allowed to enlist in the Army– d^d – and he
        was attested.

        Sus^a Worrall by Will: Payne C. chd by Thos Harden on suspi-
        cion of feloniously stealing a pair of silver Tea Tongs, the
        property of Gedaliah Gatfield – there was no Proof – d^d.

1s.   Morris Linnahan [blank] by Ja^s Barker C. chd by Marg^t Carter
        (on the Lord Mayor's W^t 8th Inst:) for an Ass^t – they withdrew
        & d^d

        Will: Prosser[175] PC by Will: Mulsey C. chd by Monkhouse
        Davidson Esqr and John Stapleton for ~~feloniously~~ stealing
        from his person a cambrick handkerchief of the Value of 2s.
        & upwards s^d Davidson on their Oaths com^d to [blank]
RX   Monkhouse Davidson of Fench:[urch] Str: Esqr   10
        John Stapleton New Str: Square L. Carp^r   10
        Will: ~~Catchpole &c.~~ Mulsey Grocers Alley   10

---

175. The case proceeds to the Old Bailey. See *OBP*, July 1781, trial of William Prosser
     (t17810711-9).

Marg^t Churchill by Will: Catchpole C. chd by Ann Townsend (on Ald^n Peckham's W^t Yesterday) for an Ass^t – friv^s and d^d.

1s.   Marg^t Lock by d^{o}C. chd by Jane Wilkins (on the Lord Mayor's W^t 8th Inst:) for an Ass^t – d^d

1s.   Richard Harding PC by John Fleming C. chd by him with riding upon his Dray, no Person ~~him hav^g~~ on foot driv^g same, they withdrew and on making Satisfaction – d^d

        Mr Nash attended   Evan Pugh

Mr Alderman Newnham by Mr Alderman Gill. Wednesday 13 June
        1781.
p^d 3s./6d.   Chas Thompson PC, Mary Young WC } by John Fleet
for an   C. chd by Sus^a Ux: John Watts for feloniously stealing
advertizem^t a metal Watch with a steel Chain and silver Seal, two
              silver Table Spoons, two silver Tea Spoons, a pair of
              silver Sugar Tongs, a black sattin Cloak, a linen Table
              Cloth Val: £5 the property of the said John Watts – no
              part of the Goods co^d be traced, and Mr Watts was left
              to his Indictment if any sho^d be fo^d

              They were further chd by Thos Churchill with felo-
              niously stealing in his dwelling House, situate in the
              County of Middlesex, two silver table Spoons, 3 silver
              tea Spoons, two silk Gowns, one linen Gown, 4 linen
              Shirts, one pair of silk Breeches, ~~one~~ 2 pair of ~~brown~~
              cloth Breeches, one cloth Coat, 4 cloth Waistcoats, 6
              pair of linen Sheets, 36 damask Napkins, and several
              other things Val £10 & upw^{ds} his property – rem^{d}ed till
              Monday.

1s.   Hector McCoy by John Barker C. chd by Mary Ux: (on Ald^n
        Alsop's W^t 23^d May) for an Ass^t – the Parties having ag^d – d^d.

Ald^n Thos Crawley, Abraham Crawley} WC by Aaron Hale
Newnham C. chd by a Watchman (not now present) for lodging in the
         open Air – their Uncle appeared – d^d.

         Mr Houstoun att^d

Mr Alderman Clark. Thursday 14 June 1781.
        ~~Richd Hazell WC~~ John Doe WC Wm Blackbourn C. Ch^d by R^d
        Hazell

1s.   W^t v. Wm Evans ads Dirk New Efterck for assaulting & beating him

Mr Joseph Beckley Sum^d ads Mr James Nealson to produce Driver of H[ackne]^y Coach N° 153 he standing Charg'd for wilfully misbehaving himself the 12th Inst^t by taking more than his Fare for Carrying s^d Mr Nealson in s^d Coach from the Adelphi to Buckingham S^t & from thence to the Royal Exchange Adj^d true and Convicted 5s.

Mr Rhodes attended   R.C.

Aldⁿ   Ann Mason by John Edwards C. chd by Ja^s Dowsett for
Wooldridge   an Ass^t – also for making a disturbance – she promised
            to behave well in future – d^d

Fra^s Appleton sum^d by Thos Griffin, Carman, for refusing to pay the Cartage of sundry Loads – ag^d to give an Order on Marsh and Hudson for the Money

Thos Hall chd on suspicion of stealing 4 Chests & one Bag of Tea – was ord^d to the King's Head, Tower Hill, to go to Sea.

Sus^a Clayton WC by Will: Rogers C. chd by Thos Deykin for feloniously stealing a linen handkerchief for want of Proof – d^d she was (on Deykin's Oath) com^d to B:

Benj: Jandrell by John Dickenson C. chd by Saml Marjorum, Overseer of the Poor of the Parish of Saint Helen – for deserting Ann & Mary his Infant Children, who are become chargeable thereto – ag^d to provide for them – d^d.

Mr Alderman Wooldridge by Mr Alderman Plomer. Friday 15 June
      1781.
      Mary Lambert WC by Jos: Thompson C. chd by him for
      picking up Men – rem^ded for her Aunt to appear, to take her
      home

Ann Kingham by Walter Prosser C. chd by Mary Watson (not now present) on suspicion of feloniously stealing a Shift & a pair of Shoes – d^d.

Ann Tate, Eliz: Dawes} WC by Jos: Thompson C. chd by him for picking up Men on Tuesday Night at the End of Fleet Market – d^d.

Mary Green d°C by Will: Martin C. chd by Rob: Trotter on Suspicion of feloniously stealing a flour Sack – there was no Proof of a felony – the Sack was restored & pris^r was d^d.

Ann Green d°C by d°C. chd by Jos: Cookson for feloniously stealing 3lb W^t of Bacon Val: 1s./6d. his Property – rem^{d}ed for Mr Cookson to enquire the prisoner's Character

Randall McDonald by John Fletcher C. chd by Ja^s Nutt on suspicion of stealing a Suit of cloth Cloaths, Val: 40s & upw^{ds}, his property – for want of Proof – d^d.

Will: Noel by Jno King C. chd by Oliver Lumley a W^{ch}man belonging to the India Warehouse in Leadenhall Mket for loitering about there under suspicious Circumstances – d^d.

John Doe WC by Will: Blackburn C. chd by R^d Hasel, a Publican on Suspicion of stealing about 20s. in Silver – also a silver tea Spoon Val: 2s. his Property – rem^{d}ed 'till Monday

John Stovell, Ticket Porter sum^d by Zachariah Holmes, Street Keeper, for working an unlicensed Cart for hire within this City on Saturday last – it app^d to be a hand barrow and not a Cart – d^d.

Will: Harris the Driver of a Cart N° [blank] sum^d by Rice Thomas for driving the said Cart ag^t the Cart & Horse of the s^d Rice Thomas & damaging the Horse – d^d.on Agreement.

1s.   W^t ag^t Thos Benfield ads Ann Dawbiggin Ass^t etc.

7s. 6d.[176]

Mr Alderman Hart by Mr Alderman Gill. Monday 18 June 1781.
   Chas Thompson PC, Mary Young WC[177]} by John Fleet C. chd by Thos Churchill with feloniously stealing in his dwelling House, situate in the County of Middlesex, 2 silver Table Spoons 3 silver Tea Spoons 2 silk Gowns, one linen Gown, 4 linen Shirts, one pair of silk Breeches, 2 pair of cloth Breeches, one cloth Coat, 4 cloth Waistcoats, 6 pair of linen Sheets, 36 damask Napkins & sev^l other things Val: £10 & upwards his property. On the Oaths of Churchill & Will: Ward com^d to take
Middx their Trial

---

176. This appears very faintly in the left margin.
177. See entry on 8 June 1781 above.

RX   Thos Churchill of St. Agnes leClare, Middx Lab^r £20
       Will: Ward Holborn Hill London ~~for self~~ Pawnbroker   £10
       John Fleet Aldersgate Street Bdings W^{ch}maker   £10

They were further chd by John Hill on suspicion of feloniously stealing one pair of silver Salts 2 silver Table Spoons, 4 silver tea Spoons, a silver Tea Strainer, a silver milk Pot – there was no Evidence of the felony – the Goods not being traced to either of the Prisoners

They were further chd by John Watkins & Ann his Wife with feloniously stealing in the dwelling House of s^d John Watkins, sit: in the County of Middlesex, a table Clock, 3 silver table Spoons, 8 tea Spoons – Watkins wished for time to consider

They were further chd by Eliz: Ux: John Chambers with feloniously stealing in his dwelling House a gold Watch, a silver Milk Pot & other things – there was no Proof – Chambers was left to prosecute or not, at the Sessions

They were further charged by Ann Hall for feloniously stealing a pair of Sheets, 2 pillow biers 3 window Curtains – left to consider whether to prosecute.

Ja^s Rigby by Peter Ashmore C. chd by Will: Maxwell for feloniously stealing a silk Handkerchief – Val. [blank] his property – Ord^d to Tower Hill – Mr Maxwell lives at Hounslow.

6s.   Affidavits Johan Trot, Simon Vegen & 2 others

       Ann ~~Green~~ Morgan[178] WC by Will: Martin C. chd by Jos: Cookson for feloniously stealing 3 lb 6 Ozs of bacon Value 1s./6d. his property – com^d to d^{o}C (on his Oath)
RX   Jos: Cookson Fleet Mket L. Cheesemonger   £ 10
       Will: Martin – ~~Fleet L.~~ 3 Tuns Snow Hill   £ 10

John Farby d^{o}C by d^{o}C. chd by Stephen Mercer for wilfully driving a Waggon agst his Cart, driving over his Wife – rem^{d}ed to have her ex^d by a Surgeon

Chch Wdns of St Catharine Coleman sum^d by Sarah Alloe for relief

---

178. The case proceeds to the Old Bailey. See *OBP*, July 1781, trial of Ann Morgan (t17810711–40).

Mr Beach attended   W.G

Mr Alderman Wright. Tuesday 19 June 1781.

1s.   Aff^t Thos Hankins

1s.   W^t ag^t Hen: Leader ads Ann Roberts Ass^t etc.

        W^t ag^t [blank] Laird (Tapster at the Bell Savage Inn Ludgate Hill) ads Mary Hewitt – Ass^t

P   D^o against Hector McCoy ads Mary Ux: Ass^t etc.

P̶ 1s.   D^o agt Ann Manning ads Constant Caruss Ass^t etc.

        John Doe WC by Will: Blackburn C. chd by R^d Hasel on suspicion of feloniously stealing 15s. in Silver and a silver tea Spoon Val: [blank] his Property

1s.   Aff^t Brice

1s.   Aff^t Matthias Tunffooin

1s.   Affirmation Will: Storrs Fry

        R^d Kirkham[179] PC by Will: Ginn C. chd by John Pearson & John Stubley on suspicion of feloniously stealing 14lb W^t of Indico Val: £4 & upw^{ds}, the property of Paul Amsinck Esq^e and Geo: Will: Soltau Partners in Trade – on their Oaths & also of Edwd Hanson committed to d^{o}C.

RX   ~~Geo. Wm Soltau Suffolk Lane~~
        John Stubley Watchman at the Steel Yard   £10
        John Pearson – Cousin Lane, Bull Porter   £10
        Edwd Hanson – Botolph Lane L.   £10
        ~~Will: Ginn~~ – Cousin Lane Peruke Maker   £10

        John Farby d^{o}C. by Will: Martin C. chd by Stephen Mercer & John Payne for driving a Waggon agst his Cart, whereby it run over Mercer's Wife – they withdrew & d^d.

1s.   W^t ag^t Eleanor O'Brien ads Ann Winn Ass^t etc.

        Mary Williams WC by Will: Martin C. chd by Mary Geary for assaulting her, the Pris^r being guilty of great misbehav^r was remanded till tomorrow

---

179. The case proceeds to the Old Bailey. See *OBP*, July 1781, trial of Richard Kirkham (t17810711–8).

1s.   W^t ag^t Francis Rickards ads Samuel Cheesewright Ass^t etc.

Eliz: Price WC by Rob: Benham C. chd by Will: ~~Hampshire~~ Tucker Churchwarden of St Mary Somerset for obtaining Money of him by fraudulent Pretences— & also for abusing him – on his Oath com^d to B and on the Oath of John Holyland

John Laird by Jno Bradley C. chd by Mary Hewitt (on his Wp's W^t) for an Ass^t – the Alderman thought Hewitt blame-able – d^d.

T.W   Mr Nash attended.

Mr Alderman Pugh, Sir Thomas Hallifax. Wednesday 20 June 1781.
~~Sir Thos Halli~~[180] Wm Coroday sum^d ads Jos^h Gates – for not marking his Barge, navigating on the River Thames, as the Law Directs – he had done it—after receiving the Sum^s— & having behaved well – he recommended the man to make Sat^n to Gates for his Trouble – he was d^d.

Thos Edis Produced his Son John sum^d ads R^d Read for driving his hand Barrow on the foot pavem^t 16 Inst– it was recom-mended to refer the Mre to Mr Jacob the Com^r of pavements within this ward—& the Mre was now d^d.

Mary Dunbar by Dan. Currier C. chd by Mr Ald^n Clark for making a disturbance – John Aylward a Patrole was sworn – committed to B.

on Thompson's   Chas Thompson, Mary Young} by John Fleet C.
Trial – Humphries chd by Jno Crawford
RX   John Crawford at Will: Windsor's Pawnbroker
                   Minories   } £20

John Dee WC by Will: Blackburn C. chd by Richd Hasel Thos Hasel and John Squire on suspicion of feloniously stealing 15s. in silver and a silver tea Spoon Val: 1s. 6d. his property – Hasel declined a Prosecution – d^d.

Mary Williams d^{o}C by Will: Martin C. chd by Mary Geary for assaulting her – she promised not to behave so in future – d^d

---

180. 'Sir Thomas Halli' appears with strikethrough at the start of this case. Perhaps Hallifax presided over this and the following case, as the clerk's hand changes on the third entry and Pugh signs off at the end of the day.

Henry Leader by Thos Spratley C. chd by Ann Roberts (on a W^t Per Ald^n Wright Yesterday) for an Ass^t – friv^s and d^d.

1s. W^t ag^t Ann Thornton & Ja^s Chambers ads Mary Baker Ass^t etc.

1s. Fra^s Rickards by John Fleet C. chd by Thomas Cheesewright (on Ald^n Wright's W^t Yesterday) for an Ass^t – friv^s and d^d

John Atkins by Will: Catchpole C. chd by Philip Edridge (on the Lord Mayor's W^t Yesterday) on suspicion of feloniously ~~stealing~~ receiving four bottles of Brandy & two Bottles of Rum stolen from him, knowing the same to have been stolen – it app^d that Atkin's Wife was the Receiver – d^d

1s. W^t ag^t Solomon Sheffield ads David Dakers Ass^t

Chas Thompson, Mary Young} were further charged by [blank] Waller for feloniously stealing a silver Watch, a linen Gown and Coat, a linen Shift – they were rem^{d}ed to make Enquiry of the Pawnbrokers, until Tuesday next at 11 O'Clock.

1s. W^t ag^t Sarah Mortimer ads Elizabeth Hart Ass^t etc.

2s. Ann Thornton, Ja^s Chambers} by John Clarke C. chd by Mary Baker (on his Wp's W^t of this day) for an Ass^t – friv^s & d^d

Mr Houston attening EP

Mr Alderman Kitchin. Thursday 21 June 1781.

Ald^n Pugh Wm Moore & Henry Young} WC Chas Delegall C. Ch^d by Willm Hubbart with assaulting him – with a drawn Sword

nil – John Wootton also charged ~~them~~ Moore with cutting him on the head – Jno Deacon saw this Ass^t com^d – Will: Spence also chd them with cutting him – they withdrew and ag^d – d^d.

~~Thos Barnsley, Will: Smallwood, Patrick Crockhall} doC by John Newman C. chd by him~~

P Mary Thomas by Will: Martin C. chd by Ann Smith (on the Lord Mayor's W^t) for an Ass^t

Rhodes Att^y attended

Mr Alderman Burnell. Friday 22 June 1781.
(No Attendance)

Mr Rhodes attended   RH

Mr Alderman Alsop. Friday 28 September 1781.
~~Sarah Rogers WC by Rob Jones C. ch by William Miller for feloniously stealing a Quantity of Silk~~

~~Eliz: Bainbridge by Will: Catchpole C. chd by Mary Thompson (on Aldn Turner's Wt Yesterday) for an Asst~~

~~Ann Powell by Rob: Roe C. chd by Geo: Kilney~~

(No Attendance)

16s. 4d.[181]   Mr Houstoun att^{d}ed

The Right Honourable Thomas Harley by Mr Alderman Wooldridge.
Monday 1 October 1781.
1s   W^t ag^t Will: Vincent ads Roger Griffin Ass^t etc.

Owen Smith WC by John Edwards C. chd by Sam Ayres, a Watchman of Cripplegate Ward for ass^{t}ing and beating him on his Duty – he ask'd Pardon and was d^d

Mr Beach attended   TW

Mr Alderman Crosby.   Tuesday 2 October 1781.
John Wood WC by Jno Carter C. chd by Watkin Morgan for assaulting & beating him – (on a W^t granted in Middx by Justice Girdler & back'd by Ald^n Pugh) – they withdrew & co^d not agree
RX   John Wood N° 4 White Hart C^t Long Lane Cordwainer £20
Middx   R^d Wall N° 22 Middle St Cloth Fair Middx D^o } £
3s./4d.   Abram Harris – N° 3 White Hart C^t super – Linen   } 10
Draper

Peter Eaton Sum^d by Eliz Lilley for assaulting her – they withdrew, but co^d not agree & the Husband saying, he sho^d apply to a superior Court – the Sum^s was d^d – afterw^{ds} ag^d & d^d.

Ja^s Harvey WC by Thos Cochran C. chd by George Bailey on Suspicion of feloniously stealing some mahogany boards – there was no reason to take the Pris^r into Custody – d^d

---

181. This appears very lightly in the left margin.

Will: Walker WC by R^d Finch C. chd by Ja^s Manly for making a great Noise & Disturbance in his Ho: and refusing to go out of his Shop when required– he was d^d

John Taylor PC by Will: Govan C. chd by Will: Plestow for feloniously stealing a Man's Hat – for want of Proof—d^d.

Mary Knowles WC by John Colliton C. chd by him for wandering abroad & lodging in the open Air, not giving a good Account of herself – being ill with the foul distemper, recommended to the Hospital.

Jos: Gerrer by Walter Prosser C. chd by Marg^t Ux: Thos Sharp for an Ass^t – they withdrew & ag^d – d^d.

Dominick Brennock by John Nick C. chd by Richd Hussey – being fo^d Yesterday Afternoon in his Parlour under suspicious Circumstances – d^d.

1s.   Mary Green by Hen: Hancock C. chd by Ann Ux: Jos: Lovegrove (on Ald^n Pugh's W^t Yesterday) for an Ass^t – discharged

Chas Gantley WC by John Sadgley C. chd by Rob: Hog for throwing a handful of Mud at him – he was d^d

Mary Penn WC by Will: Martin C. chd by Jno Hollingsworth, a W^{ch}man, for calling out thieves & Murder – d^d.

Mr Houstoun att^d B.C.

Mr Alderman Townsend by Mr Alderman Pugh. Wednesday 3 October 1781.
    Mary Scrivens WC by [blank] Patten[182] C. chd by [blank]

Mary Penn d^{o}C by Will: Martin C. chd by John Hollingsworth, a W^{ch}man, for making a disturbance – Ridnell near Bewley Bridge by Servitude – rem^{d}ed by ~~Servil~~ to be pass'd

Ann Buxton d^{o}C

Jane Davis d^{o}C by [blank] Rathbone C. chd by [blank]

Mary Glyn WC by [blank] Maitland C.

---

182. Possibly Joseph Patten.

Chch Wdns of Saint Sepulchre sum^d by Mary Vergis for relief
– Ord^d to be relieved.

Mr Houstoun att^d   EP

Mr Alderman Bull by Mr Alderman Wooldridge. Thursday 4 October
1781.

1s.   W^t to search the Apartments of Eliz: Jones N° 14 Union Court,
Holborn,—on Oath of John Sheers for a clouded Gown, a
Piece of Callico &c. stolen from him.

1s.   D^o agt John Grinder ads Walter Batley Ass^t etc.

Jane Davis WC by Jno Rathbone C. chd by him for abusing
him – on promising to keep out of the Streets at unseasonable
Hours – d^d

1s.   W^t ag^t Jos: Rodd ads Ja^s Bembo Ass^t etc.

Mr Alderman Bull adhuc Thursday 4 October 1781.
Mary Pugh by Will: Catchpole C. chd by Ja^s Clarke and John
Sherwood for feloniously stealing 12^lb of Cheese Val: 3s.—the
property of the s^d Ja^s Clarke – rem^ded 'till tomorrow to enquire
of Mr Ald^n Pugh (to whom she referred) respecting her.

Eliz: Wootton by Nath: Jewson C. chd by John Greaves &
Mich^l Clark, Overseers of the Poor of the Parish of Allhallows,
Barking, for feloniously stealing one Shirt – she confess'd
under a Promise of Favour – rem^ded 'till Monday.

1s.   John Grinder by Rob: Wheelwright C. chd by Walter Batley
(on a W^t by his Wp this day) for an Ass^t – they withdrew &
ag^d – d^d.

Eliz: Ward by Will: Wood C. chd by Rob: Young for being a
disorderly Woman, & abusing him and for making a disturbance – d^d

Hen: Corp WC by Jno Mears C. chd by Nathan Veazey for
offering to sell bad half Pence, at a lower Rate than the same
is purported to be – rem^ded 'till Saturday

Will: Thorp by Saml Roberts C. chd by Will: Martin for feloniously stealing 3 Stone Dishes & 6 Stone Plates Value [blank]
his Property, remanded till tomorrow for fur^r Examicon

F.B.   Rhodes Att^y attended

1s.   John Morris by John Feakins C. chd by Hester Ux: Jos: Cletter (on the Lord Mayor's W^t) for an Ass^t – John Perkins & Eliz: Boucher saw the fact com^d – it app^d that Cletter encouraged a Mob to break Morris's Windows – d^d.

Mr Alderman Wilkes. Friday 5 October 1781.
       John Gray WC by Peter Ashmore C. chd by Valentine Jones for attempting to pick his Pocket – rem^ded to be examined, if fit for Service

       Thos Plato by Will: Catchpole C. chd by John Manning for obtaining four Sheep from him, by saying they were paid for – rem^ded 'till tomorrow

1s.   Will: Jones by Jos: Thompson C. chd by Will: Newell (on the Lord Mayor's W^t 3^d Inst) for an Ass^t – Thos Drew s^d Newell made the 1st Ass^t – d^d

       Will: Thorp by Saml Roberts C. chd by Eliz: Ux: Will: Martin & Thos Pickering for feloniously stealing ~~two~~ three earthen Dishes & 6[?] Earthen Plates – Val: 2s. the property of the said Will: Martin
RX   Saml Roberts N° 4 Cock L. Turner for Eliz: Martin
       & self   } £ 10
       Thos Pickering – Nags Head Wine Porter   } £ 10

       Mary Pugh by Will: Catchpole C. chd by James Clarke (as Yesterday) rem^ded 'till Monday

       Eliz: Ware by Will: Cook C. chd by Geo: Hogg for attempting to defraud her of a riding Habit – she app^d to be insane – d^d

1s.   W^t ag^t Peter Ward ads John Saunders Ass^t etc.

       John Webb by Jos: Thompson C. chd by And^w Burton for behaving indecently to him, by feeling his private Parts – Webb says: he's an Engraver in Monmouth Street N° 8 – rem^ded 'till Monday

12s. 4d.[183]   Mr Beach attended.   John Wilkes

---

183. This appears very faintly in the left margin.

Mr Alderman Sawbridge by Mr Alderman Wooldridge. Monday 8 October 1781.

John Gray WC by Peter Ashmore C. chd by Valentine Jones for attempting to pick his Pocket – rem^{d}ed.

Hen: Corp d^{o}C by John Mears C. chd by Nathan Veazey for offering to sell bad half Pence – the Pris^r is a Hat Maker – rem^{d}ed 'till tomorrow

~~Ann Adams~~, Thos Plato, ~~John Bannister~~} d^{o}C by Will: Catchpole C. chd by John Manning for obtaining four Sheep – rem^{d}ed

Ann Bowen d^{o}C by David Ranken C. chd by Will: Ponting & Chas Millifey for pilfering a Tart – on account of her Age she was forgiven – d^d

Ann McCormack d^{o}C by [blank] Cass C. chd by [blank]

Jonathan Lawton, Jane Smith} d^{o}C by Thos Clark C. chd by Ja^s Liddiard – being fo^d together in an indecent Situation – d^d.

John Phillips by Fra^s Phipps C. chd by Hen: Tickell on suspicion of feloniously stealing a half Hogshead – he lives at Mr Meredith's, the Pilgrim in Holborn – Mr Vaughan N° 40 Eagle Street, his Master – the Alderman took his Word 'till tomorrow

John Webb WC by Jos: Thompson C. chd by And^w Burton for ass^{t}ing him, with Intent to commit the detestable Crime of Buggery – he was com^d to d^{o}C for want of Sureties.

RX   Danl Taylor, Servant to Mr Evans Fleet Street   £ 20[184]

Peter Ward by Jno Bradley C. chd by John Saunders (on a W^t Per Ald^n Wilkes on Friday last) for an Ass^t – Saunders app^d blameable –d^d.

Eliz: Petty, Saml Thompson} WC by Fra^s Penny C. chd by Will: Pigot for refusing to pay for a Pot of Beer after they drank it – also for assaulting him – they were d^d

Sarah Murphy by Will: Hunt C. chd by Chris^r Beane for felo-

---

184. Though clearly a separate entry, this recognizance may relate to the Webb case immediately above.

niously stealing a Hat – there was no Pretence for the Charge – d^d.

Mr Beach attended   T.W

Sir Thomas Hallifax. Tuesday 9 October 1781.
Aldⁿ Pugh   W^t ag^t Eliz Ellick ads Hester Wells Ass^t
P

Hen: Corp rem^ded Yesterday, was d^d by desire of Mr Vernon, Solicitor of the Mint

John Williams by John Wootton C. chd by Mary Williams (on Aldⁿ Pugh's W^t 14th August) for an Ass^t – ag^d & d^d

John Gray rem^ded Yesterday, was d^d the felony not being compleat

1s.   W^t ag^t Moses Levy ads Simon Rochelle Ass^t.

Samuel Slaughter[185] by Jos: Thompson C. chd by Ann Lanthorne for feloniously stealing two copper Sauce Pans & a copper Quart Pot Val: 2s. her Property—on Oath of s^d Lanthorne & Zephaniah Lambert com^d to WC.

R RX   Ann Langthorn of Fleet street N° 99 widow Victualler   £10
Zephaniah Lambert of Poppins Co^t N° 27 Fleet street,   £10 Porter

W^t v. [blank] Davis [blank] ats of [blank] L[?]

1s.   ~~W^t v~~ Thos Lermit & Henry Boice upon Suspicion of feloniously stealing two pieces of figured Velvet of the Value of 10s & upwards the property of Lermit.

~~W^t agt [blank] Davis ads Thos Lermitt on suspicion~~

Thos Davis by Rob: Aston C. chd by Jno Boscomb for feloniously stealing an Umbrella Val. 2s. – Geo: Johns & John Worrall saw it in his Custody & drop it – ~~rem^ded~~ com^d to WC.

Mr Alderman Wooldridge adhuc Tuesday 9 October 1781
Thos Plato by Will: Catchpole C. chd by John Manning for feloniously stealing four Sheep Val. £3 his property – rem^ded

185. The case proceeds to the Old Bailey. See *OBP*, October 1781, trial of Samuel Slaughter (t17811017–63).

Mary Pugh pr by [blank] Catchpole by James Clarke upon Susp^n of stealing some Cheese dismissed

Mr Houston attended T.W

Sir James Esdaile. Wednesday 10 October 1781.
Ald^n Pugh W^t ag^t Isaac Lepine ads Mary Hetherley Ass^t
1s.

1s.   D^o ag^t John Wilson ads Sarah Holdridge D^o

Ald^n Isaac Sakey PC by Nathan Lyon C. chd by Thos Lermit &
Plomer Hen: Boyce on suspicion of feloniously stealing 20 Yards
of figured Velvet Val: £10 – Sarah Myers knows nothing of
this Matter – the Pris^r denied all knowledge of the Velvets –
rem^{d}ed 'till Friday to have the Woman

P   Sarah Casey by Jno Newman C. chd by Mary Askew (on Ald^n
Hart's W^t Yesterday) for an Ass^t—d^d.

Moses Levy by Thos Fenner C. chd by Simon Rochelle (on
Ald^n Pugh's W^t Yesterday) for an Ass^t– ~~bailed Moses Levy
White Street Woolpack Alley Dealer £20~~ they withdrew – ag^d
& d^d.

The Lord Mayor Elect. adhuc Wednesday 10 October 1781.
Francis Murden sum^d to produce the Driver of his Cart N^o
[blank] to answer the Complaint of Jno Andrews for taking a
Load away out of Turn – d^d.

Mr Houston attended WP

1s.   W^t ag^t Thos Ryder ads Thos Weschart, Ass^t etc.

Mr Alderman Plumbe. Thursday 11 October 1781.
~~W^t to search the Lodgings of Eliz: Jones in Union Court,
Holborn, for Callico Gowns &c on Oath of Jno Shires~~

(No Attendance.)

Rhodes Att^y att^d

Mr Alderman Kennett by The Lord Mayor Elect. Friday 12 October
1781
Isaac Sakey PC by Nathan Lyon C. chd by Thos Lermitte and
Hen: Boyce on Suspicion of feloniously stealing 20 Yards of

figured Velvet Val: [blank] the Property of the said Thos Lermitte
– Mary Davis Says, the Pris^r came on Sunday Morning to her
Mother's Lodgings & bro^t two Pieces of Velvet, one a green
Ground, the other a light Ground with pale coloured Stripes
– co^d not agree in Price – went away – her Brother call'd the
Pris^r back, and told him, she wo^d give him the Price, but don't
know what the Price was – Sarah Simons was coming into
the Room when the Pris^r was going out with the Velvet 1st
time – Simons came to desire Rachael Davis to go an Errand
– afterw^ds fetched her Hat & Cloak, returned & was shewn
the Velvet – then Rachel Davis & Simons went out together –
Groves was backwards & forwards the time Sakey was in the
Room – her Brother was not in the Room when Sakey 1st bro^t
the Velvet

Sarah Simons Says—She came up to Mrs Davis's Lodgings
on Sunday Morning – saw the Prisoner in the Room.

Jacob Simons run after the Pris^r & fo^d him in Hounsditch

Ann Groves saw Sakey offer something to Mrs Davis –
Sakey has been there often before – rem^ded 'till Monday

Eliz: Jones, Geo: Fosset} by Jos: Gates C. chd by John Shires
(on a Search W^t Yesterday Per the Lord Mayor) on Suspicion of feloniously stealing several Pieces of Callico a muslin
Apron, &c. – rem^ded 'till Monday to have the Pawnbroker

Jos: Williams by Will: Hunt C. chd by Cath: Lowe on suspicion of feloniously stealing a Cloak and a Shirt – he said, he
pawned the Cloak for 1s. at Mr Brooks's Fleet Market – rem^ded
'till Monday to enquire of the Pawnbroker

5s.[186]   Mr Houston attended   WP

The Lord Mayor Elect. Monday 15 October 1781.

Sarah Davis, Isaac Sakey} PC by Nathan Lyon C. chd by Thos
Lermitte & Hen: Boyce on suspicion of feloniously stealing 20
Yards of figured Velvet Val: [blank] the property of the s^d Thos
Lermitte – Boyce declared he bo^t the velvet now Produced (ab^t
[blank] Yards) of Sarah Davis, who being present acknowl-
edged selling them to him – & declared she bought about 20
Yards want^g a Quar^r, of which this was part, of Isaac Sakey
the pris^r – she gave £5 all but 2s. for it – sold 6 Yards to one
Paterson a dealer of Rochester – 3 Yards to two Lads – Ann
Groves remembers seeing Sakey in the Lodgings – rem^ded

_____

186. This appears faintly in the left margin.

Geo: Fosset, Eliz: Jones} WC by Jos: Gates C. chd by John Shires & Alice Ux: (on a Search W^t Per the Lord Mayor) on suspicion of feloniously stealing sev^l Pieces of Callico a muslin Apron, a piece of Linen, containing 13 Yards – rem^{d}ed 'till tomorrow

Jos: Williams by Will: Hunt C. chd by Cath: Lowe on suspicion of feloniously stealing a Cloak and a Shirt

Sarah Black by John Collinson C. chd by Sarah Decosta (on Ald^n Pugh's W^t of Saturday last) for an Ass^t – they withdrew and d^d upon an Agreement

~~Thos Allison~~, Isaac Collins} WC by Will: Catchpole C. chd by Philip Edridge, Vict. Hosier Lane for attempting to cheat Hen: Crowther his Errand Boy by giving him Order to fetch half a pint of Brandy & change for half a Gua for one Laban a Neighbour – the Boy went back but Edridge, suspecting it to be a Fraud, put Water in a Bottle & gave it with some Change to the Boy – Pris^r came up to him & wanted to have the Change from him – on wch Edridge apprehended him – there was nothing effected,

Margaret Dunn d^{o}C by [blank] Williams C. chd by [blank]

1s.   Aff^t Rob Woolcombe

1s.   D^o Wm Brown

1s.   D^o R^d Davis

1s.   Back'd a Middx W^t Per Mr Greene

2s.   John Chapel, Ja^s Kirshaw} WC Edm^d Wells C. chd by Saml Thomas & John Darnell for an Ass^t – they withdrew – d^d

        Ben: Hill, Will: Rogers} D^{o}C: Saml Roberts C. chd by him for wandering in Smithfield at ½ past 3 this Morning – their Friends app^d – d^d.

P   ~~John Taylor~~ Thos Mose by Ja^s Drummond C. chd by John Taylor (on the Lord Mayor's W^t 11th Inst.) for an Ass^t – agreed & d^d. Taylor was called & did not appear.

1s.   Aff^t Thos Aston

276

John Williams by Thos Jones C. chd by Will: Cattle for getting into a Waggon with a felonious Intent—at the Blossoms Inn Lawrence Lane – on unloading the Waggon this Morning a Rope wch tyed the Load in was found cut, on unloading it this Morning, the Waggon was loaded with Cheese; –he was rem^ded to give an Acco^t of himself & Mr Wilmot a plaisterer in Drury Lane (with whom Prisoner said he work'd) to be sent to [blank].

Wm Parsons WC ~~John~~ Mich^l Brodnix C. chd by Tim^o Whaley on suspicion of stealing a Bag of Oats (ab^t a Bushell & a half) wch he found him carrying on his Shoulder at 4 this Morning, near puddle Dock, rem^ded 'till Wednesday – his acco^t was not satisfactory

P   Ann Green – John Clements C. chd by Martha Collins on suspⁿ of stealing ~~some~~ a Sauce pan, Tea Kettle & a sheet out of her ready furnished Lodgings – Prosx did not chuse to swear ag^t her, she was d^d.

1s.   Marg^t Dunn [blank] Thos Williams C. chd by Ja^s Welch (on Ld Mayor's W^t 11 Inst.) for an Ass^t – the Compl^t app^d friv^s – she was d^d.

1s.   W^t ag^t Jos^h ~~Balling~~ ads Judith Davis Ass^t etc.

Ja^s King by Aaron Coates C. chd by John Beaumont (on Aldⁿ Pugh's W^t 13 Inst) for an Ass^t – Jos: Knowell did'nt see a blow struck – Beaumont was sworn – com^d to WC for want of Sureties – afterw^{ds} ag^d & d^d.

Mr Beach attended   WP

Will: Clark by Edwd Stratton C. chd by Geo: Hudson on Suspicion of being concerned with other persons in feloniously stealing 4 Bushels of Oats & a Quantity of Hay – his Cart was employed to take the Corn & Hay there was no Proof – d^d.

Mary Tame WC by Thos Massey C. chd by Chris^r Brown for attempting to steal a pint pewter Pot – a Quantity of Pewter was fo^d in a room behind her Lodgings – rem^ded to give an Acc^t of herself – 'till Friday next.

Mr Alderman Turner. Tuesday 16 October 1781.
Sarah Davis, Isaac Sakey} PC by Nathan Lyon C. chd by Thos Lermitte & Hen: Boyce on suspicion of feloniously stealing 20

Yards of figured Velvet Val: [blank] the Property of the said Tho[s] Lermitte

Mary Tame WC by Tho[s] Massey C. chd by Chris[r] Brown

Will: Hudson WC by Jos: Thompson C. chd by Will: Garrard for feloniously stealing a looking Glass in a mahogany Frame, and a mahogany Tea Caddy Val: [blank] his Property

1s.   W[t] against Geo: Fayle ads Joshua Hill Ass[t].

Lord Mayor   Cha[s] Dunn WC by Cha[s] Delegal C. chd by Fra[s] Scott for
Elect   ass[t]ing & beating him – Dunn alledged his Ma[r] collared him – d[d].

Ald[n] Hart   Jos: Ballin by Will: Govan C. chd by Judith Davis (on the Lord Mayor's Elect's W[t] Yesterday) for an Ass[t] – Davis app[d] to be to blame – d[d].

1s.   Rich[d] Dighton by Jno Fleming C. chd by John Wagstaff (on a Surry W[t] Per Justice Levy 12th Inst. back'd by Ald[n] Kitchin) for an Ass[t] – it app[d] that Wagstaff gave the 1st Assault – d[d]

M[r] Houstoun att[d].   JH

M[r] Alderman Peckham by M[r] Alderman Wooldridge. Wednesday 17 October 1781.
Sarah Davis, Isaac Sakey[187]} PC by Nathan Lyon C. chd by Tho[s] Lermitte & Hen: Boyce on suspicion of feloniously stealing 21 Yards of figured Velvet Val: £10 the property of the s[d] Tho[s] Lermitte – Edward Mason proved the Goods to belong to Lermitte

RX   Moses Levi of Winkworth Str: Par: Christ Ch:
Spitalfields Chandler   £ 40
for Sarah Ux: Moses Davis, Sarah Davis, Sarah
Simons & Ann Groves Tho[s] Lermitte &c.   40

Geo: Fosset, Eliz: Jones} WC by Jos: Gates C. chd by John Shires and Alice Ux: (on a Search W[t] by the Lord Mayor the 11th Inst.) on suspicion of feloniously stealing a muslin Apron, two Pieces of Linen Val: 20s. the Property of the s[d] John Shires– there was no Proof.

---

187. The case proceeds to the Old Bailey. See *OBP*, December 1781, trial of Isaac Sakie, Sarah Davis (t17811205–7).

W^t ag^t Ja^s Somers ads John Vincent Ass^t etc.

Wm Hudson WC Jos^h Thompson C. Ch^d by Wm Garrard for feloniously Stealing a looking Glass Set in a Mahogany frame and a Mahogany Tea Caddy Value [blank] the Property of the said Will: Garrard – he ag^d to go to Sea

1s.   Geo: Fayle by John Prockter C. chd by Joshua Hill (on Ald^n Hart's W^t Yesterday) for an Ass^t – upon an Agreement d^d

Thos Allison by Wm Catchpole C. chd by John Webster & John Moseley for feloniously stealing a smock frock – sent to Sea

James Ironmonger by Will: Clark C. chd by Will: Smart for getting over a Wall, to break into his House – he agreed to go to Sea.

Charlotte Rood by Ja^s Drummond C. chd by him on suspicion of feloniously stealing a Coat – there was no Proof – d^d

John Williams by Thos Jones C. chd by Will: Cattle for getting into a Waggon with a felonious Intent – rem^{d}ed to go to Sea

Will: Parsons rem^{d}ed on Monday, was brought up – rem^{d}ed to go to Sea – afterw^{ds} discharged upon producing Persons who gave him a Character.

Mr Rhodes attended   TW

Mr Alderman Turner. Thursday 18 October 1781.

1s.   Francis Wm Augustus Cranfield WC Edm^d Wells C. chd by Wm King – at the 3 Tons in Fleet Street for making a Disturbance at his House & for ass^{t}ing him, on an Agreement d^d.

1s.   W^t ag^t Hezekiah Tindall ads Betty Bennett Ass^t etc.

1s.   Ja^s Somers (on Ald^n Wooldridge's W^t yesterday) ads Jno Vincent for an Ass^t – ag^d & d^d

Thos Totman PC Nathan Lyons C. on Mr Ald^n Pughs W^t Ch^d by Overseers of St Botolph Aldgate for deserting his Wife and 4 Infant Children Whereby they are become Chargeable to the said Pish ag^t the Statute. He was discharge'd on his Promise of returning to take Care in future of his Wife and Children.

1s.   Warr^t v Martha Cole ads Margary Hobson Per Ass^t

1s.   D° v Catherine Murphy ads Mary ux Mich^l Desmond Ass^t

Mr Rhodes attended   BT

Mr Alderman Newnham by Mr Alderman Sainsbury. Friday 19 October 1781.
Charles Gandley, Jos: Watts} WC by Dan. Wells C. chd by Ralph Smith on suspicion of feloniously stealing a pair of silver shoe Buckles – there was no Evidence – d^d.

P   Warr^t v Hannah Cox ads Hannah Preston Per Ass^t

Mary Tame rem^{d}ed on Monday till this Day for fur^r Examicon Thos Massey Const Ch^d by Chr^r Brown for attempting to steal a Pewter Pint Pot his Property For Want of Proof D^d.

1s.   Peace Warr^t v J Evans Att^y in John St^t London ads. Anth^y Songa

18s.[188] Mr Rhodes attended NN

Mr Alderman Hart. Monday 22 October 1781.
Mary Gomus WC by John Carter C. chd by Mary Barton for feloniously stealing a cotton Gown & a black Sattin Cloak – by consent she was d^d.

Will: Jones d°C by Edwd Stratton C. chd by Han^h Ux: (on a W^t 30th August last Per Ald^n Pugh) for an Ass^t – the Wife did not appear – d^d.

Maria Alexander d°C by John Collinton C. chd by Thos Stay for fraudulently obtaining 1 Yard & half of Jebe – there was no Colour for the Charge – she app^d to have gained Credit in her own Name – d^d

She was a second time chd by Mary Evans for obtaining some Apparel & pawning it—she said (as the Pretence) that Mr Chas Gray of Grays Inn was to pay her £500 on 24th August – that the Money came to her in right of her Husband – upon Enquiry no such Person as Gray lives in Grays Inn – rem^{d}ed to produce the Pawnbrokers tomorrow – the Offence being com^d in the County of Middx – deliv^d over

188. This appears faintly in the left margin.

1s.   Back'd a Yorkshire W^t by Mr Robinson

1s.   D° a Middx W^t

Eliz: Lewis, Mary Gandy} WC by Will: Fleet C. chd by a Watchman (not present) for picking up Men – d^d.

1s.   Thos Fitkin PC by John Jarman C. chd by Geo: Dias the Younger for knocking at his Door & ass^ting him on Saturday Night – between the hours of 10 & 11 – he ask'd Pardon & was d^d

John Holland by Thos Clark C. chd by John Stewart for an Ass^t – they withdrew and ag^d – d^d

John Cole sum^d by John Levi for unlawfully detaining his wearing Apparel – d^d.

Gave 2s.   Mary Forret WC by John Fletcher C. chd by him for
to this   wandering abroad & begging – she belongs to St James
Woman   Garlickhithe – ord^d 2s. 'till tomorrow & then to be pass'd

P   Eliz: Phillips by Nich^s Kidder C. chd by Thos Wilson for defrauding him of 2s. about a Year ago – d^d.

1s.   W^t ag^t Thos Hawkins ads Wm Scutt Ass^t etc.

1s.   D° agt [blank] Savage ads Sarah Rooksby D°

1s.   D° agt [blank] Langdon ads Marg^t Ward D°

Michael Connor from PC by Walter Prosser C. chd by William Coates for imbezling six Dozen of Worsted Sheets which he was intrusted with to weave Value 15s. the Property of the s^d Walter Prosser, rem^ded till tomorrow

1s.   Jos: Gill by Thos Spratley C. chd by Ja^s Whitson for an Ass^t – they withdrew & ag^d

Mr Beach attended   JH.

Ja^s Ironmonger WC by Thos Spratley C. chd by John Beck, a Watchman of Cripplegate Ward, on suspicion of stealing a great Coat with which he was stopt at an unseasonable hour – rem^ded 'till tomorrow

John Gover by Will: Pascall C. chd by John Radford for assaulting him– he app^d to be insane– d^d.

Mr Alderman Wright. Tuesday 23 October 1781.

1s.   W^t ag^t John Merrick ads Will: Sealey Ass^t etc.

Ald^n Turner   Eliz: Frasier an Appr: sum^d by Saml Higgins her Ma^r for being an idle & disorderly Appr: & particularly, for disobeying his lawful Commands – postponed to inform Mr Maxwell of the Asylum, of the Misconduct of the Girl.

1s.   W^t ag^t Jane Taylor ads Eliz: Reeves

Mich^l Connor PC by Walter Prosser C. chd by Wm Coates for embezzling six doz: of worsted Shute[189] – John Palmer delivered it & it was deficient 6 doz: – he ~~had~~ alledged he was robbed of the Shute

1s.   Back'd a Bench W^t Per Justices Girdler & Gregson.

1s.   W^t ag^t James Hodges & Thos Golding Journeymen Basket Makers ads John Rippengall, a Basket Maker, for leaving their Work unfinished

1s.   John Merrick by Thos Emery C. chd by Will: Sealey (on his Wp's W^t this day) for an Ass^t – Sealey app^d to be blameable – Sealey app^d to be the Aggressor – d^d.

Will: Hudson WC by Jos: Thompson C. chd by Will: Garrard for feloniously stealing a looking Glass in a mahogany Frame & a mahogany Tea Caddy Val: 3s. his Property – d^d.

1s.   Richd Brocksop by J Stevens C. chd by Will: Ross (on Ald^n Turners W^t Yesterday) for knowingly & designedly by false pretences obtaining from him four Pounds in Money, with Intent to cheat & defraud him of the same – ag^d & d^d

2s.   Will: Bull, Dan. Hill} WC by Thos Clark C. chd by Eliz: Purcell for making a disturbance in her House – the Horns in Gutter Lane – they withdrew and on settling the Matter – they were d^d.

---

189. For weaving.

P   Thos Hawkins by John Casbolt C. chd by Will: Scutt (on Ald^n Hart's W^t Yesterday) for an Ass^t – Scutt was to blame – d^d.

Ja^s Ironmonger WC by Thos Spratley C. chd by John Beck, a Watchman on suspicion of stealing a blue great Coat – rem^{d}ed 'till Friday

1s.   John Taggard PC by Moses Orme C. chd by Ja^s Patrole, for an Ass^t – ag^d & d^d.

Mr Houstoun attended   TW

Mr Alderman Pugh. Wednesday 24 October 1781.
Ald^n Will: Pinnick, John Pedley} by Edm^d Wells C. chd by
Wooldridge   Will: Stock for making a great Noise & Disturbance, & fighting before his Door in Fleet Street – d^d.

Jos: Clisset by Jos: Thompson C. chd by Jno Wood (on Ald^n Hart's W^t Yesterday) for standing Indicted last Sessions for ass^{t}ing him – to which he has not app^d or pleaded – bailed to plead
3s./4d. Jos: Clisset N° 11 Hughes C^t Black Friars   £ 20
RX   Rob: Griffiths   Salisbury C^t Vict.   £ 10
     Will: Hickson   D^o Chandler   £ 10

1s.   Aff^t Marg^t Frail

Chas Bocock sum^d by Elias Bishop for driving his Cart upon the foot Pavement—in Bow Lane – it was a Case of Necessity – d^d.

Mich^l Connor PC by Walter Prosser C. chd by Wm Coates for embezzling 6 doz. of worsted Shute – a Letter from Mr Provey was read, giving the Man a good Character – d^d.

W^t v. John Diaper ats Jane Grey Assault etc.

Mr Houstoun att^d. TW

1s.   Peace W^t agst Richd Eward ads Ja^s Allard.

Mr Alderman Sainsbury. Thursday 25 October 1781.
1s.   W^t v. John Gautier a Journeyman in the Weaving Business ats Thos Sebastian Mason for imbezling half a Guinea, and other misbehaving.

1s.   W^t v. Wm Dixon upon the Certificate of the Deputy Cl of the Peace for assaulting Frances the Wife of Mordecai Lazerus.

1s.   D^o v. Joseph Mountefiore ats Isaac de Ximes Assault.

Thos Gibbs by John Fletcher C. chd by Winifred Ux: (on Ald^n Harts W^t 23d. Inst:) for an Ass^t – ag^d to allow her 1s. a Week.

Ja^s Scott sum^d by Will: Prentice for taking a Load away out of Turn with his Cart N° 312, at the Steel Yard on Saturday

Mr Houstoun attended   TS.

Mr Alderman Kitchin. Friday 26 October 1781.

P^{s190} Back'd a Middx W^t Per Mr Justice Penleaze

nil   W^t upon a Certif: agst Hen: Isaacs for standing Indicted for ass^{t}ing John Spencer

1s.   James Ironmonger WC by Thos Spratley C. chd by Hen: Siddons & John Beck & John Williams for feloniously stealing a blue cloth box Coat Val: 20s. the property of the s^d Hen: Siddons – he said he bo^t the Coat a fortnight ago – he was allowed to enlist in the East India Company's Service and was attested.

Thos Wheeley, Luke Watkins, Will: Moody, Ja^s Hall, Chris^r Beck, Peter Usher, Betty Norman, Will: Dawes, Richd Smith, Rob Jones} sum^d by Ja^s Slatford, Overseer of the Poor of the Parish of St Botolph without Aldersgate, for refusing to pay their several Proportions of the Poor's Rate of the s^d Parish – Beck excus'd not being a Tenant the Quarter in Question – Usher was allowed three Weeks

1s.   John Diaper by Will: Catchpole C. chd by Jane Grey (on Ald^n Wright's W^t) for an Ass^t – ag^d & d^d.

Geo: Hartley by Thos Wall C. chd by Saml Singleton & Fra^s Cattell for feloniously stealing a Man's Hat Val: 5s. the Property of the s^d Sam. Singleton – enlisted

1s.   W^t ag^t John Bostock & Mary Topping Ass^t

---

190. It is possible that 1s. was entered initially.

Hen: Mackrell by Jno Marriott C. chd by Geo: Watson for an Ass^t – upon a Woman (not now present) rem^{d}ed – Thos Surry King Street, Snow's Fields.

1s.   Aff^t Hen: Isherwood

Thos Finch by Ja^s Barker C. chd by John Connor for stealing six Pence & a fowl – there was no Pretence for the Charge – d^d

£1.7.4d[191]   Mr Houstoun attended   HK

Mr Alderman Burnell.   Monday 29 October 1781.
(No Alderman attended)   (Mr Beach att^d)

Mr Alderman Crichton.   Tuesday 30 October 1781.
Ald^n Hart   Henry Barelay the Driver of a hackney Coach N° 300 sum^d by Richd Dorrill for driving the same on the foot Pavement – conv^d in 10s. Penalty wch he p^d.

1s.   Aff^t Danl Morier

1s.   D^o Will: Goodwin

1s.   W^t ag^t Rob: Pedley & Thos Pedley ads Will: Stapleton – Ass^t

1s.   D^o agt Geo: Cope ads Thos Woodfield Ass^t

1s.   Thos Price PC by Will: Hunt C. chd by Will: Anderson for making a disturbance – d^d

P   Ja^s Harrison by John Colliton C. chd by Jno Steele, a Publican, for an Ass^t – d^d

P   Eleanor Reed by d^{o}C. chd by John Steele for Ass^t ing his Wife – he forgave her – d^d

John Clark pr by Wm Catchpole C. chd by Sarah the Wife of Wm Norton on Ald^n Plomers W^t per Ass^t

1s.   Peace W^t ag^t Thos Evans ats Anthoney Songa

Will: Reed by Simon Cook C. chd by Mary Ux: (on a W^t Per the Lord Mayor 11th Inst) for an Ass^t – he promised never to do so again – d^d

---

191. This appears faintly in the left margin.

Arthur Ward WC by John Larkin C. chd by Ben: Dudley for feloniously stealing a hand Saw Val: [blank]– rem^{d}ed to bring Persons to his Character

Eliz: Jones d^{o}C by Will: Catchpole C. chd by Chas Bearblock & Alex^r Bearblock for feloniously stealing a quart pewter Pot Val: 1s./6d. the Property of the s^d Chas Bearblock – com^d to d^{o}C.

R   Chas Bearblock Old Bailey Vict for self & Alex^r fils.   £10
       Will: Catchpole &c.   £10

Nath: Hinton by d^{o}C. chd by Saml Sharp on Suspicion of stealing 28^{lb} W^t of Butter – he said, he rece'd it from Mr Barnaville's Servt to sell it – remanded till tomorrow

Mr Alderman Hart adhuc Tuesday 30 October 1781.

John Love, Alice Love, Pat^k McGiurk} by Marcus Levy C. chd by Henry Wilson for feloniously publishing as true, a certain Bill of Exchange, dated Oxford 14th Septr 1781, drawn by Lane and Jackson, upon Messrs Brown, Collinson & Co. Bankers, London, payable to John Dordlen Esq^e or Order for £35 & purporting to be accepted by Messrs Brown, Collinson & Co.— they well knowing the said Acceptance to be false forged & counterfeit – John Love alledged he fo^d a Pocket Book containing the Bill, at Liphook—on Monday Se'ennight – that he was coming with a Pass to London from Portsmouth – he produced his Discharge & the Pass – he came in the Minerva from Lisbon to Plymouth, rem^{d}ed 'till Monday, to write into Oxfordshire to Mr Will: Jacobs, Woodstock & to Mr Thomas, Schoolmaster, Wanstead.

there was a Letter from Thomas to Whittaker[192]

Sarah Evans by John Edwards C. chd by Wm Spence for wilfully breaking his Windows – com^d to B.

Hen: Watkins WC by Jos: Patten C. chd by Chas Griffiths for abusing him – he ag^d to forgive him – d^d

John White d^{o}C by Geo: Cass C. chd by Sarah Clayton for stealing her Hat– they had ag^d & d^d

Marg^t Cole pr charged Alex^r Sherett C. chd by Catherine Heath

---

192. This separate entry probably refers to the previous case.

upon Susp^n of keeping a Guinea, wch she afterw^{ds} returned, dis^d.

Mr Houstoun att^d. JH

Mr Alderman Turner by Mr Alderman Sainsbury. Wednesday 31 October 1781.
Mich^l Farren the Driver of a Cart N° 10140 was produced by Messrs Sutton & Co. – sum^d ads Nich^s Davison for driving the said Cart on the Foot Pavement in Wood Street – he ask'd Pardon – settled

Thos Evans by Thos Linton C. chd by Anth^y Songa (on a peace W^t Yesterday by Mr Ald^n Hart) for using threats whereby &c.. Barth^w Songa declared he could[?] give a Horse whip for the Consul. Saml Rasing heard him say he wo^d get a Horse whip for Mr Songa, the Consul he offered to give it under his Hand – Mr Evans allowed the Expressions improper – the W^t was d^d.

John Lucas sum^d by Will: Stapleton for an Ass^t – William Longford saw Geo: Pedley & Thos Pedley assault Stapleton – Geo: Greene – John Bentley saw Stapleton strike Pedley, after he declared he would fight no more Morris Williams heard Stapleton call Rob: Pedley and Mr Lucas, a Scoundrel – Richd Hart saw Stapleton knock Rob: Pedley down, twice, after he had given out – John Lane saw Stapleton knock down Rob: Pedley – didn't hear Mr Lucas say a Word – Thos Taylor heard Stapleton say to Pedley, that he co^d beat six or seven of 'em – saw Stapleton knock down Rob: Pedley, after he had given out.
Will: Higgens didn't hear Mr Lucas encourage – Saml Barrow saw nothing of the Matter – Geo: Giles saw Stapleton & Pedley engaged – Rob: Meeke saw the same – Mr Lucas did not appear to encourage the Fighting – saw Stapleton knock down Thos Pedley.
The Ald^n said, he saw no reason to require Sureties of Mr Lucas, & the Sum^s was d^d.

Geo: Hartley by Thos Wall C. chd by Saml Singleton & Fra^s Cattell for feloniously stealing a Man's Hat Val: 5s. – the property of the s^d S. Singleton – to go to Sea

Nathl Hinton WC by Wm Catchpole C. chd by a Person not now pres^t on Susp^n of stealing a firkin of Butter – the man alledged he had it from Mr Barneuelt, Edwd Wheeler warehouse keeper to Mr Barneuelt app^d & declared he gave him the Butter & that the Pris^r did not steal it he was d^d.—the Butter was the Property of Wheeler – he declared he came from Mr Barneuelt.

Arthur Ward WC John Larkin C. chd by Ben: Dudley – (rem^{d}ed Yesterday) on Susp^n of stealing a Hand Saw – Val: 3s. his Property; Saml Hog of Bow Lane, with whom he had served 2 Years ago, gave pris^r a good Cha^r says he left him, after working 2 years with him & behaving well, to work with his Father—he was on Dudley's Oath com^d to DoC:

RX   Ben: Dudley of Fell Street L. Carpenter to Prosecute   £ 10
     Jno Larkin of same place Leather Gilder   10

Mary Pinchon [blank] Wm Wray C. chd by Sus^a Ellison for stealing a Pair of Old Shoes of trifling Val: the Pros^x begg'd to forgive her – she was reprim^{d}ed & d^d.

W^t ag^t Thos Roberts ads Sarah Price Ass^t etc.

Mr Houstoun attended   TS

Mr Alderman Alsop. Thursday 1 November 1781.
Ald^n Richd Yelverton sum^d by Geo: Fothergill for an Ass^t – it app^d
Kitchin   that Fothergill behaved insolently to his Ma^r who, therefore, corrected him – d^d

Geo: Massey sum^d by John Martin, Carman, for refusing to pay him his Fare for refusing to pay the Cartage of half a Load of Butter from the Keys to lower East Smithfield—& waiting three hours – Ord^d 2s./3d.

Han^h Baker, Carwoman, sum^d by Edwd Lee, for loading a greater Load than is allowed by Law – it was not proved to be more than a Load – d^d

P   W^t ag^t Jane Swingwood ads Eliz: Gethin Ass^t etc.

R^d Peachey the Driver of a Cart N° 371 produced by Rob: May – sum^d by Thos Cooper, Carman, for taking a Load out of Turn at Custom Ho: Key – adj^d.

2s.   Aff^t Will: Fox bis.

1s.   D^o Will: Jones

Will: Haywood sum^d by John Martin, Carman, for refusing to pay the Cartage of a Load of Staves – ag^d

1s.   Warr[t] v Ann Riley ads. John Emmerton Per Ass[t]

Rhodes Att[y]   Edw[d] Bradley, a Journeyman Hat Maker by Tho[s] Fenner
attended.   C. chd by Tho[s] Hobson his Master for purloining
R.A.   Embezzling or otherwise unlawfully disposing of two
P[ds] Weight of Coney Wool & other Materials entrusted
with him to make into Hats – rem[d] 'till tomorrow (being
drunk).

John Gray by Tho[s] Smith C. chd by Edw[d] French for feloniously stealing a silk handkerchief Val: 3s. his Property –
rem[d]ed to produce Persons to his Character

John Wainwright by Marcus Levi C. chd by W[m] Shaw for feloniously stealing a purple & white Jacket & Coat, one muslin
Gown, two cloth Aprons, two muslin Aprons, two Shifts –
there was no reason to suspect the Pris[r] – d[d]

1s.   Warr[t] v W[m] Ford ads W[m] Ward (a Pawn B[r] opposite S[t] And[ws]
Holborn) on Susp[n] of feloniously stealing a Blew[sic] Silk
Gown Value £2 his Property

(NB. Attendance noted above)[193]

The Right Honourable Thomas Harley by M[r] Alderman Newnham.
Friday 2 November 1781.
Edw[d] Bradley, a Journeyman Hatter by Tho[s] Fenner C. chd by
Tho[s] Hobson, his Ma[r] (on Ald[n] Plomer's W[t] 29th October) for
purloining, embezzling, or otherwise unlawfully disposing of
2lb. W[t] of Coney Wool, 18 Ozs. of Quarter Wool – 9 Ozs. of
Hare's Wool, 6 Ozs. of Toy Wool, 6 Ozs. ¾ of Fine Hair, 1 Oz.
of Vigonia Wool, & 10 Ozs. ½ of Beaver, being the Materials
with which he the said Edw[d] Bradley was entrusted to make
13 Hats

John Parker sum[d] by Rachel Johnson for refusing to deliver to
her a Cotton Gown pawned for 2s. within two Years – there
was no Proof – d[d]

Ald[n] Pugh. John Bletcher by Sam[l] Roberts C. chd by Tho[s] James for
ass[t]ing him – under the Authority of being an Officer of
Excise – the Ald[n] went away

193. Rhodes' signature appears on an earlier page beside the Edward Bradley case in the original,
hence the nota bene that appears here at the end of the day's business.

11s.[194]

Mr Alderman Crosby. Monday 5 November 1781.

John Love, Alice Ux:, Patk McQuirk} by Marcus Levy C. chd by Henry Wilson, for feloniously publishing as true, a certain Bill of Exchange, dated Oxford 14th Sept. 1781 with a forged Acceptance, purporting to be the Acceptance of Messrs Brown, Collinson & Co. Bankers, London, knowing the same to be False forged and counterfeit

David Harris by Edmd Wells C. chd by Charles Pinto for feloniously stealing ~~four~~ three fustick Violin Bows Val: [blank] his property

Will:Jones WC by doC. chd by Will: King for [blank]

(No Attendance)
(Mr Beach attded.)

Mr Alderman Townsend. Tuesday 6 November 1781.

~~John Love, Alice Ux:, Patrick McQuirk} by Marcus Levy C. chd by Hen: Wilson for feloniously uttering & publishing as true, a certain Bill of Exchange, drawn by Lane and Jackson, upon Messrs Brown, Collinson and Co., Bankers, London payable to John Dowlen Esqe or Order for the Sum of £35~~ [blank] ~~after Date, and purporting to be accepted by the said Brown, Collinson and Co they well knowing the said Acceptance to be false forged & counterfeit~~

~~Edwd Bradley a Journeyman Hatter WC by Thos Fenner C. chd by Thos Hobson, his Mar (on Aldn Plomer's Wt 29th October) for purloining embezzling or otherwise unlawfully disposing of 2lb. Wt of Coney Wool, 18 Ozs. of Quarter Wool, 9 Ozs. of Hare's Wool, 6 Ozs. of Toy Wool, 6 Ozs. ¼ of fine Hair 1 Oz. of Vigonia Wool, & 10 Ozs. ½ of beaver, being the Materials with which he was entrusted to make 13 Hats~~

~~David Harris by Edmd Wells C. chd by Charles Pinto for feloniously stealing 3 fustick violin Bows Val~~ [blank] ~~his property~~

~~Will: Jones WC by Edmund Wells C. chd by Wm King~~

Chas Wilkins sumd ads Joseph Ricketts a Hackney Coachman for refusing to pay him his Fare from the Tower to Tower Street, thence to Laytonstone – adjd 'till Tuesday

194. This appears faintly in the left margin.

John McKeirnan WC by John Buttermere C. chd by Tho[s] Golder, for working a private Still, [illegible] in a Cellar belonging to a Ho: in Watling Street, the Still holds 100 Gall[s] & upw[ds] – Tho[s] Trimby saw him after he had broke through into ano[r] Cellar, & it was, as he declared to him, travers'd being seized by the Excise Officers, who had catch'd him working the private Stills – he was rem[d]ed 'till tomorrow.

~~Sarah Marshal do~~C. ~~by~~ [blank] ~~Gilbert C. chd by~~ [blank]

~~Ja[s] Brickhall do~~C. ~~by Geo: Cruthers C. charged by~~ [blank]

~~Will: Pegler do~~C. [blank] ~~Alexander C. chd by~~ [blank]

M[r] Nash attended   John Wilkes

M[r] Alderman Bull. Wednesday 7 November 1781.
    Edw[d] Bradley a Journeyman Hatter WC by Tho[s] Fenner C. chd by Tho[s] Hobson, his Ma[r], (on Ald[n] Plomer's W[t] 29th October) for purloining, embezzling or otherwise unlawfully disposing of 2 lb. W[t] of Coney Wool, 18 Ozs of Quarter Wool, 9 Ozs of Hare's Wool, 6 Ozs of Toy Wool, 6 Ozs ¾ of Fine Wool 1 Oz. of Vigonia Wool, & 10 Ozs ½ of beaver, being the Materials with which he entrusted to make 13 Hats

The Lord   W[t] ag[t] Jos: Isaacs ads Jacob Judah, Ass[t] etc.
Mayor Elect[195]
1s.
    John Love, Alice Ux:, Patrick Mcquirk} by Marcus Levy C. chd by Henry Wilson [blank]

    Will: Downes by Edm[d] Wells C. chd by John Plaw on suspicion of feloniously stealing a Quantity of Lead, he was carrying – he alledged that he was taking it by direction of his Ma[r] – Plaw s[d], there was a Man in Company – rem[d]ed.

1s.   Will: Jones WC by doC. chd by Will: King, a Publican at the 3 Tons in Fleet Street, for being a disorderly Person – King not being present – d[d].

    John McKeirnan WC by John Buttemere C. chd by Tho[s] Golder for working a private Still in a Cellar belonging to a Ho: in Watling Street – he s[d] he was employed by a M[r] Smith

195. William Plomer.

– that he was hired to work the Still – had worked it about a Month – didn't know who Smith is – nor where he lives – he (the Pris^r) lives in Church Lane, White Chapel – rem^{d}ed 'till tomorrow

Sarah Marshal doC. by Isaac Gilbert C. chd by Ann Boot for pilfering some Sugar, Rum & other things – also for stealing a pair of Sheets & a bason – rem^{d}ed 'till tomorrow

The Lord Mayor Elect adhuc Wednesday 7 November 1781.
John Gray WC by ~~Edwd French~~ Thos Smith C. chd by Edwd French for feloniously stealing a silk handkerchief Val: 2s. his property – com^d to doC –enlisted

RX ~~Edwd French N° 99 Hounsd^{ch} Coppersmith~~
~~Thos Smith N° 102 D^o Watch maker~~

Richd Jones doC by Thos Henley C. chd by Robt Cooper for threatening to shoot him with a Pistol – Stephen Stevens, Brandy Merchant charged Cooper with coining half Pence – he & Jones detained

Mr Houston has attended   WP

Mr Alderman Wilkes. Thursday 8 November 1781.

Sir Thos Hallifax — Edwd Bradley a Journeyman Hatter by Thos Fenner C. chd by Thos Hobson for purloining, embezzling, or otherwise unlawfully disposing of 2 lb. W^t of Coney Wool, 18 Ozs. of Quarter Wool, 9 Ozs of Hare's Wool, 6 Ozs of Toy Wool 6 Ozs ¾ of Fine Wool, 1 Oz of Vigonia Wool & 10 Ozs. ½ of beaver, being the Materials with which he was entrusted to make 13 Hats – Edwd Wing on the 13th Novr deliv^d Stuff for 3 Hats, wch he made – afterw^{ds} deliv^d him Materials for six Hats – never saw him 'till apprehended – rem^{d}ed to enquire into the Security

John McKeirnan WC by John Buttermere C. chd by Thos Golder for working a private Still in a Cellar belonging to a House in Watling Street – the Clk of the Solicitor s^d there was no Authority to hold him – d^d.

Mr Alderman Wilkes adhuc Thursday 8 November 1781.
Sarah Marshal WC by Isaac Gilbert C. chd by Alex^r Boot & Ann Boot for feloniously stealing a pair of Sheets, a bason— rem^{d}ed.

Sarah O'Brien, Jane Wallis} WC by R^d Mardell C. chd by Jno

Ja^s Moore for feloniously stealing a pint pewter Pot Val: 8d. his property – rem^{d}ed 'till Saturday, except Wallis who was d^d.

Richd Jones, Rob: Cooper } WC by Thos Henley C. chd by John Clark on suspicion of coining half pence at Chelsea in the County of Middx – referred to a Justice of that County.

2s.   Thos Flude, Saml Sharp} by Ja^s Drummond C. chd by Rob: Bassam (on the Lord Mayor's W^t) for an Ass^t – they withdrew & ag^d – d^d

John Love, Alice ux, Patrick McQuirk} PC Marcus Levy C. Chd by Henry Wilson (Vide Entry made Tuesday 6th Inst.) Hearing adjourn'd a material Witness not attend^g.

Thos Pritchard & Wm Downs} PC Edmund Wells C. Chd by John Plaw on Susp^n of feloniously Stealing one hundred & 50 Pounds Weight of Leaden Pipe Value [blank] Property unknown rem^d till Tuesday for fur^r Examicon

Thos Windsor, Joseph Moss} PC Thos Parrott C. chd by him for being idle & disorderly Boys & susp^d Pilferers– Adj^d true & Sent to the Marine Society

Mr Rhodes attended   John Wilkes

Mr Alderman Sawbridge.   Friday 9 November 1781.
    (No Attendance) being Lord Mayor's Day

Sir Thomas Hallifax. Monday 12 November 1781.
    (No Attendance)
    Mr Beach att^{d}ed.

Sir James Esdaile. Tuesday 13 November 1781.
Mr Ald^n Hart   Edwd Bradley, a Journeyman Hat Maker by Thos
Mr Ald^n Pugh   Fenner C. chd by Thos Hobson, his Master for embezzling & unlawfully disposing of 2lb. W^t of Coney Wool, 18 Ozs of Quarter Wool, 9 Ozs of Hare's Wool, 6 Ozs of Toy Wool, 6 Ozs ¾ of Fine Wool, 1 Oz. of Vigonia Wool, & 10 Ozs ½ of Beaver – the same being Materials with which he the s^d Edwd Bradley, was intrusted by him the s^d Thos Hobson to be wrought into Hats – upon the oath of the s^d Thos Hobson com^d to B p^r W^t for six Weeks.

M[r] Alderman Hart adhuc Tuesday 13 November 1781

John Love, Alice Ux:, Pat[k] McQuirk} WC by Marcus Levy C. chd by Hen: Wilson for feloniously uttering and publishing as true, a Bill of Exchange, purporting to be accepted by Mess[rs] Brown Collinson & Co., Bankers, London – they knowing the said Acceptance to be false forged & counterfeit – rem[d]ed 'till tomorrow.

M[r] Ald[n] Pugh — Sarah Evans by ~~Will: Spencer C~~ Jno Edwards C. chd by Will: Spencer for wilfully breaking his Windows – she promised not to do the like in future – d[d].

Ald[n] Hart — Sarah Davis[196] WC by Will: Payne C. chd by Margaret Ux Jos[h] Smith on suspicion of feloniously stealing a lace Cloak Val: 10s. the property of Joseph Smith on the Oaths of Mrs. Smith & Payne committed to DoC:

RX — Jos[h] Smith of Fleet St[r] Temple Bar L: Vintner £10 / W[m] Payne 10

Tho[s] Pritchard, W[m] Downes} WC by Edm[d] Wells C. chd by John Plaw on susp[n] of fel[y] steal[g] 150 lb weight of Lead Pipes, they were remanded on Thursday to this day. John Gunbies appeared & proved the Lead Pipe his property. Pritchard inlisted for a Soldier

David Harris by same C. charged by Charles Pinto for feloniously steal[g] 3 fustick Violin Bows value 10s. his property, for want of evidence d[d].

1s. — W[t] ag[t] James Raleigh ads Tho[s] Cunningham Ass[t] &c.

M[r] Nash attended. JH

M[r] Alderman Plumbe. Wednesday 14 November 1781.

Ald[n] Wilkes Sainsbury — Tho[s] Frost sum[d] to answer the Complaint & Information of Jos: Toone for wilfully & knowingly aiding & assisting one John Scott in fraudulently & clandestinely removing and conveying away from the dwelling House of s[d] Scott certain Goods & Chattels, not exceeding the Value of £50 for the purpose of preventing the said Goods and Chattels from being distrained for Arrears of Rent due & owing – neither the Landlord nor Agent appeared to complain – the present Sum[s] was therefore d[d].

196. The case proceeds to the Old Bailey. See *OBP*, December 1781, trial of Sarah Davis (t17811205–53).

Ald^n Ja^s Underwood WC by Jno Bradley C. chd by Jere^h Wher-
Sainsbury lings for feloniously stealing a live Duck – Val: 1s. his
property –Will: Brown saw the Pris^r with the Duck in
his Possession – on their Oaths & also of Geo: Fletcher
committed to d^oC

RX Jere^h Wherlings – Bell Inn Smithfield Innholder } £10
for <u>Geo: Fletcher</u> – his Servt } ~~£10~~
Will: Brown – Finchley Middx Farmer £10

Mr Rhodes excused 540[197] John Wilkes

Mr Alderman Kennett by Mr Alderman Kitchin. Thursday 15 November
1781.
1s. Warr^t v Timothy Foley ads. Alice Langley Per Ass^t

Ja^s Raleigh by John Collison C. chd by Thos Cunningham
(on a W^t Per Ald^n Hart 13th Inst.) for an Ass^t – it app^d that
~~Cunningham was ye Aggressor~~ Raleigh was the Aggressor on
his own Confession & Oath of s^d Cunningham Adj^d true, The
Prisoner made Satisfaction & Was D^d.

Sarah Turner WC Joseph Thompson C. chd by Ja^s Goddard
per Suspicion of feloniously stealing a Silk Handkerchief, 2
linnen handkf^s 2 Towels & o^r Goods his Property. For Want
of Evidence she was D^d

2s. Affidavits Cazenove and ano^r

Mr Alderman Plumbe by Mr Alderman Kitchin Adhuc Thursday 15
November 1781.
Mary Harris Joseph Thompson C. Chd by Jane Evans on
Suspicion of feloniously Stealing a Table Cloth Two Towells
one white handkf & other Goods her Property, For want of
Evidence She was D^d.

Mary Harris (on Mr Ald^n Pughs Warr^t) WC Robt Rowe C.
Chd by Thos Foresight for Embezzling pawning or Otherwise
unlawfully disposing of 75 Scotch Cloth Shirts, with wch She
had been Entrusted to make up Value £15 his Property ag^t the
Stat. Remanded for fur^r Examicon 'till tomorrow

John Love, Alice his Wife, Patrick McQuirk[198]} WC Marcus
Levi C. Chd by Hen^y Wilson for feloniously publishing as True

197. Possibly the time he was excused.
198. The clerk may have it as 'McGurk'.

a certain Bill of Exchange dated Oxford 14th Septr 1781 Drawn by Lane and Jackson upon Messrs Brown Collinson & Co. Bankers in London Payable to John Dowlen Esqr or Order for £35 and purporting to be accepted By Messrs Brown, Collinson and Co. They the s^d John Love Alice his Wife and Patrick McQurk, Well knowing the s^d Acceptance to be false forged & Counterfeited – John Love alledg'd he found a Pocket Book contain^g the Bill in que[sti]on at Liphook near Petersfield in his Way from Portsmouth to London on Monday 22d Octr last with a Pass – He produc'd his Discharge & the Pass they were d^d.

1s.	Will: Carter by Wm Catchpole C. chd by Joseph Mann (on the Lord Mayor's W^t 13th Nov^r) for an Ass^t – ag^d & d^d

1s.   Cath. Swinney by John Collison C. chd by Eleanor Newman (on Aldⁿ Turner's W^t 27th Octo^r) for an Ass^t – ag^d & d^d

1s.   ~~Mary~~ Edwd Thompson by John Collington C. chd by Mary Bragg (on the Lord Mayor's W^t 13th Inst.) for ~~an~~ Assaulting Thos Bragg her Husband, Mre Sett^d & D^d.

Robt Cuthbert, WC Thos Wall C. chd by John Horten a Watchman for being a disorderly Person – rem^ded 'till tomorrow

Mary Lewis by Ja^s Drummond C. chd by Mary Hillyard for stealing the Cuff of her linen Gown & a linen Apron – d^d

Mr Rhodes attended   HK

The late Lord Mayor.[199] Friday 16 November 1781.
     (No Attendance)
     (Mr Rhodes att^ded)

Mr Alderman Peckham. Monday 19 November 1781.
     Rob: Cuthbert WC by Thos Wall C. chd by John Horton, a Watchman, for being a disorderly Person – Ja^s Sangar, Poulterer in Blackmoor Street, app^d to give him a good Character – d^d.

2s.   Lucy Ann Pullen, Paul Wray} WC by Will: Catchpole C. chd ~~by~~ each other – Wray 1st chd Pullen with ass^ting him – then she gave Charge – d^d

199. Sir Watkin Lewes.

Mary Harris WC by Rob: Roe C. chd by Thomas Foresight (on M[r] Ald[n] Pugh's W[t] 14[th] April last) for embezzling, pawning, or otherwise unlawfully disposing of 75 scotch cloth Men's Shirts Val: £15 – with which she was entrusted to make up – rem[d]ed 'till tomorrow.

1s.   Aff[t] Tho[s] Hall

John Barrett doC by [blank][200] Hunt C. chd by [blank]

John Knight d°C by Martin Platts C. chd by Tho[s] Bambridge for feloniously stealing a linen handkerchief Val: 1s. his Property – M[r] Bambridge College of Physicians – rem[d]ed to enter (if fit) in the Navy.

Eliz: Griffith[201] d°C by Jos: ~~Gates~~ Thompson C. chd by Tho[s] Gardiner & Jno Pammill for feloniously stealing a copper Turbot Pan & Cover Val: 14s. the Property of the s[d] Tho[s] Gardiner – on the Oath of Pummel – committed to d°C.

RX   Tho[s] Gardiner of Harp Alley L. Broker   £10
Jno Pummill of the Queens Head Fashion St[r] Spitallf[ds] £10

Sophia Owen d°C by d°C. chd by Rachel Matthews for feloniously stealing a pair of Pattens, & a copper Sausepan Val: 14s. her Property – Matthews wished not to prosecute & the Pris[r] appearing to be a poor destitute Object – rem[d]ed to be pass'd

Rob: Jordan sum[d] to answer the Complt & Information of Simon Jeakins for bringing a Load of Hay into Smithfield Market – 25 ~~Loads~~ Trusses of which were not sound Hay & made up of the same which the Outisde did import – Jeakins was sworn –Will: Nowe examined the Trusses & found 24 worse in the Inside than without – conv'd in & p[d] the Penalty of £1.16._. which was p[d] – Money p[d] to M[r] J. Ch: Wdn

Will: Oram WC by Will: Catchpole C. chd by Sam. Durant on suspicion of feloniously stealing a pair of Sheets – there was no Proof – d[d]

Price Devereux Prosser d°C by Tho[s] Massey C. chd by Sam. Wordsworth for stealing a Woman's Cloak – d[d]

M[r] Beach attended   RP.

---

200. Probably William Hunt.
201. The case proceeds to the Old Bailey. See *OBP*, December 1781, trial of Elizabeth Griffiths (t17811205–50).

Mr Alderman Newnham. Tuesday 20 November 1781.

Ald^n Wright   Sarah Adams sum^d by Will: Bacchus a hackney Coachman, for refusing to pay him his Fare for carrying you in his hackney Coach from Hatton Garden to the Minories – ag^d to have the Gro[un]^d measured

Eleanor Cohen WC by Jos: Thompson C. chd by [blank] Schofield on suspicion of stealing a quart & pint pewter Pot – there was no Proof – d^d

Mary Harris WC by Robert Roe C. chd by Thos Foresight (on Mr Ald^n Pugh's W^t 14th April last) for embezzling, pawning, or otherwise unlawfully disposing of 75 scotch cloth Men's Shirts Val: £15 – with wch she was entrusted to make up – by Consent of Mr Foresight d^d

1s.   Aff^t David Ximenes

Mr Alderman Wright adhuc Tuesday 20th November 1781.

Thos Teber WC by Hen: Golding C. chd by [blank] Tucker & Geo: Russel, Patrole of the Ward of Queenhith, for being apprehended last Night with some Coals, which they suspect him to have pilfered – remanded.

Will: Jenkins, a Journeyman Stickdresser by Will: Martin C. chd by Thos Wright, his Ma^r (on Ald^n Turner's W^t 27th Septr last) for pawning, or otherwise unlawfully disposing of 6 doz. of Dragon Canes Val: £1.4._. entrusted with him the s^d W. Jenkins to be manufactured – the Mre was settled

Mr Nash attended   RW

Mr Alderman Clark. Wednesday 21 November 1781.
(No Alderman)
(Mr Houstoun att^{d}ed)

Mr Alderman Wooldridge. Thursday 22 November 1781.
Barbara Wright WC by Chas Staples C. chd by [blank]

(No Attendance)
(Mr Houstoun att^{d}ed.)

Mr Alderman Hart. Friday 23 November 1781.
2s.   Aff^t John Hayes, D^o John Cox

Will: Austin sum^d by John Fleming, Street Keeper for using his narrow wheeled Cart in this City – they withdrew & ag^d.

John Knight WC by Martin Platts C. chd by Thos Bambridge (not now present) for Feloniously stealing a linen handkerchief – rem^ded 'till Monday

James Scot Sum^d for wilfully misbehaving by loading a load out of turn – contrary to the Order of Sessions – ordered to pay 3.6 being the Value of the load

Attended Mr Houstoun   J H

Mr Alderman Wright. Monday 26 November 1781.
~~Stephen~~ Chris^r Trusty WC by John Edwards C. chd by Will: Hancock for driving & beating an Ox from a drove of seven – also for ass^ting the said Will: Hancock – com^d for want of Sureties to d^oC.

Thos Butler[202] d^oC. by Will: Bailey C. chd by Ja^s Lyon for feloniously stealing 8 bushels ~~a Quarter~~ of Malt – Val £1.6.. & upw^ds – his Property – on his Oath com^d to d^oC.
RX   Ja^s Lyon – Queenhith London, Lighterman   £20

1s.   ~~Mattw~~ Richd Baylis d^oC. by John Edwards C. chd by Will: Pretty for making a disturbance at the Plough in Fore Street – also for ass^ting him – they withdrew & d^d.

Marg^t Eves by Will: Cass C. chd by Eliz: Turner (on the Lord Mayor's W^t 17th Inst) for an Ass^t – d^d.

1s.   W^t ag^t John Trusty ads Sarah Clewes Ass^t etc.

1s.   D^o agt Uriah Whitecoat ads Frances Ux: John Gale Ass^t etc.

P   Peace W^t ag^t Will: Carey ads Lydia Ux: D^o

        Mr Beach att^d.   TW

Mr Alderman Pugh by Mr Alderman Kitchin. Tuesday 27 November 1781
        Saml Holt sum^d ads Thos Fenton C^h W^n of St. Bart^w the Great for not pay^g Poors Rate. prom^d to pay in 14 days – promised to pay

---

202. The case proceeds to the Old Bailey. See *OBP*, December 1781, trial of Thomas Butler (t17811205–54).

Richd Harper sum^d for the like – to consider whether to consider

Sarah Jones sum^d for the like – allowed a Month

Mary Marshal by Jos: Thompson C. chd by Mary Locke (on the Lord Mayor's W^t Yesterday) for an Ass^t – friv^s & d^d

2s.   George Phillis, Will: Herne} WC by Charles Delegal C. chd by each other – Phillis 1st charged Herne with ass^ting him – Herene then chd Phillis with the like – d^d

1s.   Chas Rushton by Chas Delegal C. chd by John Hayley (on the Lord Mayor's W^t 20th Nov^r) for an Ass^t – Hayley not appearing – d^d.

Ann King by Edmund Wells C. chd by Wm Charlton Church-warden of the Parish of St Dunstan in the West, for making a great Disturbance – d^d.

1s.   W^t ag^t Eliz: Wicks ads. Jane Ryland Ass^t etc.

Mr Nash Attending   EP

Mr Alderman Sainsbury by Mr Alderman Kitchin. Wednesday 28th November 1781.
      Eliz: Wicks by John Fletcher C. chd by Jane Ryland (on Ald^n Pugh's W^t Yesterday) for an Ass^t – they withdrew but co^d not agree – com^d for want of Sureties to WC.

Ald^n Turner   Chch Wdns of St Botolph without Bishopsgate, sum^d to shew Cause why they sho^d not be ordered to allow a Provision to the Churchwardens & Overseers of the Poor of the Parish of St Botolph without Aldersgate for the Maintenance of Edwd Burrow, a Bastard, born in the s^d Parish of St Botolph without Bishopsgate, & removed for Nurture to the s^d Parish of St. Botolph without Aldersgate – allowed 2s. a Week.

Chch Wdns of St Mildred in Bread Street sum^d by Jos: Mawtass for refusing to relieve him, his Wife & three Children – they ag^d to take 'em into the Workhouse

1s.   W^t ag^t Rob: Hughes ads Eliz: Ux: Edward Lewis – Ass^t

Mr Houstoun attended. HK

300

Mr Alderman Kitchin. Thursday 29 November 1781.

Ann Hutin sum^d by Josiah Foster for knowingly & designedly by false Pretences obtaining linen drapery Goods Val: £9 & upw^{ds} – with Intent to cheat & defraud him thereof – Adjourn'd for fur^r Hearing till Tuesday next

John Wiseman, Selwood Taverner} WC Thos Wall C. Ch^d by James Davids for wilfully breaking his Windows   They made Satisfaction, askt Pardon, & were d^d

John White WC Joseph Wray C. Ch^d by Joseph Walley with Secreting himself yesterday in the Basket of a the Bristol Stage Coach then standing at the 3 Cups Inn Bread Street with Intent on Suspicion to committ Felony. He was reprim^d & D^d

Will: Wright WC by Will: Hartley C. chd by him for making a great Disturbance in the Watch Ho: of the Ward of Farringdon within – Tho askt Pardon   Was reprimanded & Disch^d.

1s.   Warr^t v Alexander English ads. Elizth Hayes Ass^t

Rhodes Att^y attended   HK

Mr Alderman Burnell. Friday 30 November 1781.
(No Attendance)

Mr Alderman Crichton. Monday 3 December 1781.

2s.   John Mills, And^w Carey} WC by John Prockter C. chd by Thos Page for an Ass^t – ag^d & d^d

John Hevey WC by [blank] C. chd by Edward Beauchamp & Will: Masters upon Suspicion of having feloniously published as true in the County of Middlesex knowing it to be false forged & counterfeited a certain Bill of Exchange, purporting to be the Bill of Exchange of Jere: Connell for Smith, Moore & Co. to Barnard McCarty or Order on Richd Beatty & Co. for the payment of £30, thirty one days after Sight – Mr Beauchamp was sworn & the Pris^r was com^d to WC.

Ja^s Burnham a Journeyman Brazier by [blank] Catchpole C. chd by John Taylor (on Ald^n Pugh's W^t 1st Inst) a Master Brazier for leaving certain work of his unfinished wch he had contracted to Perform – ag^d & d^d

1s.   Back'd a Middx W^t Per Justice Blackborow

John Kinnaird PC by Will: Govan C. chd by John Kinnaird for running away from his Ma^r Rob Leslie – d^d

1s.   W^t ag^t Thos Nash ads. Mary Ux: Ass^t etc.

1s.   W^t ag^t Mary Julin ads Mary Fitzgerald Ass^t etc.

1s.   D^o against John Telford an Appr: ads Saml Tyler his Ma^r for running away & deserting his Service

1s.   D^o ag^t Mary Faircloth ads Alex^r Knight Ass^t

George Holden from PC by William Wood C. chd by Joseph Coward for making a disturbance in his Publick Ho: – Eliz: Bray the Maid Servant chd him with an Ass^t – Remanded till tomorrow.

Anth^y Reboul[203] by Jos: Sheppard C. chd by Fabrot Geering with defrauding him of 5 Guas– under false Pretences – com^d for want of Sureties to WC.

RX   Fabrot Geering Tower Street L. Merch^t £20

Mr Beach attended   W.C.

Mr Alderman Turner. Tuesday 4 December 1781
Ald^n Pugh. Thos Nash by Will: Payne C. chd by Mary Ux: (on Ald^n
1s.   Crichton's W^t Yesterday) for an Ass^t – ag^d & d^d

1s.   W^t ag^t John Moore ads Sus^a Moore Ass^t

Ald^n Harley   Marg^t Walden WC by Martin Platt C. chd by him for wandering abroad in Par: St Vedast – to be pass'd

Ja^s Griffiths d^{o}C by Geo: Caruthers C. chd by Thos Pettit, a W^{ch}man for an Ass^t – ag^d & d^d

Mr Alderman Turner by Mr Alderman Harley adhuc Tuesday 4 December 1781
1s.   W^t ag^t Ben: Benjamin, Rose Benjamin, & Jane Levy ads Judith Levy Ass^t

Mr Nash attended   TH.

---

203. The case proceeds to the Old Bailey. See *OBP*, December 1781, trial of Anthony Reboul (t17811205–62).

Joseph Roberts, Sarah Ux:} WC by Thos Spratley C. chd by Ja^s Curtis, their Landlord, on suspicion of stealing one pair of Sheets &c. in their ready furnished Lodgings – d^d

David Hart PC by Thos Parrott C. chd by John Cole on suspicion of stealing a silver Tankard – d^d the Tankard being afterw^ds fo^d.

Edwd Ellard by Luke Herod C. chd by Mary Ux: (on a W^t 30th Novr Per Ald^n Pugh) for an Ass^t – they withdrew but co^d not agree – rem^ded

Ald^n Wilkes, Kitchin	Thos Frost, Thos Burgess} sum^d to answer the Complaint & Information of Joseph Toone for wilfully & knowingly aiding & assisting one John Scott in fraudulently & clandestinely removing certain Goods out of his dwelling Ho: in Lombard Street, in order to prevent the Landlords from distraining for Rent – the same not exceeding the Value of £50 – Edward Edwards was present with Mr Toone – Toone told Frost if he took the Goods away, it wo^d be worse for him – that Toone informed Frost of the Consequence of removing the Goods – it app^d, that the Goods were taken back to the House & locked up, & were not removed to any other Place – Toone denied, that he saw the Goods returned & declared he believed they were not put into their original Situation – Eliz: Pratt & Will: Lamb saw these goods put into the Ho: of Scott – they were sworn – the Compl^t was d^d.

Mr Alderman Kitchin adhuc Tuesday 4 December 1781.
    Eliz: Smith PC by Moses Hyam C. chd by Han^h Levi for feloniously stealing two cotton Gowns, Val: 10s. her Property – rem^ded 'till tomorrow.

N.B. Attendance Certify'd in preceding Margin.

Mr Alderman Alsop. Wednesday 5 December 1781.
Ald^n Wooldridge And^w James Pratt by Thos Clark C. chd by Sus^a Ux: Will: Collins for feloniously stealing a pair of blankets, a copper Tea Kettle, Val: [blank] d^d as he never occupied the Lodgings, nor took the Goods.

Richd Beatty PC by John Dickenson C. chd by John Heather for accepting in the Name of Beatty and Co. sundry Bills of Exchange, when he was only Clerk in the House – rem^ded

Ald^n Kitchin   Eleanor Marne by John Collison C. chd by Jos: Clifford
1s.   (on Ald^n Crichton's W^t Yesterday) for an Ass^t – d^d.

Matthew Berry the Driver of a Dray N^o [blank] produced by his Mas^r S. Whitbread Esq^e – sum^d by Geo: Elkins for driving the s^d Dray agst a Coach & damaging the same – John Cook said it was the Fault of Elkins who might have cleared the Dray – d^d.

Sarah Simpson, Sarah Tomkins} WC by Will: Cass C. chd by John Lingard, a Waggoner at the Blossoms Inn, Lawrence Lane for stealing 8s. – Lingard not appearing – they were d^d

1s.   W^t ag^t Ja^s Welch & Mary Ragan ads Mich. Power on suspicion of Feloniously stealing a silver Watch, two pair of silver Buckles, 4 Coats, 4 Waistcoats, 2 pair of breeches, 2 Hats Val: £10.

Mr Alderman Kitchin adhuc Wednesday 5 December [1781]
1s.   W^t ag^t Dan Cook ads Eliz: Young Ass^t etc.

Edwd Ellard by Luke Herod C. chd by Mary his Wife (on a W^t Per Ald^n Pugh 30th Nov^r) for an Ass^t – ag^d to allow 6s. a Week – he was thereupon d^d

Ald^n Thos Noake was complained agst by Henry Baldwin, his Ma^r to
Wilkes whom he is an Appr: for being an idle & disorderly Apprentice & refusing to obey lawful Commands – adjourned.

Mr Houstoun excused being ill – HK

1s.   W^t ag^t Lazarus Lee ads Bridget Ux of James Baxter for feloniously assaulting her & by Force & agst her Will having carnal Knowledge of her Body

The Right Honourable Thomas Harley. Thursday 6th December 1781.
Ald^n John Hevey WC by [blank] C. chd by Edwd Beauchamp
Crichton & Will: Masters (on Mr Ald^n Crichton's Commitment 3^d Inst.) on a violent Suspicion of knowingly defrauding several Persons out of large Sums of Money under False Pretences. McCarty lives in Dyot Street St Giles's & is now at Bath, Westgate Street – Smith, Moore, McCarty Beatty & himself are the Partners in the House at Bath – rem^{d}ed 'till tomorrow

Esther Timberwell PC Moses Hyems C. Ch[d] by Han[h] Levy on Suspicion of feloniously Stealing a linnen Gown Value 5s. her Property – M[r] Hurford undertook for her Appearance – d[d].

Sarah Pockington, Mary Robinson, Sarah Hayley} WC by Cha[s] Delegal C. chd by Will Hull, W[ch]man of the Ward of Farringdon without for being in the Street at an unseasonable Hour & abusing him – d[d]

M[r] Rhodes attended. R.H.

M[r] Alderman Crosby by M[r] Alderman Crichton. Friday 7 December 1781
John Hevey[204] WC chd by Edw[d] Beauchamp (on his Wp's Commitment 3[d] Inst.) on a violent Suspicion of knowingly defrauding several Persons out of large Sums of Money, under false pretences. Beauchamp's says on Monday Se'enight the Pris[r] came to Shop at ~~Temple~~ Holborn Barr & wanted to purchase some gold Watches – he fixed on one marked 18 Guas – he produced a Bill upon the Bath Bank for £30 – Beauchamp objected to taking it – Pris[r] said McCarty (wch appeared upon the back of the Bill) was his Name & that was his own Indorsement – asked him who Rich[d] Beatty was – s[d] "he was our Agent to the Bath Bank" – Said, he chused to see the Acceptance was good – Sent John Bartrum his Appr: to enquire if the Acceptance was good – the Boy returned & s[d] it was a good Bill – John Heather saw the Pris[r] sign his Name John Hevey.

1s.   Aff[t] Will: Cole

Rich[d] Beatty PC by Jno Dickenson C. chd by John Heather for accepting sundry Bills of Exchange in the Name of Beatty and C[o] S[t] Helens, where he was not a Partner but a Clerk – and confederating with other Persons to defraud the said John Heather & others of large Sums of Money—McCarty lives in Dyot Street, recommend[d] Pris[r] to Hevey, to accept their Bills – was to have a Ga a Week & after a Trial & approved of, to be admitted a Partner & have a Share of the Profits – has p[d] to Mess[rs] Coates & Crompton, Panton Street, Haymarket, two Bills, one for £10, the other for £30 – M[r] Hevey at one time gave the Pris[r] Money, at another time a Bank Note for £20 was sent from Bath – don't know where M[r] Smith lives – can't say

---

204. The case proceeds to the Old Bailey. See *OBP*, January 1782, trial of John Hevey (t17820109–22).

he ever saw McCarty or Connell write – Hevey, McCarty are
the C° with Smith & Moore – the Books of the Compting Ho:
Pris^r sent on Saturday by a Porter who came from Hevey –
Dickenson s^d that when he went to apprehend the Pris^r he ask'd
him, if he was Mr Hevey's Clerk—the Pris^r answered Yes.

Will: Masters & Rob: Orford chd the Pris^r with defrauding
said Masters of a gold Watch & £10 in Money – Saml Read
chd Hevey with fraudulently obtaining a gold Watch & giving
a Note for £20 accepted by the Prisoner

Beatty was remanded till Tuesday next for further Examination on the Oath of Saml Read

Will: Price[205] PC by Ja^s Munday C. chd by Francis Morales
for knowingly & designedly by false Pretences obtaining from
him 5 Yards & a half of Cotton Val: 13s. – the property of Will:
Davis Esq. with Intent to cheat & defraud him thereof – Jos:
Portal also sworn.

R	Fra^s Morales – Servt to W. Davis Tower Hill Esq	£10
	Jos: Portal – Linen Draper Bpsgate Street	10

next	Will: Stanton Blake engraved the Plate from which the Notes	
Sess^s	were ~~printed~~ cast off – com^d to WC. (Vide the Commitment)	

RX	Edwd Beauchamp Holborn Barrs L. Pawnbroker	£ 40
	John Heather – Long Acre in the Co: of Middx D°	£ 20
	Will: Stanton Blake – Abchurch Lane L. Engraver	£ 20
	~~John Kirby &c.~~	

(Mr Nash att^ded)

---

205. The case proceeds to the Old Bailey. See *OBP*, December 1781, trial of William Price
(t17811205–61).

INDEX

[---] indicates a 'blank' or unrecorded given name or surname.
Variants of the same given name are indicated by an abbreviation of otherwise
(oth.) while identifiable aliases for individual surnames are indicated as such.

[---],
   [---]   64, 87
   [---], called Little Bob   79
   [---], constable   259
   Alexander   45
   Hurst   202
   Reb   51
Aaron,
   Aaron (alias Aarons)   198
   Aaron, constable   190
   Elias, constable   134
   Isiah   118
   Jacob, constable   25, 27, 43
   Jane   69
   Mathias   53
Aarons, Mary   181
Abel,
   Dan¹   219
   Mark   58
Aberdeen, John   214
Abingdon   121
Abney, John   210
Abraham,
   Hannah Beal 36
   Michael   19
Abrahams,
   Abraham   56
   Dinah   220
   Edwᵈ   60
   Jacob   36
   Judith w. Abraham   56
   Lemon   222
   Samuel   163
Acton,
   Jno   111, 124
   John   108
   Saml   129
Acton Wells   257
Acts of Parliament
   10 Geo. II, c. 31   33
Adair, Margᵗ   182
Adderley, Wᵐ   100
Adey, Alice   102
Adley,
   Amey   163
   Eliz   27

John   27
Adams,
   Ann   272
   Barbarah   170
   Dan¹   105
   Dᵒ   247
   Dudley   227
   Jane   142
   Joseph   201
   Rᵈ   118
   Rob   239
   Sam¹   251
   Sarah   298
   Will   142
Adamson,
   Henry   38
   Jarvis   176
   Jno   80
   Thoˢ   100
Adderley, Wᵐ   100
Addington, Mʳ [---] justice   179, 185, 242
advertisement, in newspapers   xx, 7, 8, 13,
   16, 17, 18, 76, 111, 119, 150, 198, 211,
   261
Ailsworth, Eliz   256
Aislabie, Rawson   218
Aked,
   Charity w. John   199
   John   128, 199
Akers, Sarah   114
Alchorn,
   Prudence w. Sam¹   171
   Sam¹   171
Aldbourn, Thoˢ   103
Alden, Timʸ   147
Alder,
   Eliz   155
   Sarah   155, 156
aldermen
   Alexander, William   xxvii, 24, 25, 27, 35
     38, 40, 48
   Alsop, Robert   4, 30, 33, 36, 45, 50, 58,
     60, 65, 68, 70, 85, 99, 133, 150, 167,
     168, 176, 194, 216, 217, 231, 251,
     261, 268, 288, 303

307

313

315

Index

Cockle, R^d 127
Cockman,
Will 190, 191
W^m, constable 129
Codner, Loveday 61
Cogar, John 256
Cohen,
Easter 48
Eleanor 298
Hen, constable 132, 149
Simon 204
Coker,
Mary 180
Mary w. Thos 89
Thos 89
Cole,
Alice 150, 150n
Ann 153, 154
Benj 241
James 92
Jas 106, 219
John 281, 303
Joseph 60
Marg^t 286
Martha 279
Sus^a 81, 82
Thos 30
Will 99, 305
Coleman,
Catherine 264
Eliz 179
George 171
Jo^s oth. Jos^h, constable 103, 106
Joseph 142
Collett,
Ann 94
Hannah 159
Henry 159
Mary 39
Collier,
Andrew 201
John 141, 146, 147, 148
Mary 136
Collington, John, constable 240, 296
Collins,
Ann 217
Eliz 132, 200
Isaac 276
James 4
Martha 277
Mary 154
Sus^a w. Will 303
Will 303
Collinson, John, constable 56, 190, 276
Collinton,
Jno oth. John, constable 192, 232, 280
Collis, Mary 149
Collison,
John 138
John constable 242, 295, 296, 304
Colliton, John, constable 223, 258, 269, 285

Colman, Mary 97
Colston, Robt 56
Comerford, [---] 127
Comfort, John 42
committal procedures xviii
Common Council 29
Commorell, Fred^k 56, 58
compounding xviii
Compton,
James, constable 39
Will, constable 244, 245, 257
Con, Sarah 36
Conan, R^d, constable 235
Condon, Isabella 71
Conen, R^d, constable 217, 226
confessions xxi
Conion, Rich^d, constable 200
Connell, Jere 301, 306
Connelley, Terence 33
Connolly, Ann 73
Connoway, James 3
constables xix, xx, xxiii, xxiii-xxiv
Connor,
John 285
Lawrence 70
Marg^t 83
Michael 281, 282, 283
Will 90
W^m 7
Conway, Geo 130
Cook,
Dan 304
Geo 190
Jane 106, 107
Jno 97
John, constable 7
John 237, 304
Joseph 111
Jos^h 241
Mary w. John 237
Osmond 42
Simon, constable 112, 142, 285
Sophia 207
Sus^a 82
Will 271
W^m 18
Cooke,
Eliz^a 6
Ja^s 44
Jno 74
John 49
Mary 60, 63
Mary w. Will 147
Thos 77, 87
Will 147
William (alias Cook), constable xxiv, 154, 165, 174, 175
Cookson
Isaac 8
Jos 154, 263, 264
Joseph 127

319

340

347

351

LONDON RECORD SOCIETY

The London Record Society was founded in December 1964 to publish transcripts, abstracts and lists of the primary sources for this history of London, and generally to stimulate interest in archives relating to London. Membership is open to any individual or institution; the annual subscription is £18 (US $22) for individuals and £23 (US $35) for institutions. Prospective members should apply to the Hon. Secretary, Dr Helen Bradley, London Record Society, PO Box 691, Exeter, EX1 9PH (email londonrecordsoc@btinternet.com)

The following volumes have already been published:

1. *London Possessory Assizes: a Calendar*, edited by Helena M. Chew (1965)
2. *London Inhabitants within the Walls, 1695*, with an introduction by D. V. Glass (1966)
3. *London Consistory Court Wills, 1492–1547*, edited by Ida Darlington (1967)
4. *Scriveners' Company Common Paper, 1357–1628, with a Continuation to 1678*, edited by Francis W. Steer (1968)
5. *London Radicalism, 1830–1843: a Selection from the Papers of Francis Place*, edited by D. J. Rowe (1970)
6. *The London Eyre of 1244*, edited by Helena M. Chew and Martin Weinbaum (1970)
7. *The Cartulary of Holy Trinity Aldgate*, edited by Gerald A. J. Hodgett (1971)
8. *The Port and Trade of Early Elizabethan London: Documents*, edited by Brian Dietz (1972)
9. *The Spanish Company*, edited by Pauline Croft (1973)
10. *London Assize of Nuisance, 1301–1431: a Calendar*, edited by Helena M. Chew and William Kellaway (1973)

11. *Two Calvinistic Methodist Chapels, 1748–1811: the London Tabernacle and Spa Fields Chapel*, edited by Edwin Welch (1975)
12. *The London Eyre of 1276*, edited by Martin Weinbaum (1976)
13. *The Church in London, 1375–1392*, edited by A. K. McHardy (1977)
14. *Committees for the Repeal of the Test and Corporation Acts: Minutes, 1786–90 and 1827–8*, edited by Thomas W. Davis (1978)
15. *Joshua Johnson's Letterbook, 1771–4: Letters from a Merchant in London to his Partners in Maryland*, edited by Jacob M. Price (1979)
16. *London and Middlesex Chantry Certificate, 1548*, edited by C. J. Kitching (1980)
17. *London Politics, 1713–1717: Minutes of a Whig Club, 1714–17*, edited by H. Horwitz; *London Pollbooks, 1713*, edited by W. A. Speck and W. A. Gray (1981)
18. *Parish Fraternity Register: Fraternity of the Holy Trinity and SS. Fabian and Sebastian in the Parish of St. Botolph without Aldersgate*, edited by Patricia Basing (1982)
19. *Trinity House of Deptford: Transactions, 1609–35*, edited by G. G. Harris (1983).
20. *Chamber Accounts of the Sixteenth Century*, edited by Betty R. Masters (1984)
21. *The Letters of John Paige, London Merchant, 1648–58*, edited by George F. Steckley (1984)
22. *A Survey of Documentary Sources for Property Holding in London before the Great Fire*, by Derek Keene and Vanessa Harding (1985)
23. *The Commissions for Building Fifty New Churches*, edited by M. H. Port (1986)
24. *Richard Hutton's Complaints Book*, edited by Timothy V. Hitchcock (1987)
25. *Westminster Abbey Charters, 1066–c.1214*, edited by Emma Mason (1988)
26. *London Viewers and their Certificates, 1508–1558*, edited by Janet S. Loengard (1989)
27. *The Overseas Trade of London: Exchequer Customs Accounts, 1480–1*, edited by H. S. Cobb (1990)
28. *Justice in Eighteenth-Century Hackney: the Justicing Notebook of Henry Norris and the Hackney Petty Sessions Book*, edited by Ruth Paley (1991)
29. *Two Tudor Subsidy Assessment Rolls for the City of London: 1541 and 1582*, edited by R. G. Lang (1993)
30. *London Debating Societies, 1776–1799*, compiled and introduced by Donna T. Andrew (1994)
31. *London Bridge: Selected Accounts and Rentals, 1381–1538*, edited by Vanessa Harding and Laura Wright (1995)

Previously published titles in the series are available from Boydell and Brewer; please contact them for further details, or see their website, www.boydellandbrewer.com